Frommer's

W9-AAX-410

Los Cabos & Baja

1st Edition

by Lynne Bairstow

Here's what the critics say about Frommer's:

"Amazingly easy to use. Very portable, very complete."

—*Booklist*

"Detailed, accurate, and easy-to-read information for all price ranges."
—*Glamour Magazine*

"Hotel information is close to encyclopedic."
—*Des Moines Sunday Register*

"Frommer's Guides have a way of giving you a real feel for a place."
—*Knight Ridder Newspapers*

WILEY
Wiley Publishing, Inc.

Published by:

Wiley Publishing, Inc.

111 River St.
Hoboken, NJ 07030-5774

ISBN-13: 978-0-7645-8975-1
ISBN-10: 0-7645-8975-X

Editor: Kendra L. Falkenstein and Marc Nadeau
Production Editor: Suzanna R. Thompson
Cartographer: Tim Lohnes
Photo Editor: Richard Fox
Production by Wiley Indianapolis Composition Services

Front cover photo: Kayaking toward a natural arch
Back cover photo: Cabo Real Golf Course in Cabo San Lucas

For information on our other products and services or to obtain technical support, please contact our Customer Care Department within the U.S. at 800/762-2974, outside the U.S. at 317/572-3993 or fax 317/572-4002.

Wiley also publishes its books in a variety of electronic formats. Some content that appears in print may not be available in electronic formats.

Manufactured in the United States of America

5 4 3 2

Contents

List of Maps

This book is dedicated to my many friends in Mexico who, through sharing their insights, anecdotes, knowledge, and explorations of Mexico, have shared their love of this country. In particular, Ricardo, Silver, Carlos, Claudia, and Alejandra have shared with me and have shown me what a magical place Mexico is, and how much more I have to discover and enjoy.

Acknowledgments

Many thanks to the people who helped me gather the information, tips, and treasures that have made their way into this book. I am especially grateful for the assistance of Alejandra Macedo, my friend and research assistant, whose tireless work ensured that the information in this book is correct and that no grain of sand was left unturned in seeking out the fun there is to have in Los Cabos and Baja.

—Lynne Bairstow

About the Author

For **Lynne Bairstow**, Mexico has become more home to her than her native United States. After exploring the country and living in Puerto Vallarta for most of the past 14 years, she's developed a true love of Mexico and its complex, colorful culture. Her local friends now claim she has *patas saladas*—a term translated as "salty feet" and which means that she has become a true Vallarta local. Her travel articles on Mexico have been published in the *New York Times,* the *San Francisco Chronicle,* the *Los Angeles Times, Private Air, Luxury Living,* and the Mexicana and Alaska Airlines in-flight magazines. In 2000, Lynne was awarded the Pluma de Plata, an honor granted by the Mexican government to foreign writers, for her work with the Frommer's guide to Mexico.

An Invitation to the Reader

In researching this book, we discovered many wonderful places—hotels, restaurants, shops, and more. We're sure you'll find others. Please tell us about them, so we can share the information with your fellow travelers in upcoming editions. If you were disappointed with a recommendation, we'd love to know that, too. Please write to:

Frommer's Los Cabos & Baja, 1st Edition
Wiley Publishing, Inc. • 111 River St. • Hoboken, NJ 07030-5774

An Additional Note

Please be advised that travel information is subject to change at any time—and this is especially true of prices. We therefore suggest that you write or call ahead for confirmation when making your travel plans. The authors, editors, and publisher cannot be held responsible for the experiences of readers while traveling. Your safety is important to us, however, so we encourage you to stay alert and be aware of your surroundings. Keep a close eye on cameras, purses, and wallets, all favorite targets of thieves and pickpockets.

Frommer's Star Ratings, Icons & Abbreviations

Every hotel, restaurant, and attraction listing in this guide has been ranked for quality, value, service, amenities, and special features using a **star-rating system.** In country, state, and regional guides, we also rate towns and regions to help you narrow down your choices and budget your time accordingly. Hotels and restaurants are rated on a scale of zero (recommended) to three stars (exceptional). Attractions, shopping, nightlife, towns, and regions are rated according to the following scale: zero stars (recommended), one star (highly recommended), two stars (very highly recommended), and three stars (must-see).

In addition to the star-rating system, we also use **seven feature icons** that point you to the great deals, in-the-know advice, and unique experiences that separate travelers from tourists. Throughout the book, look for:

Finds	Special finds—those places only insiders know about
Fun Fact	Fun facts—details that make travelers more informed and their trips more fun
Kids	Best bets for kids and advice for the whole family
Moments	Special moments—those experiences that memories are made of
Overrated	Places or experiences not worth your time or money
Tips	Insider tips—great ways to save time and money
Value	Great values—where to get the best deals

The following **abbreviations** are used for credit cards:

AE	American Express	DISC	Discover	V	Visa
DC	Diners Club	MC	MasterCard		

Frommers.com

Now that you have the guidebook to a great trip, visit our website at **www.frommers.com** for travel information on more than 3,000 destinations. With features updated regularly, we give you instant access to the most current trip-planning information available. At Frommers.com, you'll also find the best prices on airfares, accommodations, and car rentals—and you can even book travel online through our travel booking partners. At Frommers.com, you'll also find the following:

- Online updates to our most popular guidebooks
- Vacation sweepstakes and contest giveaways
- Newsletter highlighting the hottest travel trends
- Online travel message boards with featured travel discussions

The Best of Los Cabos & Baja

Although many consider Baja Mexico as an extension of Southern California, it is actually a region rich with its own culture, history, and attractions. The area's tremendous variety attracts every kind of traveler with an unequaled mix of sophisticated resorts, rustic inns, exquisite beaches, desert landscapes, and exhilarating adventures. Following are my personal favorites—the best places to go, the best restaurants, the best hotels, and my picks for must-see, one-of-a-kind experiences.

1 The Most Unforgettable Travel Experiences

- **Harvest Festival in the Valle de Guadalupe:** Mexico's wine country comes alive in true fiesta style each year, late August to early September, during this annual wine festival. The celebrations combine wine tastings with parties, concerts, blessings of the grapes, and other events. See p. 147.

- **Exploring Baja's Missions:** From the late 17th through the 19th centuries, Jesuit, Franciscan, and Dominican friars founded a succession of missions in Baja California. The missions were part of the many institutions that the Spanish crown used to colonize the territories of "Nuevo España." Explore one or several along the "Camino Real Misionero." See p. 118.

- **Arts Festival in Todos Santos:** Although Todos Santos is filled with a creative, artistic ambience at any time, it reaches a peak each February during the annual Arts Festival. Held since the early 1990s, the festival continues to grow in popularity and content. See p. 87.

- **Centro Cultural Tijuana:** The ultramodern complex houses an impressive combination of cultural venues, including the Museo de las Identidades Mexicanas (Museum of Mexican Identities), gallery space for changing exhibitions, a concert hall, and an OMNIMAX theater, all showcasing the best of Mexico's culture and performing arts. See p. 146.

- **Foxploration!:** When the 1997 movie *Titanic* was filmed here, at a seaside sound stage created for the production of the movie, Hollywood turned its attention to Rosarito Beach for even more movie making. The original production facility has been turned into an interactive museum and entertainment center that brings into focus the art of moviemaking and special effects, especially those made along Baja's coastline. See p. 160.

- **Bullfights in Tijuana:** No matter what your opinion of bullfighting may be, the pastime is an undeniable part of the sporting culture of Mexico, drawing from its Spanish heritage. Considered among the best venues for watching this sport in North America, Tijuana's dual bullrings feature top matadors in their contest against bulls. The season runs from May to September. See p. 149.

- **Cave Paintings of Central Baja:** Primitive rock paintings on the walls of caves in central Baja are the only examples of this type of art on the North American continent. Their origin remains a mystery, and researchers say they could date back as far as 10,000 years, created during the Prehistoric Age. Regardless of who created them, or when they were created, the colorful, mystical murals are impressive. The journey to reach them is also an adventure in itself. See "Baja's Cave Paintings: An Exploration of the Mysterious" on p. 116.

- **Carnaval in La Paz:** The best Carnaval (or Mardi Gras) party in Baja takes place in La Paz, where round-the-clock revelries take place just prior to Lent. The oceanfront *malecón* is the site of most of the festivities as this generally tranquil town swings into party mode. See p. 94.

2 The Best Beach Vacations

- **Los Cabos Corridor:** Dramatic rock formations and crashing waves mix with wide stretches of soft sand and a rolling break here. This stretch of coast is also home to Baja's most luxurious resorts, verdant golf greens, and even a specialty surf camp. Start at San José del Cabo and work your way down to the famed Playa de Amor at Land's End in Cabo San Lucas. Some beaches here are more suitable for contemplation than for swimming, which isn't all bad. See chapter 4.

- **Todos Santos:** Although the town of Todos Santos itself is just inland from the beach, it's near enough to beautiful stretches of pristine beaches, where whales can easily be sighted offshore during the months of December through May. During summer months, these shores are home to nesting turtles. Year-round, an eco–surf camp specializes in teaching the art of surfing to women, though they usually have lessons for both sexes. The town itself is part artist outpost, part pure relaxation. See chapter 4.

- **La Paz:** If laid-back is what you're after, this town—the official capital of Baja Sur—offers peaceful, small-town beach life at its best. Most accommodations are smaller, inexpensive inns, with a few unique, more luxurious places tossed in. Explore a succession of rocky coves and sandy beaches, or focus your efforts on underwater vistas or the offshore islands, where you'll encounter a wealth of marine life, as well as great diving and snorkeling. You can also visit nearby Isla Espíritu Santo, where you can mingle with the resident colony of sea lions. See chapter 5.

- **Loreto:** Once the center of the mission movement in Baja, Loreto is both a town of historical interest as well as a naturalists' dream. Offshore islands provide abundant opportunities for kayaking, snorkeling, diving, and exploring, and the beaches to the south of town are downright dreamy. If you tire of the big blue, there are plenty of inland explorations nearby as well. See chapter 6.

- **Rosarito to Ensenada:** Northern Baja's beach towns may be primarily known for attracting a rowdy party crowd on weekends, but whether or not you're here for the revelry, you'll also find this stretch of coast ideal for great surfing and dramatic diving. See chapter 7.

3 The Best Museums

- **Museo Histórico Comunitario:** It's a little-known fact that this region—now known as Mexico's wine country—was originally settled by Russian immigrants who were granted political asylum by Mexico in the early 1900s. A tribute to these pioneers of grape cultivation in the area, this small but intriguing museum tells the story of this curious time. An adjacent restaurant serves traditional Russian food. See p. 174.

- **Museo de las Misiones, Loreto:** The missionaries who came to Baja in the 17th through 19th centuries did more than work on converting the local populations to Christianity. This museum features a complete collection of historical and anthropological exhibits pertaining to the Baja peninsula, and includes the zoological studies and scientific writings of the friars. It also documents the contribution of these missions to the demise of indigenous cultures. See p. 118.

- **Museo de Antropología (Anthropology Museum), La Paz:** If you can't make it to see the actual cave paintings of central Baja, this museum has large, although faded, photographs of them along with a number of exhibits on various topics concerning the geology and history of Baja California. See p. 101.

- **Serpentarium, La Paz:** Reptiles are the star of this mostly open-air natural museum that offers plenty of opportunities to get up close and personal with the snakes, iguanas, lizards, crocodiles, and other reptilians of Baja. Children seem especially happy to explore here. See p. 102.

- **Museo Regional de Historia, Mulegé:** It's not so much this museum that fascinates me; it's more about the fact that it was once a state penitentiary that allowed its inmates to leave during the day—on the condition they return at dusk! For some reason, escape attempts were rare in this honor-system prison. The museum details the operation of this unique entity and the town of Mulegé. See p. 130.

- **Museo de Cera, Tijuana:** Many of the figures in this wax museum are creepy, but it's hard not to be fascinated by the eclectic mix of personalities memorialized in wax that range from Aztec warriors and Dominican friars to Bill Clinton and Whoopi Goldberg. Don't miss the Chamber of Horrors. See p. 145.

- **Museo de las Identidades Mexicanas (Museum of Mexican Identities), Tijuana:** Located inside the Centro Cultural Tijuana, this permanent collection of artifacts from pre-Hispanic through modern times displays the gamut of Mexican historical and cultural influences, leaving visitors with a better understanding of this complex society. See p. 146.

4 The Best Outdoor Adventures/Active Vacations

- **Whale-Watching in Magdalena Bay:** Few sights are as awe-inspiring as watching whales in their natural habitat, and few places in the world can offer as complete an experience as Mexico's Baja peninsula, especially in Magdalena Bay. It's part of the El Vizcaíno Biosphere Reserve, where a large number of whales can be seen easily. The various protected bays and lagoons in this area on the Pacific coast are the preferred winter waters for migrating gray whales as they journey south to mate and give birth to their calves. See chapter 6.

- **Scuba Diving off Los Cabos:** Great dive sites are very accessible from Los Cabos, with the favorites being Gordo Banks and Cabo Pulmo. Most impressive, however, are the "sandfalls" (similar to a waterfall, but instead of water flowing over a ledge, sand flows in an underwater current) that even Jacques Cousteau couldn't figure out. See chapter 4.

- **Surfing the Northern Baja Coast:** Northern Baja has the perfect combination of perpetual right-breaking waves, cheap places to stay, and a community of fellow surfers. It's also home to Killers at Todos Santos Island, a legendary wave that takes a boat ride to reach, as well as many other great breaks. See chapter 7.

- **Kayaking the Islands off Loreto:** The offshore islands and inlets surrounding Loreto are a kayaker's paradise, and numerous outfitters are equipped to take you on day trips or overnight kayak excursions. Especially popular is exploring Isla del Carmen, a mostly inaccessible and private island just offshore. See chapter 6.

- **Snorkeling with Sea Lions at Los Islotes:** A playful, curious colony of more than 250 California brown sea lions resides on Los Islotes, a cluster of red-rock islands offshore from La Paz. Numerous tour operators can take you there, a 2½-hour trip by boat, after which you can snorkel or dive while watching the underwater antics of these sea mammals. See chapter 5.

- **Golf in Los Cabos:** Los Cabos has evolved as one of the world's top golf destinations. It currently has seven courses open to challenge golfers and several more under construction. The master plan calls for a total of 207 holes of play. In addition to the championship design, quality, and exquisite desert-and-sea scenery of these courses, Cabo offers very reliable weather. The ample and intriguing variety of courses challenges golfers of all levels. See chapter 4.

- **Exploring the Caves in Central Baja:** The goal of a trip to these caves is to see the mysterious cave paintings that potentially date back to the Prehistoric Age, but the journey itself to the caves in Central Baja is a fascinating adventure. Depending upon your destination, treks can be mildly challenging to difficult. These treks will take you through the canyons, crossing streams, and up challenging climbs. In many protected areas, access is allowed only with an authorized guide. The caves are in the San Francisco de la Sierra and Santa Martha mountains in Central Baja. See chapter 6.

- **Sportfishing in the Sea of Cortez:** You're as likely to reel in the big one here as anywhere in the world, where bringing in a 45-kilogram (100-lb.) marlin is considered routine. The Sea of Cortez has abundant sport fishing—which was the original lure to adventure travelers years before easier access brought more traditional tourism. Among your likely catches are sailfish, wahoo, tuna, and the famed marlin, in black, blue, and striped varieties. See chapter 4.

- **Hiking the National Parks of Northern Baja:** In northern Baja, several national parks provide ample opportunities for hiking, camping, climbing, and other explorations. Among the most notable is the **Parque Nacional Constitución de 1857,** a 5,000-hectare (12,350-acre) preserve at an altitude that averages 1,200m (3,936 ft.), and, contrary to what you may expect in Mexico, has a large lake in an alpine setting. In the **Parque Nacional Sierra San Pedro Mártir,** you'll find the Picacho del Diablo (Devil's Peak), a mountain with a summit at 3,095m (10,152 ft.) from which you can see both oceans and an immense stretch of land. See chapter 7.

5 The Best Places to Get Away from It All

- **Rancho La Puerta:** In 1940, well before resort spas were the rage—or even an acceptable form of vacationing—Rancho La Puerto opened its doors. It was called a "health camp" then, and today it is considered a pioneer of the modern spa and fitness movement. In the more than 50 years it's been in operation it has consistently been at the cutting edge of promoting health and wellness. It emphasizes a mind/body/spirit philosophy in one of the most relaxing and pristine settings you can imagine. For those looking to get away from it all in search of your best self, this is the place. See p. 155.

- **Mulegé:** Literally an oasis in the desert, Mulegé attracts those looking for a small, funky, and lovely town where one can slow down the pace of life to a crawl. You'll find an assortment of accommodations here, plus nearby places to park an RV or pitch a tent, with opportunities nearby for nature explorations. And if you feel the need to connect with others, there's the ubiquitous Mulegé pig roast, which is more than a meal here—it's a tradition. See chapter 6.

- **Camping near Loreto:** The beautiful succession of tranquil coves and beaches bordering Loreto makes for great places to set up camp. Once settled you can kayak the coast or indulge in other opportunities to explore this magnificent landscape. See chapter 6.

- **La Playita:** Although it's close to the easy air access and diversions of Los Cabos, La Playita is a quiet beach to use as a starting point for fishing expeditions. Located just to the north of the town of San José del Cabo, it's a great spot to get away—yet still be near to dining, golf, and other activities, should you feel so inclined. See chapter 4.

- **Valle de Guadalupe:** Mexico's wine country bears little resemblance to the tourism-oriented wineries of Northern California. Here you'll find plenty of peace and quiet in the midst of acres of vineyards. A couple of small inns welcome visitors who want to stop and smell the grapes—or vintages produced here. And, its eclectic history makes exploring the area a treat. See chapter 7.

- **Danzante Adventure Resort:** This resort's location, 40km (25 miles) north of Loreto on pristine Ensenada Blanca Bay makes it far away from most everything, but you won't miss a thing. Lovely suites filled with handmade furnishings are perched on a hill facing the sea, while ocean breezes gently rock the hammocks found on every palm-thatched terrace. All meals and a host of activities are included in the rate. Getting to know the engaging and adventurous couple that owns Danzante is one of the main reasons to book a stay here. See p. 120.

- **Todos Santos:** This artists' outpost is becoming increasingly popular for those looking for the climate and beaches of southern Baja without the crowds of Los Cabos. It's both a cultural oasis as well as an oasis in the true sense of the word: In this desert landscape, Todos Santos enjoys an almost continuous water supply that supports verdant groves of palms, mangos, avocados, and papayas. The quaint inns, creative cuisine, and lovely colonial-style architecture prevalent in the town cultivate an ambience of the artistic. See chapter 4.

6 The Best Shopping

Some tips on bargaining: Although haggling over prices in markets is expected and part of the fun, don't try to browbeat the vendor or bad-mouth the goods. Vendors won't bargain with people they consider disrespectful unless they are desperate to make a sale. For best results be insistent but friendly.

- **Carved Furniture in Rosarito:** Rosarito Beach's Bulevar Benito Juarez has become known for its selection of shops featuring ornately carved wooden furniture. Comparing the offerings has become easy, with so many options in one central location. See p. 158.

- **Art in Todos Santos:** Whether it's oil on canvas, pottery, or weavings, you'll find very high quality original works of art in this town that is building a reputation as a truly cultural community. The annual Arts Festival, held every February, brings an even greater selection of works to choose from. See p. 87.

- **Chinatown in La Paz:** Although small in size, La Paz's Chinatown is authentic, drawing from the days when Chinese immigrants were brought to Baja to work the mines here. From dim sum to shops selling Chinese herbs and medicines, you'll feel transported to another culture in this unique Mexican shopping experience. See p. 103.

- **Ibarra's Pottery, La Paz:** Not only can you shop for hand-painted tiles, tableware, and decorative pottery here, but you can also watch it being made. Each piece offered for sale in this popular shop is individually made. See p. 103.

- **San José's boutiques:** As San José del Cabo becomes increasingly gentrified, so does its shopping experience. In southern Baja, the best boutiques and shops offering clothing, jewelry, and decorative items for the home are found within the lovely colonial buildings in this tree-lined town. See p. 56.

- **Avenida Revolución in Tijuana:** This rowdy drive is shopping central for the entire Baja peninsula. The most popular items offered here are electronics, traditional Mexican souvenirs, T-shirts, and prescription medicines—sans prescription. See p. 146.

- **Mercado de Artesanías, Tijuana:** For a more authentic and spirited marketplace atmosphere to pick up your colorful sombrero or serape, head to this collection of over 200 stalls in Tijuana, where bargaining is both accepted and expected. You'll also find pottery, clothing, and crafts from throughout Mexico. See p. 151.

- **Duty-Free in Cabo San Lucas:** Fine jewelry, watches, perfumes, and cosmetics are offered at duty-free prices in Cabo's UltraFemme store, the largest duty-free shop in Mexico. See p. 79.

7 The Hottest Nightlife

Although, as expected, Cabo San Lucas is home to much of Baja's nightlife, that resort city isn't the only place to have a good time after dark. Along the northern Pacific coast, beachside dance floors with live bands and extended happy hours in seaside bars dominate the nightlife. Here are some of my favorite hot spots:

- **Nikki Beach, Los Cabos:** The global haven of the hip has recently arrived in Cabo San Lucas, on the beachfront of the Meliá San Lucas hotel on Medano Beach. Lounge on oversize beds draped in white, day or night, while sipping colorful cocktails and watching the beautiful people groove to music spun by the worlds' hottest DJs. See p. 84.
- **Cabos's Cantinas:** The nightlife scene in Los Cabos originated in a collection of rowdy beach bars, which still hold their appeal to this day, regularly packing in the crowds until the first fishing boats head out to sea. The Giggling Marlin and El Squid Roe still rank as the top spots for revelers looking for the laid-back but riotous good time that seems only to happen here. See chapter 4.
- **Tijuana's Avenida Revolución:** This street ranks among the world's most famous—or infamous—for nighttime carousing. "La Revo," as it's commonly known, is probably the single most common introduction

tourists have to Mexico, though it offers only a glimmer of the country's wealth of attractions. No matter the night, you're likely to find a party atmosphere here on par with the best of a Mardi Gras celebration in full swing. Bring plenty of aspirin for the next morning—as overindulgence is the norm. See chapter 7.
- **The Tijuana Club Scene:** Tijuana's nightlife is not limited to Avenida Revolución: Increasingly, the city is hosting a sophisticated club scene that welcomes internationally renowned DJs and the requisite selection of martinis. Most of these clubs are concentrated in the Zona Río. See chapter 7.
- **Beach Bars of Rosarito and Ensenada:** It doesn't have to be spring break in Rosarito or Ensenada to find a similar let-loose party atmosphere here. The favored spot is Papas & Beer, which has a location in both of these beach towns. And both regularly draw a young and spirited crowd for endless-summer style fun. See chapter 7.

8 The Most Luxurious Hotels

- **Las Ventanas al Paraíso** (Los Cabos Corridor; ℭ 888/525-0483 in the U.S., or 624/144-0300; www.lasventanas.com): Understated luxury by the sea, Las Ventanas perfectly melds desert landscapes and sophisticated pampering in this elegant yet intimate resort. Special extras like telescopes and fireplaces to private pools and rooftop terraces make each suite a slice of heaven. Their seaside infinity pool is one of my favorite places in the world, helped, in no small part, by the exceptional service offered by the resort's pool butlers. See p. 62.
- **Esperanza** (Los Cabos Corridor; ℭ 866/331-2226 in the U.S., or

624/145-6400; www.esperanzaresort.com): A creation of the famed Auberge Resorts group, this dramatically designed resort, set on a bluff overlooking two small coves, feels more like a collection of villas than a hotel. Hallmarks are its exceptional spa, award-winning restaurant, and impeccable service. See p. 62.
- **One&Only Palmilla** (Los Cabos Corridor; ℭ 800/637-2226 in the U.S., or 624/146-7000; www.oneandonlypalmilla.com): Currently the most popular Mexican resort with the Hollywood crowd, the completely renovated Palmilla has regained its spot as the most deluxe hotel in this

seaside playground known for sumptuous accommodations and great golf. The new, exceptional spa, fitness center, and yoga garden, as well as a restaurant by renowned chef Charlie Trotter, are added bonuses. See p. 63.

- **Camino Real Loreto Baja Beach & Golf Resort** (Loreto; © 800/873-7484 in the U.S., or 613/133-0010; www.caminoreal.com): Set on its own private cove just south of the historic town of Loreto, this is central Baja's most luxurious place to stay. An adjacent golf course and a calm beach for swimming add to its appeal. See p. 119.

- **Camino Real Tijuana** (Tijuana; © 877/215-3051 in the U.S., or 664/633-4000; www.caminoreal.com/tijuana): Bold architecture in vibrant colors are signature Camino Real, as is the collection of fine Mexican art that graces the lobby here. This city hotel is considered Tijuana's most popular, with spacious, work-friendly rooms and a selection of services that cater to taking care of business. See p. 152.

9 The Best Budget Inns

- **Cabo Inn** (Cabo San Lucas; © 624/143-3348; www.caboinnhotel.com): This former bordello is the best budget inn in the area. Rooms are small but extra clean and invitingly decorated, amenities are generous, and the owner-managers are friendly and helpful. Ideally located, close to town and near the marina, the inn caters to sportfishers. See p. 80.

- **Posada Señor La Mañana** (San José del Cabo; © 624/142-1372; www.srmanana.cam): Set in a grove of tropical trees, this simple and simply inviting inn offers guests an abundance of hammocks strewn about the property as well as the use of a community kitchen, which encourages impromptu get-togethers. See p. 58.

- **Hotel Mediterrane** (La Paz; © 612/125-1195; www.hotelmed.com): Mixing Mexican with Mediterranean decor details, the result here is a stylish, economical inn. The location near the *malecón* means you're close to everything. The on-site Trattoria La Pazta restaurant is a favorite of mine in La Paz. See p. 105.

- **Hotel Las Trojes** (Loreto; © 613/135-0277; www.loreto.com/costa2.htm): This unusual bed-and-breakfast is built from authentic wooden granaries *(trojes)* from the Tarascan Indians, brought over from the state of Michoacán. A beach bar and the friendly service are additional reasons to stay. See p. 121.

- **Hotel Hacienda Mulegé** (Mulegé; © 615/153-0021): Right in the heart of Mulegé, this former 18th-century hacienda is a comfortable and value-priced place to stay, complete with a small shaded pool, restaurant, and popular bar. See p. 132.

- **La Fonda** (South of Rosarito Beach; no phone): Since the 1950s, La Fonda has welcomed repeat guests drawn to its dramatic setting perched on a cliff above breaking surf and the quiet of a place with no phones. The best rooms have fireplaces, which are a welcome addition during winter months. See p. 162.

10 The Best Unique Inns

- **Casa Natalia** (San José del Cabo; © 888/277-3814 in the U.S. or 624/142-5100; www.casanatalia.com): This renovated historic home, now a charming inn, is an oasis of palms, waterfalls, and flowers against the desert landscape. Each room and suite is an artful combination of modern architecture and traditional Mexican touches. The restaurant is the hottest in town. See p. 57.

- **Hotel California** (Todos Santos; ℂ 612/145-0525 or -0522): After undergoing a complete renovation in 2003, the Hotel California has now emerged as the hippest place to stay in the area. Jewel-tone rooms and a profusion of candles and eclectic accents make this a study in creative style. Although you can check out any time you please, chances are you won't want to after being lured in by the inviting pool area and the popular La Coronela Restaurant and Bar. See p. 88.

- **Adobe Guadalupe** (Valle de Guadalupe; ℂ 649/631-3098; www.adobe guadalupe.com): The six rooms of this inn are among the only places to stay in Mexico's wine country, and are inviting in their own right. It's also a boutique winery, offering its vintages with the four-course dinners served each evening (for an extra charge, though breakfasts are included). See p. 175.

- **Posada de las Flores** (Loreto; ℂ 877/245-2860 or 613/135-1162; www.posadadelasflores.com): Adjacent to the main plaza in this town steeped in history, this inn is the perfect setting from which to explore—rooms are individually decorated in fine Mexican antiques and arts and crafts. It also boasts a rooftop glass-bottomed swimming pool. See p. 120.

- **Punta Chivato** (north of Mulegé at Punta Chivato; ℂ 615/153-0188; www.posadadelasflores.com): Enjoy the 3 hectares (7½ acres) of desert landscape and tranquil, private beach that come with a stay in the large and beautifully decorated suites and guest rooms here. Meals are included, as are a host of light activities. There's even a private airstrip to make it more accessible. See p. 130.

11 The Best Dining Experiences

In this section, best doesn't necessarily mean most luxurious. Although some of the restaurants listed here are fancy affairs, others are simple places to get fine, authentic Mexican cuisine.

- **"C," at the One&Only Palmilla** (Los Cabos Corridor; ℂ 624/146-7000): Under the direction of celebrated chef Charlie Trotter, a meal at "C" is a fusion of exquisite flavors, perfectly melding Mexican and Continental cuisine. See p. 63.

- **Laja** (Valle de Guadalupe; ℂ 646/155-2556): This lovely adobe-and-stone gourmet restaurant has become a reason in and of itself to visit Mexico's wine country. A daily fixed menu of four to eight courses is prepared, which regularly draws a crowd and wins mounting accolades. See p. 176.

- **Café Santa Fe** (Todos Santos; ℂ 612/145-0300): Excellent northern Italian cuisine prepared in the exhibition kitchen of this gracious cafe has been a driving factor in drawing people to Todos Santos over the past decade. Enjoying lunch here in the flower-filled courtyard is a particularly wonderful way to pass an afternoon. See p. 90.

- **Mi Cocina** (San José del Cabo; ℂ 624/142-5100; www.casanatalia.com/dining.cfm): It could be the creative menu, the captivating garden setting, the hibiscus-infused martinis, or it could be the gracious hospitality of owners Nathalie and Loic. Whatever the reason, Mi Cocina at Casa Natalia gets my vote for the single best dining experience in Los Cabos.

There may possibly be better restaurants in the area, but for me, the combination of winning elements can't be topped. See p. 60.

- **The Mulegé Pig Roast** (Mulegé): It doesn't matter where you stay in Mulegé, you'll invariably be confronted with the possibility of a pig roast. As they say here, it's more than a pig, it's a party; and it's the must-do tourist activity in town, one in which the pig is roasted Polynesian-style in a palm-lined open pit for hours while guests enjoy libations. See p. 132.

- **El Boleo** (Santa Rosalía; © 615/ 152-0310): Throughout Mexico, bakeries offer a small version of the French baguette known as *boleos,* and I've concluded that they've been named after this bakery, in Santa Rosalía. This bakery has been operating since the late 1800s when the French Compañía de Boleo (part of the Rothschild family holdings) obtained a 99-year lease from the Mexican government to operate the area's copper mines in exchange for creating employment opportunities. Of course, the French executives

running the operation needed their bread, which continues to be addictive to this day. See p. 135.

- **Cien Años** (Tijuana; © 664/633-3900): One of the finest gourmet Mexican restaurants in Baja, Cien Años will intrigue even the most adventurous of diners with regional specialties that may include garlicky ant eggs or buttery *guisanos* (cactus worms). See p. 15.

- **La Embotelladora Vieja** (Ensenada; © 646/174-0807): In the Bodegas de Santo Tomás winery, this stylish restaurant features a Baja-French menu carefully crafted to complement wine. See p. 171.

- **Lobster in Puerto Nuevo** (Puerto Nuevo): It seems almost every restaurant or simple shack serving food in this tiny seaside town has locally caught lobster on the menu—and there's good reason why. It's fresh, and it's delicious. The Puerto Nuevo way of serving it is grilled and accompanied with fresh tortillas, salsa, limes, beans and rice, and the price is just over $10, making it well worth a stop in this town. See p. 164.

2

Planning Your Trip to Los Cabos & Baja

A little planning can make the difference between a good trip and a great trip. When should you go? What's the best way to get there? How much should you plan on spending? What festivals or special events will be taking place during your visit? What safety or health precautions are advised? I'll answer these and other questions for you in this chapter. In addition to these basics, I highly recommend taking a little time to learn about the culture and traditions of Mexico and the Baja. It can make the difference between simply getting away for a few days and truly adding cultural understanding to your trip. See appendix A for more details.

1 Baja California at a Glance

The Baja peninsula is part of Mexico—and yet it is not. Attached to the mainland United States and separated from the rest of Mexico by the Sea of Cortez (also called the Gulf of California), the Baja peninsula is longer than Italy, stretching 1,410km (874 miles) from Mexico's northernmost city of Tijuana to Cabo San Lucas at its southern tip. Volcanic uplifting created the craggy desertscape you see today. Whole forests of cardón cactus, spiky Joshua trees, and spindly ocotillo bushes populate the raw, untamed landscape.

Culturally and geographically, Baja is set apart from mainland Mexico, and it remained isolated for many years. Now the state of Baja California del Sur has developed into a vacation haven that offers spectacular golf, fishing, diving, and whale-watching. Great sportfishing originally centered attention on Los Cabos, and it remains a lure today, although golf has overtaken it as the principle attraction. Once accessible only by water, Baja attracted a hearty community of cruisers, fishermen, divers, and adventurers starting in the late 1940s. By the early 1980s, the Mexican government realized the growth potential of Los Cabos and invested in new highways, airport facilities, golf courses, and modern marine facilities. Expanded air traffic and the opening of Carretera Transpeninsular in 1973 paved the way for the area's spectacular growth.

BAJA SUR Of the peninsula's three regions, Baja Sur has attracted the most attention and travelers, and is increasingly known as a haven for golfers. Twin towns with distinct personalities sit at the tip of the peninsula: **Cabo San Lucas** and **San José del Cabo.** The two Cabos are the center of accommodations and activities.

The road that connects Cabo San Lucas and San José del Cabo is the centerpiece of resort growth. Known as **the Corridor,** this stretch of four well-paved lanes offers cliff-top vistas but has no nighttime lighting. The area's most deluxe resorts and renowned golf courses are here, along with a collection of dramatic beaches and coves.

Although Los Cabos often feels like the southern playground of the United States' West Coast, other areas of Baja Sur can seem like the least crowded corners of Mexico. **Todos Santos,** an artistic community on the Pacific side of the coastal curve, just north of the tip, draws travelers who find that Cabo San Lucas has outgrown them. **La Paz,** the capital of Baja Sur, remains an easygoing maritime port, with an interesting assortment of small lodgings and a growing diversity of eco- and adventure tours.

MID-BAJA   Among the highlights of the mid-Baja region are the east coast towns of **Loreto, Mulegé,** and **Santa Rosalía.** Although they have a much richer historic and cultural heritage than Baja Sur's resort towns, they've been eclipsed by the growth of tourism infrastructure and services in the two Cabos. Loreto currently stands at the center of attention of the Mexican government's promotional and investment focus, so expect this quiet town to be growing soon.

This area's natural attractions have made it a center for sea kayaking, sportfishing, and hiking—including excursions to view indigenous cave paintings, which UNESCO has named a World Heritage Site. This is also the place to come if you're interested in whale-watching; many tour companies operate out of Loreto and smaller neighboring towns. For more information, see "Whale-Watching in Baja: A Primer," in chapter 6.

BAJA NORTE   **Tijuana** has the dubious distinction of being the most visited and perhaps most misunderstood town in all of Mexico. Dog racing, free-flowing tequila, and a sin-city reputation have all been hallmarks of this classic border town, a favored resort for the Hollywood elite during Prohibition. New cultural and sporting attractions, extensive shopping, and strong business growth—of the reputable kind—are helping to brighten Tijuana's image.

Tranquil **Rosarito Beach** is also reemerging as a resort town, given a boost after the movie *Titanic* was filmed here (the set is now a movie-themed amusement park). Farther down the Pacific coast is the lovely port town of **Ensenada,** also known for its prime surfing and spirited sportfishing. The nearby vineyards of Mexico's wine country are a new and growing attraction.

2 Visitor Information

The **Mexico Hot Line** (✆ 800/44-MEXICO) is an excellent source for general information; you can request brochures on the country and get answers to the most common questions from the exceptionally well-trained, knowledgeable staff.

More information (15,000 pages' worth) about Mexico is available on the official site of Mexico's Tourism Promotion Board, **www.visitmexico.com.** The **U.S. State Department** (✆ 202/647-5225;** http://travel.state.gov) offers a **Consular Information Sheet** on Mexico (http://travel.state.gov), with safety, medical, driving, and general travel information gleaned from reports by its offices in Mexico, and consistently updated. You can also request the Consular Information Sheet by fax (✆ 202/647-3000). The same website also provides other consular information sheets and warnings as well as *Tips for Travelers to Mexico.* Another source is the Department of State's background notes series. Visit the State Department home page (www.state.gov) for information.

The **Centers for Disease Control and Prevention Hot Line** (✆ 800/311-3435 or 404/639-3534; www.cdc.gov) is a source of medical information for travelers to Mexico and elsewhere. For travelers to Mexico and Central America, the number with recorded messages is © **877/FYI-TRIP.** The toll-free fax number for requesting information is © 888/232-3299. Information by fax is also available at **www.cdc.gov/travel**. The U.S. State Department offers medical information for Americans traveling abroad and a list of air ambulance services at **http://travel.state.gov**.

MEXICAN GOVERNMENT TOUR-IST BOARD   The board has offices in major North American cities, in addition to the main office in Mexico City (© **555/203-1103**).

United States: Chicago (© **312/606-9252**), Houston (© **713/772-2581**, ext. 105, or 713/772-3819), Los Angeles (© **310/282-9112**), and New York (© **212/308-2110**). The Mexican Embassy is at 1911 Pennsylvania Ave. NW, Washington, DC 20005 (© **202/728-1750**).

Canada: 1 Place Ville-Marie, Suite 1931, Montreal, QUE H3B 2C3 (© **514/871-1052**); 2 Bloor St. W., Suite 1502, Toronto, ON M4W 3E2 (© **416/925-0704**); 999 W. Hastings, Suite 1110, Vancouver, BC V6C 2W2 (© **604/669-2845**). The Embassy office is at 1500-45 O'Connor St., Ottawa, ON K1P 1A4 (© **613/233-8988;** fax 613/235-9123).

3 Entry Requirements & Customs

ENTRY REQUIREMENTS
All travelers to Mexico are required to present **proof of citizenship,** such as an original birth certificate with a raised seal, a valid passport, or naturalization papers. Those using a birth certificate should also have current photo identification, such as a driver's license or official ID. If the last name on the birth certificate is different from your current name, bring a photo identification card *and* legal proof of the name change, such as the original marriage license or certificate. *Note:* Photocopies are *not* acceptable.

The best ID is a passport. Safeguard your passport in an inconspicuous, inaccessible place like a money belt, and keep a copy of the critical pages with your passport number in a separate place. If you lose your passport, visit the nearest consulate of your native country as soon as possible for a replacement.

ONCE YOU'RE IN MEXICO
You must carry a **Mexican Tourist Permit (FMT),** the equivalent of a tourist visa, which Mexican border officials issue, free of charge, after proof of citizenship is accepted. Airlines generally provide the

necessary forms aboard your flight to Mexico. The FMT is more important than a passport in Mexico, so guard it carefully. If you lose it, you may not be permitted to leave the country until you can replace it—a bureaucratic hassle that can take anywhere from a few hours to a week.

The FMT can be issued for up to 180 days. Sometimes officials don't ask but just stamp a time limit, so be sure to say "6 months," or at least twice as long as you intend to stay. If you decide to extend your stay, you may request that additional time be added to your FMT from an official immigration office in Mexico.

Note: Children under 18 traveling without parents or with only one parent must have a notarized letter from the absent parent(s) authorizing the travel.

CUSTOMS
WHAT YOU CAN BRING INTO MEXICO
When you enter Mexico, Customs officials will be tolerant as long as you have no illegal drugs or firearms. You're allowed to bring in two cartons of cigarettes or 50 cigars, plus 1 kilogram (2.2

> ### (Tips) A Few Words on Prices in Mexico
>
> The peso's value continues to fluctuate—at press time it was close to 11 pesos to the dollar. Prices in this book (which are always given in U.S. dollars) have been converted to U.S. dollars at 11 pesos to the dollar. Most hotels in Mexico—with the exception of places that receive little foreign tourism—quote prices in U.S. dollars. Thus, currency fluctuations are unlikely to affect the prices charged by most hotels.
>
> Mexico has a **value-added tax** of 15% (*Impuesto al Valor Agregado,* or IVA, pronounced "ee-bah") on almost everything, including restaurant meals, bus tickets, and souvenirs. One of the exceptions is Los Cabos, where the IVA is 10%; as ports of entry, the towns receive a break on taxes. Hotels charge the usual 15% IVA, plus a locally administered bed tax of 2% (in many but not all areas), for a total of 17%. In Los Cabos, hotels charge the 10% IVA plus 2% room tax. Prices quoted by hotels and restaurants will not necessarily include IVA. You may find that upper-end properties quote prices without IVA included, while lower-priced hotels include IVA. Always ask to see a printed price sheet, and always ask if the tax is included.

lb.) of smoking tobacco; two 1-liter bottles of wine or hard liquor, and 12 rolls of film. A laptop computer, camera equipment, and sports equipment that could feasibly be used during your stay are also allowed. The underlying guideline is: Don't bring anything that looks as if it's meant to be resold in Mexico.

WHAT YOU CAN TAKE HOME
U.S. citizens who want specifics on what they can bring back should download the invaluable free pamphlet *Know Before You Go* from **www.customs.gov**. (Click "Traveler Spotlight," then "Know Before You Go.") Or contact the **U.S. Customs Service,** 1300 Pennsylvania Ave. NW, Washington, DC 20229 (© **877/287-8867**) and request the pamphlet.

For a clear summary of **Canadian** rules, request the booklet *I Declare* from the **Canada Customs and Revenue Agency** (© **800/461-9999** in Canada, or 204/983-3500; www.ccra-adrc.gc.ca).

U.K. citizens should contact **HM Customs & Excise** (© **0845/010-9000,** or 020/8929-0152 from outside the U.K.; www.hmce.gov.uk).

A helpful brochure for **Australian citizens,** available from Australian consulates or Customs offices, is *Know Before You Go.* For more information, contact the **Australian Customs Services** (© **1300/363-263;** www.customs.gov.au).

For information on **New Zealand Customs,** contact The Customhouse, 17–21 Whitmore St., Box 2218, Wellington (© **04/473-6099** or 0800/428-786; www.customs.govt.nz).

4 Money

The currency in Mexico is the Mexican **peso.** Paper currency comes in denominations of 20, 50, 100, 200, 500, and 1,000 pesos. Coins come in denominations of 1, 2, 5, 10, and 20 pesos, and 20 and 50 **centavos** (100 centavos = 1 peso).

The current exchange rate for the U.S. dollar, and the one used in this book, is around 11 pesos; at that rate, an item that costs 11 pesos would be equivalent to US$1.

Getting **change** is a problem. Small-denomination bills and coins are hard to come by, so start collecting them early in your trip. Shopkeepers everywhere always seem to be out of change and small bills; that's doubly true in markets.

Many establishments that deal with tourists, especially in coastal resort areas, quote prices in dollars. To avoid confusion, they use the abbreviations "Dlls." for dollars and "M.N." (*moneda nacional,* or national currency) for pesos. All dollar equivalencies in this book were based on an exchange rate of 11 pesos per dollar.

The rate of exchange fluctuates daily, so you probably are better off not exchanging too much currency at once. Don't forget to have enough pesos to carry you over a weekend or Mexican holiday, when banks are closed. In general, avoid carrying the U.S. $100 bill, the bill most commonly counterfeited in Mexico and therefore the most difficult to exchange, especially in smaller towns. Because small bills and coins in pesos are hard to come by in Mexico, the $1 bill is very useful for tipping. A tip of U.S. coins, which cannot be exchanged into Mexican currency, is of no value to the service provider.

The bottom line on exchanging money: Ask first, and shop around. Banks generally pay the top rates.

Exchange houses (*casas de cambio*) are generally more convenient than banks because they have more locations and longer hours; the rate of exchange may be the same as at a bank or slightly lower.

Before leaving a bank or exchange-house window, count your change in front of the teller before the next client steps up.

Large airports have currency-exchange counters that often stay open whenever flights are operating. Though convenient, they generally do not offer the most favorable rates.

A hotel's exchange desk commonly pays less favorable rates than banks; however, when the currency is in a state of flux, higher-priced hotels are known to pay higher rates than banks, in an effort to attract dollars. In almost all cases, you receive a better rate by changing money first, then paying.

BANKS & ATMs   Banks in Mexico are rapidly expanding and improving services. They tend to be open weekdays from 9am until 5pm, and often for at least a half-day on Saturday. In larger resorts and cities, they can generally accommodate the exchange of dollars (which used to stop at noon) anytime during business hours. During times when the currency is in flux, a particular bank may not exchange dollars, so check before standing in line. Some, but not all, banks charge a service fee of about 1% to exchange traveler's checks. However, you can pay for most purchases directly with traveler's checks at the establishment's stated exchange rate. Don't even bother with personal checks drawn on a U.S. bank—the bank will wait for your check to clear, which can take weeks, before giving you your money.

Travelers to Mexico can easily withdraw money from **ATMs** in most major cities and resort areas. The U.S. State Department has an advisory against using ATMs in Mexico for safety reasons, stating that

Money Matters
The universal currency sign ($) is used to indicate pesos in Mexico. The use of this symbol in this book, however, denotes U.S. currency.

they should only be used during business hours, but this pertains primarily to Mexico City, where crime remains a significant problem. In most resorts in Mexico, the use of ATMs is perfectly safe—just use the same precautions you would at any ATM. Universal bank cards (such as the Cirrus and PLUS systems) can be used. This is a convenient way to withdraw money and avoid carrying too much with you at any time. The exchange rate is generally more favorable than that at a currency house. Most machines offer Spanish/English menus and dispense pesos, but some offer the option of withdrawing dollars. Be sure to check the daily withdrawal limit before you depart.

For Cirrus locations abroad, check © **800/424-7787** or www.mastercard.com. For PLUS outlets abroad, check © **800/843-7587** or www.visa.com. Before you leave home, check your daily withdrawal limit, and make sure that your personal identification number (PIN) works in international destinations. Also keep in mind that many banks impose a fee every time a card is used at a different bank's ATM, and that fee can be higher for international transactions (up to $5 or more) than for domestic ones.

You can also get cash advances on your credit card at an ATM. Keep in mind that credit card companies try to protect themselves from theft by limiting the funds someone can withdraw outside their home country, so call your credit card company before you leave home. And keep in mind that you'll pay interest from the moment of your withdrawal, even if you pay your monthly bills on time.

CREDIT CARDS   Credit cards are a safe way to carry money: They also provide a convenient record of all your expenses, and they generally offer relatively good exchange rates. You can also withdraw cash advances from your credit cards at banks or ATMs, provided you know your PIN. If you've forgotten yours, or didn't even know you had one, call the number on the back of your credit card and ask the bank to send it to you. It usually takes 5 to 7 business days, though some banks will provide the number over the phone if you tell them your mother's maiden name or some other personal information.

Keep in mind that when you use your credit card abroad, most banks assess a 2% fee above the 1% fee charged by Visa or MasterCard or American Express for currency conversion on credit charges. But credit cards still may be the smart way to go when you factor in things like exorbitant ATM fees and higher traveler's check exchange rates (and service fees).

In Mexico Visa, MasterCard, and American Express are the most accepted cards. You'll be able to charge most hotel, restaurant, and store purchases, as well as almost all airline tickets, on your credit card. You generally can't charge gasoline purchases in Mexico. You can get cash advances of several hundred dollars on your card, but there may be a wait of 20 minutes to 2 hours.

Charges will be made in pesos, then converted into dollars by the bank issuing the credit card. Generally you receive the favorable bank rate when paying by credit card. However, be aware that some establishments in Mexico add a 5% to 7% surcharge when you pay with a credit card. This is especially true when using American Express. Many times, advertised discounts will not apply if you pay with a credit card.

For tips and telephone numbers to call if your wallet is stolen or lost, go to "Lost & Found" in the "Fast Facts" section of this chapter.

5 When to Go

High season on the Baja peninsula begins around December 20 and continues to Easter. This is the best time for calm, warm weather; snorkeling, diving, and fishing (the calmer weather means clearer and more predictable seas); and for visiting the ruins that dot the interior of the peninsula. Book well in advance if you plan to be in Los Cabos around the holidays.

Low season begins the day after Easter and continues to mid-December; during low season, prices may drop 20% to 50%.

The weather in Baja, land of extremes, can be unpredictable. It can be sizzling hot in summer and cold and windy in winter—so windy that fishing and other nautical expeditions may be grounded for a few days. Though winter is often warm enough for watersports, bring a wet suit if you're a serious diver or snorkeler, as well as warmer clothes for unexpectedly chilly weather at night.

BAJA CALENDAR OF EVENTS

Note: Banks, government offices, and many stores close on national holidays.

January

Día de Año Nuevo (New Year's Day). This national holiday is perhaps the quietest day in all of Mexico. Most people stay home or attend church. All businesses are closed. In traditional indigenous communities, new tribal leaders are inaugurated with colorful ceremonies rooted in the pre-Hispanic past. January 1.

Día de los Reyes (Three Kings Day). This day commemorates the Three Kings bringing gifts to the Christ Child. On this day, children receive gifts, much like the traditional Christmas gift-giving in the United States. Friends and families gather to share the Rosca de Reyes, a special cake. Inside the cake is a small doll representing the Christ Child; whoever receives the doll must host a tamales-and-*atole* party on February 2. January 6.

February

Día de la Candelaria (Candlemas). Music, dances, processions, food, and other festivities lead up to a blessing of seed and candles in a ceremony that mixes pre-Hispanic and European traditions marking the end of winter. Those who attended the Three Kings celebration reunite to share *atole* and tamales at a party hosted by the recipient of the doll found in the Rosca. February 2.

Día de la Constitución (Constitution Day). This national holiday is in honor of the current Mexican constitution, signed in 1917 as a result of the revolutionary war of 1910. It's celebrated through small parades. February 5.

Carnaval. Carnaval takes place over the 3 days before the beginning of Lent. La Paz celebrates with special zeal, and visitors enjoy a festive atmosphere and parades. The 3 days preceding Ash Wednesday.

Miércoles de Ceniza (Ash Wednesday). The start of Lent and time of abstinence, this is a day of reverence nationwide; some towns honor it with folk dancing and fairs.

March

Semana Santa (Holy Week). Celebrates the last week in the life of Christ from Palm Sunday through Easter Sunday with somber religious processions almost nightly, spoofing of Judas, and reenactments of biblical events, plus food and craft fairs. Businesses close during this traditional week of Mexican national vacations.

If you plan on traveling to or around Mexico during Holy Week, make reservations early. Seats on flights into and out of the country will be reserved months in advance. The week following is a traditional vacation period. Late March or April.

May

El Día del Trabajo (Labor Day). Workers' parades take place countrywide, and everything closes. May 1. National holiday.

La Paz Foundation. Celebrates the founding of La Paz by Cortez in 1535, and features *artesanía* exhibitions from throughout southern Baja. May 1 to 5. La Paz.

Cinco de Mayo. A national holiday that commemorates the defeat of the French at the Battle of Puebla. May 5.

June

Día de la Marina (Navy Day). Celebrated in all coastal towns, with naval parades and fireworks. June 1.

August

Fiestas de la Vendimia (Wine Harvest Festival). Ensenada's food-and-wine festival celebrates the annual harvest, with blessings, seminars, parties, and wine tastings. Call ℂ **800/ 44-MEXICO** for details and schedule. Mid- to late August.

September

Día de la Independencia (Independence Day). Celebrates Mexico's independence from Spain. A day of parades, picnics, and family reunions throughout the country. At 11pm on September 15, the president of Mexico gives the famous independence *grito* (shout) from the National Palace in Mexico City. At least half a million people crowd into the *zócalo* (town square), and the rest of the country watches the event on TV. September 15 and 16. September 16 is a national holiday.

October

Festival Fundador. Celebrates the founding of the town of Todos Santos

in 1723. Streets around the main plaza fill with food, games, and wandering troubadours. October 10 to 14.

Día de la Raza ("Ethnicity Day," or Columbus Day). This day commemorates the fusion of the Spanish and Mexican peoples. October 12.

November

Día del los Muertos (Day of the Dead). This national holiday (Nov 1) actually lasts for 2 days: All Saints' Day—honoring saints and deceased children—and All Souls' Day, honoring deceased adults. Relatives gather at cemeteries countrywide, carrying candles and food, and often spend the night beside graves of loved ones. Weeks before, bakers begin producing bread in the shape of mummies or round loaves decorated with bread "bones." Sugar skulls emblazoned with glittery names are sold everywhere. Many days ahead, homes and churches erect altars laden with bread, fruit, flowers, candles, favorite foods, and photographs of saints and of the deceased. On both nights, costumed children walk through the streets, often carrying mock coffins and pumpkin lanterns, into which they expect money will be dropped. November 1 and 2.

Día de la Revolución (Revolution Day). This national holiday commemorates the start of the Mexican Revolution in 1910 with parades, speeches, rodeos, and patriotic events. November 20.

December

Feast of the Virgin of Guadalupe. Religious processions, street fairs, dancing, fireworks, and Masses honor the patroness of Mexico. It is one of the country's most moving and beautiful displays of traditional culture. The Virgin of Guadalupe appeared to a young man, Juan Diego, in December

1531 on a hill near Mexico City. It's customary for children to dress up as Juan Diego, wearing mustaches and red bandanas. December 12.

Christmas Posadas. On each of the 9 nights before Christmas, it's customary to reenact the Holy Family's search for an inn. Door-to-door candlelit processions pass through cities and villages nationwide, especially Querétaro and Taxco. Hosted by businesses and community organizations, these take the place of the northern tradition of a Christmas party. December 15 to 24.

Navidad (Christmas). Mexicans extend this celebration and leave their jobs, often beginning 2 weeks before Christmas and continuing all the way through New Year's. Many businesses close, and resorts and hotels fill. December 23 to 25.

Víspera de Año Nuevo (New Year's Eve). As in the rest of the world, New Year's Eve in Mexico is celebrated with parties, fireworks, and plenty of noise. December 31.

6 Health & Safety

STAYING HEALTHY
GENERAL AVAILABILITY OF HEALTH CARE

In most of Mexico's resort destinations, health care meeting U.S. standards is now available. Mexico's major cities are also known for their excellent health care, although the facilities available may be sparser, and equipment older than what is available at home. Prescription medicine is broadly available at Mexico pharmacies; however, be aware that you may need a copy of your prescription, or need to obtain a prescription from a local doctor. This is especially true in the border towns, such as in Tijuana, where many Americans have been crossing into Mexico specifically for the purpose of purchasing lower-priced prescription medicines.

Contact the **International Association for Medical Assistance to Travelers (IAMAT; © 716/754-4883,** or 416/ 652-0137 in Canada; www.iamat.org) for tips on travel and health concerns in the countries you're visiting, and lists of local, English-speaking doctors. The United States **Centers for Disease Control and Prevention** (© **800/311-3435;** www. cdc.gov) provides up-to-date information on health hazards by region or country and offers tips on food safety.

COMMON AILMENTS

HIGH-ALTITUDE HAZARDS Travelers to certain regions of Mexico occasionally experience **elevation sickness,** which results from the relative lack of oxygen and the decrease in barometric pressure that characterizes high elevations (more than 1,500m/5,000 ft.). Symptoms include shortness of breath, fatigue, headache, insomnia, and even nausea. Mexico City is at 2,121m (6,957 ft.) above sea level, and mountainous points within central Baja are also at high elevations. At high elevations, it takes about 10 days to acquire the extra red blood corpuscles you need to adjust to the scarcity of oxygen. To help your body acclimate, drink plenty of fluids, avoid alcoholic beverages, and don't overexert yourself during the first few days. If you have heart or lung problems, talk to your doctor before going above 2,400m (8,000 ft.).

BUGS, BITES & OTHER WILDLIFE CONCERNS Mosquitoes and **gnats** are prevalent along the coast. Insect repellent *(repelente contra insectos)* is a must, and it's not always available in Mexico. If you'll be in these areas and are prone to bites, bring along a repellent that contains the active ingredient DEET. Avon's Skin So Soft also works extremely well.

Another good remedy to keep the mosquitoes away is to mix citronella essential oil with basil, clove, and lavender essential oils. If you're sensitive to bites, pick up some antihistamine cream from a drugstore at home.

Most readers won't ever see a scorpion (*alacrán*). But if one stings you, go immediately to a doctor. In Mexico you can buy scorpion toxin antidote at any drugstore. It is an injection and it costs around $25. This is a good idea if you plan to camp in a remote area where medical assistance can be several hours away.

MORE SERIOUS DISEASES You shouldn't be overly concerned about tropical diseases if you stay on the normal tourist routes and don't eat street food. However, both dengue fever and cholera have appeared in Mexico in recent years. Talk to your doctor or to a medical specialist in tropical diseases about precautions you should take. You can also get medical bulletins from the U.S. State Department and the Centers for Disease Control and Prevention (see "Visitor Information," earlier). You can protect yourself by taking some simple precautions: Watch what you eat and drink; don't swim in stagnant water (ponds, slow-moving rivers, or wells); and avoid mosquito bites by covering up, using repellent, and sleeping under netting. The most dangerous areas seem to be on Mexico's west coast, away from the big resorts.

STAYING SAFE

CRIME I have lived and traveled in Mexico for over a decade, have never had any serious trouble, and rarely feel suspicious of anyone or any situation. You will probably feel physically safer in most Mexican cities and villages than in any comparable place at home. However, crime in Mexico has received attention in the North American press over the past several years. Many feel this unfairly exaggerates the real dangers, but it should be noted that crime rates, including taxi robberies, kidnappings, and highway carjackings, have risen in recent years. The most severe problems have been concentrated in Mexico City, where even longtime foreign residents will attest to the overall lack of security. Isolated incidents have also occurred in Ixtapa, Baja, Cancún, and even traditionally tranquil Puerto Escondido. Check the U.S. State Department advisory before you travel for any notable hot spots. See "Visitor Information," earlier in this chapter, for information on the latest **U.S. State Department advisories.**

Precautions are necessary, but travelers should be realistic. Common sense is essential. You can generally trust people whom you approach for help or directions—but be wary of anyone who approaches you offering the same. The more insistent the person is, the more cautious you should be. The crime rate is, on the whole, much lower in Mexico than in most parts of the United States, and the nature of crimes in general is less violent. Random, violent, or serial crime is essentially unheard of in Mexico. You are much more likely to meet kind and helpful Mexicans than you are to encounter those set on thievery and

---

Tips **Over-the-Counter Drugs in Mexico**

Antibiotics and other drugs that you'd need a prescription to buy in the States are available over the counter in Mexican pharmacies. Mexican pharmacies also carry a limited selection of common over-the-counter cold, sinus, and allergy remedies.

Tips Treating & Avoiding Digestive Trouble

It's called "travelers' diarrhea" or *turista*, the Spanish word for "tourist": persistent diarrhea, often accompanied by fever, nausea, and vomiting, that used to attack many travelers to Mexico. (Some in the U.S. call this "Montezuma's revenge," but you won't hear it called that in Mexico.) Widespread improvements in infrastructure, sanitation, and education have practically eliminated this ailment, especially in well-developed resort areas. Most travelers make a habit of drinking only bottled water, which also helps to protect against unfamiliar bacteria. In resort areas, and generally throughout Mexico, only purified ice is used. If you do come down with this ailment, nothing beats Pepto Bismol, readily available in Mexico. Imodium is also available in Mexico and is used by many travelers for a quick fix. A good high-potency (or "therapeutic") vitamin supplement and even extra vitamin C can help; yogurt is good for healthy digestion.

Since dehydration can quickly become life threatening, the Public Health Service advises that you be careful to replace fluids and electrolytes (potassium, sodium, and the like) during a bout of diarrhea. Drink Pedialyte, a rehydration solution available at most Mexican pharmacies, or natural fruit juice, such as guava or apple (stay away from orange juice, which has laxative properties), with a pinch of salt added.

How to Prevent It: The U.S. Public Health Service recommends the following measures for preventing travelers' diarrhea: **Drink only purified water** (boiled water, canned or bottled beverages, beer, or wine). **Choose food carefully.** In general, avoid salads (except in first-class restaurants), uncooked vegetables, undercooked protein, and unpasteurized milk or milk products, including cheese. Choose food that is freshly cooked and still hot. In addition, something as simple as **clean hands** can go a long way toward preventing *turista*.

deceit. (See also "Emergencies" under "Fast Facts," later in this chapter.)

BRIBES & SCAMS As is the case around the world, there are the occasional bribes and scams in Mexico, targeted at people believed to be naive—such as the telltale tourist. For years Mexico was known as a place where bribes—called *mordidas* (bites)—were expected; however, the country is rapidly changing. Frequently, offering a bribe today, especially to a police officer, is considered an insult, and it can land you in deeper trouble.

If you believe a **bribe** is being requested, here are a few tips on dealing with the situation. Even if you speak Spanish, don't utter a word of it to Mexican officials. That way you'll appear innocent, all the while understanding every word.

When you are crossing the border, should the person who inspects your car ask for a tip, you can ignore this request—but understand that the official may suddenly decide that a complete search of your belongings is in order. If faced with a situation where you feel you're being asked for a *propina* (literally, "tip"; colloquially, "bribe"), how much should you offer? Usually $3 to $5 or the equivalent in pesos will do the trick. Many tourists have the impression that everything works better in Mexico if you "tip"; however, in reality, this only perpetuates the *mordida* attitude. If you are pleased with a service, feel free to tip, but you shouldn't tip simply to attempt to get away with something illegal or inappropriate, whether it is crossing the border without having your car inspected or not getting a ticket that's deserved.

Whatever you do, **avoid impoliteness;** under no circumstances should you insult a Latin American official. Extreme politeness, even in the face of adversity, rules Mexico. In Mexico, *gringos* have a reputation for being loud and demanding. By adopting the local custom of excessive courtesy, you'll have greater success in negotiations of any kind. Stand your ground, but do it politely.

As you travel in Mexico, you may encounter several types of **scams,** which are typical throughout the world. One involves some kind of a **distraction** or feigned commotion. While your attention is diverted, a pickpocket makes a grab for your wallet. In another common scam, an **unaccompanied child** pretends to be lost and frightened and takes your hand for safety. Meanwhile the child or an accomplice plunders your pockets. A third involves **confusing currency.** A shoeshine boy, street musician, guide, or other individual might offer you a service for a price that seems reasonable—in pesos. When it comes time to pay, he or she tells you the price is in dollars, not pesos. Be very clear on the price and currency when services are involved.

7 Specialized Travel Resources

FAMILY TRAVEL

I can't think of a better place to introduce children to the exciting adventure of exploring a different culture. Among the best destinations for children in Mexico is La Paz (see chapter 5). The larger hotels in Los Cabos can often arrange for a babysitter. Some hotels in the moderate-to-luxury range have small playgrounds and pools for children and hire caretakers with special activity programs during the day. Few budget hotels offer these amenities.

Before leaving, you should check with your doctor to get advice on medications to take along. Disposable diapers cost about the same in Mexico but are of poorer quality. You can get Huggies Supreme and Pampers identical to the ones sold in the United States, but at a higher price. Many stores sell Gerber's baby foods. Dry cereals, powdered formulas, baby bottles, and purified water are all easily available in midsize and large cities or resorts.

Cribs, however, may present a problem—only the largest and most luxurious hotels provide them. Rollaway beds are often available for children staying in the room with parents. Child seats or high chairs at restaurants are common, and most restaurants will go out of their way to accommodate your child.

Because many travelers to Baja will rent a car, it is advisable to bring your car seat. Leasing agencies in Mexico do not rent car seats.

Every country's regulations differ, but in general children traveling abroad should have plenty of documentation on hand, particularly if they're traveling with someone other than their own parents (in which case a notarized form letter from a parent is often required). For details on entry requirements for children traveling abroad, go to the U.S. State Department website (travel.state.gov/foreignentryreqs. htm).

Throughout this book, the "Kids" icon distinguishes attractions, hotels, restaurants, and other destinations that are particularly attractive and accommodating to children and families.

Familyhostel (✆ **800/733-9753;** www.learn.unh.edu/familyhostel) takes the whole family, including kids ages 8 to 15, on moderately priced domestic and international learning vacations. Lectures, fields trips, and sightseeing are guided by a team of academics.

Recommended family travel Internet sites include **Family Travel Forum** (www.familytravelforum.com), a comprehensive site that offers customized trip planning; **Family Travel Network** (www.familytravelnetwork.com), an award-winning site that offers travel features, deals, and tips; **Traveling Internationally with Your Kids** (www.travelwithyourkids.com), a comprehensive site offering sound advice for long-distance and international travel with children; and **Family Travel Files** (www.thefamilytravelfiles.com), which offers an online magazine and a directory of off-the-beaten-path tours and tour operators for families.

TRAVELERS WITH DISABILITIES

Mexico may seem like one giant obstacle course to travelers in wheelchairs or on crutches. At airports, you may encounter steep stairs before finding a well-hidden elevator or escalator—if one exists. Airlines will often arrange wheelchair assistance to the baggage area. Porters are generally available to help with luggage at airports and large bus stations, once you've cleared baggage claim.

Mexican airports are upgrading their services, but it is not uncommon to board from a remote position, meaning you either descend stairs to a bus that ferries you to the plane, which you board by climbing stairs, or you walk across the tarmac to your plane and ascend the stairs. Deplaning presents the same problem in reverse.

Escalators (and there aren't many in the country) are often out of order. Stairs without handrails abound. Few restrooms are equipped for travelers with disabilities; when one is available, access to it may be through a narrow passage that won't accommodate a wheelchair or a person on crutches. Many deluxe hotels (the most expensive) now have rooms with bathrooms for people with disabilities. Those traveling on a budget should stick with one-story hotels or hotels with elevators. Even so, there will probably still be obstacles somewhere. Generally speaking, no matter where you are, someone will lend a hand, although you may have to ask for it.

Most disabilities shouldn't stop anyone from traveling. There are more options and resources out there than ever before.

Many travel agencies offer customized tours and itineraries for travelers with disabilities. **Flying Wheels Travel** (✆ **507/451-5005;** www.flyingwheelstravel.com) offers escorted tours and cruises that emphasize sports and private tours in minivans with lifts. **Access-Able Travel Source** (✆ **303/232-2979;** www.access-able.com) offers extensive access information and advice for traveling around the world with disabilities. **Accessible Journeys** (✆ **800/846-4537** or 610/521-0339; www.disabilitytravel.com) caters specifically to slow walkers and wheelchair travelers and their families and friends.

Organizations that offer assistance to disabled travelers include **MossRehab** (www.mossresourcenet.org), which provides a library of accessible-travel resources online; **SATH (Society for Accessible Travel & Hospitality;** ✆ **212/447-7284;** www.sath.org; annual membership fees: $45 adults, $30 seniors and students), which offers a wealth of travel resources for all types of disabilities and informed recommendations on destinations, access guides, travel agents, tour operators, vehicle rentals, and companion services; and the **American Foundation for the Blind**

(AFB) (© **800/232-5463;** www.afb.org), a referral resource for the blind or visually impaired that includes information on traveling with Seeing Eye dogs.

For more information specifically targeted to travelers with disabilities, the community website **iCan** (www.ican online.net/channels/travel/index.cfm) has destination guides and several regular columns on accessible travel. Also check out the quarterly magazine **Emerging Horizons** ($15 per year, $20 outside the U.S.; www.emerginghorizons.com); and *Open World* magazine, published by SATH (see above; subscription: $13 per year, $21 outside the U.S.).

SENIOR TRAVEL

Mexico is a popular country for retirees. For decades, North Americans have been living indefinitely in Mexico by returning to the border and re-crossing with a new tourist permit every 6 months. Mexican immigration officials have caught on, and now limit the maximum time in the country to 6 months within any year. This is to encourage even partial residents to acquire proper documentation.

Some of the most popular places for long-term stays in Baja are in the mid-Baja region, including Loreto and Mulegé. Also, northern Baja is becoming a popular place, especially around the Ensenada region.

AIM, Apdo. Postal 31–70, 45050 Guadalajara, Jal., is a well-written, informative newsletter for prospective retirees. Subscriptions are $18 to the United States and $21 to Canada. Back issues are three for $5.

Sanborn Tours, 2015 S. 10th St., Post Office Drawer 519, McAllen, TX 78505-0519 (© **800/395-8482**), offers a "Retire in Mexico" orientation tour.

Mention the fact that you're a senior citizen when you make your travel reservations. Although all of the major U.S. airlines except America West have canceled their senior discount and coupon-book programs, many hotels still offer discounts for seniors.

Members of **AARP** (formerly known as the American Association of Retired Persons), 601 E St. NW, Washington, DC 20049 (© **888/687-2277;** www.aarp. org), get discounts on hotels, airfares, and car rentals. AARP offers members a wide range of benefits, including *AARP: The Magazine* and a monthly newsletter. Anyone over 50 can join.

Many reliable agencies and organizations target the 50-plus market. **Elderhostel** (© **877/426-8056;** www.elderhostel. org) arranges study programs for those aged 55 and over (and a spouse or companion of any age) in the U.S. and in more than 80 countries around the world. Most courses last 5 to 7 days in the U.S. (2–4 weeks abroad), and many include airfare, accommodations in university dormitories or modest inns, meals, and tuition. **ElderTreks** (© **800/741-7956;** www. eldertreks.com) offers small-group tours to off-the-beaten-path or adventure-travel locations, restricted to travelers 50 and older. **INTRAV** (© **800/456-8100;** www. intrav.com) is a high-end tour operator that caters to the mature, discerning traveler, not specifically seniors, with trips around the world that include guided safaris, polar expeditions, private-jet adventures, and small-boat cruises down jungle rivers.

Recommended publications offering travel resources and discounts for seniors include: the quarterly magazine *Travel 50 & Beyond* (www.travel50andbeyond. com); *Travel Unlimited: Uncommon Adventures for the Mature Traveler* (Avalon); *101 Tips for Mature Travelers,* available from Grand Circle Travel (© **800/221-2610** or 617/350-7500; www.gct.com); and *Unbelievably Good Deals and Great Adventures That You Absolutely Can't Get Unless You're Over 50* (McGraw-Hill), by Joann Rattner Heilman.

GAY & LESBIAN TRAVELERS

Mexico is a conservative country, with deeply rooted Catholic religious traditions. Public displays of same-sex affection are rare and still considered shocking for men, especially outside of urban or resort areas. Women in Mexico frequently walk hand in hand, but anything more would cross the boundary of acceptability. However, gay and lesbian travelers are generally treated with respect and should not experience any harassment, assuming they give the appropriate regard to local culture and customs.

The International Gay and Lesbian Travel Association (IGLTA) (℃ **800/448-8550** or 954/776-2626; www.iglta.org) is the trade association for the gay and lesbian travel industry, and offers an online directory of gay- and lesbian-friendly travel businesses; go to their website and click on "Members."

Many agencies offer tours and travel itineraries specifically for gay and lesbian travelers. **Above and Beyond Tours** (℃ **800/397-2681;** www.abovebeyond tours.com) is the exclusive gay and lesbian tour operator for United Airlines. **Now, Voyager** (℃ **800/255-6951;** www.nowvoyager.com) is a well-known San Francisco–based gay-owned and -operated travel service. **Olivia Cruises & Resorts** (℃ **800/631-6277;** www.olivia.com) charters entire resorts and ships for exclusive lesbian vacations and offers smaller group experiences for both gay and lesbian travelers.

The following travel guides are available at most travel bookstores and gay and lesbian bookstores, or you can order them from **Giovanni's Room** bookstore, 1145 Pine St., Philadelphia, PA 19107 (℃ **215/923-2960;** www.giovannisroom.com): *Out and About* (℃ **800/929-2268;** www.gay.com), which offers guidebooks and a newsletter ($20 a year; 10 issues) packed with solid information on the global gay and lesbian scene; *Spartacus International Gay Guide* (Bruno Gmünder Verlag; www.spartacusworld.com/gayguide) and *Odysseus: The International Gay Travel Planner* (Odysseus Enterprises Ltd.), both good, annual English-language guidebooks focused on gay men; the *Damron* guides (www.damron.com), with separate, annual books for gay men and lesbians; and *Gay Travel A to Z: The World of Gay & Lesbian Travel Options at Your Fingertips* by Marianne Ferrari (Ferrari International; Box 35575, Phoenix, AZ 85069), a very good gay and lesbian guidebook series.

STUDENT TRAVEL

Because Mexicans consider higher education more a luxury than a birthright, there is no formal network of student discounts and programs. Most Mexican students travel with their families rather than with other students, so student discount cards are not commonly recognized.

If you're a student planning to travel outside the U.S., you'd be wise to arm yourself with an **International Student Identity Card (ISIC),** which offers substantial savings on rail passes, plane tickets, and entrance fees. It also provides you with basic health and life insurance and a 24-hour help line. The card is available for $22 from **STA Travel** (℃ **800/781-4040** in North America; www.sta.com), the biggest student travel agency in the world. If you're no longer a student but are still under 26, you can get a **International Youth Travel Card (IYTC)** for the same price from the same people, which entitles you to some discounts (but not on museum admissions). (*Note:* In 2002, STA Travel bought competitors **Council Travel** and **USIT Campus** after they went bankrupt. It's still operating some offices under the Council name, but it's owned by STA.) **Travel CUTS** (℃ **800/667-2887** or 416/614-2887; www.travelcuts.com) offers similar services for both Canadians and U.S. residents.

Tips Advice for Female Travelers

As a female traveling alone, I can tell you firsthand that I feel safer traveling in Mexico than in the United States. But I use the same common-sense precautions I follow traveling anywhere else in the world and am alert to what's going on around me.

Mexicans in general, and men in particular, are nosy about single travelers, especially women. If a taxi driver or anyone else with whom you don't want to become friendly asks about your marital status, family, and so forth, my advice is to make up a set of answers (regardless of the truth): "I'm married, traveling with friends, and I have three children." Saying you are single and traveling alone may send the wrong message. U.S. television—widely viewed now in Mexico—has given many Mexican men the image of American single women as being sexually promiscuous. Check out the award-winning website **Journeywoman** (www.journeywoman.com), a "real-life" women's travel information network where you can sign up for a free e-mail newsletter and get advice on everything from etiquette and dress to safety; or the travel guide *Safety and Security for Women Who Travel* by Sheila Swan and Peter Laufer (Travelers' Tales, Inc.), offering common-sense tips on safe travel.

8 Planning Your Trip Online

SURFING FOR AIRFARES

The "big three" online travel agencies, **Expedia, Travelocity,** and **Orbitz,** sell most of the air tickets bought on the Internet. (Canadian travelers should try expedia.ca and Travelocity.ca; U.K. residents can go for expedia.co.uk and opodo.co.uk.) Each has different business deals with the airlines and may offer different fares on the same flights, so it's wise to shop around. Expedia and Travelocity will also send you **e-mail notification** when a cheap fare becomes available to your favorite destination. Of the smaller travel agency websites, **SideStep** (www.sidestep.com) has gotten the best reviews from Frommer's authors. It's a browser add-on that purports to "search 140 sites at once," but in reality only beats competitors' fares as often as other sites do.

Also remember to check **airline websites,** especially those for low-fare carriers such as Southwest or STS, whose fares are often misreported or simply missing from travel agency websites. Even with major airlines, you can often shave a few bucks from a fare by booking directly through the airline and avoiding a travel agency's transaction fee. But you'll get these discounts only by **booking online:** Most airlines now offer online-only fares that even their phone agents know nothing about. For the websites of airlines that fly to and from your destination, go to "Getting There," below.

Great **last-minute deals** are available through free weekly e-mail services provided directly by the airlines. Most of these are announced on Tuesday or Wednesday and must be purchased online. Most are only valid for travel that weekend, but some (such as Southwest's) can be booked weeks or months in advance. Sign up for weekly e-mail alerts at airline websites or check megasites that compile comprehensive lists of last-minute specials, such as **SmarterTravel.com.** For last-minute trips, **site59.com** and **lastminutetravel.com** in the U.S. and **lastminute.com** in Europe often have better air-and-hotel package deals than the major-label sites. A website listing numerous bargain sites and airlines around the world is **www.itravelnet.com**.

If you're willing to give up some control over your flight details, use what is called an "**opaque" fare service** like **Priceline** (www.priceline.com; www.priceline.co.uk for Europeans) or its smaller competitor **Hotwire** (www.hotwire.com). Both offer rock-bottom prices in exchange for travel on a "mystery airline" at a mysterious time of day, often with a mysterious change of planes en route. The mystery airlines are all major, well-known carriers—and the possibility of being sent from Philadelphia to Chicago via Tampa is remote; the airlines' routing computers have gotten a lot better than they used to be. But your chances of getting a 6am or 11pm flight are pretty high. Hotwire tells you flight prices before you buy; Priceline usually has better deals than Hotwire, but you have to play their "name our price" game. If you're new at this, the helpful folks at **BiddingForTravel** (www.biddingfortravel.com) do a good job of demystifying Priceline's prices and strategies. Priceline and Hotwire are great for flights within North America and between the U.S. and Europe. But for flights to other parts of the world, consolidators will almost always beat their fares. *Note:* In 2004 Priceline added nonopaque service to its roster. You now have the option to pick exact flights, times, and airlines from a list of offers—or opt to bid on opaque fares as before.

For much more about airfares and savvy air-travel tips and advice, pick up a copy of *Frommer's Fly Safe, Fly Smart* (Wiley Publishing, Inc.).

SURFING FOR HOTELS

Shopping online for hotels is generally done one of two ways: by booking through the hotel's own website or through an independent booking agency (or a fare-service agency like Priceline; see below). These Internet hotel agencies have multiplied in mind-boggling numbers of late, competing for the business of millions of consumers surfing for accommodations around the world. This competitiveness can be a boon to consumers who have the patience and time to shop and compare the online sites for good deals—but shop they must, for prices can vary considerably from site to site. And keep in mind that hotels at the top of a site's listing may be there for no other reason than that they paid money to get the placement.

Of the "big three" sites, **Expedia** offers a long list of special deals and "virtual tours" or photos of available rooms so you can see what you're paying for (a feature that helps counter the claims that the best rooms are often held back from bargain booking websites). **Travelocity** posts unvarnished customer reviews and ranks its properties according to the AAA rating system. Also reliable are **Hotels.com** and **Quikbook.com.** An excellent free program, **TravelAxe** (www.travelaxe.net), can help you search multiple hotel sites at once, even ones you may never have heard of—and conveniently lists the total price of the room, including the taxes and service charges. Another booking site, **Travelweb** (www.travelweb.com), is partly owned by the hotels it represents (including the Hilton, Hyatt, and Starwood chains) and is therefore plugged directly into the hotels' reservations systems—unlike independent online agencies, which have to fax or e-mail reservation requests to the hotel, a good portion of which get misplaced in the shuffle. More than once, travelers have arrived at the hotel, only to be told that they have no reservation.

To be fair, many of the major sites are undergoing improvements in service and ease of use, and Expedia will soon be able to plug directly into the reservations systems of many hotel chains—none of which can be bad news for consumers. In the meantime, it's a good idea to **get a** **confirmation number** and **make a print-out** of any online booking transaction.

9 Getting There

BY PLANE

The airline situation in Mexico is rapidly improving, with many new regional carriers offering scheduled service to areas previously not served. In addition to regularly scheduled service, charter service direct from U.S. cities to resorts is making Mexico more accessible. For information about saving money on airfares using the Internet, see "Planning Your Trip Online," above.

THE MAJOR INTERNATIONAL AIRLINES The main airlines operating direct or nonstop flights from the United States to points in Baja include **AeroCalifornia** (© 800/237-6225; www.reservaciones.com/airlines/aerocalifornia), **Aeromexico** (© 800/237-6639; www.aeromexico.com), **Alaska Airlines** (© 800/252-7522; www.alaskaair.com), **America West** (© 800/235-9292; www.americawest.com), **American Airlines** (© 800/433-7300; www.aa.com), **Continental** (© 800/525-0280; www.continental.com), **Frontier Airlines** (© 800/432-1359; www.frontierairlines.com), **Mexicana** (© 800/531-7921; www.mexicana.com), **Northwest/KLM** (© 800/225-2525; www.nwa.com), **United** (© 800/241-6522; www.united.com), and **US Airways** (© 800/428-4322; www.usairways.com). **Southwest Airlines** (© 800/435-9792; www.ifly swa.com) serves San Diego.

The main departure points in North America for international airlines are Atlanta, Chicago, Dallas/Fort Worth, Denver, Houston, Los Angeles, Las Vegas, Miami, New York, Orlando, Philadelphia, Phoenix, Raleigh/Durham, San Antonio, San Francisco, Seattle, Toronto, and Washington, D.C.

BY CAR

Driving is not the cheapest way to get to Mexico, but it is the best way to see the country. Even so, you may think twice about taking your own car south of the border once you've pondered the bureaucracy involved. One option is to rent a car once you arrive and tour around a specific region. Rental cars in Mexico are generally new, clean, and well maintained. Although they're pricier than in the United States, discounts are often available for rentals of a week or longer, especially when you make arrangements in advance from the United States. (See "Car Rentals," later in this chapter, for more details.)

If, after reading the section that follows, you have additional questions or you want to confirm the current rules, call your nearest Mexican consulate or the Mexican Government Tourist Office. Although travel insurance companies are generally helpful, they may not have the most accurate information. To check on road conditions or to get help with any travel emergency while in Mexico, call © **01-800/903-9200,** or 555/250-0151 in Mexico City. English-speaking operators staff both numbers.

In addition, check with the **U.S. State Department** (see "Visitor Information," earlier in this chapter) for warnings about dangerous driving areas.

CAR DOCUMENTS To drive your car into Mexico (even for the day), you'll need a **temporary car-importation permit,** which is granted after you provide a required list of documents (see below). The permit can be obtained through Banco del Ejército (Banjercito) officials, who have a desk, booth, or office at the

⌜Tips⌝ **Carrying Car Documents**

You must carry your temporary car-importation permit, tourist permit (see "Entry Requirements," earlier in this chapter), and, if you purchased it, your proof of Mexican car insurance (see below) in the car at all times. The temporary car-importation permit papers will be issued for 6 months to a year; the tourist permit is usually issued for 30 days. It's a good idea to overestimate the time you'll spend in Mexico, so that if something unforeseen happens and you have to (or want to) stay longer, you'll avoid the hassle of getting your papers extended. Whatever you do, don't overstay either permit. Doing so invites heavy fines and confiscation of your vehicle, which will not be returned. Remember also that 6 months does not necessarily work out to be 180 days.

Mexican Customs *(aduana)* building after you cross the border into Mexico.

The following strict requirements for border crossing were accurate at press time:

- **A valid driver's license,** issued outside of Mexico.
- **Current, original car registration and a copy of the original car title.** If the registration or title is in more than one name and not all the named people are traveling with you, a notarized letter from the absent person(s) authorizing use of the vehicle for the trip is required; have it ready. The registration and your credit card (see below) must be in the same name.
- **A valid international major credit card.** With a credit card, you are required to pay only a $23 car-importation fee. The credit card must be in the same name as the car registration. If you do not have a major credit card (American Express, Diners Club, MasterCard, or Visa), you must post a bond or make a deposit equal to the value of the vehicle. Check cards are not accepted.
- **Original immigration documentation.** This is either your tourist permit (FMT) or the original immigration booklet, FM2 or FM3, if you hold more permanent status.

- **A signed declaration promising to return to your country of origin with the vehicle.** Obtain this form *(Carta Promesa de Retorno)* from AAA or Sanborn's before you go, or from Banjercito officials at the border. There's no charge. The form does not stipulate that you must return by the same border entry through which you entered.
- **Temporary Importation Application.** By signing this form, you state that you are only temporarily importing the car for your personal use and will not be selling it. This is to help regulate the entry and restrict the resale of unauthorized cars and trucks. Make sure the permit is canceled when you return to the U.S.

If you receive your documentation at the border, Mexican officials will make two copies of everything and charge you for the copies. For up-to-the-minute information, a great source is the Customs office in Nuevo Laredo, or *Módulo de Importación Temporal de Automóviles, Aduana Nuevo Laredo* (© **867/712-2071**).

Important reminder: Someone else may drive, but the person (or relative of the person) whose name appears on the car-importation permit must *always* be in the car. (If stopped by police, a non-registered family member driving without the registered driver must be prepared to prove familial relationship to the registered driver—no joke.) Violation of this rule subjects the car to impoundment and the driver to imprisonment, a fine, or both. You can drive a car with foreign license plates only if you have a foreign (non-Mexican) driver's license.

MEXICAN AUTO INSURANCE Liability auto insurance is legally required in Mexico. U.S. insurance is invalid; to be insured in Mexico, you must purchase Mexican insurance. Any party involved in an accident who has no insurance may be sent to jail and have his or her car impounded until all claims are settled.

See Baja by Boat: Cruising the Sea of Cortez

John Steinbeck made this journey famous, recording his observations and philosophies on a 4,000-mile expedition during which he collected marine specimens in the 1951 classic *The Log from the Sea of Cortez*. These days, a few companies offer small-ship cruises from Cabo San Lucas north to the colonial town of Santa Rosalía, an ideal way to sample the best of Baja. Any travel agent can price or book Sea of Cortez cruises.

Cruise West (© **800/888-9378** or 206/441-8687 in the U.S.; fax 206/441-4757; www.cruisewest.com) offers several voyages that explore the interior Baja coast. Along the way, the ship pulls into small, pristine coves where passengers can participate in nature walks, hiking, snorkeling, and kayaking. One itinerary has stops at Loreto, Santa Rosalía, Mulegé, and La Paz, and an overland side trip to Bahía Magdalena for a day of whale-watching. There are two ships: the 65m (213-ft.) *Spirit of Endeavor,* with 51 cabins, all with double accommodations and full facilities; and the 58m (190-ft.) *Spirit of '98,* with 48 double cabins with full facilities. Prices range from $2,095 to $4,695 per person (based on double occupancy) for the 7-night cruise; all meals and activities are included. This cruise is oriented toward a slightly older passenger; there's an exceptional educational orientation aimed at learning about the areas explored, especially the regional flora and fauna. Photography-themed cruises also are available.

Baja Expeditions, 2625 Garnet Ave., San Diego, CA 92109 (© **800/843-6967** or 858/581-3311; www.bajaex.com), offers natural-history cruises, whale-watching, sea kayaking, and scuba-diving trips out of La Paz.

Classic American Safari Cruises (© **888/862-8881**; fax 425/776-8889; www.amsafari.com) offers 3- and 4-night luxury yacht cruises in the Sea of Cortez. Sailing round-trip from La Paz, the cruise explores the protected waters of the area, stopping in small, pristine coves on it's way to Loreto, where it turns back south. The yacht comes equipped with standard amenities and a variety of stateroom options, all with private bathroom and shower. It's ideal for families, small groups, or corporate events. Prices range from $3,995 to $5,995 per person, based on double occupancy, and include all transfer, private tours, kayak and boat adventures, gourmet meals, and beverages including wines and premium liquors. Full yacht charters are also available.

> **Finds Out-of-the-Ordinary Places to Stay**
>
> Mexico lends itself beautifully to the concept of small, private hotels in idyllic settings. They vary in style from grandiose estate to palm-thatched bungalow. **Mexico Boutique Hotels** (www.MexicoBoutiqueHotels.com) specializes in smaller places to stay with a high level of personal attention and service. Most options have less than 50 rooms, and the accommodations consist of entire villas, *casitas,* bungalows, or a combination.

This is true even if you just drive across the border to spend the day. U.S. companies that broker Mexican insurance are commonly found at the border crossing, and several quote daily rates.

You can also buy car insurance through **Sanborn's Mexico Insurance,** P.O. Box 52840, 2009 S. 10th, McAllen, TX (© **956/686-3601;** fax 800/222-0158 or 956/686-0732; www.sanbornsinsurance.com). The company has offices at all U.S. border crossings. Its policies cost the same as the competition's do, but you get legal coverage (attorney and bail bonds if needed) and a detailed mile-by-mile guide for your proposed route. Most of the Sanborn's border offices are open Monday through Friday, and a few are staffed on Saturday and Sunday. **AAA** auto club also sells insurance. Another good source is **www.mexico-car-insurance.com.**

RETURNING TO THE UNITED STATES WITH YOUR CAR You must return the car papers you obtained when you entered Mexico when you cross back with your car, or at some point within 180 days. (You can cross as many times as you wish within the 180 days.) If the documents aren't returned, heavy fines are imposed ($250 for each 15 days late), and your car may be impounded

and confiscated or you may be jailed if you return to Mexico. You can only return the car documents to a Banjercito official on duty at the Mexican Customs building before you cross back into the United States. Some border cities have Banjercito officials on duty 24 hours a day, but others do not; some also do not have Sunday hours.

BY SHIP
Numerous cruise lines serve Mexico, with many ships (including specialized whale-watching trips) originating in California and traveling down to the Baja peninsula. If you don't mind taking off at the last minute, several cruise-tour specialists arrange substantial discounts on unsold cabins. One such company is **The Cruise Line,** 150 NW 168 St., North Miami Beach, Miami, FL 33169 (© **800/777-0707** or 305/521-2200).

BY BUS
Greyhound-Trailways (or its affiliates) offers service from around the United States to the Mexican border, where passengers disembark, cross the border, and buy a ticket for travel into Mexico. Many border crossings have scheduled buses from the U.S. bus station to the Mexican bus station.

10 The Active Traveler

Los Cabos, where several championship tournaments are held each year, has become the preeminent golf destination in Mexico. Visitors to Baja can enjoy

tennis, racquetball, squash, water-skiing, surfing, bicycling, and horseback riding. Scuba diving is excellent in the Sea of Cortez.

OUTDOORS ORGANIZATIONS & TOUR OPERATORS AMTAVE, or Asociación Mexicana de Turismo de Aventura y Ecoturismo, A.C. (© **800/ 509-7678;** www.amtave.org or www. turismoaventura.com), is an association of eco- and adventure tour operators. It publishes an annual catalog of participating firms and their offerings, all of which must meet criteria for security, quality, and training of the guides, as well as for sustainability of natural and cultural environments.

Baja Expeditions, 2625 Garnet Ave., San Diego, CA 92109 (© **800/843- 6967** or 858/581-3311; www.bajaex. com), offers natural-history cruises, whale-watching, sea kayaking, camping, and scuba-diving trips out of Loreto, La Paz, and San Diego. Small groups and special itineraries are the firm's specialty.

Mexico Travel Link Ltd., 300-3665 Kingsway, Vancouver, BC V5R 5W2 Canada (© **604/454-9044;** fax 604/454- 9088; www.mexicotravel.net), offers cultural, sports, and adventure tours to Baja and other destinations.

Mexico Motorcycle Adventures, Inc., 697 18th St., Beaumont, Texas 77706 (© **409/838-9983;** fax 409/833-2550), offers off-road motorcycle tours to the Baja and other parts of Mexico.

Mountain Travel Sobek, 6420 Fairmount Ave., El Cerrito, CA 94530 (© **800/227-2384,** 888/687-6235, or 510/527-8100; www.mtsobek.com), takes groups kayaking in the Sea of Cortez and whale-watching in Baja. Sobek is one of the world's leading eco-tour outfitters.

Natural Habitat Adventures, 2945 Center Green Court, Suite H, Boulder, CO 80301 (© **800/543-8917** or 303/ 449-3711; www.nathab.com), offers naturalist-led natural history and adventure travel. Expeditions focus on whale-watching in Baja.

Naturequest, 30872 South Coast Highway, Suite 185, Laguna Beach, CA 92651 (© **800/369-3033** or 949/499- 9561; natureqst@aol.com), offers Baja trips that get close to nature with special permits for venturing by two-person kayak into sanctuaries for whales and birds, and slipping among mangroves and into shallow bays, estuaries, and lagoons.

One World Workforce, P.O. Box 3188, La Mesa, CA 91944 (© **800/451- 9564**), has weeklong "hands-on conservation trips" that offer working volunteers a chance to help with sea-turtle conservation at Bahía de Los Angeles, Baja (spring, summer, and fall).

For more than 20 years, local resident Trudi Angell has guided sea-kayaking tours in the Loreto area with **Tour Baja,** P.O. Box 827, Calistoga, CA 94515 (© **800/398-6200** or 707/942-4550; fax 707/942-8017; www.tourbaja.com). She and her guides offer firsthand knowledge of the area, its natural history, and local culture. Her company's kayaking, mountain biking, pack trips, and sailing charters combine these elements with great outdoor adventures.

Sea Kayak Adventures, 1036 Pine Avenue, Coeur d'Alene, ID 83814 (© **800/616-1943** or 208/765-3116; fax 208/765-5254; www.seakayakadventures. com), features kayak trios in both the Sea of Cortez and Magdalena Bay, with a focus on whale-watching. This company has the exclusive permit to paddle Magdalena Bay's remote northern waters, and they guarantee gray whale sightings. Trips combine paddling of 4 to 5 hours per day, with hiking across dunes and beaches, while nights are spent camping.

By alternating sea-kayaking trips between Alaska and Baja for 2 decades, **Sea Trek Sea Kayaking Center** (© **415/ 488-1000;** fax 415/488-1707; www.sea trekkayak.com) has gained an intimate knowledge of the remote coastline of Baja. Eight-day trips depart from and return to Loreto; a 12-day expedition travels from Loreto to La Paz. An optional day excursion to Bahía Magdalena for whale-watching is also available. Full boat support is provided, and no previous paddling experience is necessary.

11 Tips on Accommodations

MEXICO'S HOTEL RATING SYSTEM

The hotel rating system in Mexico is called "Stars and Diamonds." Hotels may qualify to earn one to five stars, or five diamonds. Many hotels that have excellent standards are not certified, but all rated hotels adhere to strict standards. The guidelines relate to service, facilities, and hygiene more than to prices.

Five-diamond hotels meet the highest requirements for rating: The beds are comfortable, bathrooms are in excellent working order, all facilities are renovated regularly, infrastructure is top-tier, and services and hygiene meet the highest international standards.

Five-star hotels usually offer similar quality, but with lower levels of service and detail in the rooms. For example, a five-star hotel may have less luxurious linens, or perhaps room service during limited hours rather than 24 hours.

Four-star hotels are less expensive and more basic, but they still guarantee cleanliness and basic services such as hot water and purified drinking water. Three-, two-, and one-star hotels are at least working to adhere to certain standards: Bathrooms are cleaned and linens are washed daily, and you can expect a minimum standard of service. Two- and one-star hotels generally provide bottled water rather than purified water.

The nonprofit organization Calidad Mexicana Certificada, A.C., known as **Calmecac** (**www.calmecac.com.mx**), is responsible for hotel ratings. For additional details about the rating system, visit Calmecac's website or www.starsanddiamonds.com.mx.

HOTEL CHAINS

In addition to the major international chains, you'll run across a number of less-familiar brands as you plan your trip to Mexico. They include:

- **Fiesta Americana** and **Fiesta Inn** (www.posadas.com). Part of the Mexican-owned Grupo Posadas company, these hotels set the country's midrange standard for facilities and services. They generally offer comfortable, spacious rooms and traditional Mexican hospitality. Fiesta Americana hotels offer excellent beach-resort packages. Fiesta Inn hotels are usually more business oriented.

- **Hoteles Camino Real** (www.caminoreal.com). The premier Mexican hotel chain, Camino Real maintains a high standard of service at its properties, all of which carry five stars (see "Mexico's Hotel Rating System," above). Its beach hotels are traditionally on the best beaches in the area. This chain also focuses on the business market. The hotels are famous for their vivid and contrasting colors.

12 Getting Around

An important note: If your travel schedule depends on an important connection, use the telephone numbers in this book or other resources mentioned here to find out whether the connection you are depending on is still available. Although we've done our best to provide accurate information, transportation schedules can and do change.

BY PLANE

To fly from point to point within Mexico, you'll rely on Mexican airlines. Mexico has two privately owned large national carriers: **Mexicana** (© 01-800/ 366-5400) and **Aeromexico** (© 01-800/ 021-4000), in addition to several up-and-coming regional carriers. Mexicana and Aeromexico both offer extensive connections to the United States as well as within Mexico.

Several new regional carriers are operated by or can be booked through Mexicana or Aeromexico. Regional carriers are Mexicana's **Aerocaribe** and **Aero Mar**, and Aeromexico's **Aerolitoral.** The regional carriers are expensive, but they go to difficult-to-reach places. In each applicable section of this book, we've mentioned regional carriers with all pertinent telephone numbers.

Because major airlines can book some regional carriers, read your ticket carefully to see if your connecting flight is on one of these smaller carriers—they may use a different airport or a different counter.

AIRPORT TAXES   Mexico charges an airport tax on all departures. Passengers leaving the country on international flights pay $18—in dollars or the peso equivalent. It has become a common practice to include this departure tax in your ticket price, but double-check to make sure so you're not caught by surprise at the airport. Taxes on each domestic departure within Mexico are around $13, unless you're on a connecting flight and have already paid at the start of the flight.

Mexico charges an $18 "tourism tax," the proceeds of which go into a tourism promotional fund. Your ticket price may not include it, so be sure to have enough money to pay it at the airport upon departure.

RECONFIRMING FLIGHTS   Although Mexican airlines say it's not necessary to reconfirm a flight, it's still a good idea. To avoid getting bumped on popular, possibly overbooked flights, check in for an international flight 1½ hours in advance of travel.

BY CAR

Most Mexican roads are not up to U.S. standards of smoothness, hardness, width of curve, grade of hill, or safety markings. Driving at night is dangerous—the roads are rarely lit; trucks, carts, pedestrians, and bicycles usually have no lights; and you can hit potholes, animals, rocks, dead ends, or uncrossable bridges without warning.

The spirited style of Mexican driving sometimes requires super vision and reflexes. Be prepared for new customs, as when a truck driver flips on his left turn signal when there's not a crossroad for miles. He's probably telling you the road's clear ahead for you to pass. Another custom that's very important to respect is turning left. Never turn left by stopping in the middle of a highway with your left signal on. Instead, pull onto the right shoulder, wait for traffic to clear, then proceed across the road.

GASOLINE   There's one government-owned brand of gas and one gasoline station name throughout the country—**Pemex** (Petroleras Mexicanas). There are two types of gas in Mexico: *magna,* 87-octane unleaded gas, and premium 93 octane. In Mexico, fuel and oil are sold by the liter, which is slightly more than a quart (40 liters equals about 11 gal.). Many franchise Pemex stations have bathroom facilities and convenience stores—a great improvement over the old ones.

Important note: No credit cards are currently accepted for gas purchases.

BREAKDOWNS   If your car breaks down on the road, help might already be on the way. Radio-equipped green repair trucks operated by uniformed English-speaking officers patrol major highways during daylight hours. These **"Green**

Angels" perform minor repairs and adjustments free, but you pay for parts and materials.

Your best guide to repair shops is the Yellow Pages. For repairs, look under "Automóviles y Camiones: Talleres de Reparación y Servicio"; auto-parts stores are under "Refacciones y Accesorios para Automóviles." To find a mechanic on the road, look for a sign that says TALLER MECANICO.

Places called *vulcanizadora* or *llantera* repair flat tires, and it is common to find them open 24 hours a day on the most traveled highways.

MINOR ACCIDENTS When possible, many Mexicans drive away from minor accidents or try to make an immediate settlement, to avoid involving the police. If the police arrive while the involved persons are still at the scene, everyone may be locked in jail until blame is assessed. In any case, you have to settle up immediately, which may take days. Foreigners who don't speak fluent Spanish are at a distinct disadvantage when trying to explain their version of the event. Three steps may help the foreigner who doesn't wish to do as the Mexicans do: If you were in your own car, notify your Mexican insurance company, whose job it is to intervene on your behalf. If you were in a rental car, notify the rental company immediately and ask how to contact the nearest adjuster. (You did buy insurance with the rental, right?) Finally, if all else fails, ask to contact the nearest Green Angel, who may be able to explain to officials that you are covered by insurance. See also "Mexican Auto Insurance" in "Getting There," earlier in this chapter.

CAR RENTALS You'll get the best price if you reserve a car at least a week in advance in the United States. U.S. car-rental firms include **Advantage** (© 800/777-5500 in the U.S. and Canada; www.advantagerentacar.com), **Avis** (© 800/331-1212 in the U.S., 800/TRY-AVIS in Canada; www.avis.com), **Budget** (© 800/527-0700 in the U.S. and Canada; www.budget.com), **Hertz** (© 800/654-3131 in the U.S. and Canada; www.hertz.com), **National** (© 800/CAR-RENT in the U.S. and Canada; www.nationalcar.com), and **Thrifty** (© 800/367-2277 in the U.S. and Canada; www.thrifty.com), which often offers discounts for rentals in Mexico. For European travelers, **Kemwel Holiday Auto** (© 800/678-0678) and **Auto Europe** (© 800/223-5555) can arrange Mexican rentals, sometimes through other agencies. These and some local firms have offices in Mexico City and most other large Mexican cities. You'll find rental desks at airports, all major hotels, and many travel agencies.

Cars are easy to rent if you are 25 or over and have a major credit card, valid driver's license, and passport with you. Without a credit card you must leave a cash deposit, usually a big one. One-way rentals are usually simple to arrange but more costly.

Car-rental costs are high in Mexico because cars are more expensive. The condition of rental cars has improved greatly over the years, however, and clean, comfortable, new cars are the norm. At press time, the basic cost of a 1-day rental of a Volkswagen Beetle, with unlimited mileage (but before 15% tax and $15 daily insurance), was $58 in Los Cabos. Renting by the week gives you about a 15% lower daily rate. Rental prices may be considerably higher around a major holiday. Also double-check charges for insurance—some companies will increase the insurance rate after several days. Always ask for detailed information about all charges you will be responsible for.

Car-rental companies usually write up a credit card charge in U.S. dollars.

Deductibles Be careful—these vary greatly in Mexico; some are as high as

Travel Tip

Little English is spoken at bus stations, so come prepared with your destination written down, then double-check the departure.

$2,500, which comes out of your pocket immediately in case of car damage. Hertz's deductible is $1,000 on a VW Beetle; Avis' is $500 for the same car.

Insurance   Insurance is offered in two parts: **Collision and damage** insurance covers your car and others if the accident is your fault, and **personal accident** insurance covers you and anyone in your car. Read the fine print on the back of your rental agreement and note that insurance may be invalid if you have an accident while driving on an unpaved road.

Damage   Always inspect your car carefully and note every damaged or missing item, no matter how minute, on your rental agreement, or you may be charged.

BY TAXI

Taxis are the preferred way to get around in almost all the resort areas of Mexico, but are very expensive in the Los Cabos area. One-way travel between Cabo San Lucas and San José del Cabo averages $35. Short trips within towns are generally charged by preset zones and are quite reasonable compared with U.S. rates. For longer trips or excursions to nearby cities, taxis can generally be hired for around $10 to $15 per hour, or for a negotiated

daily rate. Even drops to different destinations can be arranged. A negotiated one-way price is usually much less than the cost of a rental car for a day, and service is much faster than travel by bus. For anyone who is uncomfortable driving in Mexico, this is a convenient, comfortable alternative. A bonus is that you have a Spanish-speaking person with you in case you run into any car or road trouble. Many taxi drivers speak at least some English. Your hotel can assist you with the arrangements.

BY BUS

Bus service is not as well developed in the Baja peninsula as in other parts of the country, although it is available between principle points. Travel class is generally labeled *segunda* (second), *primera* (first), and *ejecutiva* (deluxe). The deluxe buses often have fewer seats than regular buses, show movies en route, are air-conditioned, and make few stops; some have complimentary refreshments. Many run express from origin to the final destination. They are well worth the few dollars more that you'll pay. In rural areas, buses are often of the school-bus variety, with lots of local color.

13 Recommended Books & Films

Studying up on Mexico can be one of the most fun bits of "research" you'll ever do. If you'd like to learn a bit more about this fascinating country before you go— which I encourage—these books and movies are an enjoyable way to do it.

BOOKS

HISTORY & CULTURE   For an overview of pre-Hispanic cultures, pick

up a copy of Michael D. Coe's *Mexico: From the Olmecs to the Aztecs* (Thames & Hudson, 1994) or Nigel Davies's *Ancient Kingdoms of Mexico* (Penguin, 1991). Richard Townsend's *The Aztecs* (Thames & Hudson, 2000) is a thorough, well-researched examination of the Aztec and the Spanish conquest. For the Maya, Michael Coe's *The Maya* (Thames &

Hudson, 2005) is probably the best general account. For a survey of Mexican history through modern times, *A Short History of Mexico* by J. Patrick McHenry (Doubleday, 1970) provides a complete, yet concise account.

John L. Stephens' *Incidents of Travel in Yucatan, Vol. I and II* (Dover Publications, 1963) are considered among the great books of archeological discovery, as well as being travel classics. The two volumes chart the course of Stephens' discoveries of the Yucatán, beginning in 1841. Before his expeditions, little was known of the region, and the Mayan culture had not been discovered. During his travels, Stephens found and described 44 Mayan sites, and his account of these remains the most authoritative in existence.

For a more modern explorations of the archaeology of the region, Peter Tompkins *Mysteries of the Mexican Pyramids* (HarperCollins, 1987) is a visually rich book, which explores not only the ruins of the Maya in the Yucatan, but the whole of Mexico's archeological treasures.

For contemporary culture, start with Octavio Paz's classic, *The Labyrinth of Solitude* (Grove Press, 1985), which still generates controversy among Mexicans. For a recent collection of writings by Subcomandante Marcos, leader of the Zapatista movement, try *Our Word is Our Weapon* (Seven Stories Press, 2002). Another source is *Basta! Land and the Zapatista Rebellion* by George Collier (Food First, 1999), et al. For those already familiar with Mexico and its culture, Guillermo Bonfil's *Mexico Profundo: Reclaiming a Civilization* (University of Texas Press, 1996) is a rare bottom-up view of Mexico today.

Lesley Byrd Simpson's *Many Mexicos* (University of California Press, 1966) provides a comprehensive account of Mexican history with a cultural context. A classic on understanding the culture of this country is *Distant Neighbors,* by Alan Riding (Vintage, 1989).

ART & ARCHITECTURE

Art and Time in Mexico: From the Conquest to the Revolution, by Elizabeth Wilder Weismann (Harper & Row, 1985), covers religious, public, and private architecture. *Casa Mexicana,* by Tim Street-Porter (Stewart, Tabori & Chang, 1989), takes readers through the interiors of some of Mexico's finest homes-turned-museums, public buildings, and private homes.

Folk Treasures of Mexico, by Marion Oettinger (Harry N Abrams, 1990), is the fascinating story behind the 3,000-piece Mexican folk-art collection amassed by Nelson Rockefeller over a 50-year period.

Maya Art and Architecture, by Mary Ellen Miller (Thames and Hudson, 1999) showcases the best of the artistic expression of this culture, with interpretations into its meanings.

For a wonderful read on the food of the Yucatan and Mexico, pick up *Mexico, One Plate at a Time,* by celebrity chef and Mexico aficionado Rick Bayless (Scribner, 2000).

NATURE

A Naturalist's Mexico, by Roland H. Wauer (Texas A&M UP, 1992), is a fabulous guide to birding. *Mexico: A Hiker's Guide to Mexico's Natural History,* by Jim Conrad (Mountaineers Books, 1995), covers flora and fauna and tells how to find the easy-to-reach as well as out-of-the-way spots he describes. *A Field Guide to Mexican Birds,* by Roger Tory Peterson and Edward L. Chalif (Houghton Mifflin, 1999), is an excellent guide.

MOVIES

Mexico has served as a backdrop for countless movies. Here are just a few of my favorites, all available on DVD.

The 2003 blockbuster *Frida* starring Salma Hayek and Alfred Molina is not only an entertaining way to learn about two of Mexico's most famous personalities, but also of its history. The exquisite cinematography perfectly captures Mexico's inherent spirit of magic realism.

Que Viva México is a little-known masterpiece by Russian filmmaker Sergei Eisenstein, who created a documentary of Mexican history, politics and culture, out of a series of short *novellas,* which ultimately tie together. Although Eisenstein's budget ran out before he could complete the project, in 1979 this film was completed by Grigory Alexandrov, the film's original producer. It's an absolute must for anyone interested in Mexico or Mexican cinema.

Mexico's contemporary filmmakers are creating a sensation lately, and none more so than director Alfonso Cuarón. One of his early and highly acclaimed movies is the 2001 classic *Y Tu Mamá También (And Your Mother, Too),* featuring current heartthrobs Gael Garcia Bernal and Diego Luna. This sexy, yet compelling, coming-of-age movie not only showcases both the grit and beauty of Mexico, but the universality of love and life lessons.

Like Water for Chocolate is the 1993 film based on the book of the same name by Laura Esquivel, filmed by the author's husband, acclaimed contemporary Mexican director Alfonso Arau. Expect to be very hungry after watching this lushly visual film, which tells the story of a young woman who suppresses her passions under the watchful eye of a stern mother, and channels them into her cooking. In the process, we learn of the traditional norms of Mexican culture, and a great deal of the country's culinary treasures.

FAST FACTS: Baja California

Abbreviations Dept. (apartments); Apdo. Postal (post office box); Av. (*Avenida;* avenue); c/ (*calle;* street); Calz. (*Calzada;* boulevard). C on faucets stands for *caliente* (hot), F for *fría* (cold). PB (*planta baja*) means ground floor; most buildings count the next floor up as the first floor (1).

Business Hours In general, businesses in larger cities are open between 9am and 7pm; in smaller towns many close between 2 and 4pm. Most close on Sunday. In resort areas it is common to find stores open at least in the mornings on Sunday, and for shops to stay open late, often until 8pm or even 10pm. Bank hours are Monday through Friday from 9 or 9:30am to anywhere between 3 and 7pm. Increasingly, banks open on Saturday for at least a half-day.

Doctors & Dentists Every embassy and consulate is prepared to recommend local doctors and dentists with good training and modern equipment; some of the doctors and dentists speak English. See the list of embassies and consulates under "Embassies & Consulates," below. Hotels with a large foreign clientele can often recommend English-speaking doctors. Almost all first-class hotels in Mexico have a doctor on call.

Drug Laws To be blunt, don't use or possess illegal drugs in Mexico. Mexican officials have no tolerance for drug users, and jail is their solution, with very little hope of getting out until the sentence (usually a long one) is completed or heavy fines or bribes are paid. Remember, in Mexico the legal system assumes you are guilty until proven innocent. *Important note:* It isn't uncommon to be befriended by a fellow user, only to be turned in by that "friend," who's collected a bounty. Bring prescription drugs in their original containers. If possible, pack a copy of the original prescription with the generic name of the drug.

U.S. Customs officials are also on the lookout for diet drugs sold in Mexico but illegal in the U.S., possession of which could land you in a U.S. jail. If you buy antibiotics over the counter (which you can do in Mexico) and still have some left, you probably won't be hassled by U.S. Customs.

Electricity The electrical system in Mexico is 110 volts AC (60 cycles), as in the United States and Canada. In reality, however, it may cycle more slowly and overheat your appliances. To compensate, select a medium or low speed on hair dryers. Many older hotels still have electrical outlets for flat two-prong plugs; you'll need an adapter for any plug with an enlarged end on one prong or with three prongs. Many better hotels have three-hole outlets (*trifásicos* in Spanish). Those that don't may have loan adapters, but to be sure, it's always better to carry your own.

Embassies & Consulates They provide valuable lists of doctors and lawyers, as well as regulations concerning marriages in Mexico. Contrary to popular belief, your embassy cannot get you out of a Mexican jail, provide postal or banking services, or fly you home when you run out of money. Consular officers can provide you with advice on most matters and problems, however. All embassies listed here are in Mexico City. The **Embassy of Australia** (© 55/1101-2200); the **Embassy of Canada** (© 55/5724-7900; www.canada.org.mx); the **Embassy of New Zealand** (© 55/5283-9460; kiwimexico@compuserve.com.mx); the **Embassy of the United Kingdom** (© 555/242-8500; www.embajada britanica.com.mx); and the **Embassy of Ireland** (© 55/5520-5803). The **Embassy of the United States** in Mexico City is at Paseo de la Reforma 305, next to the Hotel María Isabel Sheraton at the corner of Río Danubio (© 55/5080-2000 or 55/5511-9980). Visit www.usembassy-mexico.gov for a list of U.S. consulates in Mexico. There is a **U.S. Consulate General** in Tijuana, at Tapachula 96 (© 664/622-7400), and a consular agency in Cabo San Lucas (© 624/143-3566).

Emergencies In case of emergency, dial 065 from any phone within Mexico. No coin is needed. For police emergency numbers, turn to "Fast Facts" in the chapters that follow. You should also contact the closest consular office in case of an emergency.

Internet Access In large cities and resort areas, a growing number of top hotels offer business centers with Internet access. You'll also find cybercafes in destinations that are popular with expats and business travelers. Even in remote spots, Internet access is common. Note that many ISPs will automatically cut off your Internet connection after a specified period of time (say, 10 min.) because telephone lines are at a premium.

Language Spanish is the official language in Mexico. English is spoken and understood to some degree in most tourist areas, and in Los Cabos you'll generally find more people speaking English than Spanish. Mexicans are very accommodating with foreigners who try to speak Spanish, even in broken sentences. For basic vocabulary, refer to appendix B.

Liquor Laws The legal drinking age in Mexico is 18; however, asking for ID or denying purchase is extremely rare. Grocery stores sell everything from beer and wine to national and imported liquors. You can buy liquor 24 hours a day, but during major elections, dry laws often are enacted for as much as 72 hours in advance of the election—and they apply to tourists as well as local residents. Mexico does not have laws that apply to transporting liquor in cars, but authorities are beginning to target drunk drivers more aggressively. It's a good idea to drive defensively.

It is not legal to drink in the street; however, many tourists do so. Use your judgment—if you are getting drunk, you shouldn't drink in the street, because you are more likely to get stopped by the police. As is the custom in Mexico, it is not so much what you do, but how you do it.

Lost & Found   To replace a **lost passport,** contact your embassy or nearest consular agent. You must establish a record of your citizenship and fill out a form requesting another FMT (tourist permit) if it, too, was lost. If your documents are stolen, get a police report from local authorities; having one *might* lessen the hassle of exiting the country without all your identification. Without the FMT, you can't leave the country, and without an affidavit affirming your passport request and citizenship, you may have problems at U.S. Customs when you get home. It's important to clear everything up *before* trying to leave. Mexican Customs may, however, accept the police report of the loss of the FMT and allow you to leave.

If you lose your **wallet** anywhere outside of Mexico City, before panicking, retrace your steps—you'll be surprised at how honest people are, and you'll likely find someone trying to find you to return your wallet.

If your wallet is stolen, the police probably won't be able to recover it. Be sure to notify all of your credit card companies right away, and file a report at the nearest police precinct. Your credit card company or insurer may require a police report number or record of the loss. Most credit card companies have an emergency toll-free number to call if your card is lost or stolen; these numbers are not toll-free within Mexico (see "Telephone & Fax," below, for instructions on calling U.S. toll-free numbers). The company may be able to wire you a cash advance off your credit card immediately, and, in many places, can deliver an emergency credit card in a day or two. Visa's U.S. emergency number is ⓒ 800/ **847-2911** or 410/581-9994. American Express cardholders and traveler's check holders should call ⓒ **800/221-7282.** MasterCard holders should call ⓒ **800/ 307-7309** or 636/722-7111. For other credit cards, call the toll-free number directory at ⓒ **800/555-1212.**

If you need emergency cash over the weekend when all banks and American Express offices are closed, you can have money wired to you via **Western Union** (ⓒ 800/325-6000; www.westernunion.com).

Mail   Postage for a postcard or letter is 1 peso; it may arrive anywhere from 1 to 6 weeks later. A registered letter costs $1.90. Sending a package can be quite expensive—the Mexican postal service charges $8 per kilo (2.2 lb.)—and unreliable; it takes 2 to 6 weeks, if it arrives at all. The recommended way to send a package or important mail is through FedEx, DHL, UPS, or another reputable international mail service.

Newspapers & Magazines   In southern Baja, a number of local English-language papers are available, including *Baja Life, Baja Sun,* and the irreverent, entertaining *Gringo Gazette.*

Pharmacies Farmacias will sell you just about anything you want, with a prescription or without one. Most drugstores are open Monday through Saturday from 8am to 8pm. Generally, the major resort areas have one or two 24-hour pharmacies. If you are in a smaller town and need to buy medicine after normal hours, ask for the name of the nearest 24-hour pharmacy; they are becoming more common.

Smoking Smoking is permitted and generally accepted in most public places, including restaurants, bars, and hotel lobbies. Nonsmoking areas and hotel rooms for nonsmokers are becoming more common in higher-end establishments, but they tend to be the exception rather than the rule.

Taxes There's a 15% IVA (*Impuesto al Valor Agregado,* or value-added tax) on goods and services in most of Mexico, and it's supposed to be included in the posted price. This tax is 10% in Los Cabos. There is a 5% tax on food and drinks consumed in restaurants that sell alcoholic beverages with an alcohol content of more than 10%; this tax applies whether you drink alcohol or not. Tequila is subject to a 25% tax. Mexico imposes an exit tax of around $18 on every foreigner leaving the country (see "Airport Taxes" under "Getting Around," earlier in this chapter).

Telephone & Fax Mexico's telephone system is slowly but surely catching up with modern times. All telephone numbers have 10 digits. Every city and town that has telephone access has a two-digit (Mexico City, Monterrey, and Guadalajara) or three-digit (everywhere else) area code. In Mexico City, Monterrey, and Guadalajara, local numbers have eight digits; elsewhere, local numbers have seven digits. To place a local call, you do not need to dial the area code.

To call long distance within Mexico, dial the national long-distance code **01** before dialing the area code and then the number. Mexico's area codes (*claves*) are listed in the front of telephone directories. Area codes are listed before all phone numbers in this book. For long-distance dialing, you will often see the term "LADA," which is the automatic long-distance service offered by Telmex, Mexico's former telephone monopoly and its largest phone company. To make a person-to-person or collect call inside Mexico, dial 𝄞 **020.** You can also call 020 to request the correct area codes for the number and place you are calling.

Many fax numbers are also regular telephone numbers; ask whoever answers for the fax tone (*"me da tono de fax, por favor"*). Cellular phones are very popular for small businesses in resort areas and smaller communities. To call a cellular number inside the same area code, dial 044 and then the number. To dial the cellular phone from anywhere else in Mexico, first dial 01, then the 3-digit area code and the seven-digit number. To dial it from the U.S., dial 011-52, plus the three-digit area code and the seven-digit number.

The **country code** for Mexico is **52.**

To call Mexico: If you're calling Mexico from the United States:

1. Dial the international access code: 011
2. Dial the country code: 52
3. Dial the two- or three-digit area code, then the eight- or seven-digit number. For example, if you wanted to call the U.S. consulate in Acapulco, the

whole number would be 011-52-744-469-0556. If you wanted to dial the U.S. Embassy in Mexico City, the whole number would be 011-52-55-5209-9100.

To make international calls: To make international calls from Mexico, first dial 00, then the country code (U.S. or Canada 1, U.K. 44, Ireland 353, Australia 61, New Zealand 64). Next, dial the area code and number. For example, to call the British Embassy in Washington, you would dial 00-1-202-588-7800.

For directory assistance: Dial ℭ **040** if you're looking for a number inside Mexico. *Note:* Listings usually appear under the owner's name, not the name of the business, and your chances to find an English-speaking operator are slim to none.

For operator assistance: If you need operator assistance in making a call, dial 090 to make an international call, and 020 to call a number in Mexico.

Toll-free numbers: Numbers beginning with 800 within Mexico are toll-free, but calling a U.S. toll-free number from Mexico costs the same as an overseas call. To call an 800 number in the U.S., dial 001-880 and the last 7 digits of the toll-free number. To call an 888 number in the U.S., dial 001-881 and the last 7 digits of the toll-free number. For a number with an 887 prefix, dial 882; for 866, dial 883.

Time Zone Central Standard Time prevails throughout most of Mexico. The state of Baja California Norte is on Pacific Standard Time, but Baja California Sur is on Mountain Standard Time. Mexico observes daylight savings time.

Tipping Most service employees in Mexico count on tips to make up the majority of their income—especially bellboys and waiters. Bellboys receive the equivalent of 50¢ to $1 per bag; waiters generally receive 10% to 20% of the bill, depending on the level of service. In Mexico, it is not customary to tip taxi drivers, unless they are hired by the hour or provide touring or other special services.

Toilets Public toilets are not common in Mexico, but an increasing number are available, especially at fast-food restaurants and Pemex gas stations. These facilities and restaurant and club restrooms commonly have attendants, who expect a small tip (about 50¢).

Water Most hotels have decanters or bottles of purified water in the rooms; the better hotels have either purified water from regular taps, or special taps marked *agua purificada*. Some hotels will charge for in-room bottled water. Virtually any hotel, restaurant, or bar will bring you purified water if you specifically request it, but you'll usually be charged for it. Bottled purified water is sold at drugstores and grocery stores (popular brands include Santa María, Ciel, and Bonafont). Evian and other imported brands are also widely available.

3

Suggested Los Cabos & Baja Itineraries

The vast majority of travelers to Baja either park themselves in lively Los Cabos or experience a brief border visit to the temptations of Tijuana. However, the peninsula offers much more, and it's easy to combine several of its attractive destinations into a single visit. I've designed most of the suggested itineraries described below to combine some resort-style relaxation with explorations of the natural treasures of Baja, sampling some small-town Mexican life along the way. Note that it is now possible to enter through one airport and leave through another without having to pay any extra in many cases. For explorations in northern Baja, you may choose to fly directly into Tijuana or to San Diego, crossing the border via one of the regular shuttle buses or in a car.

Unlike the rest of Mexico, Baja does not have regular bus service between the major towns. You'll either need to drive—rental cars are widely available—or participate in an organized tour with a chartered bus, though I personally wouldn't choose this option, as there's less flexibility to linger in places you're enjoying. In many areas, a four-wheel-drive vehicle, or one that sits higher up, such as an SUV, are the best bets—it's still a rugged landscape here.

None of the below itineraries can be called exhaustive explorations of Baja, but neither are they exhausting. Consider them as a sampler of the best of Baja, so that upon a return visit you'll know more about where you'd like to spend a concentration of time.

1 Northern Baja in 1 Week

This trip takes you to Mexico's most infamous town, Tijuana, and then down the coast to sample more authentic Baja. The early part of this journey takes in a few kitschy sites—consider it a sampling of the singular Mexican vision of magic realism—then on to some lovely places that will give you an appreciation of the natural beauty and range of experiences available here. The area that this itinerary covers is relatively compact, not requiring a lot of travel time, but you should cater the trip to suit your needs, spending more time in the places you like best.

Days ❶ & ❷: Arrive in Tijuana

Although most people equate Tijuana with **Avenida Revolución,** there is truly a wealth of places to visit here, which you can choose between depending upon your preferences—the Centro Cultural Tijuana, watching a bullfight, or shopping are a few of the favored activities. If you're traveling with children, a visit to the **Mundo Divertido La Mesa** amusement center (p. 147) will be highly appreciated. I recommend a stop at the **Museo de Cera** (**Wax Museum;** p. 145) or a generous sampling of Baja's wines at the **Cava de Vinos L.A. Cetto** (**L.A. Cetto Winery;** p. 147). Your first evening here should be dedicated to taking in the color and revelry of **Avenida Revolución** (p. 146) so you can truly say you've been to Tijuana.

Day ❸: Rosarito Beach

Drive just 20 minutes (29km/18 miles) south of Tijuana and you'll find a complete departure in ambience as you start to relax into the beauty of this area. The drive itself on a wide, modern coastal highway is lovely. Stop for a break at the **Rosarito Beach Hotel** (p. 158), which attracted scores of celebrities and other notables during the later days of Prohibition. Then continue on a few miles south of Rosarito proper to Fox Studio's **Foxploration!** (p. 156), a cinema-themed museum and entertainment center. You can lose yourself for hours in the interactive exhibits, but the main event remains the Titanic Expo. When you're finished, head back to Rosarito Beach for the evening, where enjoying a sunset *cerveza* at **Papas & Beer** (p. 159) on the beach is de rigueur.

Days ❹ & ❺: Exploring Ensenada

Driving south from Rosarito, choose the toll road for efficiency or the local-access road that parallels it for more local color as you head south toward Ensenada. Don't miss a stop in **Puerto Nuevo** for a sampling of the local lobster. After passing the La Fonda resort, be sure to get back on the toll road, because the old road veers inland. Eighteen kilometers (11 miles) from here, stop off at **El Mirador** to admire the dramatic coastal views, and if you dare to look straight down, take a gander at the collection of cars that lie on the rocks at the bottom. A few miles beyond the lookout point is Salsipuedes Bay, and 24 km (15 miles)

beyond this you'll arrive in Ensenada. If you arrive early enough, spend the afternoon exploring this classic town so the next day can be free for fishing, kayaking, surfing, or a visit to either of the two national parks, the **Parque Nacional Constitución de 1857** (p. 167) or the **Parque Nacional Sierra San Pedro Mártir** (p. 168). At some point, you'll want to be sure to visit the **La Bufadora** sea spout (p. 167). For an unforgettable meal in Ensenada, dine at **La Embotelladora Vieja** (p. 171) at the Bodegas de Santo Tomás Winery—it will prepare you for what's on the agenda for the next day. For a more casual good time, you have your choice of **Hussong's Cantina** (p. 172) or the Ensenada location of **Papas & Beer** (p. 172), both institutions of the partying crowd.

Day ❻: Valle de Guadalupe (Mexico's Wine Country)

With 1 day to spend here, you'll only get a small (but sufficient) survey of Mexico's wine country. I'd start with a visit to the **Museo Comunitario del Valle de Guadalupe** (p. 174) and the **Museo Histórico Comunitario** (p. 174), just across the street, to gain an appreciation of the odd history of this region. They're both quite small, so this won't take much time. Then choose two to three vineyards to visit to partake in wine tastings. My preferred wineries are the boutique **Monte Xanic** (p. 175), **Chateau Camou** (p. 175), or **Mogor Badan** (p. 175), but you may enjoy visiting one of the large establishments at **L.A. Cetto** (p. 175) or **Domecq** (p. 175). Highly recommended is a stop for lunch (reservations recommended) at **Laja** (p. 176). Just driving through this exquisite and easily navigable valley is a pleasure. I would also recommend staying the evening here, at the **Adobe Guadalupe** (p. 175), but you can also head back to Ensenada, or anywhere along the coast back north.

Suggested Los Cabos & Baja Itineraries

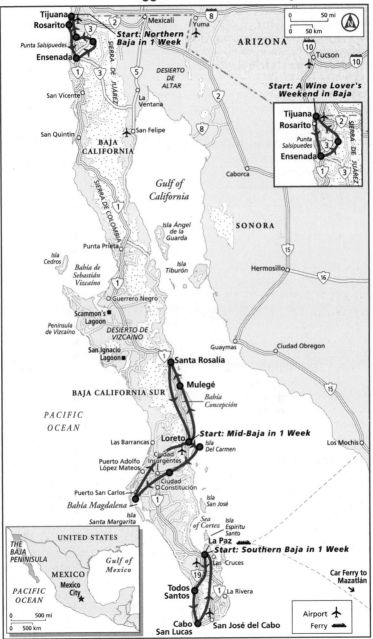

Tijuana
Rosarito
Mexicali
Yuma
Start: Northern Baja in 1 Week
ARIZONA
Tucson
Punta Salsipuedes
Ensenada

Start: A Wine Lover's Weekend in Baja

Tijuana
Rosarito
Punta Salsipuedes
Ensenada
SIERRA DE JUÁREZ

San Vicente
La Ventana
DESIERTO DE ALTAR

San Quintín
San Felipe
BAJA CALIFORNIA
Caborca

SIERRA DE COLOMBIA
SONORA

Gulf of California

Isla Ángel de la Guarda
Isla Tiburón

Punta Prieta
Hermosillo

Isla Cedros
Bahía de Sebastián Vizcaíno
Guerrero Negro
Ciudad Obregon

Scammon's Lagoon
DESIERTO DE VIZCAÍNO
Guaymas

Península de Vizcaíno
San Ignacio Lagoon
Santa Rosalía
BAJA CALIFORNIA SUR
Mulegé
Bahía Concepción

PACIFIC OCEAN

Las Barrancas
Loreto
Start: Mid-Baja in 1 Week
Isla Del Carmen
Los Mochis

Puerto Adolfo López Mateos
Ciudad Insurgentes
Ciudad Constitución

Puerto San Carlos
Bahía Magdalena
Isla San José

Isla Santa Margarita
Isla Espíritu Santo
Sea of Cortez
La Paz
Start: Southern Baja in 1 Week

THE BAJA PENINSULA
UNITED STATES
Gulf of Mexico
Las Cruces
Car Ferry to Mazatlán

MEXICO
Mexico City
La Rivera

PACIFIC OCEAN
Todos Santos
San José del Cabo
Airport
Ferry

Cabo San Lucas

45

Day ❼: Bajamar & Return to Tijuana

On your way back up the coast, stop in at either **Bajamar** (32km/20 miles north of Ensenada; p. 161) or **Real del Mar** (16km/10 miles south of Tijuana; p. 150) to play a round of golf or relax with a spa treatment. You may choose to spend your last night at either of these places, which offer "Americanized" accommodations. Alternatively, head back to Tijuana for one final evening of its seductive charms. And, if you bypassed the Puerto Nuevo lobsters on the way down the coast, don't miss them on the return trip.

2 Mid-Baja in 1 Week

This trip takes you into the heart of Baja and showcases the region's wild, natural beauty. It's an especially appealing trip for those who prefer their travels with a generous dose of activity in the mix.

Day ❶: Arrive in Loreto

Upon arrival in Loreto, you'll want to take the afternoon to explore this small, lovely town, and stop in the **Misión Nuestra Señora de Loreto** (p. 118), the first mission established in Baja, dating back to 1699. The town is remarkably easy to navigate, with one main road that runs parallel to the waterfront boardwalk. Most attractions are near the central square and old mission, but take the time to walk the short pedestrian-only length of Salvatierra to look at the wood homes that date back to the 1800s. For your first evening in town, I'd recommend dinner at **Vecchia Roma,** at the Posada de las Flores hotel (p. 121).

Day ❷: Isla del Carmen

You'll need to arrange this trip through one of Loreto's authorized tour companies, but plan on an enchanting day of kayaking, snorkeling, or hiking at Isla del Carmen, the largest of Loreto's offshore islands. Even if your preference is for water-bound activities, a visit to the abandoned salt-mining town on the northeastern tip of the island is also recommended. See p. 114.

Day ❸: San Javier

Explore a bit of Baja's interior by visiting the **Misión San Francisco Javier** (p. 118), about 2 hours from Loreto along the old Camino Real road. From here, if you're traveling with an authorized guide, you can stop to view some of the **indigenous cave paintings** (p. 116), or you may choose to combine your trip with a visit to **Primer Agua** for a picnic, swimming in the natural spring, or hiking the area. See p. 118.

Day ❹: Whale-Watching in Magdalena Bay (or Alternate Exploration)

Although **Magdalena Bay** is on the opposite side of the peninsula (on the Pacific Coast), it's an easy trip and once there you can board a skiff and spend a few hours watching the gray whales that migrate to this area in large numbers. It's a remarkable sight (p. 117). If you're traveling in months other than December to May, however, the whales won't be there, so you'll need to plan an alternate activity, perhaps a round of tennis or golf. For the truly adventurous, I'd pick the challenging 12-hour trip offered by Las Parras Tours to the foothills of the Guadalupe Mountains, where you'll hike up and view the mystical cave paintings (p. 116).

Day ❺: Kayaking, Fishing, or More Island Explorations

Use this day to explore more of what Loreto has to offer, whether it is offshore fishing, kayaking, snorkeling, diving, or hiking or horseback riding in the surrounding area.

Day ❻: Mulegé & Santa Rosalía

Although Mulegé is closer to Loreto, I'd recommend driving to Santa Rosalía first and stopping in Mulegé on your return trip. Santa Rosalía is 61km (38 miles) north of Loreto. The main reason to visit Santa Rosalía is to view its historical sites of interest, including the Gustave Eiffel–designed **Iglesia de Santa Barbara** (p. 134), the **Museo Histórico Minero de Santa Rosalía** (p. 134), and, of course, the **El Boleo** bakery (p. 135). If you prefer activities to sightseeing, you may want to forego Santa Rosalía and concentrate your time in Mulegé instead, where you can visit, with a guide, the series of caves in **La Trinidad,** a remote ranch 29km (18

miles) west of Mulegé (p. 128), or at **San Borjitas** (p. 128). Literally an oasis in the desert, Mulegé is a lovely, small town, with a large English-speaking community, but beyond the **Misión Santa Rosalía de Mulegé** and the **Museo Regional de Historia** (p. 129 and 130 respectively), the town itself doesn't offer much in the way of sightseeing. Time spent here generally revolves around visiting its lovely surrounding beaches or indulging in the famed Mulegé pig roast. See p. 132. The return trip from Mulegé to Loreto is 137km (85 miles), taking about an hour and a half.

Day ❼: Departing Loreto

Use your final day to relax, or, if it's your pleasure, play a round of golf at the **Campo de Golf Loreto** (p. 112) or tennis at the **Centro Tenístico Loreto** (p. 113).

3 Southern Baja in 1 Week

Baja's most popular areas are, of course, the twin towns at its tip, San José del Cabo and Cabo San Lucas. This itinerary combines the best of these resorts with stops at southern Baja's more traditional towns. I've planned this trip for you to arrive in La Paz and depart from Los Cabos, but you can choose to fly round-trip into Los Cabos and then drive the 177km (110 miles) north to La Paz to reach my suggested starting point.

Days ❶ & ❷: La Paz

Settle into the relaxed pace of Baja California Sur's state capital, a traditional Mexican town. You'll find plenty of interesting sights around town, but you can also explore the lovely beaches to the north. There are also several intriguing natural museums in the area, including the **Serpentarium** (p. 102) at the southernmost end of the *malecón,* or the **Aquarium** (p. 101), next to the Hotel Concha. For your second day here, book a trip to one of the offshore islands, either **Los Islotes** or **Espíritu Santo,** for snorkeling, diving, kayaking, or visiting the resident colony of sea lions. See p. 97.

Day ❸: El Triunfo to Todos Santos

Head south from La Paz toward El Triunfo, an old mining town. On the way, you may want to plan a stop at the **Cactus Sanctuary** (p. 102), a fascinating natural sanctuary where you can educate yourself about the area's flora and fauna. Stop in **El Triunfo** for a break, or even a hike to view the old mines (p. 100). Then head south to **Todos Santos** and explore this charming town, with an intriguing selection of art galleries. I highly recommend lunch at the **Café Santa Fe** (p. 90). Stay the night here—you may even choose to check in to the **Hotel California** (p. 88).

Days ❹ to ❼: Los Cabos

Continue heading south along Carretera Transpeninsular to Cabo San Lucas (68 km/42 miles) along a beautiful, mostly coastal highway. No matter whether you stay in Cabo, the Corridor, or San José, you'll no doubt explore all three areas. Devote a day to golf, if you're a golfer (p. 54). If not, indulge in one of the area's sumptuous spas or take a surf lesson at the **Cabo Surf Hotel,** on Playa Acapulquito (p. 77). Be sure to spend an evening reveling in Cabo's nightlife, starting at **Nikki Beach** (p. 84) at sunset. A cruise to **El Arco,** where you can see the famed rock formation, and on to **Playa de Amor** is a singular Cabo experience. And, of course, don't forget just relaxing at the beach. See chapter 4.

4 A Wine Lover's Long Weekend in Baja

Admittedly, Mexico is not the first country to come to mind when thinking of wine, but the emerging wine country in Baja does make for a memorable exploration and a unique and easy trip from Southern California. Take a long weekend and indulge in an exploration of the spirits here.

Day ❶: Tijuana to Ensenada

Cross the border into Mexico, and make a stop in Tijuana for a generous sampling of Baja's wines at the **Cava de Vinos L.A. Cetto** (**L.A. Cetto Winery;** p. 147). Cava is big and commercial, but it will give you an introduction to what Mexican wines have traditionally been known for. The cork-covered building is certainly a sight to see in and of itself. When you're finished (making sure you're sober enough to drive), head down the coast to Ensenada, but not before enjoying a truly wonderful meal at **La Embotelladora Vieja** (p. 171) at the Bodegas de Santo Tomás winery, which crafts its menu to complement wines. Be sure to book a room in advance at the **Adobe Guadalupe** (p. 175) if you want to truly immerse yourself in the wines of the Valle de Guadalupe. You also can stay in Ensenada, as it's just a 29km (18 mile) drive between Cabo San Lucas and San José del Cabo along Highway 3.

Days ❷ & ❸: Valle de Guadalupe

To orient yourself and ensure that you start your explorations with some knowledge of the area's unusual history, pay a visit to the **Museo Comunitario del Valle de Guadalupe** (p. 174) and the **Museo Histórico Comunitario** (p. 174). Try lunch at the Museo Communitario's adjacent Russian restaurant. Fill the rest of your days with visits to the various wineries where you can view bottling processes and partake in tastings. My preference are visits to the smaller, boutique wineries, such as **Monte Xanic, Chateau Camou,** or **Mogor Badan,** but you may also enjoy visiting one of the large establishments at **L.A. Cetto** or **Domecq.** Be certain to plan a meal (reservations are recommended) at **Laja** before heading back. Get more information on all of the above in "Exploring the Valle de Guadalupe—Mexico's Wine Country" on p. 172.

4

Los Cabos

The most popular destinations in Baja Sur are the twin towns at the peninsula's tip: Cabo San Lucas and San José del Cabo. Collectively they are known as Los Cabos (the Capes), although they couldn't be more different from one another. Cabo San Lucas is an extension of Southern California, with luxury accommodations, ubiquitous golf courses, endless shopping, franchise restaurants, and spirited nightlife. San José del Cabo remains rooted in the traditions of a quaint Mexican town, although it's rapidly becoming gentrified.

Thirty kilometers (19 miles) of smooth highway known as the Corridor lie between the two Cabos. Along this stretch, major new resorts and residential communities, including some of the world's finest golf courses, have been developed. And what has always been here continues to beckon: dozens of pristine coves and inlets with a wealth of marine life just offshore.

Great sportfishing originally brought attention to Los Cabos, which were once accessible only by water. It remains a lure today, although golf has overtaken it as the principal attraction. As early as the 1940s, the area attracted a hearty community of cruisers, fishermen, divers, and adventurers. By the early 1980s, the Mexican government realized the growth potential of Los Cabos and invested in new highways, airport facilities, golf courses, and modern marine facilities. The increase in air access and the opening of Carretera Transpeninsular 1 (in 1973) paved the way for spectacular growth.

Still more activities to keep you busy in the area are sea kayaking, whale-watching, diving, surfing, and hiking, as well as the chance to explore ancient cave paintings and to camp on isolated, wild beaches.

The Los Cabos area has earned a deserved reputation for being much more expensive than other Mexican resorts. Although there has been a boom in hotel construction, these have all been luxury resorts, only solidifying Los Cabos' higher average room prices, and not adjusting prices downward with the added supply of rooms. The other factor driving up prices is that compared to mainland Mexico, there's little agriculture in Baja; most foodstuffs and other items must be shipped in. U.S. dollars are the preferred currency here, and it's not uncommon to see price listings in dollars rather than pesos.

With more than 33km (20 miles) separating the two Cabos and numerous attractions in between, you should consider renting a car, even if only for a day. Transportation by taxi is expensive, and if you are at all interested in exploring, a rental car is your most economical option. Because of the distinctive character and attractions of the two towns and the Corridor between, they are treated separately here. It is common to stay in one and make day trips to the other two.

1 San José del Cabo ⭑⭑⭑

180km (112 miles) SE of La Paz; 33km (20 miles) NE of Cabo San Lucas; 1,760km (1,091 miles) SE of Tijuana

San José del Cabo, with its pastel cottages and flowering trees lining the narrow streets, retains the air of a provincial Mexican town. Originally founded in 1730 by Jesuit missionaries, it remains the seat of the Los Cabos government and the center of its business community. The main square, adorned with a wrought-iron bandstand and shaded benches, faces the cathedral, which was built on the site of an early mission.

San José is becoming increasingly sophisticated, with a collection of noteworthy cafes, art galleries, and intriguing small inns adding a newly refined flavor to the central downtown area. This is the best choice for those who want to enjoy the paradoxical landscape but still be aware that they're in Mexico.

ESSENTIALS
GETTING THERE & DEPARTING

BY PLANE   **Aeromexico** (© 800/237-6639 in the U.S., or 800/021-4000, 624/146-5098, or 624/146-5097 in Mexico; www.aeromexico.com) flies nonstop from San Diego, Ontario, and Los Angeles, and has connecting flights from other cities. **Aero California** (© 800/237-6225 in the U.S., or 624/143-3700) offers flights from Los Angeles; **American Airlines** (© 800/433-7300 in the U.S., or 624/146-5300; www.aa.com) flies from Dallas/Ft. Worth, Los Angeles, and Chicago; **America West** (© 800/235-9292 in the U.S., or 624/146-5380; www.americawest.com) operates connecting flights through Phoenix, Las Vegas, and San Diego; **Alaska Airlines** (© 800/426-0333 in the U.S., or 624/146-5210 or 624/146-5212; www.alaskaair. com) flies from Los Angeles, San Diego, Seattle, and San Francisco; **Continental** (© 800/525-0280 in the U.S., or 624/146-5040; www.continental.com) flies from Houston and Newark; **Delta** (© 800/221-1212 in the U.S.; www.delta.com) has flights from Atlanta and Salt Lake City; **Frontier** (© 800/432-1359 in the U.S.; www.frontier airlines.com) has direct service from Denver; **Mexicana** (© 800/531-7921 in the U.S., or 624/146-5001, 624/143-5352, or -5353; www.mexicana.com) has direct or connecting flights from Denver, Guadalajara, Los Angeles, Sacramento, Las Vegas, and Mexico City; and **United Airlines** (© 800/864-8331 in the U.S.; www.united.com) flies direct from both San Francisco and Denver.

Aéreo Calafia (© 624/143-4302; www.aereocalafia.com) is a small regional airline that offers regularly scheduled service on Cessna Grand Caravans between Los Cabos and Mazatlán, Puerto Vallarta, Culiacán, and Los Mochis, as well as charter services within Mexico.

BY CAR   From La Paz, take Carretera Transpeninsular south, a scenic route that winds through foothills and occasionally skirts the coast; the drive takes 3 to 4 hours. From La Paz, you can also take Carretera Transpeninsular south just past the village of San Pedro, then take Highway 19 south (a less winding road than the Carretera Transpeninsular) through Todos Santos to Cabo San Lucas, where you pick up Carretera Transpeninsular east to San José del Cabo; this route takes 2 to 3 hours. From Cabo San Lucas, it's a half-hour drive.

BY BUS   The *terminal de autobuses* (bus station), on Valerio González, a block east of the Carretera Transpeninsular (© 624/142-1100), is open daily from 5:30am to 7pm, although buses can arrive and depart later. Buses between Cabo San Lucas and La Paz run almost hourly during the day. For points farther north you usually change

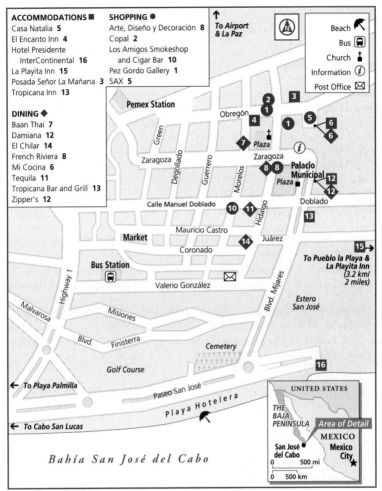

San José del Cabo

ACCOMMODATIONS ■
Casa Natalia **5**
El Encanto Inn **4**
Hotel Presidente
InterContinental **16**
La Playita Inn **15**
Posada Señor La Mañana **3**
Tropicana Inn **13**

DINING ◆
Baan Thai **7**
Damiana **12**
El Chilar **14**
French Riviera **8**
Mi Cocina **6**
Tequila **11**
Tropicana Bar and Grill **13**
Zipper's **12**

SHOPPING ●
Arte, Diseño y Decoración **8**
Copal **2**
Los Amigos Smokeshop
and Cigar Bar **10**
Pez Gordo Gallery **1**
SAX **5**

↑
To Airport
& La Paz

Beach 🏖
Bus 🚌
Church ✝
Information ⓘ
Post Office ✉

Pemex Station

Obregón

Plaza

Green

Zaragoza

Degollado

Guerrero

Morelos

Zaragoza

Palacio
Municipal
Plaza

Calle Manuel Doblado

Doblado

Hidalgo

Mauricio Castro

Market

Coronado

Juárez

To Pueblo la Playa &
La Playita Inn
(3.2 km/
2 miles)

Bus Station

Highway 1

Valerio González

Estero
San José

Malvarosa

Misiones

Blvd. Mijares

Blvd.

Finisterra

Cemetery

Golf Course

← To Playa Palmilla

Paseo San José

Playa Hotelera

← To Cabo San Lucas

Bahía San José del Cabo

UNITED STATES

THE
BAJA
PENINSULA

Area of Detail

MEXICO

San José
del Cabo

Mexico
City

0   500 mi

0   500 km

buses in La Paz. The trip to Cabo San Lucas takes 40 minutes; to La Paz, 3 hours.
Buses also go to Todos Santos; the trip takes around 3 hours.

ORIENTATION

ARRIVING The one airport (🕿 **624/146-5111**) that serves both Cabos and the
connecting Corridor is 12km (7½ miles) northwest of San José del Cabo and 35km
(22 miles) northeast of Cabo San Lucas. It was expanded in 1999, and now has separate terminals for national and international flights—be sure to request the correct
terminal when you return. Upon arrival at the airport, buy a ticket inside the building for a *colectivo* (minivan) or a taxi, which up to four passengers may share. *Colec-*
tivo fares run about $9 for up to eight passengers and are only available from the
airport. A private van for up to five passengers is $70. Taxis charge about $15 to San

José. Timeshare resorts have booths in the airport's arrival/baggage area. The promoters hook visitors with a free ride to their hotel in return for listening to their sales presentation.

The major car-rental agencies all have counters at the airport, open during flight arrivals: **Avis** (℃ **800/331-1212** from the U.S., or 624/146-0201; avissjd@avis.com.mx; Mon–Sat 7am–9pm, Sun 6am–9pm); **Budget** (℃ **800/527-0700** from the U.S., 624/146-5333 at the airport, or 624/143-4190 in Cabo San Lucas; daily 8am–6pm); **Hertz** (℃ **800/654-3131** from the U.S., 624/146-5088 or 624/142-0375 in San José del Cabo; daily 8am–8pm); and **National** (℃ **800/328-4567** from the U.S., 624/146-5022 at the airport, or 624/142-2424 in San José; daily 8am–8pm). Advance reservations are not always necessary.

If you arrive at the bus station, it's too far from the hotels to walk with luggage. A taxi from the bus station to downtown or the hotel zone costs $2 to $4.

VISITOR INFORMATION   The city tourist information office (℃ **624/142-3310,** 624/142-0465, or 624/142-9628) is in the old post office building on Zaragoza at Mijares. It offers maps, free local publications, and other basic information about the area. It's open Monday through Friday from 8am to 2pm. Prior to arrival, contact the **Los Cabos Tourism Board** (℃ **866/567-2226** from the U.S.).

CITY LAYOUT   San José del Cabo consists of two zones: downtown, where sophisticated inns as well as traditional budget hotels are located, and the hotel zone along the beach.

Zaragoza is the main street leading from the highway into town; Paseo San José runs parallel to the beach and is the principal boulevard of the hotel zone. The 1.6km (1-mile) Bulevar Mijares connects the two areas, and is the center of most tourist activity in San José.

GETTING AROUND

There is no local bus service between downtown and the beach; **taxis** (℃ **624/142-0910** or 624/142-0580) connect the two.

For day trips to Cabo San Lucas, catch a bus (see "Getting There & Departing," above) or a cab.

FAST FACTS: San José del Cabo

Area Code The local area code is **624.**

Banks Banks exchange currency during business hours, generally Monday through Friday from 8:30am to 6pm and Saturday from 10am to 2pm. There are several banks on Zaragoza between Morelos and Degollado.

Emergencies Call the local police at city hall (℃ **624/142-0361**) or dial **066.**

Hospital **Hospital General** is at Retorno Atunero s/n, in the Col. Chamizal neighborhood (℃ **624/142-0013**).

Internet Access **CaboOnline,** at Malvarosa and Gobernadora (℃ **624/142-2905**), is open Monday through Saturday from 10am to 8pm and charges $7.50 per hour for access. **Trazzo Internet,** on the corner of Zaragoza and Morelos, 1 block from the central plaza (no phone), is open Monday through Saturday from 10am to 8pm and charges $2.50 for 30 minutes or less of high-speed access.

Pharmacy **Farmacia ISSSTE,** Carretera Transpeninsular Km 34, Plaza California Local 7, San José del Cabo (© **624/142-2645**), is open daily from 8am to 8pm.

Post Office The *correo,* at Bulevar Mijares 1924 and Valerio González (© **624/ 142-0911**), is open Monday through Friday from 8am to 4pm and Saturday from 9am to noon.

BEACHES & OUTDOOR ACTIVITIES

The relaxed pace of San José del Cabo makes it an ideal place to unwind and absorb authentic Mexican flavor. Beach aficionados who want to explore the beautiful coves and beaches along the 35km (22-mile) coast between the two Cabos should consider renting a car for a day or so (from $50 per day). Frequent bus service between San José del Cabo and Cabo San Lucas also makes it possible to visit both towns (see "Getting There & Departing," above).

BEACHES

The nearest beach that's safe for swimming is **Pueblo la Playa** (also called La Playita), about 3.2km (2 miles) east of town. From Bulevar Mijares, turn east at the small sign for PUEBLO LA PLAYA and follow the dusty dirt road through cane fields and palms to a small village and beautiful beach where fishermen pull their *pangas* (skiffs) ashore. La Playita Resort and its adjacent restaurant (see "Where to Stay," below) offer the only formal sustenance on the beach. There are no shade *palapas.*

Estero San José, a nature reserve with at least 270 species of birds, is between Pueblo la Playa and the Hotel Presidente InterContinental. The estuary is a protected ecological reserve that does not offer beach access (it's where the estuary runs into the ocean, so the water is brown and murky at the mouth).

A fine swimming beach with beautiful rock formations, **Playa Palmilla,** 8km (5 miles) west of San José, is near the Spanish colonial–style One&Only Palmilla (p. 63). To reach Playa Palmilla, take a taxi to the road that leads to the Hotel Palmilla grounds, then take the fork to the left (without entering the hotel grounds) and follow signs to Pepe's restaurant on the beach.

For a list of other nearby beaches worth exploring if you have a rental car, see "Beaches & Outdoor Activities" under "Cabo San Lucas," later in this chapter.

CRUISES

Boats depart from Cabo San Lucas; prices and offerings vary, but cruises generally include music, open bar, and snacks for $30 to $40 per person. Daytime and sunset cruises are available. Arrange cruises through a travel agency, or call **Xplora Adventours** (© **624/142-9135** or 624/142-9000, ext. 8050; www.xploraloscabos.com).

Moments Festivals & Special Events in Los Cabos

San José del Cabo celebrates the feast of its patron saint on March 19. June 19 is the festival of the patron saint of San Bartolo, a village 100km (62 miles) north. July 25 is the festival of the patron saint of Santiago, a village 55km (34 miles) north. These festivals usually feature fairs, music, dancing, feasting, horse races, and cockfights.

Tips **Swimming Safety**

Although this area is ideal for watersports, occasional strong currents and undertows can make swimming dangerous at **Playa Hotelera,** the town beach—check conditions before entering the surf. Swimming is generally safe at **Pueblo la Playa** (see "Beaches," above), though it, too, occasionally experiences a strong undertow. The safest area beach for swimming is **Playa El Medano** in Cabo San Lucas.

Xplora handles all tour providers in the area and can give unbiased information. It's open daily from 8am to 10pm.

LAND SPORTS
ADVENTURE TOURS Tío Sports (© 624/143-3399; www.tiosports.com) arranges a variety of land- and water-based adventure and nature tours, including popular ATV tours to La Candelaria, parasailing, kayak, catamaran, snorkeling, and diving trips. The website gives current prices. **Gray Line Los Cabos** (© 624/146-9410; www.graylineloscabos.com) is another great contact for a complete rundown of what's available. They offer all the tours from all the local companies rather than working with only a select few. For a broad selection of tours, go with Gray Line, but if you're interested in adventure excursions or renting equipment to explore on your own, go with Tío.

GOLF Los Cabos has become one of the world's leading golf destinations, with a collection of top courses and others under construction. The lowest greens fees in the area ($64 for 9 holes; $109 for 18 holes, or two rounds on the course) are at the beautifully maintained 9-hole **Mayan Palace Golf Los Cabos** (previously the Club Campo de Golf San José), © 624/142-0901 or 624/142-0905, Paseo Finisterra 1, across from the Howard Johnson Hotel. The 7th hole offers a wonderful view with the ocean on your left and mountains facing you as you approach the green. There's a large lake at the bottom and to the left of the green and a lateral sand trap at the back of the green challenging overachievers. The 9th is a good finishing hole with a wide sloping fairway with sand traps to the top, right, and bottom of the green. The course doesn't take reservations for tee times. It is open daily from 6:30am to 4pm (to 4:30pm in summer). Club guests can also use the swimming pool. Club rentals are $25 to $45; cart rentals are included in the greens fees. For more information about playing golf in Los Cabos, see "The Lowdown on Golf in Cabo" on p. 74.

HORSEBACK RIDING You can rent horses near the Presidente InterContinental, Fiesta Inn, and Palmilla hotels for $15 to $20 per hour. Most people choose to ride on the beach. For a more organized riding experience, I highly recommend **Cuadra San Francisco Equestrian Center,** Km 19.5 along the Corridor, in front of the Casa del Mar resort (© 624/144-0160; www.loscaboshorses.com). The owner is master horseman Francisco Barrena, who has over 30 years of experience in training horses and operating equestrian schools, and will assist any level rider in selecting and fitting a horse to his or her skill level. Your choice of English or Western saddles are available on well-trained, exceptional horses. A 2-hour canyon ride in and around Arroyo San Carlos or Venado Blanco costs $70; a 1-hour ride to the beach or desert is $35.

TENNIS   You can play tennis at the two courts of the **Club Campo de Golf San José,** Paseo Finisterra 1 (© 624/142-0905), for $13 an hour during the day, $22 an hour at night. Club guests can also use the swimming pool. Tennis is also available at the **Hotel Presidente InterContinental** (two lit courts); see "Where to Stay," below.

WATERSPORTS

FISHING   The least expensive way to enjoy deep-sea fishing is to pair up with another angler and charter a *panga,* a 7m (23-ft.) skiff used by local fishermen from Playa la Puebla. Several panga fleets offer 6-hour sportfishing trips, usually from 6am to noon, for $25 per hour (there's a 3-hr. minimum). Two or three people can divide the cost. For information, visit the fisherman's cooperative in Pueblo la Playa (no phone). For larger charter boats, you'll depart from the marina in Cabo San Lucas (see below).

SEA KAYAKING   Fully guided, ecologically oriented **ocean kayak tours** are available through **Baja's Moto Rent** (© 624/143-2050), **Cabo Expeditions** (© 624/143-2700), and **Aqua Deportes** (© 624/143-0117). Most ocean kayaking tours depart from Cabo San Lucas.

SNORKELING/DIVING   **Gray Line Los Cabos** (© 624/146-9410; www.graylineloscabos.com) and **Amigos del Mar** in Cabo San Lucas (© 800/344-3349 in the U.S., or 624/143-0505; www.amigosdelmar.com) arrange snorkeling and diving trips starting at $50 per person. Among the area's best dive sites are **Cabo Pulmo** and **Gordo Banks.** Cabo Pulmo has seven sites geared for divers of all experience levels, so it never feels crowded. It also offers the possibility to snorkel with sea lions, depending on the currents and the animals' behavior. Gordo Banks is an advanced dive site where you can see whale sharks and hammerhead sharks. It's a deep dive—27 to 30m (89–98 ft.)—with limited visibility (9–12m/30–39 ft.). Most dives are drift dives, and wetsuits are highly recommended.

SURFING   **Playa Costa Azul,** at Km 29 on Carretera Transpeninsular just south of San José, is the most popular surfing beach in the area. A few bungalows are available for rent, or surfers can camp on the beach. The **Costa Azul Surf Shop,** Km 28, Playa Costa Azul (© 624/142-2771; www.costa-azul.com.mx), rents surfboards by the day. It charges $20 per day for a short or long board, leash, and rack for your rental car. Spectators can watch from the highway lookout point at the top of the hill south of Costa Azul. **Baja Wild** (© 624/142-5300; www.bajasalvaje.com) offers both surf lessons as well as surf tours, so you can get right to the best waves in the briefest amount of time. Trips take you to any of 15 breaks within the Sea of Cortez, to the big breaks on the Pacific Ocean, or even combine surfing and kayaking.

You can find good surfing from March through November all along the beaches west of Cabo, and **Playa Chileno,** near the Cabo San Lucas Hotel east of town, has a famous right break. Other good surfing beaches along the corridor are **Acapulquito, El Tule,** and **La Bocana.** *Warning:* Several accidents have involved visiting surfers who are not familiar with the rocky break, so surf with care!

When summer hurricanes spin off the southern end of the peninsula, they send huge surf northward to beaches like Zipper's, Punta Gorda, and Old Man's. Surfers have compared Zipper's (near the Brisa del Mar Trailer Park and the Costa Azul Surf Shop outside San José del Cabo) with places like Pipeline, on the north shore of Oahu. That may be a bit of an exaggeration, but there are great waves nonetheless.

WHALE-WATCHING From January through March, whales congregate offshore. Fishermen at Pueblo la Playa will take small groups out to see the whales; a 4-hour trip runs about $45 per person. Organized half-day tours on sportfishing boats, glass-bottom boats, and cruise catamarans depart from Plaza las Glorias in Cabo San Lucas and cost $35 to $50, depending on the type of boat. The price includes snacks and beverages. The ultimate whale excursion is a trip to **Magdalena Bay.** Tours from San José take you by plane—a 75-minute flight—to Magdalena, where you board a *panga* and spend 3 hours watching gray whales and humpbacks loll around the coastal lagoons. This tour is $385, including air transportation, and can be arranged through **Xplora Adventours** (© 624/142-9135; www.xploraloscabos.com). You can also spot the whales from shore; good spots include the beach by the Solmar Suites hotel on the Pacific and the beaches and cliffs along the Corridor. For more information, see "Whale-Watching in Baja: A Primer," in chapter 6.

SHOPPING

The town has a growing selection of unique design shops, hip boutiques, and collections of fine Mexican *artesanía* (handicrafts) clustered around Bulevar Mijares and Zaragoza, the main street. The municipal market, on Mauricio Castro and Green, sells edibles and utilitarian wares. The following businesses accept credit cards (American Express, MasterCard, and Visa).

ADD (Arte, Diseño y Decoración) This shop sells creative home accessories and furnishings mostly made of rustic wood, pewter, and Talavera ceramics. Shipping is available. Open weekdays from 9am to 8pm, Saturdays from 10am to 6pm. Zaragoza at Hidalgo. © 624/142-2777.

Copal Traditional and contemporary Mexican artesanía and silver jewelry are the specialties in this former residence, which has been tastefully converted into a contemporary shop. Open weekdays from 9am to 10:30pm, weekends 10am to 2pm and 4 to 10:30pm. Plaza Mijares 10, off Av. Obregón. © 624/142-3070.

Los Amigos Smokeshop and Cigar Bar For fine Cuban cigars and cigarettes, as well as Veracruz cigars, a visit here is a must. They sell not only high-quality cigars but also a whole range of smoking accessories, including humidors and cutters, with friendly assistance from their knowledgeable staff. Also available are private lockers, a bar with an excellent selection of single malts, Wednesday evening cigar tastings, and a VIP club for frequent visitors. Open Monday through Wednesday 9am to 8pm, Thursday to Saturday from 9am to 1pm. Calle Manuel Doblado and Morelos (across from the French Riviera bakery). © 624/142-1138.

Pez Gordo Gallery The premier contemporary art gallery in the Los Cabos area, Pez Gordo showcases the works of more than 40 regional artists in a variety of mediums ranging from oils to photography. Open Monday through Saturday from 10am to 8pm; Thursday until 9pm. On Saturdays, from 10am to 3pm, watch artists work in the gallery's garden patio. 19 Alvaro Obregón (next to Fandango Restaurant, in the Historic Center). © 624/142-5788. www.pezgordogallery.com.

SAX For unusual and well-priced jewelry, visit this small shop where two local designers create one-of-a-kind pieces using silver, coral, and semiprecious stones. They'll even create a special request design for you, ready in 24 hours. Open Monday through Saturday from 10am to 9pm. Mijares 2. © 624/142-6053. www.allaboutcabo.com/sax/index.htm.

WHERE TO STAY

There's more demand than supply for hotel rooms in Baja Sur, so prices tend to be higher than those for equivalent accommodations in other parts of Mexico. San José has only a handful of budget hotels, so it's best to call ahead for reservations. A new trend here is toward smaller inns, or bed-and-breakfasts, offering stylish accommodations in town. The beachfront hotel zone often offers package deals that bring room rates down to the moderate range, especially during summer months. Check before making your payment.

EXPENSIVE

Casa Natalia ★★★ *(Finds)*   This acclaimed boutique hotel is exquisite. Owners Nathalie and Loic have transformed a former residence into a beautiful amalgam of palms, waterfalls, and flowers that mirrors the beauty of the land. The inn is a completely renovated historic home, which combines modern architecture with traditional Mexican touches. Each room's name reflects the decor, such as Conchas (seashells), Azul (blue), or Talavera (ceramics); all have sliding glass doors that open onto small private terraces, with hammocks and chairs, shaded by bougainvillea and bamboo. The two spa suites each have a private terrace with a Jacuzzi and hammock. California palms surround the small courtyard pool; the terraces face this view. Casa Natalia offers its guests privacy, style, and romance. It's in the heart of the Bulevar Mijares action, just off the central plaza.

Bulevar Mijares 4, 23400 San José del Cabo, B.C.S. © **888/277-3814** in the U.S., 866/826-1170 in Canada, or 624/142-5100. Fax 624/142-5110. www.casanatalia.com. 16 units. High season $295 standard, $475 spa suite; low season $180 standard, $305 spa suite. AE, MC, V. Children under 14 not accepted. **Amenities:** Gourmet restaurant (see Mi Cocina, below); bar; heated swimming pool w/waterfall and swim-up bar; concierge; room service; massage; laundry service. *In room:* A/C, TV, fan, hair dryer, safe.

Hotel Presidente InterContinental ★★ *(Kids)*   Serenity, seclusion, and luxury are the hallmarks of the Presidente, set on a long stretch of beach next to the Estero San José. Low-rise, Mediterranean-style buildings frame the beach and San José's largest swimming pool, which has a swim-up bar. If possible, select a ground-floor oceanfront room; the lower level offers spacious terraces, but upper-level units have tiny balconies. The rooms have light-wood furnishings and brightly colored accents, with satellite TV and large bathrooms; suites include a separate sitting area. The all-inclusive resort is a good choice for those who principally want to stay put in one place and enjoy it; it's also popular with families.

Bulevar Mijares s/n, 23400 San José del Cabo, B.C.S. © **800/327-0200** in the U.S., or 624/142-0211. Fax 624/142-0232. http://loscabos.interconti.com. 395 units. High season $285 standard double, $315 oceanfront double, $511–$693 double suite; low season rates from $250 double. Rates include all meals, beverages, and many sports. AE, DC, MC, V. **Amenities:** 5 restaurants; garden cafe; 4 swimming pools (2 heated, w/swim-up bars); children's pool; golf clinics; tennis; gym; bicycles; tour desk; twice-daily shuttle to Cabo San Lucas (fee); room service; laundry service; horseback riding; yoga, Tai Chi, and Pilates classes. *In room:* A/C, TV, hair dryers.

MODERATE

El Encanto Inn ★★ *(Value)*   On a quiet street in the historic downtown district, this charming small inn borders a grassy courtyard with a fountain, offering a relaxing alternative to busy hotels. Rooms are attractively and uniquely decorated, with rustic wood and contemporary iron furniture. The nice-size bathrooms have colorful tile accents. Rooms have two double beds; suites have king-size beds and an added sitting room. A pool area with *palapa* bar and 14 poolside suites were recently added. These new suites have minibars and other extras, while all rooms offer satellite DirecTV. El Encanto's welcoming owners, Cliff and Blanca, can help arrange fishing packages and golf and diving outings. Blanca is a lifelong resident of San José, so she's a great resource for information and dining tips. This place is best for those looking for a peaceful place from which to explore historic San José. Room rates include continental breakfast at Jazmin's restaurant, half a block away. The inn is a half-block from the church.

Morelos 133 (between Obregón and Comonfort), 23400 San José del Cabo, B.C.S. ℂ **624/142-0388.** www.elencantoinn.com. 19 units. $75 double; $89–$169 suites. MC, V. Limited street parking available. **Amenities:** Small outdoor pool; *palapa* bar. *In room:* A/C, TV, coffeemaker, fan.

La Playita Inn   Removed from even the slow pace of San José, this older yet impeccably clean and friendly courtyard hotel is ideal for fishermen and those looking for something removed from a traditional hotel vacation. It's the only hotel on San José's only beach that's safe for swimming. Steps from the water and the lineup of fishing *pangas,* the two stories of sunlit rooms frame a patio with a pool just large enough to allow you to swim laps. Each room is spacious, with high ceilings, high-quality if basic furnishings, screened windows, and nicely tiled bathrooms, plus cable TV. Two large suites on the second floor have small refrigerators. If you catch a big one, there's a fish freezer for storage. Services include coffee every morning and a golf-cart shuttle to the beach. Next door, the hotel's La Playita Restaurant is open daily from 11am to 10pm and serves a great mix of seafood and standard favorites, plus occasional live jazz or tropical music.

Pueblo la Playa, Apdo. Postal 437, 23400 San José del Cabo, B.C.S. ℂ/fax **624/142-4166.** www.laplayitahotel.com. 26 units. $60–$75 double. Rates include continental breakfast. MC, V. Free parking. From Bulevar Mijares, follow sign pointing to PUEBLO LA PLAYA, taking dirt road for about 3.2km (2 miles) to the beach. The hotel is on the left, facing water at edge of the tiny village of Pueblo la Playa. **Amenities:** Adjoining restaurant; pool; fish freezer; morning coffee service. *In room:* A/C, TV.

Tropicana Inn ⚐   This handsome colonial-style hotel, a long-standing favorite in San José, welcomes many repeat visitors. Just behind (and adjacent to) the Tropicana Bar and Grill, it frames a plant-filled courtyard with a graceful arcade bordering the rooms and inviting swimming pool. Each nicely furnished, medium-size room in the L-shaped building (which has a two- and three-story wing) has tile floors, two double beds, a window looking out on the courtyard, and a brightly tiled bathroom with shower. Each morning, freshly brewed coffee, delicious sweet rolls, and fresh fruit are set out for hotel guests. There's room service until 11pm from the adjacent Tropicana Bar and Grill (owned by the hotel).

Bulevar Mijares 30 (1 block south of the town square), 23400 San José del Cabo, B.C.S. ℂ **624/142-0907** or 624/142-1580. Fax 624/142-1590. 38 units. $79 double. Rates include continental breakfast. AE, MC, V. Free limited parking. **Amenities:** Restaurant/bar; small pool; tour desk; room service; laundry service. *In room:* A/C, TV, minibar, coffeemaker.

INEXPENSIVE

Posada Señor La Mañana   This comfortable two-story guesthouse, in a grove of tropical fruit trees, offers basic rooms with tile floors and funky furniture and an abundance of hammocks strewn about the property. Guests have cooking privileges in a large, fully equipped common kitchen set beside two *palapas.* Upstairs rooms have two full-size beds plus room for an extra single bed; downstairs rooms were remodeled in late 2004, and have one queen bed plus either one or two single beds. The hotel is next to the Casa de la Cultura, behind the main square.

Alvaro Obregón 1, 23400 San José del Cabo, B.C.S. ⓒ/fax **624/142-1372**. Fax 624/142-5761. www.srmanana.com. 8 units. $38–$58 double. No credit cards. **Amenities:** Community kitchen; pool table; half-court basketball. *In room:* Fan.

WHERE TO DINE
EXPENSIVE

Baan Thai ★★ *Finds* MEXICAN   Pan-Asian cuisine seems to be in the spotlight worldwide these days, and Baan Thai, set in one of San José's lovely historic buildings, does an impressive job of innovating these flavors to blend in a hint of Mexico in this exceptional restaurant, under the direction of chef/owner Carl Marts. Move beyond traditional starters like spring rolls or satay to one of Baan Thai's more unique offerings, such as blue crab stir-fried with chile, garlic, and tomatoes, or mild chilies stuffed with smoked marlin and served with a soy-ginger dipping sauce. From there, move on to entrees such as wok-tossed Chilean salmon with chiles and basil, steamed Baja mussels in a coconut-herb broth, or seared steak tossed with mangos, green apples, and chiles. An impressive wine list and full bar service are available to complement your meal. For more than a decade prior to opening Baan Thai, Chef Marts presided over the kitchen at the Corridor's Twin Dolphin resort. Air-conditioned indoor dining, as well as outdoor dining in an exotic garden patio, is available.

Morelos s/n, 1 block behind the church and plaza. ⓒ **624/142-3344**. www.loscabosguide.com/baanthai. Main courses: $8–$21. MC, V. Mon–Sat noon–10:30pm.

Damiana ★ SEAFOOD/MEXICAN   This casually elegant restaurant in an 18th-century hacienda is decorated in the colors of a Mexican sunset: There are deep-orange walls and tables and chairs clad in bright rose, lavender, and orange cloth. The favored tables are in the tropical courtyard, where candles flicker under the trees and the bougainvillea. For an appetizer, try mushrooms diablo, a moderately zesty dish. For a main course, ranchero shrimp in cactus sauce and grilled lobster tail are flavorful choices. You can also enjoy brunch almost until the dinner hour. There is an interior dining room, but the courtyard is the most romantic dining spot in San José. Damiana is on the east side of the town plaza.

San José town plaza. ⓒ **624/142-0499** or 624/142-2899. Fax 624/142-5603. damiana@1cabonet.com.mx. Reservations recommended during Christmas and Easter holidays. Main courses lunch $9–$20, dinner $10–$50. AE, MC, V. Daily 11am–10:30pm.

El Chilar ★★ MEXICAN   In this rustically casual restaurant, chef Armando Montano is so welcoming you may feel like you're dining at a friend's home. His passion for Mexican cuisine is evident, as he blends the traditional flavors of this country—including an array of chiles—into imaginative and heavenly offerings. Among the most popular dinner options are shrimp in a roasted garlic and *guajillo* chile sauce, or the creative grilled tortilla and salmon Napoleon, accompanied by a mango *pico de gallo*. These choices may not be offered when you arrive, however, as Chef Armando is known to frequently change his menu. At night, candlelight adds a sparkle of romance to the setting. El Chilar also offers a full bar and an ample selection of wines, with suggestions for pairings with your meal. Air-conditioned indoor dining is available.

Benito Juárez 1497, at Morelos near the Telmex tower. ⓒ **624/142-2544** or 624/146-9798. Main courses $5–$29. No credit cards. Mon–Sat 3–10pm.

French Riviera ★★ FRENCH/PASTRIES/COFFEE   This is a great place to start the day . . . or end it. A casual restaurant in a classic historic building in San José, French Riviera serves tempting French fare but absolutely irresistible sweets. Its on-site bakery, with an exhibition window for watching the pastry chefs at work, results in smells so delectable I dare you to leave without a sweet something. Start the day with a croissant and cappuccino, or any number of coffee and pastry choices, or end it with a full meal of delectable French fare. A second location in Cabo San Lucas offers a more traditional restaurant setting, with a great selection of wines. It's found in Plaza del Rey, next to the Misiones del Cabo entrance on the highway at Km 6, and it's open from noon until 11pm (𝒞 **624/104-3125**).

Corner of Hidalgo and Manuel Doblado s/n. 𝒞 **624/142-3350**. www.frenchrivieraloscabos.com. Breakfast $1.50–$4; dinner $2.50–$6.50. No credit cards. Daily 7:30am–11pm.

Mi Cocina ★★★ NOUVELLE MEXICAN/EURO CUISINE   Without a doubt, Mi Cocina is the best dining choice in the entire Los Cabos area. This restaurant doesn't rely solely on the romance of its setting—the food is also superb, creative, and consistently flavorful. Notable starters include steamed baby clams topped with a creamy cilantro sauce and served with garlic croutons, or a healthy slice of Camembert cheese, fried and served with homemade toast and grapes. Among the favorite main courses are the baked baby rack of lamb served with grilled vegetables, and the Provençal-style shrimp served with risotto, roasted tomato, basil, and cilantro-fish consommé. Save room for dessert; choices include their famous chocolate-chocolate cake and a perfect crème brûlée. The full-service *palapa* bar offers an excellent selection of wines, premium tequilas, and single-malt scotches. Be adventurous and try one of their special martinis—like the Flor de México, an adaptation of the cosmopolitan, using Jamaica (hibiscus-flower infusion) rather than cranberry juice.

In the Casa Natalia hotel, Bulevar Mijares 4. 𝒞 **624/142-5100**. www.casanatalia.com/dining.cfm. Main courses $15–$32. AE, MC, V. Daily 6:30–10pm (to hotel guests only 6:30am–6pm).

Tequila ★ MEDITERRANEAN/ASIAN   Contemporary Mexican cuisine with a light and flavorful touch is the star attraction here, although the garden setting is lovely, with rustic *equipal* furniture and lanterns scattered among palms and giant mango trees. Try the specialty, shrimp in tequila sauce. Other enjoyable options include perfectly seared tuna with cilantro and ginger, ribs topped with tamarind sauce, and baked lobster with tequila sauce. Vegetarians can enjoy bell peppers stuffed with ricotta in tomato sauce or one of several pasta dishes. The accompanying whole-grain bread arrives fresh and hot, and attentive service complements the fine meal. Cuban cigars and an excellent selection of tequilas are available, as is an extensive wine list emphasizing California vintages.

Manuel Doblado s/n, near Hidalgo. 𝒞 **624/142-1155**. Main courses lunch $9–$22, dinner $10–$45. AE. Daily 5:30–10:30pm.

MODERATE

Tropicana Bar and Grill SEAFOOD/MEAT   The Tropicana remains a popular mainstay, especially for tourists. The recently remodeled restaurant/bar retains its steady clientele day and night and offers live music and special sporting events on satellite TV. The dining area is in a garden (candlelit in the evening) with a tiled mural at one end. Cafe-style sidewalk dining is also available. The menu is too extensive to lay claim to any specialty; it aims to please everyone. All meats and cheeses are imported; dinners include thick steaks and shrimp fajitas. Paella is the Sunday special.

Bulevar Mijares 30, 1 block south of the Plaza Mijares. 𝒞 **624/142-1580**. Breakfast $4–$6; main courses $10–$25. AE, MC, V. Daily 6am–11pm.

Zipper's BURGERS/MEXICAN/SEAFOOD   At the far south end of the beach heading toward Cabo San Lucas and fronting the best surfing waters, this casual hangout owned by Mike Posey and Tony Magdaleno has become popular with gringos in search of American food and TV sports. Burgers have that back-home flavor—order one with a side of spicy curly fries. Steaks, lobster, beer-battered shrimp, deli sandwiches, and Mexican combination plates round out the menu, which is printed with dollar prices.

Playa Costa Azul just south of San José (Km 28.5 on Carretera Transpeninsular). No phone. Burgers and sandwiches $7–$10; main courses $7–$18. MC, V. Daily 11am–11pm.

SAN JOSE AFTER DARK

San José has no nightlife outside of the restaurant and hotel bars. Those intent on real action will find it in Cabo San Lucas. Of particular note here are the bars at **Casa Natalia** (p. 57) and **Tropicana Bar and Grill** (p. 60)—the former caters to sophisticated romantics (it's just a small restaurant bar where locals come, since it's one of the few places open for a drink after 10pm), the latter to those in search of livelier good times. The longstanding Tropicana bar recently completed an extensive renovation and now offers a more elegant ambience—rather than simply rustic, it is now "rustic chic." Don't worry, the Tropicana still features all types of American sports events; now, however, they're on plasma TV screens, and a new area segregates drinkers from diners. Live mariachi music plays nightly from 6 to 9pm, with live Mexican and Cuban dance music playing from 9:30pm until about 1am. Truly, this is your sole nightlife option in tranquil San José. The Tropicana is open daily from 7am to 1am, and drinks are priced from $4.

Several of the larger hotels along the beach have Mexican fiestas and other weekly theme nights that include a buffet (usually all you can eat), drinks, live music, and entertainment for $25 to $35 per person. There's also a large disco on Mijares that seems to be under different ownership each year—it was closed at press time, undergoing yet another renovation.

2 The Corridor: Between the Two Cabos ★★

The Corridor between the towns of San José del Cabo and Cabo San Lucas contains some of Mexico's most lavish resorts. Most growth at the tip of the peninsula is occurring along the Corridor, which has already become a major locale for championship golf. The four major resort areas are **Palmilla, Querencia, Cabo Real,** and **Cabo del Sol,** each a self-contained community with golf courses, elegant hotels, and million-dollar homes (or the promise of them).

If you plan to explore the region while staying at a Corridor hotel, you'll need a rental car for at least a day or two; cars are available at the hotels. Even if you're not staying here, the beaches and dining options are worth visiting. Hotels—all of which qualify as "very expensive"—are listed in the order in which you'll encounter them as you drive from San José to Cabo San Lucas. Rates listed are for the high season (winter); typically they're 20% lower in the summer. Most resorts offer golf and fishing packages.

WHERE TO STAY

Casa del Mar ★ *(Finds* A little-known treasure, this intimate resort is one of the best values along the Corridor. The hacienda-style building offers luxury accommodations in an intimate setting as well as an on-site spa and nearby golf facilities. It's also convenient

The Two Cabos & the Corridor

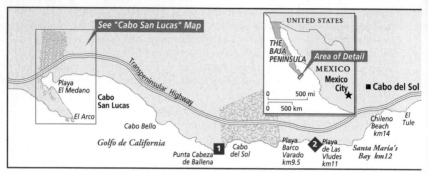

to the 18-hole championship Cabo Real golf course. Guest rooms have a bright feel, with white marble floors, light wicker furnishings, a separate sitting area, and a large whirlpool tub plus separate shower. Balconies have oversize chairs with a view of the ocean beyond the pool. It's a romantic hotel for couples and honeymooners, known for welcoming, personalized service.

Carretera Transpeninsular Km 19.5, 23410 Cabo San Lucas, B.C.S. ☎ **800/221-8808** in the U.S., or 624/144-0030. Fax 624/144-0034. www.casadelmarmexico.com. 56 units. High season $430 double, $480 suite; low season $290 double, $340 suite. AE, MC, V. Free secured parking. **Amenities:** Restaurant; lobby bar; beach club (adults only) w/pool, hot tub, pool bar, open-air restaurant; 6 other pools (2 w/whirlpools and swim-up bars); privileges at Cabo Real and El Dorado golf clubs; 2 lighted tennis courts; small workout room; full-service spa; tour desk; room service; in-room massage; babysitting; laundry; dry cleaning. *In room:* A/C, TV, dataport, minibar, hair dryer, safe, Jacuzzi.

Esperanza 👧👧👧   Although this new luxury resort along Cabo's over-the-top Corridor sits on a bluff overlooking two small, rocky coves, the absence of a real beach (though they are still sandy) doesn't seem to matter much to its guests—the hotel more than makes up for it in terms of pampering services and stylish details. Created by the famed Auberge Resorts group, the architecture of this hotel is similar in style to that of Careyes, on Mexico's Pacific coast, meaning it's dramatic, elegant, and comfortable. The casitas and villas are spread across 17 acres, designed to resemble a Mexican village, and are connected to the resort facilities by stone footpaths. The top-floor suites have handmade *palapa* ceilings and a private outdoor whirlpool spa. All rooms are exceptionally spacious, with woven wicker and tropical wood furnishings, original art, rugs and fabrics in muted colors with jeweled-tone color accents, and Frette linens gracing the extra-comfortable feather beds. Terraces are large, extending the living area to the outdoors, and all have hammocks and views of the Sea of Cortez. The oversize bathrooms have separate tub and showers with dual showerheads.

Carretera Transpeninsular Km 7, at Punta Ballena, 23140 Cabo San Lucas, B.C.S. ☎ **866/311-2226** U.S. toll-free, or 624/145-6400. Fax 624/145-6403. www.esperanzaresort.com. 50 suites, 6 villas. Valet parking (pay a tip only) or self-parking. High season $575–$925 double, $775–$1,050 beachfront suite, $3,500–$5,000 villas; low season $375–$650 rooms, $500–$775 beachfront suite, $2,000–$3,000 villas. AE, MC, V. **Amenities:** Oceanfront restaurant; bar; infinity swimming pool; golf privileges; fitness center; deluxe European full-service spa; concierge w/tour services; gourmet market; 24-hr. room service; in-room massage; babysitting; laundry; dry cleaning; private beach w/club. *In room:* A/C, plasma TV w/DVD, high-speed Internet access, hair dryer, safe, stereo.

Las Ventanas al Paraíso 👧👧👧   Las Ventanas is known for its luxury accommodations and attention to detail. The architecture, with adobe structures and rough-hewn wood accents, provides a soothing complement to the desert landscape. The

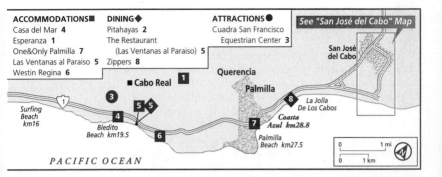

See "San José del Cabo" Map

ACCOMMODATIONS■
Casa del Mar **4**
Esperanza **1**
One&Only Palmilla **7**
Las Ventanas al Paraiso **5**
Westin Regina **6**

DINING◆
Pitahayas **2**
The Restaurant
 (Las Ventanas al Paraiso) **5**
Zippers **8**

ATTRACTIONS●
Cuadra San Francisco
 Equestrian Center **3**

only color comes from the dazzling *ventanas* (windows) of pebbled rainbow glass handmade by regional artisans. Richly furnished, Mediterranean-style rooms are large (starting at 93 sq. m/1,000 sq. ft.) and appointed with every conceivable amenity, from wood-burning fireplaces to computerized telescopes for star- or whale-gazing. Rooms contain satellite TVs with VCRs, stereos with CD players, and dual-line cordless phones. Sizable whirlpool tubs can have views of the rest of your room or the ocean, or may be closed off for privacy. Larger suites offer extras like rooftop terraces, sunken whirlpools on a private patio, or a personal pool. The spa is among the best in Mexico. With a staff that outnumbers guests by four to one, this is the place for those who want (and can afford) to be seriously spoiled. It even has special packages for pampered pets that can't be left behind.

Carretera Transpeninsular Km 19.5, 23410 San José del Cabo, B.C.S. 𝒞 **888/525-0483** in the U.S., or 624/144-0300. Fax 624/144-0301. www.lasventanas.com. 61 suites. High season $600 gardenview double, $800 oceanview double, $950 split-level oceanview suite w/rooftop terrace, $1,150 split-level oceanfront suite w/rooftop terrace, luxury suites (1 and 3 bedrooms) $2,600–$4,500; summer $450 gardenview double, $550 oceanview double, $675 split-level oceanview suite w/rooftop terrace, $900 split-level oceanfront suite w/rooftop terrace, luxury suites (1 and 3 bedrooms) $1,800–$3,800. Spa and golf packages and inclusive meal plans available. AE, DC, MC, V. Free valet parking. **Amenities:** Oceanview restaurant; seaside grill; terrace bar w/live music; fresh-juice bar; access to adjoining championship Cabo Real golf course; deluxe European spa w/complete treatment and exercise facilities; watersports; sportfishing and luxury yachts available; tour services; car rental; shuttle services; 24-hr. room service; laundry; dry cleaning; pet packages, including treats and massages. *In room:* A/C, TV, dataport, minibar, hair dryer, iron, safe.

One&Only Palmilla ★★★   One of the most comfortably luxurious hotels in Mexico, the One&Only Palmilla is the grande dame of Los Cabos resorts, and a complete renovation in 2003 made it among the most spectacular resort hotels anywhere. Perched on a cliff top above the sea (with beach access), the resort is a series of white buildings with red-tile roofs, towering palms, and flowering bougainvillea. The feeling here remains one of classic resort-style comfort, but the new sophisticated details bring it up-to-date with the most modern of resorts. The new decor features muted desert colors and luxury fabrics, with special extras such as flat-screen TVs with DVD/CD players and Bose surround-sound systems. Bathrooms feature inlaid-stone rain showers and sculpted tubs. Ample private balconies or terraces have extra-comfortable, overstuffed chairs, and each room also has a separate sitting area. Guests receive twice-daily maid service, a personal butler, and an aromatherapy menu—to ensure you leave completely relaxed or rejuvenated. Their new "C" restaurant (which also offers 24-hr. in-room dining) is under the direction of the renowned chef Charlie Trotter of Chicago.

The Los Cabos Spa Experience

Golfers flock to Los Cabos because of the diversity of course options available, and spa enthusiasts are right behind them. Claiming the distinction of having the most world-class luxury spas in all of Mexico, Los Cabos resorts seem to be having an unstated competition to see who can create the most intriguing spa menu. While most spas offer traditional European therapies, the trend here is to emphasize an authentic Mexican experience through signature treatments that incorporate indigenous ingredients found on the Baja peninsula. These include aloe, clay, tropical fruits, and desert flowers and herbs like damiana, sage, and plumeria, used for their detoxifying and healing properties. Added to this is the mystical wisdom of ancient indigenous cultures, which incorporate elements such as quartz crystals and shamanic rituals into certain therapies.

The setting of the spas here offers its own restorative component to the mix. Think of having a massage to the hypnotic rhythm of crashing waves or the feel of a gentle sea breeze blowing over your skin, and you'll easily imagine why these treatments are enhanced by the naturally calming environment of Los Cabos. Below are a few of my favorites, all located along the Corridor.

One of the original Cabo resorts to offer spa services was **Casa del Mar** (p. 61), and it still offers impressive services in a bright, airy atmosphere. Its Sueños del Mar Spa offers guests a mix of salon services, massages, and wraps. Specialties include the Tropical Exfoliation, which uses a combination of fine-milled coffee beans and dried coconut to soften skin, and the Chocolate and Mint Escape, which literally massages the body in chocolate and mint. (Ground cacao beans were an Aztec currency, and the source of a highly prized beverage consumed by ancient nobility.)

Just the entry to the spa at **Esperanza** (p. 62) is an exercise in relaxation—you follow a garden path illuminated by candles to the natural stone reception area. Before your treatment, enjoy the Pasaje de Aqua (water passage), which includes a visit to a seaside grotto environment with a mineral-rich pool, steam caves, and a cool, cascading waterfall. Each of the seven private treatment rooms comes with a private garden and an outdoor shower and soaking pool. Signature treatments here include the Grated Coconut and Lime Body Exfoliation and the Hibiscus Antioxidant Flower Bath. The Couple's Clay Bake starts with a Damiana liquor-based beverage, made with the

A second, more casual dining choice is the *palapa*-topped Agua restaurant, with "Mexiterranean" cuisine. The Palmilla has become renowned as a location for destination weddings and anniversary celebrations with a renewal of vows; ceremonies take place in its small, signature chapel that graces a sloped hillside. Across the highway, the resort's own championship golf course, designed by Jack Nicklaus, is available for guests, and the Palmilla also has two lighted tennis courts, a 186-sq.-m (2,000-sq.-ft.) state-of-the-art fitness center, and yoga garden. Also among the new additions is an exceptional spa, with 13 private treatment villas for one or two people.

damiana herb (which grows wild in Baja, and is considered an aphrodisiac). A warm bath and clay body mask are followed by a massage with desert sage oil. The most intriguing treatment, however, may be the Corona Beer Face-Lift—they claim this popular beverage tightens skin and refines the pores.

Las Ventanas al Paraíso (p. 62) raised the bar of the spa experience when it opened in 1997, but you won't find it resting on its laurels—an expansion is currently in progress which will double the spa's size, scheduled for completion in late 2005. Private outdoor Jacuzzis, cold plunge pools, and relaxation areas prepare you for your treatment, which may be a Desert Healer Anti-Oxidant wrap, using sage, elephant tree bark, eucalyptus, and chaparral, or perhaps a Nopal Anti-Cellulite and Detox Wrap. This treatment uses locally grown *nopal* (cactus paddles) to help transfer fluids from the tissue to the bloodstream. A body scrub of grape seeds, papaya, and pineapple, followed by a body mask of green tea, ginger root, and seaweed, is also a favorite. The Spa also has several treatments that employ quartz crystals, minerals, and stones.

During its recent renovation, the **One&Only Palmilla** (p. 63) spared no expense in launching its new 2,044-sq.-m (22,000-sq.-ft.) Mandara Spa, which comprises 13 indoor and outdoor spa villas, some with rain showers, daybeds, and whirlpool baths. Indulgent treatments include the Aztec Aromatic Ritual, a body wrap that uses spices such as clove, cinnamon, and ginger, followed by a massage with rosemary and pine essential oils.

At the **Westin Regina** (see below), two floors of spa and fitness services are available to guests, who seem to quickly book up the treatment schedule. The signature Heavenly Body Wrap, a full-body milk and honey exfoliation, is particularly popular. They also offer waterfront massage in a tented pavilion on the beach.

Impressive spa facilities can also be found at the **Marquis Los Cabos Beach** (✆ **624/144-2000**; www.marquisloscabos.com), the **Hilton Los Cabos Beach & Golf Resort** (✆ **624/145-6500**; www.hiltonloscabos.com), the **Sheraton Hacienda del Mar** (✆ **624/145-8000**; www.sheratonhaciendadelmar.com), the **Pueblo Bonito Rose Resort** (✆ **624/142-9898**; www.pueblobonito.com), and numerous other spots in the Los Cabos area. Ahhh . . . spa!

Carretera Transpeninsular Km 7.5, 23400 San José del Cabo, B.C.S. ✆ **800/637-2226** or 866/829-2977 in the U.S., or 624/146-7000 or 624/144-5000. Fax 624/144-5100. www.oneandonlypalmilla.com. 114 units. High season $475 double, from $775–$1,600 suites and villas; low season $325 double, from $575–$1,300 suites and villas. AE, MC, V. **Amenities:** 2 restaurants; terrace bar; pool bar; championship Palmilla golf course; deluxe European spa w/complete treatment and exercise facilities; watersports; sportfishing; tour services; car rental; shuttle services; 24-hr. room service; laundry; dry cleaning; yoga garden. *In room:* A/C, TV, dataport, minibar, hair dryer, iron, safe.

Westin Regina 👶 *Kids*   The architecturally dramatic Westin Regina sits at the end of a long paved road atop a seaside cliff. Vivid terra-cotta, yellow, and pink walls rise against a landscape of sandstone, cacti, and palms, with fountains and gardens lining the long pathways from the lobby to the rooms. Electric carts carry guests and their luggage through the vast property. The rooms are lovely, with both air-conditioning and ceiling fans, private balconies, satellite TV, and walk-in showers separate from the bathtubs. This is probably the best choice for families vacationing along the corridor, since it offers a wealth of activities for children.

Carretera Transpeninsular Km 22.5, Apdo. Postal 145, 23400 San José del Cabo, B.C.S. (C) **800/228-3000** in the U.S., or 624/142-9000. Fax 624/142-9010. www.westin.com. 295 units. $308 partial oceanview double; $347 full ocean-view double; $436–$705 suite. 20% low-season discount. AE, DC, MC, V. **Amenities:** 6 restaurants; 2 bars; 3 swimming pools; near Palmilla and Cabo Real golf courses; 18-hole putting course; 2 tennis courts; full fitness center and spa; children's activities; concierge; car-rental desk; business services; salon; 24-hr. room service; babysitting; laundry; dry cleaning; Xplora Adventours services; beach club. *In room:* A/C, TV, minibar, hair dryer, safe.

WHERE TO DINE

Las Ventanas al Paraíso Restaurant ★★★ INTERNATIONAL   It may just be called "The Restaurant," but that's where simplicity ends, and the extraordinary begins. Los Cabos is known for its pricy dining, but this is one restaurant that is worth every peso it charges. Start off with a cocktail before dinner in The Lounge, the casually elegant bar area bordering a stunning pool, lit from above with a constellation of tin stars illuminated by candles. Upon moving into the dining area, you'll get a sense of the Las Ventanas signature service and style (should you be wearing black, for instance, you'll be given a black napkin). As remarkable as the service is, however, the dining itself is even better. First courses may include Ensenada steamed mussels served in coconut milk with a hint of *chile árbol* and a dash of tequila, or a stone crab salad with baby watercress, mango, phyllo, and sweet mustard sauce. The constantly changing menu of main courses generally includes an ample selection of seafood, including lobster done in creative presentations, but the grilled rack of lamb with garlic potatoes, or prime filet mignon in a cabernet sauce, is as good as you'll find anywhere. A stellar selection of premium wines is served. You have your choice of alfresco dining on the patio, or in indoor, air-conditioned comfort. Reserve early, as dinner at The Restaurant is quite popular in Cabo at any time during the year.

At Las Ventanas al Paraíso, Carretera Transpeninsular Km 19.5. (C) **624/144-0300.** Reservations required. Dress is resort attire. Main courses: $35–$50. AE, MC, V. Daily 5–11pm.

Pitahayas ★★★ PACIFIC RIM   In a beachfront setting, Pitahayas offers gourmet dining under a grand *palapa* or on open-air terraces under a starlit sky. Master chef Volker Romeike has assembled a creative—if slightly pretentious—menu that blends Pacific Rim cuisine with Mexican herbs and seasonings. Notable sauces include mango, black bean, and curry. Rotisserie-barbecued duck is a house specialty, along with mesquite grill and wok cooking—all prepared in an impressive exhibition kitchen. A dessert pizza with fresh fruit, chocolate, and marzipan makes a fitting finish to a stunning meal. Pitahayas also boasts an extensive wine cellar, with vintages from around the world housed in an underground *cava*.

At the Hacienda del Mar resort, Carretera Transpeninsular Km 10, Cabo del Sol. (C) 624/145-8010. Reservations required during high season. Formal resort attire is requested. Main courses $12–$30. AE, MC, V. Daily 5–10:30pm.

3 Cabo San Lucas ★★

176km (109 miles) S of La Paz; 35km (22 miles) W of San José del Cabo; 1,803km (1,118 miles) SE of Tijuana

The hundreds of luxury hotel rooms along the corridor north of Cabo San Lucas have transformed the very essence of this formerly rustic and rowdy outpost. Although it

Cabo San Lucas

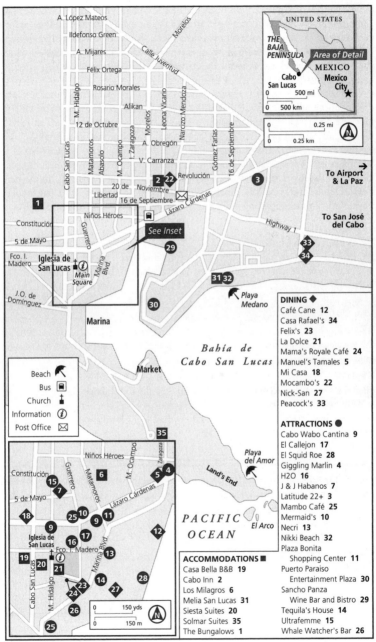

UNITED STATES

THE BAJA PENINSULA

Area of Detail

MEXICO

Cabo San Lucas

Mexico City

0   500 mi
0   500 km

0   0.25 mi
0   0.25 km

A. López Mateos
Ildefonso Green
A. Mijares
Félix Ortega
Rosario Morales
Alikan
12 de Octubre
Morelos
Calle Juventud
M. Hidalgo
Matamoros
Abasolo
M. Ocampo
J. Zaragoza
A. Morelos
Leona Vicario
Narcizo Mendoza
Gómez Farías
16 de Septiembre
A. Obregón
V. Carranza
Revolución
20 de Noviembre
16 de Septiembre
Libertad
Constitución
5 de Mayo
Fco. I. Madero
Iglesia de San Lucas
Main Square
Cabo San Lucas
Guerrero
Marina Blvd.
J.O. de Domínguez
Marina
Lázaro Cárdenas
Niños Héroes
See Inset

2 **22**
3
To Airport & La Paz
To San José del Cabo
Highway 1
33
34
1
29
31 **32**
Playa Medano
30

Bahía de Cabo San Lucas

Market

Beach
Bus
Church
Information
Post Office

35

Playa del Amor

Land's End

PACIFIC OCEAN

El Arco

Niños Héroes
Constitución
5 de Mayo
Guerrero
Matamoros
M. Ocampo
Zaragoza
Lázaro Cárdenas
Iglesia de San Lucas
Fco. I. Madero
Cabo San Lucas
Marina Blvd.
M. Hidalgo

6
15
7
5 **4**
18
25 **10**
9 **11**
9
16 **17**
13
12
19
20
21
24 **23**
14
27
28
26
25

0   150 yds
0   150 m

N

DINING ◆
Café Cane **12**
Casa Rafael's **34**
Felix's **23**
La Dolce **21**
Mama's Royale Café **24**
Manuel's Tamales **5**
Mi Casa **18**
Mocambo's **22**
Nick-San **27**
Peacock's **33**

ATTRACTIONS ●
Cabo Wabo Cantina **9**
El Callejon **17**
El Squid Roe **28**
Giggling Marlin **4**
H2O **16**
J & J Habanos **7**
Latitude 22+ **3**
Mambo Café **25**
Mermaid's **10**
Necri **13**
Nikki Beach **32**
Plaza Bonita
Shopping Center **11**
Puerto Paraiso
Entertainment Plaza **30**
Sancho Panza
Wine Bar and Bistro **29**
Tequila's House **14**
Ultrafemme **15**
Whale Watcher's Bar **26**

ACCOMMODATIONS ■
Casa Bella B&B **19**
Cabo Inn **2**
Los Milagros **6**
Melia San Lucas **31**
Siesta Suites **20**
Solmar Suites **35**
The Bungalows **1**

retains boisterous nightlife, Cabo San Lucas is no longer the simple town Steinbeck wrote about and enjoyed. Once legendary for the big-game fish that lurk beneath the deep blue sea, Cabo San Lucas now draws more people for its nearby fairways and greens—and the world-class golf being played on them. It caters to travelers getting away for a long weekend or indulging in sports and relaxation. Cabo San Lucas has become Mexico's most elite resort destination.

Travelers here can enjoy a growing roster of adventure-oriented activities, and playtime doesn't end when the sun goes down. The nightlife here is as hot as the desert in July, and oddly casual, having grown up away from the higher-end hotels. It remains the raucous, playful party scene that helped put Cabo on the map. A collection of popular restaurants and bars along Cabo's main street stay open and active until the morning's first fishing charters head out to sea. Also blossoming is its array of spas—Cabo now boasts 14 resorts with luxury spas, ranging from the holistic to the hedonistic. Despite the growth in diversions, Cabo remains more or less a one-stoplight town, with almost everything within easy walking distance along the main strip.

ESSENTIALS
GETTING THERE & DEPARTING
BY PLANE For arrival and departure information, see "Getting There & Departing," earlier in the chapter, under "San José del Cabo." Local airline numbers are: **AeroCalifornia** (© 624/143-3700 or 624/143-3915); **Alaska Airlines** (© 624/146-5166); and **Mexicana** (© **624/143-5352,** 624/143-5353, 624/142-0606, or 624/146-5001 at the airport).

BY CAR From La Paz, the best route is to take Carretera Transpeninsular south past the village of San Pedro, then Highway 19 south through Todos Santos to Cabo San Lucas, a 2-hour drive.

BY BUS The bus terminal (© **624/143-5020**) is on Niños Héroes at Morelos; it is open daily from 6am to 7pm. Buses go to San José del Cabo about every hour between 6:30am and 8:30pm, and to La Paz every 90 minutes between 6am and 6pm. To and from San José, the more convenient and economical **Suburcabos** public bus service runs every 20 minutes and costs $2.50.

ORIENTATION
ARRIVING At the airport, either buy a ticket for a *colectivo* (collective, or group taxi) from the authorized transportation booth inside the building (about $13) or arrange for a rental car, the most economical way to explore the area. Up to four people can share a private taxi; the fare to Cabo San Lucas is about $60.

The walk from the bus station to most of the budget hotels is manageable with light luggage, and taxis are readily available.

VISITOR INFORMATION The **Secretary of Tourism** functions as the information office in Cabo. It's on Madero between Hidalgo and Guerrero (© **624/146-9628** or 624/142-0446). The English-language *Los Cabos Guide, Los Cabos News, Cabo Life, Baja Sun,* and the irreverent and extremely entertaining *Gringo Gazette* are distributed free at most hotels and shops and have up-to-date information on new restaurants and clubs. On the Web, good sources include the official destination site **www.visitcabo. com.** *Note:* The many visitor-information booths along the street are actually time-share sales booths, and their staffs will pitch a visit to their resort in exchange for discounted tours, rental cars, or other giveaways.

CITY LAYOUT   The small town spreads out north and west of the harbor of Cabo San Lucas Bay, edged by foothills and desert mountains to the west and south. The main street leading into town from the airport and San José del Cabo is Lázaro Cárdenas; as it nears the harbor, Marina Boulevard branches off from it and becomes the main artery that curves around the waterfront.

GETTING AROUND

Taxis are easy to find but are expensive within Cabo, in keeping with the high cost of everything else. Expect to pay about $15 to $25 for a taxi between Cabo and the Corridor hotels.

For day trips to San José del Cabo, catch a bus (see "Getting There & Departing" under "San José del Cabo," above) or a cab. You'll see car-rental specials advertised in town, but before signing on, be sure you understand the total price, including insurance and taxes. Rates can run between $50 and $75 per day, with insurance an extra $10 per day. One of the best and most economical agencies is **Advantage Rent-A-Car** (© **624/143-0909** or ©/fax 624/143-0466), on Lázaro Cárdenas between Leona Vicario and Morelos. VW sedans rent for $50 per day, and weekly renters receive 1 free day. A collision damage waiver will add $14 per day to the price. If you pick up the car downtown, you can return it to the airport at no extra charge.

FAST FACTS: Cabo San Lucas

Area Code   The telephone area code is **624**.

Beach Safety   Before swimming in open water, it's important to check whether the conditions are safe. Undertows and large waves are common. Playa El Medano, close to the marina and town, is the principal swimming beach; it has several lively beachfront restaurant/bars. It's also easy to find watersports equipment for rent here. The Hotel Melia Cabo San Lucas, on Playa El Medano, has a roped-off swimming area to protect swimmers from jet skis and boats. Colored flags signaling swimming safety aren't generally used in Cabo, and neither are lifeguards.

Currency Exchange   Banks exchange currency during normal business hours, generally Monday through Friday from 9am to 6pm and Saturday from 10am to 2pm. Currency-exchange booths, found throughout Cabo's main tourist areas, aren't as competitive but are more convenient. ATMs are widely available and even more convenient, dispensing pesos—and in some cases dollars—at bank exchange rates.

Emergencies & Hospital   In Cabo, **Baja Médico,** Camino de la Plaza s/n, on the corner with Pedregral (© **624/143-0127** or 624/143-7777) has a 24-hour walk-in clinic, and provides air ambulance services. **Amerimed** (© **624/143-9671**) is a 24-hour, American-standards clinic (with bilingual physicians), which accepts major credit cards. Most of the larger hotels have a doctor on call.

Internet Access   **Onda net Café & Bar,** Lázaro Cárdenas 7, Edificio Posada, across from the Pemex gas station (© **624/143-5390**), charges $5 for 15 minutes, $7 for 30 minutes, or $8.50 for an hour. It's open Monday through Saturday from 8am to 6pm.

Pharmacy A drugstore with a wide selection of toiletries as well as medicine is **Farmacia Aramburo,** in Plaza Aramburo, on Lázaro Cárdenas at Zaragoza (*©* **624/143-1489**). It's open Monday through Friday from 7am to 11pm and accepts MasterCard and Visa.

Post Office The *correo* is at Lázaro Cárdenas and Francisco Villa, on the highway to San José del Cabo, east of the bar El Squid Roe (*©* **624/143-0048**). It's open Monday through Friday from 9am to 1pm and 3 to 6pm, and Saturday from 9am to noon.

BEACHES & OUTDOOR ACTIVITIES

Although superb sportfishing put Cabo San Lucas on the map, there's more to do here than drop your line and wait for the Big One. For most fishing cruises and excursions, try to make fishing reservations at least a day in advance; keep in mind that some trips require a minimum number of people. Most sports and outings can be arranged through a travel agency; fishing can also be arranged directly at one of the fishing-fleet offices at the marina, which is on the south side of the harbor.

You can take kayak and boat trips to Los Arcos (the Arches) rock formation or uninhabited beaches. (Expect to pay $65 for a sunset kayak around Los Arcos, $40 for morning kayak trips.) A variety of boats, including a replica of a pirate ship, provide all-inclusive daytime or sunset cruises. Many of these trips include snorkeling; serious divers have great underwater venues to explore. Horseback riding to Los Arcos and to the Pacific (very popular at sunset) costs $50 for 2 hours. Whale-watching, between January and March, has become one of the most popular local activities. Guided ATV (all-terrain vehicle) tours take you down dirt roads and through a desert landscape to the old Cabo lighthouse or an ancient Indian village. And then, of course, there's the challenge of world-class golf, a major attraction of Los Cabos.

For a complete rundown of what's available, contact **Gray Line Los Cabos** (*©* **624/146-9410;** www.graylineloscabos.com). It offers tours from any local company rather than working with only a select few. Most businesses in this section are open from 10am to 2pm and 4 to 7pm.

ATV TRIPS   Expeditions on ATVs to visit **Cabo Falso,** an 1890s lighthouse, and **La Candelaria,** an Indian pueblo in the mountains, are available through travel agencies. A 440-pound weight limit per two-person vehicle applies to both tours. The 3-hour tour to Cabo Falso includes a stop at the beach, a look at some sea-turtle nests (without disturbing them) and the remains of a 1912 shipwreck, a ride over 500-foot sand dunes, and a visit to the lighthouse. Guided tours cost around $45 per person on a single vehicle, or $60 for two riding on one ATV. The vehicles are also available for rent ($35 for 3 hr.).

La Candelaria is an isolated Indian village in the mountains 40km (25 miles) north of Cabo San Lucas. Described in *National Geographic,* the old pueblo is known for the practice of white and black witchcraft. Lush with palms, mango trees, and bamboo, the settlement gets its water from an underground river that emerges at the pueblo, which also has old mission-style buildings, many decayed, typical of a tiny rural village. The return trip of the tour travels down a steep canyon, along a beach (giving you time to swim), and past giant sea turtle nesting grounds. Departing at 9am, the 5-hour La Candelaria tour costs around $80 per person or $100 for two on the same ATV.

DRIVING TOURS   A uniquely Cabo experience is offered by **Outback Baja** (**© 624/142-9200;** fax 624/142-3166; www.bajaoutback.com) via their caravan-style Hummer Adventures. You drive these luxury Hummer H2s, going off-road to cruise desert and beachfront terrain in style. Communication links the 10 vehicles in the caravan, allowing you to listen to the narrations of the expert guides and learn about the surrounding area. There's a choice of four routes, which include treks to Todos Santos, the East Cape, Santiago and Cañón de la Zorra, and Rancho la Verdad. Tours depart at 9am and return at 3pm, with prices ranging from $165 to $220, depending upon the route, and include lunch. American Express, MasterCard, and Visa are accepted, and you must have your valid driver's license. Special group rates are also available.

If this sounds too tame, **Wide Open Baja Racing Experience** (**© 888/788-2252** or 949/340-1155 in the U.S., or 624/143-4170; office in Plaza Náutica; www.wide opencabo.com) gives you the chance to drive actual Chenowth Magnum race cars at their 1,500-acre racing ranch on the Pacific Coast. There's a varied terrain to drive, with twists, turns, sand washes, and plenty of bumps for thrill seekers. Session times for the **test drive** are at 10am and 1:30pm. The $250 price includes shuttle transportation from downtown Cabo to the ranch, driver orientation, and safety equipment. Private group rates are also available. Wide Open Baja also offers multiday tours driving race vehicles through Cabo, Ensenada, and the entire Baja peninsula.

BEACHES

All along the curving sweep of sand known as **Playa El Medano (Medano Beach),** on the northeast side of the bay, you can rent snorkeling gear, boats, WaveRunners ($70 per hr.), kayaks, pedal boats, and windsurf boards. (You can also take windsurfing lessons.) This is the town's main beach; it's a great place for safe swimming as well as for people-watching from one of the many outdoor restaurants along its shore.

Beach aficionados may want to rent a car (see "Getting Around," above) and explore the five more remote beaches and coves between the two Cabos: **playas Palmilla, Chileno, Santa María, Barco Varado,** and **Vista del Arco.** Palmilla, Chileno, and Santa María are generally safe for swimming—but always be careful. The other beaches are not considered safe for swimmers. Experienced snorkelers may wish to check them out, but other visitors should go for the view only. Always check at a hotel or travel agency for directions and swimming conditions. Although a few travel agencies run snorkeling tours to some of these beaches, there's no public transportation. Your only option for beach exploring is to rent a car.

CRUISES

Glass-bottom boats leave from the town marina daily every 45 minutes between 9am and 4pm. They cost $14 for a 1-hour tour, which passes sea lions and pelicans on its way to the famous "El Arco" (Rock Arch) at Land's End, where the Pacific and the Sea

---

Moments   Festivals & Events in Cabo San Lucas

An annual dive festival takes place in August. October 12 is the festival of the patron saint of Todos Santos, a town about 105km (65 miles) north. October 18 is the feast of the patron saint of Cabo San Lucas, celebrated with a fair, feasting, music, dancing, and other special events.

of Cortez meet. Boats drop you off at Playa de Amor; make sure you understand which boat will pick you up—it's usually a smaller one run by the same company that ferries people back at regular intervals. Check the timing to make sure you have the correct boat, or expect an additional $10 charge for boarding a competitor's boat.

A number of **daylong** and **sunset cruises** use a variety of boats and catamarans. They cost $30 to $45, depending on the boat, duration of cruise, and amenities. A sunset cruise on the 42-foot catamaran *Pez Gato* (© **624/143-3797** or 624/143-5297; pezgato@cabotel.com.mx) departs from the Plaza las Glorias Hotel dock at 5pm. A 2-hour cruise costs $35 and includes margaritas, beer, and sodas. The seasonal (winter) whale-watching tour leaves at 10:30am and returns at 1:30pm. It costs $35, and includes open bar and snacks. Similar boats leave from the marina and the Plaza las Glorias Hotel. Check with travel agencies or hotel tour desks for more information.

LAND SPORTS

Bicycles, boogie boards, snorkels, surfboards, and **golf clubs** are available for rent at **Cabo Sports Center** in the Plaza Náutica on Marina Boulevard (© **624/143-4272**). The center is open Monday through Saturday from 9am to 9pm, Sunday from 9am to 5pm.

GOLF Los Cabos has become the golf mecca of Mexico, and though most courses are along the Corridor, people look to Cabo San Lucas for information about this sport in Baja Sur. The master plan for Los Cabos golf calls for a future total of 207 holes. Fees listed below are for 18 holes, including golf cart, water, club service, and tax. Summer rates are about 25% lower, and many hotels offer golf packages. (For specifics on the various courses, see "The Lowdown on Golf in Cabo," below.)

Several specialty tour operators offer golf packages to Los Cabos, which include accommodations, greens fees, and other amenities. These include **Best Golf** (© **888/817-GOLF** from the U.S.); **Golf Adventures** (© **800/841-6570** from the U.S.; www.golfadventures.com); and **Sportours** (© **888/GOLF-MEX** from the U.S.; www.sportours.com).

The 27-hole course at the **Palmilla Golf Club,** at the One&Only Palmilla resort (© **800/386-2465** in the U.S., or 624/144-5250; daily 7am–7pm) was the first Jack Nicklaus Signature layout in Mexico, on 360 hectares (900 acres) of dramatic oceanfront desert. The course offers your choice of two back-9 options, with high-season greens fees of $215 (lower after 1pm), and low-season greens fees running between $130 and $210. Guests at some hotels pay discounted rates.

Just a few kilometers away is another Jack Nicklaus Signature course, the 18-hole Ocean Course at **Cabo del Sol,** at the Cabo del Sol resort development in the Corridor (© **624/145-8200**). The 7,100-yard Ocean Course is known for its challenging three finishing holes. Tom Weiskopf designed the new 18-hole Desert Course. Greens fees for both are $220 to $275.

The 18-hole, 6,945-yard course at **Cabo Real,** by the Meliá Cabo Real Hotel in the Corridor (© **624/144-0232;** caborealgolf@1cabonet.com.mx; daily 6:30am–6pm), was designed by Robert Trent Jones, Jr., and features holes that sit high on mesas overlooking the Sea of Cortez. Fees run $220 for 18 holes. After 3pm rates drop to $150.

El Dorado Golf Course (© **624/144-5451;** www.caboreal.com) is a Jack Nicklaus Signature course next to the Westin Regina hotel at Cabo Real. The course is open daily 7am to dusk. Greens fees are $256 (after 2pm, $178). Carts are included; caddies are $100.

An 18-hole course designed by Roy Dye is at the **Raven Club,** formerly the Cabo San Lucas Country Club (© **800/854-2314** in the U.S., or 624/143-4653; fax 624/143-5809). The entire course overlooks the juncture of the Pacific Ocean and Sea of Cortez, including the famous Land's End rocks. It includes the 607-yard, par-5 7th hole—the longest hole in Mexico. Greens fees are $176 for 18 holes, $130 after 2:30pm. The course was redone after a 2001 hurricane added substantial water "features." It is still a Dye-design course, with a slightly changed layout that regular players say is much improved.

The lowest greens fees in the area are at the public 9-hole **Mayan Palace Golf Los Cabos** (previously the Club Campo de Golf San José; © **624/142-0900** or 624/142-0905) in San José del Cabo (p. 54). Greens fees are just $64 for 9 holes, $109 for 18 holes, with carts included. Rates for 18 holes drops to $80 after 3pm.

HORSEBACK RIDING   For horseback riding, I highly recommend **Cuadra San Francisco Equestrian Center** (see p. 54 for more information).

You can also rent **horses** through **Rancho Colin** (© **624/143-3652**) for around $25 per hour. Tours to the Pacific for sunset riding on the beach cost $35 per person per hour. It's open daily from 8am to noon and 2 to 5pm, and is located in front of the parking lot of the Hotel Meliá Los Cabos.

ECOTOURS   There's an increasing array of offerings of adventure tours and extreme sports available in the Los Cabos area. One of the best is **Baja Wild** (© **624/142-5300;** www.bajawild.com), which offers the Waterfalls and Canyons guided hiking excursion in the Sierra de la Laguna mountains 2 hours north of Los Cabos. The range runs north to south in the Baja peninsula and reaches elevations of more than 2,100m (7,000 ft.), accommodating a unique biosphere where oak and pine trees flourish. Although you sense you are in Baja's desert landscape, you'll be awed by the amount of wildlife you'll see: frogs, doves, Monarch butterflies, giant golden eagles, lizards, and much more. There are also cool, spring-fed mountain pools for taking a dip in after the 5-mile round-trip hike. Group sizes are limited to about eight, and transportation to the hiking area is by air-conditioned minivan. This tour costs $75 per person and includes morning coffee and baked goods, snacks on the hike, and lunch upon return.

WATERSPORTS

SNORKELING/DIVING   Several companies offer snorkeling; a 2-hour cruise to sites around El Arco costs $30, and a 4-hour trip to Santa María costs $55, including gear rental. Among the beaches visited on different trips are Playas del Amor, Santa María, Chileno, and Barco Varado. Snorkeling gear rents for $10 to $15. For information on a snorkeling excursion or cruise with snorkeling possibilities, contact **Gray Line** (© **624/146-9410**). For scuba diving, contact **Amigos del Mar** (© **800/344-3349** or 310/459-9861 in the U.S., or 624/143-0505 in Mexico; fax 310/454-1686 in the U.S., or 624/143-0887 in Mexico; www.amigosdelmar.com; daily 8am–4:30pm) at the marina, near the Solmar hotel. Dives are along the wall of a canyon in San Lucas Bay, where you can see the "sandfalls" that even Jacques Cousteau couldn't figure out—no one knows their source or cause. There are also scuba trips to Santa María Beach and more distant places, including the Gordo Banks and Cabo Pulmo. Prices start at $45 for a one-tank dive, $66 for two tanks; trips to the coral outcropping at Cabo Pulmo start at $125. You'll need a wetsuit for winter dives. A 5-hour resort course is available for $100. Open-water certification costs around $450.

The Lowdown on Golf in Cabo

Los Cabos, one of the world's finest golf destinations, offers an ample and intriguing variety of courses to challenge golfers of all levels.

The reason so many choose to play here is not just the selection, quality, and beauty of the courses, but the very reliable weather. The courses highlighted below compare to the great ones in Palm Springs and Scottsdale, with the added beauty of ocean views and a wider variety of desert cacti and flowering plants.

Course fees are high in Cabo—generally over $200 per round. But these are world-class courses, worth the world-class price. Courses generally offer 20% to 30% off rates if you play after 2 or 2:30pm. This is actually a great time to play, because the temperature is cooler and play is generally faster.

The golf offerings in Los Cabos will only continue to expand; four courses are in various phases of construction. At **Puerto Los Cabos,** a new mega-development northeast of San José del Cabo, construction has started on the first of two 18-hole courses, with 9 holes designed by Jack Nicklaus, and the other 9 by Greg Norman. It's scheduled to be playable by June 2006. At the other end of the peninsula near Cabo San Lucas on the Pacific side, the **Cabo Pacifica** development will soon be launching two more championship courses.

The courses below are listed in order of location, from north to south.

PALMILLA GOLF CLUB   The original Cabo course is now a 27-hole layout. The original 18 holes are known as the Arroyo; the new holes are the Ocean 9. It's a bit of a misnomer—although the newer holes lie closer to the water, only one has a true ocean view, with a spectacular play directly down to the beach. You must play the Arroyo for your first 9 holes, then you choose between Mountain and Ocean for your back 9. If you play this course only once, choose the Mountain, which offers better ocean views. The signature hole is the Mountain 5; you hit over a canyon, then down to the green below over a forced carry. The 14th hole here is considered one of the world's most beautiful golf holes, a forced carry from the hillside tee boxes to an island. From there, players line up on a green set on the side of a steep arroyo. The hole opens up to spectacular vistas and seems a lot longer than it plays. This is target golf, on a Jack Nicklaus course that was constructed with strategy in mind. A mountaintop clubhouse provides spectacular views. Although it is currently a semiprivate club, most Corridor hotels have membership benefits.

CABO DEL SOL   The Ocean Course at Cabo de Sol was the second Jack Nicklaus course constructed in Los Cabos. It is much more difficult than the Palmilla course, with less room for error.

Don't be fooled by the wide, welcoming 1st hole. This is challenging target golf, with numerous forced carries—even from the red tees. Seven holes are along the water. At the par-3 signature 17th hole, the golfer is faced with a 178-yard shot over sandy beach and rocky outcroppings to a tiny green framed by bunkers on one side and a drop to the ocean on the other.

The finishing hole, guarded by desert and cactus on the right and rock cliffs leading to the sea on the left, is modeled after the 18th at Pebble Beach.

Cabo del Sol offers another option, the Desert Course, which is Tom Weiskopf's first course design in Mexico. It is spread out over 56 hectares (140 acres) of gently rolling desert terrain and provides sweeping ocean views.

CABO REAL   This Robert Trent Jones Jr., design is known for its holes along the Sea of Cortez; exceptional among these is the frequently photographed 12th hole, which sits high on a mesa facing the sea. Jones designed the course to test low handicappers, but multiple tees make it enjoyable for average players as well. While the first 6 holes are in mountainous terrain, others skirt the shore. Rolling greens and strategically placed bunkers on narrow terrain work their way up to the 6th tee, 460 feet above sea level. The most celebrated hole, the 15th, sits right on the beach between the Meliá Cabo Real Golf & Beach Resort and Las Ventanas al Paraíso.

THE RAVEN CLUB   The front and back 9s are the work of different members of the Dye family, so the course plays like two different courses. Characteristic of Dye designs, it has deep waste bunkers, subtle terracing up hillsides, and holes built into the natural desert terrain. The most challenging hole is the 607-yard, par-5 7th hole, around a lake; it's the longest hole in Mexico. The par-5 16th is a legendary left to right dogleg with an undulating, elevated green. The course is designed to offer a variety of play options, from a short course played on front tees to a super-long course with numerous bunkers and hazards. The whole course was redone in 2002 by the Dye family. Although the layout is essentially the same, some greens have moved slightly and some holes are a little shorter than before, but all of the bunkers and hazards have remained, and the course is now considered even better. From the greens on higher ground, you'll enjoy views overlooking the famous El Arco, the Sea of Cortez, the town of Cabo San Lucas, and the Pacific Ocean.

EL DORADO GOLF COURSE   A Jack Nicklaus Signature course at Cabo Real, El Dorado is a links-style course in the Scottish tradition. The layout is challenging—7 holes border the Sea of Cortez, and 12 are carved out of two pristine canyons. The oceanview holes are not the only water; manmade lakes are also a part of the scenery. El Dorado bills itself as the "Pebble Beach of Baja"— but then again, so does Cabo del Sol. You decide. Note that this course was recently purchased and will be redesigned. It's now scheduled to close for a period beginning summer 2005. It may reopen by 2006 as a private course.

Note: Cabo's newest course, **Querencia** (© 624/145-6670; www.bajagolf. com/querencia.html), is a Tom Fazio design. However, it is a private club, with play limited to property owners and members. Querencia embodies a championship 18-hole course, a 9-hole short course, a practice facility, and a 2,415-sq.-m (26,000-sq.-ft.) clubhouse with incredible views of the Sea of Cortez. If you can get on, greens fees are $275.

SPORTFISHING Many larger hotels, like the Solmar, have their own fleets (which are not necessarily better, only more convenient for reserving and billing). To make your own arrangements, go to the town marina on the south side of the harbor, where you'll find several fleet operators with offices near the docks. *Panga* fleets offer the best deals; 5 hours of fishing for two or three people costs $200 to $450. But stroll around the marina and talk with the captains—you may make a better deal. Try **ABY Charters** (© **624/144-4203;** www.abycharters.com; daily 10am–4pm; MasterCard and Visa are accepted) or the **Picante/Blue Water Sportfishing Fleet** (© **624/143-2474;** www.picantesportfishing.com; daily 6am–8pm; American Express, MasterCard, and Visa are accepted). Both have booths (with bathrooms) at the sportfishing dock at the far south end of the marina. A day on a fully equipped cruiser with captain and guide starts at around $1,070 for up to four people. For deluxe trips with everything included aboard a 12m (40-ft.) boat, you'll have to budget $1,455. (Also see "The Active Traveler," in chapter 2, for companies that arrange fishing in advance.) If you've traveled in your own vessel, you'll need a fishing permit. Depending on the size of the boat, it will cost $15 to $45 per month. Daily permits ($4–$10) and annual permits are also available.

The fishing here lives up to its reputation: Bringing in a 100-pound marlin is routine. Angling is good all year, though the catch varies with the season. Sailfish and wahoo are best from June through November; yellowfin tuna, May through December; yellowtail, January through April; black and blue marlin, July through December. Striped marlin are prevalent year-round.

SURFING Good surfing can be found from March through November all along the beaches west of town, and there's a famous right break at Chileno Beach, near the Cabo San Lucas Hotel east of town. (Also see "Surfing" in "San José del Cabo," earlier in this chapter, for details on Playa Costa Azul and Zipper's.) Other good surfing beaches along the corridor are Acapulquito, El Tule, and La Bocana.

The Pacific Coast has yet to face the onslaught of development that's so rapidly changed the east cape. An hour-long drive up the coast to the little towns of Pescadero and Todos Santos can be a great surf journey. They have a couple of good point breaks.

Playa San Pedrito is off the dirt road that begins 7.4 kilometers (4½ miles) south of the Todos Santos town limits. Follow the signs for SAN PEDRITO CAMPGROUND. The point is very rocky and sharp, but it's a wonderful wave on the right swell direction and tide (northwest swell, rising tide). Another stretch down the road will lead you to Playa los Cerritos (13km/8 miles south of Todos Santos), a lovely beach with a surfable point break off a big headland.

Other beach breaks are rideable at various times, but a vicious shorebreak and strong undertow characterize much of the beach around Todos Santos. While the unruliness of the ocean has helped keep industrial tourism at bay, it also means you have to hunt a little harder to find playful waves.

Tips **Don't Sweat the One That Got Away**

"Catch and release" is strongly encouraged in Los Cabos. Anglers reel in their fish, which are then tagged and released unharmed. The angler gets a certificate and the knowledge that there will still be fish in the sea when he returns.

Surf & Sleep

If you can't get enough of the surf, stay where this is the specialty, and not just an activity. The Los Cabos area has two hotels that cater to surfers, one along Los Cabos Corridor, the other on the Pacific Coast, near Todos Santos, and both fronting terrific surf breaks.

The **Cabo Surf Hotel** (© 858/964-5146 from the U.S., or 624/142-2666; www.cabosurfhotel.com) has 16 beachfront rooms in a secluded, gated boutique resort. It's 13km (8 miles) south of San José del Cabo, across from the Querencia golf course, on Playa Acapulquito, known as the best surfing beach in Los Cabos. Along with a choice of rooms and suites, it's equipped with a restaurant, surf shop, and the Mike Doyle Surf School, which offers day lessons and more intensive instruction. Rates range from $241 to $300 per night for doubles, and $265 to $550 for suites and villas. Promotional rates are available during summer months.

The **Teampaty Eco Surf Camp** (© 612/145-0882 or 612/108-0709; www.todossantos.cc/ecosurfcamp.html) is a solar-powered hostel-style surf camp that caters to instruction for women. The camp takes place at Los Cerritos beach, with a sandy bottom and gentle waves, making it ideal for beginners. Women-only camps take place over 5 days and nights, and run Monday through Friday. Their ongoing surf camp program arranges for participants to stay in private homes in Pescadero or Todos Santos with full amenities and daily transportation to and from the beach. Daily rates at the camp are also available, priced from $25 to $50 per night including kitchens and solar-heated showers. Tent access is available for $6 per person. In addition to surf instruction, participants assist in sea turtle preservation programs (July–Feb). Surfboard rentals, lessons ($20 per hr.), and excursions to nearby areas are also available through the camp.

WHALE-WATCHING   Whale-watching cruises are not to be missed. For information about the excursions, which operate between January and March, see "Whale-Watching" under "San José del Cabo," earlier in this chapter, and "Whale-Watching in Baja: A Primer," in chapter 6.

EXPLORING CABO SAN LUCAS
HISTORIC CABO SAN LUCAS

Sports and partying are Cabo's main attractions, but there are also a few cultural and historical points of interest. The Spanish missionary Nicolás Tamaral established the stone **Iglesia de San Lucas** (Church of San Lucas) on Calle Cabo San Lucas near the main plaza in 1730; a large bell in a stone archway commemorates the completion of the church in 1746. The Pericúe Indians, who reportedly resisted Tamaral's demands that they practice monogamy, eventually killed him. Buildings on the streets facing the main plaza are gradually being renovated to house restaurants and shops, and the picturesque neighborhood promises to have the strongest Mexican ambience in town.

NEARBY DAY TRIPS

Travel agencies can book day trips to the city of La Paz for around $60, including beverages and a tour of the countryside along the way. Usually there's a stop at the weaving shop of Fortunato Silva, who spins his own cotton and weaves it into wonderfully textured rugs and textiles. For more information, see chapter 5, "La Paz: Peaceful Port Town." Day trips are also available to Todos Santos ($60), with a guided walking tour of the Cathedral Mission, museum, Hotel California, and various artists' homes. For more on Todos Santos, see "Todos Santos: A Creative Oasis," later in this chapter.

SHOPPING

San José has the better shopping of the two towns when it comes to higher quality items, but if you're after a beer-themed T-shirt, Cabo San Lucas can't be topped. In Cabo San Lucas, the most notable shops are now concentrated in the **Puerto Paraíso Entertainment Plaza** (© 624/144-3000; www.puertoparaiso.com). Opened in 2002, this is now the focal point for shopping for tourists. It's a world-class mall, complete with parking, a food court, movie theaters, and a video arcade. With over 50,000 sq. m (538,195 sq. ft.) of air-conditioned space on three levels, it's too bad that the shops don't live up to the promise of this attractive mall. Although it bills itself as having an array of designer shops, this is a bit misleading; there may be only one or two name-brand items within any store, and many of the locales are vacant. It is, however, a good place to shop for swimwear or resort wear, and there are plenty of gift items to choose from, but don't expect the equivalent of a U.S. shopping mall experience. It does have some choice dining options, though, the best being the local branch of **Ruth's Chris Steak House** (adjacent to the marina; © 624/144-3232; daily 1–11:30pm). The plaza is located marina-side between the Plaza Bonita Mall and Marina Fiesta Resort—you can't miss it if you tried. Most other shops in Cabo are on or within a block or two of Boulevard Marina and the plaza.

   The Plaza Bonita Shopping Center (Cabo San Lucas, Bulevar Marina at Cárdenas) is an older shopping center that is still worth a visit. This large terra-cotta-colored plaza on the edge of the Cabo San Lucas marina has been around since 1990, and it finally has a group of successful businesses. A branch of **Dos Lunas** (© 624/143-1969) sells colorful casual sportswear. **Cartes** (© 624/143-1770) is filled with hand-painted ceramic vases and dishes, pewter frames, carved furniture, and hand-woven textiles. Most shops in the plaza are open daily from 9am to 9pm.

   In addition to the malls, I recommend the following specialty stores in Cabo:

El Callejón   This shop is stocked with Cabo's best selection of fine Mexican furniture and decor items, plus gifts, accessories, tableware, fabrics, and lamps. Open Monday to Saturday 9:30am to 7:30pm. Vicente Guerrero between Cárdenas and Madero (across from Cabo Wabo). © 624/143-3188.

H2O   Here you'll find a tempting selection of women's swimwear, casual wear, and dresses and evening wear, as well as casual resort wear for men. Open Monday to Saturday 9am to 8pm, Sunday 11am to 5pm. Vicente Guerrero and Madero. © 624/143-1219.

J & J Habanos   Cabo's largest cigar shop sells premium Cuban and fine Mexican cigars—it even has a walk-in humidor. Open Monday to Saturday 9am to 10pm, Sunday 9am to 9pm. Madero between Bulevar Marina and Vicente Guerrero. © 624/143-6160 or 624/143-3839.

Necri   Come here to find fine home accessories and Mexican handicrafts with an extensive selection of pewter and Talavera. Open Monday to Saturday 9am to 9pm. Bulevar Marina (across from Subway). © 624/143-0283.

Tequila's House   A large selection of fine tequilas and other liquors as well as cigars are sold here. There are two locations. Open Monday to Saturday 8am to 11pm. Bulevar Marina 624, in front of Caliente. © 624/143-5666. Morelos at Lázaro Cárdenas. © 624/143-9070.

UltraFemme This is Mexico's largest duty-free shop, with an excellent selection of fine jewelry and watches, including Rolex, Cartier, Omega, TAG Heuer, and Tissot; perfumes (Lancôme, Chanel, Armani, Carolina Herrera); and other gift items, all at duty-free prices. Open daily 10am to 10pm. Plaza UltraFemme, Bulevar Marina, across from Carlos & Charlies. © **624/145-6090** or 624/145-6099. www.ultrafemme.com.mx.

WHERE TO STAY

Unless otherwise indicated, all hotel rates listed here are for the high season, which runs from November through Easter; summer rates are about 20% less. Several Cabo San Lucas hotels offer package deals that significantly lower the nightly rate; ask your travel agent for information.

Budget accommodations are scarce in Cabo San Lucas, but the number of small inns and B&Bs is growing. Several notable ones have opened in the past few years. Most larger hotels are well maintained, with packages available through travel agents; these listings focus on smaller, more unique accommodations.

VERY EXPENSIVE

Solmar Suites ⭐⭐ Set against sandstone cliffs at the very tip of the Baja peninsula, the Solmar is beloved by those seeking seclusion, comfort, and easy access to Cabo's diversions. The suites are in two-story white stucco buildings along the edge of a broad beach. They have satellite TV, separate seating areas, and private balconies or patios on the sand. Guests gather by the pool and on the beach at sunset and all day long during the winter whale migration. The Solmar has one of the best sportfishing fleets in Los Cabos, including the deluxe *Solmar V,* for long-range diving, fishing, and whale-watching expeditions. A small timeshare complex adjoins the Solmar; some units are available for nightly stays.

Av. Solmar 1, 23410 Cabo San Lucas, B.C.S. © **624/143-3535.** Fax 624/143-0410. www.solmar.com. (Reservations: Box 383, Pacific Palisades, CA 90272. © **800/344-3349** or 310/459-9861. Fax 310/454-1686.) 194 units. High season $170–$330 double; low season $145–$300 double. AE, MC, V. **Amenities:** Restaurant (w/Sat Mexican fiesta); 2 bars (1 beach, 1 swim-up); 3 pools; Jacuzzi; sportfishing; concierge; tour desk; car-rental desk; salon; room service; laundry; dry cleaning. *In room:* A/C, TV, dataport, minibar, coffeemaker, hair dryer, safe.

EXPENSIVE

Meliá San Lucas ⭐⭐ If you've come to Cabo to party, this is your place. The recently renovated Meliá San Lucas has been converted into Cabo's newest hot spot, with an upgrade to its rooms and the addition of the hip Nikki Beach (a super-chic day-and-night club that hails from St. Tropez and Miami Beach; p. 84) on its beachfront. Its location on Playa El Medano is central to any other action you may want to seek out, but you'll find plenty right here as well. Rooms are awash in blues and white, with a sleek, contemporary decor. All suites have ocean views and private terraces looking across to the famed El Arco. Master suites have a separate living room area. Guests gather by the beachfront pool where the Nikki Beach trademark oversize day beds perfectly accommodate this lounge atmosphere. There are also VIP teepees, and live DJ music keeps the party here going day and night. In addition to Nikki Beach, several dining options are at the hotel, including one on the beach at sunset

Playa El Medano s/n; 23410 Cabo San Lucas, B.C.S. © **624/145-7800.** Fax 624/143-0420. www.meliasanlucas. solmelia.com. 150 units. $181–$238 double; $394 junior suite; $441 master suite. AE, MC, V. **Amenities:** Restaurant (w/Sat Mexican fiesta); 2 bars (1 beach, 1 lobby); 3 pools; Jacuzzi; concierge; tour desk; car-rental desk; boutique; room service; laundry; dry cleaning. *In room:* A/C, TV, high-speed Internet access, minibar, coffeemaker, hair dryer, safe.

MODERATE

The Bungalows ★★ *Finds*   This is one of the most special places to stay in Los Cabos. Each "bungalow" is a charming retreat decorated with authentic Mexican furnishings. Terra-cotta tiles, hand-painted sinks, wooded chests, blown glass, and other creative touches make you feel as if you're a guest at a friend's home rather than a hotel. Each room has a mini-kitchenette, purified water, VCR, and designer bedding. Rooms surround a lovely heated pool with cushioned lounges and tropical gardens. A brick-paved breakfast nook serves a gourmet breakfast with fresh-ground coffee and fresh juices. Under owner Steve's warm and welcoming management, this is Cabo's most spacious, comfortable, full-service inn. A 100% smoke-free environment, it is 5 blocks from downtown Cabo.

Miguel A. Herrera s/n, in front of Lienzo Charro, 23410 Cabo San Lucas, B.C.S. ℂ/fax **624/143-5035** or 624/143-0585. www.cabobungalows.com. 16 units. High season $115–$165 suite; low season $105–$165 suite. Extra person $20. Rates include full breakfast. AE. Street parking available. **Amenities:** Breakfast room; pool; concierge; tour desk. *In room:* A/C, TV/VCR, dataport, minifridge, coffeemaker.

Casa Bella B&B ★★★ *Finds*   This hacienda-style boutique hotel is right on the main plaza in Cabo San Lucas yet retains a sense of privacy and tranquillity, even though you're close to everything in downtown Cabo. This is made possible thanks to a wall with windows and arches that surrounds the series of white stucco buildings comprising this lovely place. The seven guest rooms and one suite surround a central courtyard and pool, landscaped paths, and terraces. The common living area has the only TV on property, and a small, lovely terraced dining area serves the complementary continental breakfast as well as other meals. Each of the rooms is individually decorated with antiques and handcrafted furnishings. The large tiled bathrooms have open showers, and some have small gardens. The hotel is open from October 15 to July 31.

Hidalgo 10, Col. Centro, 23410 Cabo San Lucas, B.C.S. ℂ/fax **624/143-6400.** Fax 624/143-6401. www.loscabos guide.com/hotels/casa-bella-hotel.htm. 8 units. High season $145–$200; low-season specials available upon request. Rates include continental breakfast. MC, V. Street parking available. **Amenities:** Restaurant; pool; concierge; Internet connection; room service; laundry facilities; TV. *In room:* A/C.

Los Milagros   The elegant white two-level buildings containing the 11 suites and rooms of Los Milagros (the Miracles) border either a grassy garden area or the small pool. Rooms contain contemporary iron beds with straw headboards, buff-colored tile floors, and artistic details. Some units have kitchenettes, and the master suite has a sunken tub. E-mail, fax, and telephone service are available through the office, and there's coffee service in the mornings on the patio. Evenings are romantic: Candles light the garden and classical music plays. Request a room in one of the back buildings, where conversation noise from people passing through the courtyard and sitting around the pool is less intrusive. It's just 1½ blocks from the Giggling Marlin and Cabo Wabo.

Matamoros 116, 23410 Cabo San Lucas, B.C.S. ℂ/fax **624/143-4566.** www.losmilagros.com.mx. 11 units. $84 double. Ask about summer discounts, group rates, and long-term discounts. No credit cards. Limited street parking. **Amenities:** Small pool. *In room:* A/C.

INEXPENSIVE

Cabo Inn ★★ *Finds*   This three-story hotel on a quiet street is a real find, and it keeps getting better. It offers a rare combination of low rates, extra-friendly management, and great, funky style. Rooms are basic and very small, with either two twin beds or one queen. Although this was a bordello in a prior incarnation, everything is kept new and updated, from the mattresses to the minifridges. Muted desert colors add a spark of personality. The rooms surround a courtyard where you can enjoy satellite TV, a barbecue grill, and free coffee. The third floor has a rooftop terrace with *palapa* and a small swimming pool. Also on this floor is "Juan's Love Palace," aka the honeymoon suite. It's a colorful, *palapa*-topped, open-air room with hanging *tapetes* (woven palm mats) for additional privacy. A large fish freezer is available, and most rooms have kitchenettes. The hotel's just 2 blocks from downtown and the marina. A lively restaurant next door will even deliver pitchers of margaritas and dinner to your room.

20 de Noviembre and Leona Vicario, 23410 Cabo San Lucas, B.C.S. ℰ/fax **624/143-3348**. www.caboinnhotel.com. 21 units. $58–$120 double; $330 double weekly (low season only). No credit cards. Street parking. **Amenities:** Small rooftop pool and sunning area; communal TV and barbecue. *In room:* A/C.

Siesta Suites ℱ   Reservations are a must at this immaculate, small inn popular with return visitors to Cabo. (It's especially popular with fishermen.) The very basic rooms have white-tile floors and white walls, kitchenettes with seating areas, refrigerators, and sinks. The mattresses are firm, and the bathrooms are large and sparkling clean. Rooms on the fourth floor have two queen beds each. The accommodating proprietors offer free movies and VCRs, a barbecue pit and outdoor patio table on the second floor, and a comfortable lobby with TV. They can also arrange fishing trips. Weekly and monthly rates are available. The hotel is 1½ blocks from the marina, where parking is available.

Calle Emiliano Zapata between Guerrero and Hidalgo, 23410 Cabo San Lucas, B.C.S. ℰ **866/271-0952** from the U.S., or 624/143-2773. www.cabosiestasuites.com. 20 suites (15 w/kitchenette). $55 per 2 people in a suite (price based on number of people in the room—most rooms can sleep up to 4). AE, MC, V. **Amenities:** Pool; barbecue pit. *In room:* VCR, fan.

WHERE TO DINE

It's not uncommon to pay a lot for mediocre food in Cabo, so try to get a couple of unbiased recommendations. If people are only drinking and not dining, take that as a clue—many seemingly popular places are long on party atmosphere but short on food. Prices decrease the farther you walk inland. The absolute local favorite is **Manuel's Tamales,** a street stand selling traditional treats of cornmeal stuffed with meat or cheese then steamed in a cornhusk. Look for him on weekend nights on the corner of Lázaro Cárdenas and Zaragoza. Streets to explore for other good restaurants include Hidalgo and Lázaro Cárdenas, plus the Marina at the Plaza Bonita. Note that many restaurants automatically add the tip (15%) to the bill.

VERY EXPENSIVE

Casa Rafael's ℱ INTERNATIONAL   Looking for a little romance? Casa Rafael's, though overpriced, is among the most romantic places (a rosy-pink château with an arched front and a patio with caged birds and a fountain) in Cabo. Dine in one of the large house's candlelit rooms and alcoves (which are air-conditioned), or outside beside the small swimming pool. Piano music plays in the background while you enjoy a leisurely meal. To start, try sublime smoked dorado pâté, or perhaps hearts of palm with raspberry vinaigrette. House specialties—a tasty combination of selections from the meat, seafood, and pasta menus—include Cornish game hen in champagne sauce. Black Angus steaks are imported from the United States; the lamb comes from New Zealand.

Calle Medano and Camino el Pescador. ℰ 624/143-0739. Fax 624/143-1679. www.allaboutcabo.com. Reservations strongly recommended. Main courses $20–$58. AE, MC, V. Daily 7–10pm. Follow Hacienda Rd. toward the ocean; when you top the hill, turn left and drive to the château.

EXPENSIVE

Nick-San ✿✿ JAPANESE/SUSHI   Exceptional Japanese cuisine and sushi are the specialties at this air-conditioned restaurant with minimalist decor. A rosewood sushi bar with royal-blue tile accents allows diners to watch the master sushi chef at work. An exhibition kitchen behind him demonstrates why this place has been honored with a special award for cleanliness. It's a favorite of mine—as well as of many local residents.

Bulevar Marina, Plaza de la Danza, Local 2. ✆ 624/143-4484. Reservations recommended. Main courses $12–$30; sushi from $3.50. MC, V. Tues–Sun 11:30am–10:30pm.

Peacocks ✿✿ INTERNATIONAL   One of Cabo's most exclusive patio-dining establishments, Peacocks emphasizes fresh seafood creatively prepared. Start with the house pâté or a salad of feta cheese with cucumber, tomato, and onion. For a main course, try one of the pastas—linguini with grilled chicken and sun-dried tomatoes is a good choice. More filling entrees include steaks, shrimp, and lamb, all prepared several ways.

Paseo del Pescador s/n, near Hotel Meliá Cabo San Lucas. ✆ 624/143-1858. Reservations recommended. Main courses $15–$35. AE, MC, V. Daily 6–10:30pm.

MODERATE

La Dolce ITALIAN   This restaurant is the offspring of Puerto Vallarta's La Dolce Vita, with authentic Italian thin-crust, brick-oven pizzas and other specialties. It seems about 80% of the business is from local customers, underscoring the attention to detail and reasonable prices. The simple menu also features sumptuous pastas and calzones plus great salads. This is the best late-night dining option in town.

Hidalgo and Zapata s/n. ✆ 624/143-4122. Main courses $8–$19. MC, V. Mon–Sat 8pm–midnight. Closed Sept.

Mi Casa ✿ MEXICAN   The building's vivid cobalt-blue facade is your first clue that this place celebrates Mexico, and the menu confirms that impression. This is one of Cabo's most renowned gourmet Mexican restaurants. Traditional specialties such as *manchamanteles* (literally, "tablecloth stainers"), *cochinita pibil,* and *chiles en nogada* (chiles stuffed with a mixture of meat, spices, nuts, and raisins then topped in a white sweet-cream sauce with walnuts and served cold) are menu staples. Fresh fish is prepared with delicious seasonings from throughout Mexico. Especially pleasant at night, the restaurant's tables, scattered around a large patio, are set with colorful cloths, traditional pottery, and glassware. It's across from the main plaza.

Calle Cabo San Lucas (at Madero). ✆ 624/143-1933. Reservations recommended. Main courses $15–$25. AE, MC, V. Daily 5:30–10pm.

INEXPENSIVE

Cafe Cane ✿ COFFEE/PASTRY/LIGHT MEALS   This cozy, tasty cafe and bistro is a welcome addition to the Cabo Marina boardwalk. Espresso drinks or fruit smoothies and muffins are good eye-openers for early risers. Enjoy a light meal or a tropical drink either inside or on the bustling waterfront terrace. The appealing menu also offers breakfast egg wraps, salads (for example, curried chicken salad with fresh fruit), sandwiches (such as blue-cheese quesadillas with smoked tuna and mango), and pastas—all reasonably priced. Full bar service is also available.

Marina boardwalk, below Plaza Las Glorias hotel. ✆ 624/143-3435. Main courses: $4–$9; coffee $1.75–$3.50. AE, MC, V. Daily 6am–5pm.

Felix's 𝒢 MEXICAN   This colorful, friendly family-run place has grown up since opening in 1958, going from just serving tacos to offering a full array of tasty Mexican and seafood dishes. Everything's fresh and homemade, including corn tortillas and the numerous and varied salsas—more than 30! Fish tacos made with fresh dorado are superb, as are the shrimp dishes—the coconut mango version, served with homemade mango chutney, is especially tasty. Don't leave without sampling the original Mexican bouillabaisse, a rich stew of shrimp, crab, sea bass, scallops, Italian sausage, and savory seasonings. Mexican specialties include chimichangas and *carne asada* (grilled marinated beef) with chile verde sauce. There is full bar service; the specialties are fresh-fruit margaritas and daiquiris. At breakfast time, this is Mama's Royale Café (see below).

Hidalgo and Zapata s/n. 𝒞 624/143-4290. Main courses $8–$15. MC, V. Mon–Sat 3–10pm.

Mama's Royale Café 𝒢𝒢 BREAKFAST   This is a great place to start the day. The shady patio decked with cloth-covered tables and the bright, inviting dining room are both comfortable places to settle in, and the food's just as appetizing. Effrain and Pedro preside over this dining hot spot with well-prepared breakfast selections that include grilled sausage; French toast stuffed with cream cheese and topped with pecans, strawberries, and orange liqueur; several variations of eggs Benedict; home fries; fruit crepes; and, of course, traditional breakfasts, plus free coffee refills. The orange juice is fresh squeezed, and there usually is live marimba or mariachi music to get your morning off to a lively start.

Hidalgo at Zapata. 𝒞 **624/143-4290.** Breakfast special $2.50; breakfast a la carte $2.50–$10. MC, V. Daily 7:30am–1pm.

Mocambo's 𝒢 SEAFOOD   The location of this longstanding Cabo favorite is not inspiring—it's basically a large cement building—but the food obviously is: The place is always packed, generally with locals tired of high prices and small portions. Ocean-fresh seafood is the order of the day, and the specialty platter can easily serve four people. The restaurant is 1½ blocks inland from Lázaro Cárdenas street.

Av. Leona Vicario and 20 de Noviembre. 𝒞 **624/143-6070.** Main courses $5–$23. MC, V. Daily noon–10pm.

CABO SAN LUCAS AFTER DARK

Cabo San Lucas is the nightlife capital of Baja. After-dark fun centers on the casual bars and restaurants on Marina Boulevard or facing the marina rather than a flashy disco scene. You can easily find a happy hour with live music and a place to dance, or a Mexican fiesta with mariachis.

MEXICAN FIESTAS & THEME NIGHTS   Some larger hotels have weekly Fiesta Nights, Italian Nights, and other buffet-plus-entertainment theme nights that can be fun as well as a good buy. Check travel agencies and the following hotels: the **Solmar Suites** (𝒞 **624/143-3535**), the **Finisterra** (𝒞 **624/143-3333**), and the **Hotel Meliá Cabo San Lucas** (𝒞 **624/143-4444**). Prices range from $22 (not including drinks, tax, and tips) to $35 (which covers everything, including an open bar with national drinks).

SUNSET WATCHING   At twilight, check out Land's End, where the two seas meet. **Whale Watcher's Bar,** in the Hotel Finisterra (𝒞 **624/143-3333**), is Los Cabos' premier place for sunset watching. Its location at Land's End offers a world-class view of the sun sinking into the Pacific. The high terrace offers vistas of both sea and beach as well as magical glimpses of whales from January to March. Mariachis play on Friday from 6:30 to 9pm. The bar is open daily from 10am to 11pm. "Whale margaritas" cost $4, beer $3. There are two-for-one drinks during happy hour from 4 to 6pm.

HAPPY HOURS & HANGOUTS

If you shop around, you can usually find an *hora alegre* (happy hour) somewhere in town between noon and 7pm. On my last visit, the most popular places to drink and carouse until all hours were the Giggling Marlin, El Squid Roe, and the Cabo Wabo Cantina. For a different vibe, try **Sancho Panza Wine Bar and Bistro** (① **624/143-3212;** see description below).

El Squid Roe   El Squid Roe is one of the late Carlos Anderson's inspirations, and it still attracts wild, fun-loving crowds of all ages with its two stories of nostalgic decor and eclectic food that's far better than you'd expect from such a party place. As fashionable as blue jeans, this is a place to see and see what can be seen—women's tops are discarded with regularity as the dancing on tables moves into high gear. There's also a patio out back for dancing when the tables, chairs, and bar spots are taken. Open daily from noon to 2am. Bulevar Marina, opposite Plaza Bonita Mall. ① **624/143-0655.** www.elsquidroe. com. Cover only during special event nights.

Giggling Marlin   Live music alternates with recorded tunes to get the happy patrons dancing—and occasionally jumping up to dance on the tables and bar. A contraption of winches, ropes, and pulleys above a mattress provides entertainment as couples literally string each other up by the heels—just like a captured marlin. The food is only fair; stick with nachos and drinks. There is live music Wednesday through Sunday from 9pm to midnight during high season. The Giggling Marlin is open daily from 8am to 2am. Beer is $1.75 to $2.50; schooner margaritas cost $4 to $6. Drinks are half-price during happy hour, from 2 to 6pm. Lázaro Cárdenas at Zaragoza, across from the marina. ① **624/143-0606.** www.gigglingmarlin.com.

Latitude 22+   This raffish restaurant and bar never closes. License plates, signs, sports caps, and a 435-kilogram (959-lb.) blue marlin are the backdrop for U.S. sports events that play on six TVs scattered among pool tables, dart boards, and assorted games. You can order dishes from hamburgers to chicken-fried steak, or breakfast anytime. Happy hour is from 4 to 6pm. Lázaro Cárdenas s/n, 1 block north of the town's only traffic light. ① **624/143-1516.** www.lat22nobaddays.com.

Mambo Café   This latest addition to the Cabo nightlife scene, opened in December 2004, is part of a chain of bars around Mexico. It features a Caribbean concept club with a marine tropical ambience playing contemporary Latin music. Live music is also featured. It's open Tuesday through Sunday from 9pm until anywhere between 2 and 5am, depending on the crowd. Bulevar Marina Local 9–10, next to the Costa Real Cabo Resort. ① **624/143-1484.** www.mambocafe.com.mx. Cover charge varies with the night.

Nikki Beach   This haven of the hip hails from South Beach, Miami, and St. Tropez, and has brought its ultracool vibe to the Meliá San Lucas resort beachfront in March 2005. White-draped bed-size lounges scatter the outdoor lounge area, under a canopy of umbrellas, surrounding a pool and overlooking Cabo's best swimming beach. A teak deck offers covered dining. The music is the latest in electronic, house, and chill, with visiting DJs often playing on weekend nights. Sundays feature the signature beach brunch. It's a great choice for catching rays during the day while sipping tropical drinks, but its real appeal is the nocturnal action. Open Sunday through Wednesday from

11am to 1am (food service stops at 11pm), Thursday through Saturday from 11am to 3am (food service stops at 1am.). On Playa El Medano at the Meliá San Lucas. ✆ **624/145-7800.** www.nikkibeach.com.

Sancho Panza Wine Bar and Bistro   Finally, an alternative to beer bars. Sancho Panza combines a gourmet food market with a wine bar that features live jazz plus an intriguing menu of Nuevo Latino cuisine (Mediterranean food with Latin flair). The place has a cozy neighborhood feel, with tourists and locals taking advantage of the selection of more than 150 wines, plus espresso drinks. During high season, make reservations. Open Monday through Saturday 3pm to midnight. Plaza las Glorias boardwalk, next to the Lighthouse. ✆ **624/143-3212.** www.sanchopanza.com.

DANCING
Cabo Wabo Cantina   Owned by Sammy Hagar (formerly of Van Halen) and his Mexican and American partners, this "cantina" packs in youthful crowds, especially when rumors (frequent, and frequently false, just to draw a crowd) fly that a surprise appearance by a vacationing musician is imminent. Live rock bands from the United States, Mexico, Europe, and Australia perform. One of Cabo's few air-conditioned dance venues, it's especially popular in the summer months. When there isn't a band, a disco-type sound system plays mostly rock and some alternative and techno. Overstuffed furniture frames the dance floor. Beer goes for $3, margaritas for $5. For snacks, the Taco-Wabo, just outside the club's entrance, stays up late, too. The cantina is open from 11am to 4am. Vicente Guerrero at Lázaro Cárdenas. ✆ **624/143-1188.** Cover charge varies—when there's just recorded music; often there is no cover.

MENS' CLUBS
There's a changing selection of strip clubs to choose from in Cabo, but the mainstays include **Mermaid's,** corner of Lázaro Cárdenas and Vicente Guerrero (✆ **624/143-5370;** www.loscabosnights.com/mermaids.htm), which offers its patrons their choice of topless stage shows or private dances. Admission is $5 for the general show or $20 for the private dances. It's open nightly from 7pm to 3am. Another popular option is **Twenty/20 Showgirls,** Lázaro Cárdenas at Francisco Villa (✆ **624/143-5380**), also with a bevy of beauties to entertain you with their dancing skills on any one of the numerous stages. It's the largest of these clubs in Cabo. In addition to a topless cabaret show, it offers topless lap dances as well as televised sports, pool tables, and food service. It's open from 8:30pm to 3am, closed Tuesdays.

4 North from Los Cabos
The coastline of the Sea of Cortez north of San José has long been a favored destination of die-hard anglers, who fly their private planes to airstrips at out-of-the-way lodges. This is a stretch of undeveloped beachfront, with nothing but beach and desert—no stores, no businesses, and only the occasional guest lodge with not much to do other than fish, surf, and sunbathe. The coastline has experienced considerable development in the past few years, however, and hotels have expanded their services to please even those who never plan to set foot on a boat. Housing developments are appearing along the main road, but there's still plenty of space for adventurous campers to find secluded beaches here.

The rough dirt Coastal Road runs along the east cape from San José to La Ribera; completing the 89km (55-mile) drive can take up to 4 hours. Along this route you pass by Cabo Pulmo, where Baja's only coral reef lies just offshore. There are no major

East Cape

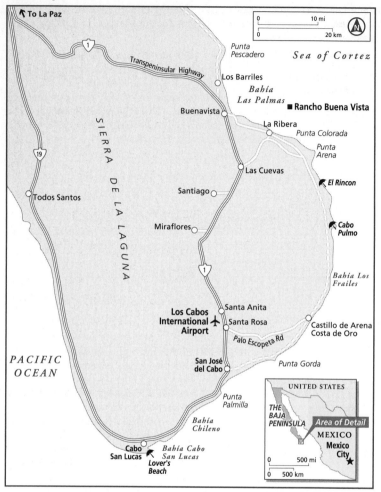

| 0 | 10 mi |
| 0 | 20 km |

To La Paz

Transpeninsular Highway

Punta Pescadero

Sea of Cortez

Los Barriles

Bahía Las Palmas

Buenavista

■ Rancho Buena Vista

La Ribera

Punta Colorada

Punta Arena

SIERRA DE LA LAGUNA

Las Cuevas

El Rincon

Todos Santos

Santiago

Miraflores

Cabo Pulmo

Bahía Los Frailes

Los Cabos International Airport

Santa Anita

Santa Rosa

Castillo de Arena
Costa de Oro

Palo Escopeta Rd

PACIFIC OCEAN

San José del Cabo

Punta Gorda

Punta Palmilla

Bahía Chileno

Bahía Cabo San Lucas

Cabo San Lucas

Lover's Beach

UNITED STATES

THE BAJA PENINSULA

Area of Detail

MEXICO

Mexico City

| 0 | 500 mi |
| 0 | 500 km |

hotels, restaurants, or dive shops here, and most divers reach the reefs on dive boats from Los Cabos. The more efficient approach to the east cape is to drive paved Carretera Transpeninsular from San José north to the dirt roads leading off the highway to resorts and communities at Punta Colorada, Buena Vista, Los Barriles, and Punta Pescadero. Public buses from San José stop at major intersections, where you'll need to catch a cab to the hotels. Most guests who stay at the more secluded hotels take a cab from the airport and remain at their hotel.

WHERE TO STAY & DINE

Rancho Buena Vista   A fishing resort with no pretensions, Rancho Buena Vista has several one-story bungalows spread about the grounds. The simple rooms have red-tiled floors, good showers, double beds, and small patios. Hammocks hang under palms and by the swimming pool, and the bar/restaurant is the center of the action. The hotel has an excellent deep-sea fishing fleet with its own dock and a private airstrip. Note that the info on the website is outdated.

Carretera Transpeninsular at Buena Vista, 69km (35 miles) north of San José del Cabo's airport. © **624/141-0177.** Fax 624/141-0055. (Reservations: P.O. Box 1408, Santa Maria, CA 93456. © **800/258-8200** outside CA, or 805/928-1719; fax 805/925-2990.) www.ranchobuenavista.com. 55 units. $185 double. Rates include 3 meals daily. MC, V. **Amenities:** Restaurant/bar; pool; fishing charters; tour desk. *In room:* A/C.

5 Todos Santos: A Creative Oasis ★★★

68km (42 miles) N of Cabo San Lucas

A few years back, Todos Santos became known as "Bohemian Baja" as it found its way onto the itineraries of those looking for the latest, the trendiest, and the hippest of artists' outposts—and of those simply weary of the L.A.-ization of Cabo San Lucas.

The art and artistry created here—from the kitchen to the canvas—seems to care less about commercial appeal than about quality, which makes it even more of a draw. Not to be overlooked are the attendant arts of agriculture, masonry, and weavings practiced by some of the town's original residents. From the superb meals at **Café Santa Fe** to an afternoon spent browsing at **El Tecolote Libros,** the best bookstore I've come across in Mexico, Todos Santos is intriguing to its core.

The town is not only a cultural oasis in Baja but an oasis in the true sense of the word—in this desert landscape, Todos Santos enjoys an almost continuous water supply from the peaks of the Sierra de la Laguna mountains. It's just over an hour's drive up the Pacific coast from Cabo San Lucas; you'll know you've arrived when verdant groves of palms, mangos, avocados, and papayas suddenly interrupt the arid coastal scenery.

During the Mission period, the reliable water supply made this valley the only area south and west of La Paz deemed worth settling. In 1723, an outpost mission was established followed by the full-fledged Misión Santa Rosa de Las Palmas, endowed by one of Spain's leading families in 1733. The town was then known as Santa Rosa de Todos Santos, eventually shortened to its current name, which translates as "All Saints."

Over the next 200 years, the town alternated between prosperity and difficulty. Its most recent boom lasted from the mid–19th century until the 1950s, when the town prospered as a sugarcane production center and began to develop a strong cultural core. Many of the buildings now being restored and converted into galleries, studios, shops, and restaurants were built during this era.

Demand for older colonial-style structures by artists, entrepreneurs, and foreign residents has resulted in a real estate boom. New shops, galleries, and cafes crop up continuously. The coastal strip south of Todos Santos is in the process of being developed, with its first luxury hotel and spa slated to open sometime in the next 2 years. For the casual visitor, Todos Santos can easily be explored in a day, but a few tranquil inns welcome charmed guests who want to stay a little longer. For additional information and current events, visit **www.todossantos-baja.com**.

WHAT TO DO IN TODOS SANTOS

During the **Festival Fundador** (Oct 10–14), which celebrates the founding of the town in 1723, streets around the main plaza fill with food, games, and wandering troubadours. Many of the shops and the Café Santa Fe close from the end of September through the festival. The Arts Festival, held in February, seems to be gaining importance, with film festivals, dance and music performances, and more.

Todos Santos is a good stopover for those traveling between Cabo and La Paz; a day's visit can be arranged through tour companies in Los Cabos or done on your own with a rental car. There are at least half a dozen galleries in town, including the noted **Galería de Todos Santos,** at the corner of Topete and Legaspi (© **612/145-0500**), which features a changing collection of works by regional artists. It's open daily 11am to 4pm (closed Sun May–Nov) and doesn't accept credit cards. The **Galería Santa Fe,** Centenario, across from the plaza (© **612/145-0340**), holds a popular collection of eclectic, kitschy, and cool-looking original, creative Mexican folk art and *artesanía* treasures that include picture frames adorned with images of Frida Kahlo and "shrines"—kid-size wooden chairs decorated in bottle caps, Virgin of Guadalupe images, *milagros* (small paintings on a tin sheet depicting the story of a "miracle" that occurred, as a kind of homage), and more. It's open Wednesday through Monday from 10am to 5pm and accepts MasterCard and Visa.

El Tecolote Libros 🐸🐸🐸 (© **612/145-0295**), though tiny, gets our vote for the best bookstore in Mexico. It carries an exceptional selection of Latin American literature, poetry, children's books, and reference books centering on Mexico. Both English and Spanish editions, new and used, are in stock, along with maps, magazines, cards, and art supplies. Information on upcoming writing workshops and local reading groups is also posted here. The shop is at the corner of Hidalgo and Juárez. It's open Monday through Saturday from 9am to 5pm, and Sunday from 10am to 3pm.

WHERE TO STAY

Hotel California   This place has been the stuff of legends—and claims to be the source of inspiration for the Eagles' song of the same name, although this myth has been mostly debunked. A few years back it was a dilapidated guesthouse; however, after an extensive renovation, it's now the hippest place to stay in the area. Think Philippe Stark in the desert—the decor here is a fusion of jewel-tone colors with eclectic Mexican and Moroccan accents. Each room features a different decor, but all of it is high style, with rich hues and captivating details. Most rooms also offer an outdoor terrace or seating area. It's so stylishly accommodating that although you can check out anytime you want—you may not want to! On the ground floor, you'll find the lobby, the low-lit library—with deep blue walls, a profusion of candles, and tin stars— and a small outdoor pool with sun chairs. Also at ground level is the Emporio Hotel California boutique and the La Coronela Restaurant and Bar, the area's current nocturnal hot spot with live guitar, jazz, and blues music on Saturday evenings. On Sundays, the restaurant serves a mixed grill of steak, fish, chicken breast, and sausage for $13 per person.

Calle Juárez, corner of Morelos, 23305 Todos Santos, B.C.S. © 612/145-0525. 11 units. $140–$195 double; off season $75–$125 double. MC, V. **Amenities:** Restaurant/bar; pool; boutique; library.

Posada La Poza   On a lagoon and bird sanctuary, the Posada La Poza (Inn at the Spring) opened its doors in 2002 and has been earning rave reviews for its artistic and serene atmosphere. Each of the seven boutique suites features a private terrace or patio, comfortable sitting areas, colorful walk-in showers, and large windows overlooking the garden, lagoon, and ocean. Two junior suites and the honeymoon suite also offer a spa or hot tub. Guest beds are fitted with fine Swiss linens. The original artwork is by Libusche Wiesendanger, who together with her Swiss-born husband Jureg created this unique inn. The honeymoon suite, which has an oversize bathroom, fireplace, and expansive terrace. Rates include a full breakfast served in the El Gusto!

Todos Santos

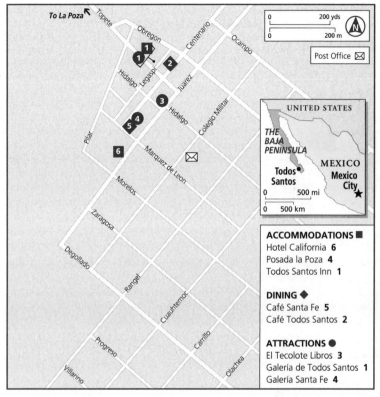

ACCOMMODATIONS ■
Hotel California **6**
Posada la Poza **4**
Todos Santos Inn **1**

DINING ◆
Café Santa Fe **5**
Café Todos Santos **2**

ATTRACTIONS ●
El Tecolote Libros **3**
Galería de Todos Santos **1**
Galería Santa Fe **4**

gourmet Mexican restaurant, part of the inn. Guests may enjoy the horseshoe-shaped saltwater swimming pool with a small waterfall, and the exercise facility (on a lovely garden patio). Hiking and walking paths surround the hotel, and bikes are available for guest use. The inn is part of a bird sanctuary that is home to more than 70 species and is also located along the migratory route of the gray whales (Nov–Mar). For more information on whale-watching, see "Whale-Watching" under "San José del Cabo," earlier in this chapter, and "Whale-Watching in Baja: A Primer," in chapter 6.

A.P. 10, Col. La Poza, 23305 Todos Santos, B.C.S. ℂ **612/145-0400.** www.lapoza.com. $120–$150 double; $225–$270 junior suite; $380–$500 honeymoon suite. MC, V. **Amenities:** Saltwater swimming pool; exercise facility; hiking paths.

Todos Santos Inn   An elegant place to stay, the inn is in a historic house that has served as a general store, cantina, school, and private residence. Now under new ownership, it retains its air of casual elegance, with luxurious white bed linens, netting draped romantically over the beds, Talavera tile bathrooms, antique furniture, and high, wood-beamed ceilings. Rooms and suites border a courtyard terrace, pool, and garden. The suites are air-conditioned but have neither television nor telephone. A new wine bar, open to the public, serves libations Tuesdays through Saturdays from 5 to 9pm, and has possibly the town's best margaritas, in addition to an excellent selection of California and other imported wines. Seasonal discounts are available.

Calle Legaspi 33, between Topete and Obregón, 23305 Todos Santos, B.C.S. ℂ 612/145-0040. 6 units. $95 double; $135 suite. No credit cards. Closed Sept. **Amenities:** Pool. *In room:* A/C in suites.

WHERE TO DINE

Café Santa Fe ℛ CAFE   For myself—and I would suspect many others—a meal here is reason enough to visit Todos Santos. Much of the attention the town has received in recent years can be directly attributed to this outstanding cafe, and it continues to live up to its lofty reputation. Owners Ezio and Paula Colombo refurbished a large stucco house across from the plaza, creating an exhibition kitchen, several dining rooms, and a lovely courtyard adjacent to a garden of hibiscus, bougainvillea, papaya trees, and herbs. My favorite room is the one in homage to Frida Kahlo, with reproductions of her work on grand canvases that flatter her more than her originals.

The excellent Northern Italian cuisine emphasizes local produce and seafood; try ravioli stuffed with spinach and ricotta in a Gorgonzola sauce, or ravioli with lobster and shrimp accompanied by an organic salad. In high season, the wait for a table can be long since everything is prepared to order.

Centenario 4. ℂ 612/145-0340. Reservations recommended. Main courses $10–$20. MC, V. Wed–Mon noon–9pm. Closed Sept to early Nov.

Café Todos Santos CAFE   The garden setting here is a more casual option, and is a magical place to start the day. Among the espresso drinks is the bowl-size caffe latte, which is accompanied by a freshly baked croissant or one of the signature cinnamon buns. Lunch or a light meal may include a frittata, a filling sandwich on home-baked bread, or a fish filet wrapped in banana leaves with coconut milk.

Centenario 33, across from the Todos Santos Inn. ℂ 612/145-0300. Main courses $3–$6. No credit cards. Mon 7am–2pm; Tues–Sun 7am–9pm.

5

La Paz: Peaceful Port Town

La Paz means "peace," and the feeling seems to float on the ocean breezes of this provincial town. Despite being an important port with almost 200,000 inhabitants and the capital of the state of Baja California Sur, La Paz remains slow-paced and relaxed. It's an easygoing yet sophisticated city and the guardian of "old Baja" atmosphere, with beautiful deserted beaches just minutes away that complement the lively beach and palm-fringed *malecón* (sea wall) that fronts the town center.

The presence of the University of South Baja California has added a unique cultural element to the area that includes museums, a theater, and an arts center. The surrounding tropical desert diversity and uncommon wildlife are also compelling reasons to visit. They lend themselves to countless options for adventurous travelers, including hiking, rock climbing, diving, fishing, and sea kayaking. Islands and islets sit just offshore; once the hiding place for looting pirates, they now attract kayakers and beachcombers. At Espíritu Santo and Los Islotes, it's possible to swim with sea lions.

Despite its name, La Paz has historically been a place of conflict between explorers and indigenous populations, traders, and pirates. Beginning in 1535, Spanish conquistadors and Jesuit missionaries arrived, leaving their influence on the architecture and traditions of La Paz. From its founding—when conquistadors saw local Indians wearing pearl ornaments—through the late 1930s, when an unknown disease killed off the oysters in the Bay of La Paz, this was the center of world pearl harvesting. Writer John Steinbeck immortalized a local legend in his novella *The Pearl*.

La Paz is ideal for anyone nostalgic for Los Cabos the way it used to be, before development and burgeoning crowds. From accommodations to taxis, it's also one of Mexico's most outstanding beach-vacation values and a great place for family travelers. Be forewarned that development activity in the areas immediately surrounding La Paz may change this in the coming years, so plan a visit now to experience the pearl of La Paz in its natural state.

1 Essentials

177km (110 miles) N of Cabo San Lucas; 196km (122 miles) NW of San José del Cabo; 1,578km (978 miles) SE of Tijuana

GETTING THERE & DEPARTING

BY PLANE **AeroCalifornia** (© **800/237-6225** in the U.S., or 612/125-1023 or 612/124-6344) has flights to La Paz from Los Angeles, Tijuana, and Mexico City. **Aeromexico** (© **800/237-6639** in the U.S., or 612/122-0091, 612/122-0093, or 612/122-1636) connects through Tucson and Los Angeles in the United States, and flies from Mexico City, Guadalajara, Tijuana, and other points within Mexico.

Tips Taking Your Car to the Mainland

Those planning to take their cars on the ferry to the Mexican mainland must meet all the requirements listed in "Getting There" in chapter 2. Additionally, every traveler going to the mainland needs a Mexican Tourist Permit (FMT).

Tourism officials in La Paz say that FMTs are available only in Mexicali, Tecate, Tijuana, Ensenada, and Guerrero Negro, and not in La Paz, although car permits to cross over into the mainland can be issued there. If you do happen to make it as far as La Paz, or anywhere outside the frontier zone, and are found not to have an FMT, you will be subject to a $40 fine.

BY CAR From San José del Cabo, Carretera Transpeninsular north is the longer, more scenic route; a flatter, faster route is Carretera Transpeninsular east to Cabo San Lucas, then Highway 19 north through Todos Santos. A little before San Pedro, Highway 19 rejoins Carretera Transpeninsular north into La Paz; the trip takes 2 to 3 hours. From the north, Carretera Transpeninsular south is the only choice; the trip from Loreto takes 4 to 5 hours.

BY BUS The Central Camionera (main bus station) is at Jalisco and Héroes de la Independencia, about 25 blocks southwest of the center of town; it's open daily from 6am to 10pm. Bus service operates from the south (Los Cabos, 2½–3½ hr.) and north (as far as Tijuana). It's best to buy your ticket in person the day before, though reservations can be made over the phone. Taxis are available in front of the station.

All routes north and south, as well as buses to Pichilingue ($1.50), the ferry pier, and to close outlying beaches, are available through the Transportes Aguila station, sometimes called the beach bus terminal, on the *malecón* at Alvaro Obregón and Cinco de Mayo (© **612/122-7898**). The station is open daily from 6am to 10pm. Buses to Pichilingue depart every hour.

More local destinations are handled from the beach bus station, where the main bus station has more long-distance trips to major points in Baja. Buses from the Central Camionera tend to be more modern and have better facilities.

BY FERRY **Baja Ferries** serves La Paz from Topolobampo (the port for Los Mochis) daily at 3pm (5-hr. crossing). In La Paz, the Baja Ferries office, Isabel La Católica and Navarro (© **612/125-7443** or 612/123-1313), sells tickets. The office is open daily 8am to 6pm. For information, call © **01-800/122-1414** toll-free within Mexico, or 612/123-0208.

The ferry departs for Topolobampo daily at 11pm. The ferries can carry 1,000 passengers as well as accommodate vehicles and trucks. Passengers pay one fee for themselves and another for their vehicles, with prices for cars varying by size. A car less than 5.4m (18 ft.) long costs $120. One-way tickets cost $65, or $33 for children, and include cabin lodging with two or four beds (bunk-style beds, like on a train) and a bathroom. The ferries offer restaurant and bar service, as well as a coffee shop and live music. Disabled access is offered as well. Passengers are requested to arrive 3 hours prior to departure time. Information and updated schedules are available at www.baja ferries.com.

La Paz Area

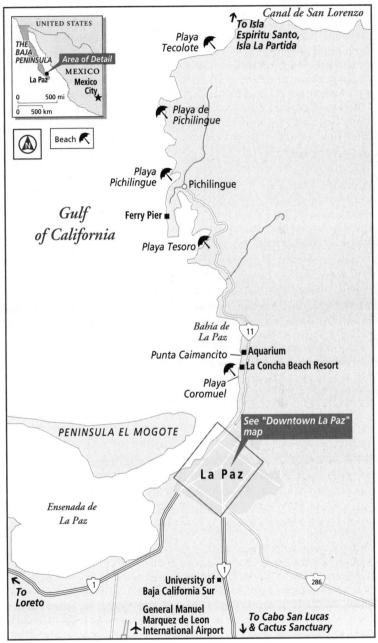

UNITED STATES

THE BAJA PENINSULA

Area of Detail

MEXICO

La Paz

Mexico City

0   500 mi
0   500 km

Beach

Canal de San Lorenzo

To Isla Espiritu Santo, Isla La Partida

Playa Tecolote

Playa de Pichilingue

Playa Pichilingue

Pichilingue

Gulf of California

Ferry Pier

Playa Tesoro

Bahía de La Paz

Punta Caimancito

Aquarium

La Concha Beach Resort

Playa Coromuel

See "Downtown La Paz" map

PENINSULA EL MOGOTE

La Paz

Ensenada de La Paz

To Loreto

University of Baja California Sur

General Manuel Marquez de Leon International Airport

To Cabo San Lucas & Cactus Sanctuary

Reserve your space on the ferry as early as possible and confirm your reservation 24 hours before departure; you can pick up tickets at the port terminal ticket office as late as the morning of the day you are leaving. **Agencia de Viajes Aome,** Cinco de Mayo 502 at Guillermo Prieto (© **612/125-2346,** ext. 1), is the only agency in La Paz authorized to sell ferry tickets. The office is open daily from 8am to 6pm. Several tour agencies in town book reservations on the ferry, but it is best to buy your ticket in person at the ferry office. The dock is at Pichilingue, 18km (11 miles) north of La Paz.

Buses to Pichilingue depart from the beach bus terminal of **Transportes Aguila** (© **612/122-7898**) on the *malecón* at Independencia on the hour, from 7am to 8pm, and cost $2 each way.

ORIENTATION
ARRIVING
BY PLANE   The airport is 18km (11 miles) northwest of town along the highway to Ciudad Constitución and Tijuana. Airport *colectivos* (minivans) run only from the airport to town ($11), not vice versa. Taxi service (around $17) is available as well. Most major car-rental agencies have booths inside the airport. Two local agencies are **Budget** (© **612/124-6433** or 612/122-7655) and **Avis** (© **612/122-6262** or 612/ 122-1813). Also available is **Local Car Rental,** Alvaro Obregón 582 (© **612/123-3622**).

BY BUS   Buses arrive at the Central Camionera, about 25 blocks southwest of downtown, or at the beach station along the *malecón.* Taxis line up in front of both.

BY FERRY   Buses line up in front of the ferry dock at Pichilingue to meet every arriving ferry. They stop at the beach bus station on the *malecón* at Independencia; it's within walking distance of many downtown hotels if you're not encumbered with luggage. Taxis also meet each ferry and cost about $8 to downtown La Paz.

VISITOR INFORMATION
The most accessible visitor information office is on Alvaro Obregón, across from the intersection with Calle 16 de Septiembre (© **612/122-5939;** info@vivalapaz.com). Open daily from 9am to 10pm, the extremely helpful staff here speaks English and can supply information on La Paz, Los Cabos, and the rest of the region. This space doubles as the office for the La Paz Tourist Police, who assist with directions or problems that visitors may encounter. The official website of the La Paz Tourism Board is www.vivalapaz.com.

Moments Festivals & Events in La Paz

February features the biggest and best *carnaval,* or Mardi Gras, in Baja, as well as a month-long Festival of the Gray Whale (starting in Feb or Mar). On May 3, La Fiesta de La Paz (Celebration of Peace) celebrates the city's founding by Cortez in 1535, and features *artesanía* exhibitions from throughout southern Baja. The annual marlin-fishing tournament is in August, with other fishing tournaments in September and November. And on November 1 and 2, the Days of the Dead, altars are on display at the Anthropology Museum. For more events, check www.bajaevents.com.

CITY LAYOUT

Although La Paz sprawls well inland from the *malecón* (the seaside boulevard, Alvaro Obregón), you'll probably spend most of your time in the older, more congenial downtown section within a few blocks of the waterfront. The main plaza, Plaza Pública (or Jardín Velasco), is bounded by Madero, Independencia, Revolución, and Cinco de Mayo. The plaza centers on an iron kiosk where public concerts frequently take place in the evening.

GETTING AROUND

Because most of what you'll need in town is on the *malecón* between the tourist information office and the Hotel Los Arcos, or a few blocks inland from the waterfront, it's easy to get around La Paz on foot. Public buses go to some of the beaches north of town (see "Beaches & Outdoor Activities," below), but to explore the many beaches within 81km (50 miles) of La Paz, your best bet is to rent a car or hire a taxi. Several car-rental agencies have offices on the *malecón*.

FAST FACTS: La Paz

Area Code The telephone area code is **612**.

Banks Banks generally exchange currency during normal business hours: Monday through Friday from 9am to 6pm and Saturday from 10am to 2pm. ATMs are readily available and offer bank exchange rates on withdrawals.

Emergencies Dial ⓒ **066** for general emergency assistance, or **060** for police. Both calls are free.

Hospitals Try **Hospital Especialidades Médicas,** no. 110 in the Fidepaz building, Carretera Aeropuerto Km 4.5 at Delfines (ⓒ **612/124-0400**), and **Hospital Juan María de Salvatierra,** Nicolás Bravo 1010, Col. Centro (ⓒ **612/122-1496**).

Internet Access The best Internet access in town is found at **Don Tomas Cyber Café,** Alvaro Obregón 229, on the corner with Constitución (ⓒ **612/128-5508;** www.jasam-net.com/don_tomas). In addition to Internet access daily from 7am to 11pm, they offer wireless and hookups for laptops, VOIP international calling, translation services, and cafe and bar service for sustenance while you surf. They charge $1.50 per hour. **BajaNet,** Madero 430 (ⓒ **612/125-9380**), charges 1 peso (11¢) per minute, with a $1 (10-min.) minimum charge. It's open Monday through Saturday 8am to 10pm, Sunday 9am to 9pm. Internet access is also available at the **Omni Services Internet Café,** on the *malecón,* Alvaro Obregón 460-C, close to Burger King (ⓒ **612/123-4888**). They also offer hookups for laptops, color printers, and copy, fax, and VOIP phone services to the U.S. and Canada for 30¢ per minute.

Marinas La Paz has two marinas: **Marina de La Paz,** at the west end of the *malecón* at Legaspi (ⓒ **612/125-2112;** marinalapaz@bajavillas.com), and **Club de Yates Palmira,** south of town at Carretera a Pichilingue Km 2.5, Edificio la Plaza (ⓒ **612/121-6172** or 612/121-2300; mpalmira@prodigy.net.mx). The large ships arrive at the commercial port of **Pichilingue,** Carretera a Pichilingue Km 2.5, Puerto Pichilingue (ⓒ **612/122-7010**), 17km (11 miles) from La Paz.

Municipal Market   The public market is 3 blocks inland, at Degollado and Revolución. It mainly sells produce, meats, and utilitarian wares. Hours are Monday through Saturday 6am to 6pm and Sunday 6am to 1pm.

Parking   In high season, street parking may be hard to find in the downtown area, but there are several guarded lots, and side streets are less crowded.

Pharmacy   One of the largest pharmacies is **Farmacia Baja California,** Independencia and Madero (© **612/122-0240** or 612/123-4408). It's open 24 hours.

Post Office   The *correo* is 3 blocks inland, at Constitución and Revolución (© **612/122-0388**); it's open Monday through Friday 8am to 2pm, Saturday 9am to 1pm.

Tourism Office   Located at Carretera al Norte Km 5.5, Edificio Fidepaz (© **612/124-0199**), it's open daily from 8am to 3pm and 5 to 7pm. A tourist information module/booth is also on the *malecón,* open Monday through Saturday from 8am to 8pm.

2 Beaches & Outdoor Activities

La Paz combines the unselfconscious bustle of a small capital port city with beautiful isolated beaches not far from town. Well on its way to becoming the undisputed adventure-tourism capital of Baja, it's the starting point for whale-watching, diving, sea kayaking, climbing, and hiking tours throughout the peninsula. Those interested in day adventures can usually arrange everything mentioned above, plus beach tours, sunset cruises, and visits to the sea lion colony, through travel agencies in major hotels or along the *malecón.* You can also arrange activities through agencies in the United States that specialize in Baja's natural history. (See "The Active Traveler," in chapter 2.)

BEACHES

Within a 10- to 45-minute drive from La Paz lie some of the loveliest beaches in Baja. Many rival those of the Caribbean with their clear, turquoise water.

The beaches that line the ***malecón*** are the most convenient in town. Although the sand is soft and white, and the water appears crystal clear and gentle, locals don't generally swim there. Because La Paz is a commercial port, the water is not considered as clean as that in the very accessible outlying beaches. With its colorful playgrounds dotting the central beachfront, as well as numerous open-air restaurants that front the water, the *malecón* is best for a casual afternoon of post-sightseeing lunch and playtime.

The best beach in the area is immediately north of town at **La Concha Beach Resort;** nonguests may use the hotel restaurant/bar and rent equipment for snorkeling, diving, skiing, and sailing. It's 10km (6¼ miles) north of town on the Pichilingue Highway, at Km 5.5. The other beaches are farther north of town, but midweek you may have these far distant beaches to yourself.

At least 10 public buses from the beach bus station at Independencia on the *malecón* depart from 8am to 5:30pm for beaches to the north. The buses stop at the small **Playa Camancito** (5km/3 miles), **Playa Coromuel** (8km/5 miles), **Playa Tesoro** (14km/8¾ miles), and **Pichilingue** (17km/11 miles); from where the bus lets you off at the ferry stop, walk north on the highway to the beach. Ask when the last bus will make the return trip. Pichilingue, Coromuel, and Tesoro beaches have *palapa*-shaded bars or restaurants, which may not be open midweek. You can pack a lunch and rent a shade umbrella for $1 per group, with tables and chairs available for a minimal additional charge.

The most beautiful of these outlying beaches is **Playa Tecolote** ᖇᖇ, approximately 29km (18 miles) from La Paz at the end of a paved road. The water is a heavenly cerulean blue and there are several restaurants. To get to Playa Tecolote on your own, take a bus to Pichilingue; from there, take a taxi the remaining 13km (8 miles). When the taxi drops you off, make arrangements for it to return. The road is paved as far as Playa Tecolote and Playa Balandra (29km/18 miles; good but with no services), and turnoffs to these and other beaches are well marked.

For more information about beaches and maps, check at the tourist information office on the *malecón*. If you want to take a general tour of all the beaches before deciding where to spend your precious vacation days, **Viajes Lybs** (✆ 612/122-4680) offers a 4-hour beach tour for $22 per person, with stops at Pichilingue, Balandra, and El Tecolote beaches.

CRUISES

A popular and very worthwhile cruise is to **Isla Espíritu Santo** and **Los Islotes** to visit the largest sea lion colony in Baja, stunning rock formations, and remote beaches, with stops for snorkeling, swimming, and lunch. If conditions permit, you may even be able to snorkel beside the sea lions. Both boat and bus tours are available to **Puerto Balandra,** where bold rock formations rising up like humpback whales frame pristine coves of crystal-blue water and ivory sand. **Viajes Palmira,** on the *malecón* across from Hotel Los Arcos (✆ 612/122-4030), **Viajes Lybs,** 16 de Septiembre 408, between Revolución and Serdán (✆ 612/122-4680; fax 612/125-9600), and other travel agencies can arrange these all-day trips, weather permitting, for $67 per person.

WATERSPORTS

SCUBA DIVING   Scuba-diving trips are best from June through September. You can arrange them through Fernando Aguilar's **Baja Diving and Services,** Obregón 1665-2 (✆ 612/122-1826; fax 612/122-8644; www.clubcantamar.com). Diving sites include the sea lion colony at Los Islotes, distant Cerralvo Island, the sunken ship *Salvatierra,* a 18m (59-ft.) wall dive, and several sea mounts (underwater mountains) and reefs. Also available is a trip to see hammerhead sharks and manta rays. Rates start at $92 per person for an all-day outing and two-tank dive. Baja Diving also has a 40-unit sports lodge and beach resort, **Club Hotel Cantamar** (✆ 612/122-7010). Rates for a double room run about $65.

Other excellent dive operators include **Baja Quest,** at Navarro 55, between Abasolo and Topete (✆ 612/123-5320; www.bajaquest.com.mx), and **Sea & Scuba,** on the *malecón,* at Ocampo (✆ 612/123-5233). Day boat trips runs approximately $77 for two tank dives. Also of note is **DeSea Adventures,** Marina Palmira L3, Carretera a Pichilingue Km 2.5 (✆ 612/121-5100; www.deseabaja.com), a complete tour company with an expertise in diving. Prices are $145 for three-tank dives including equipment, or $170 including a resort dive course. DeSea also has private boats with guides for underwater photo or video diving, and private divemaster or instructors for yachts or charters. DeSea also offers **free diving,** including instruction from internationally experienced free-dive instructors Aharon and María Teresa Solomon. Courses include yoga-based breathing exercises, mental control, and the physiology of breath hold. Beginning through advanced instruction is available, as are live-aboard charters and spear-fishing instruction.

La Paz's Top Dive Spots

La Paz is among the world's great dive destinations: More than 25 dive sites surround the islands outside La Paz's bay, such as Espíritu Santo, San José, and Cerralvo. What sets La Paz diving apart is the opportunity to view giant mantas, sea lions, and impressive numbers of sharks, including whale sharks and hammerheads. Here are the area's favorite dive sites:

• **El Bajo:** Advanced divers revel in the underwater mountain rising to 18m (60 ft.) from the surface, with a relatively flat top. It's especially notable for its schooling hammerhead sharks; six to hundreds travel clockwise around the seamount for unknown reasons. You're also likely to see Panamic green morays; over 50 live in a small canyon on the mountain. Additional seamounts nearby have peaks at between 18 and 45m (60–150 ft.) from the surface; visibility is good year-round.

• **El Bajito:** Just next to the Los Islotes sea lion colony is this beautiful dive site where crevices in the sea floor are covered in soft corals.

• **Isla Los Islotes:** Divers here can view the underwater rock caves and frolic with the friendly colony of sea lions. The two large rock islands, one of which is a natural arch whose center you can dive through, are a 1½-hour boat ride from La Paz, north of Espíritu Santo, and offer depths of 4.5 to 30m (15–100 ft.).

• **La Reina and La Reinita:** Enjoy a wreck dive and wall diving to 45m (150-ft.) depths at these islets in front of Cerralvo Island, 1½ hours from La Paz. You'll see brain coral, tropical fish, rays, and several types of morays here. During the summer you can see giant seahorses. Whale encounters are common in the channel during season while heading toward this site.

• **Las Animas:** The strong currents surrounding a collection of tiny islets in front of San José Island maintain a permanent population of pelagic fish, making for a great dive site, popular for extended live-aboard trips.

• **Salvatierra Wreck:** In 1976, this 75m (250-ft.) ferryboat sank after colliding with a nearby reef. It now lies on a sandbar at a depth of 18m (60 ft.) in the San Lorenzo Channel and the southern end of Espíritu Santo. Filled with sea life, it makes for a fascinating dive site and is good for novice divers.

• **San Francisquito:** Similar to El Bajo, this popular site for advanced divers, with varied depths, has an abundance of sea life.

• **Whale Island:** This small, whale-shaped island has dive-through caves, crevices, rocky reefs, and a coral forest at depths from 6 to 18m (20–60 ft.). Between the caves is a sand shelf containing a large "garden" of conger eels, which extend their bodies vertically from the sea floor and sway in the currents while feeding on passing morsels. This area is tranquil and protected from wind; its mild current makes it a good choice for beginning divers, or for a second dive of the day.

• Two rusting Chinese long liner boats, the *Lapas 03* and the *Fang Ming,* were sunk in 1999 near Whale Island to promote **artificial reef** development for sport diving. They're at a depth of 21m (70 ft.) and offer full penetration diving over numerous levels.

Another excellent dive operator is **Grupo Fun Baja,** Reforma 395, on the corner of Guillermo Prieto (© **612/121-5884** or 612/125-2366; www.funbaja.com; daily 8am–8pm), which offers one- or two-tank dive trips to all the top area dive sites, as well as scuba camping trips. These trips combine diving and camping on the island of Espíritu Santo. All equipment for camping is provided, with comfortable twin-size beds. A chef prepares the meals, providing a changing menu that may include fresh fish, clams, chicken, or vegetarian fare upon request. The Mini Safari scuba-camping trip lasts 2 days and 1 night, while the Big Safari trip is 4 days and 3 nights. Safari Packages include all camping gear, meals, and drinks (mineral water, soft drinks, beer, tequila), as well as basic bathroom facilities (toilet and shower with fresh water). The Mini Safari costs $440 per person with dives, or $289 without dives; the Big Safari costs $999 with dives, or $599 without dives.

Baja Expeditions, Sonora 586 (© **612/125-3828;** fax 612/125-3829; www.baja ex.com; daily 8am–8pm), runs live-aboard and single-day dive trips to the above-mentioned locations and other areas in the Sea of Cortez. The cost is $110 for a two-tank dive. See p. 32, for contact information in the U.S. and Canada.

SEA KAYAKING Kayaking in the many bays and coves near La Paz has become extremely popular, as many of the area's special sites for swimming and snorkeling are accessible only by kayak. In the waters near La Paz, you have the sensation of being suspended in the air because of the transparency of the water. Many enthusiasts bring their own equipment. Several companies from the United States can arrange kayaking trips in advance (see "The Active Traveler," in chapter 2, for more information). Locally, **Baja Quest,** at Navarro 55, between Abasolo and Topete (© **612/123-5320;** www.bajaquest.com.mx), and **Mar y Aventuras,** Topete 564, between 5 de Febrero and Navarro (© **612/122-7039** or 612/125-4794; www.kayakbaja.com), also arrange kayaking trips.

SPORTFISHING La Paz, justly famous for its sportfishing, attracts anglers from all over the world to its waters, home to more than 850 species of fish. The most economical approach is to rent a *panga* (skiff) with guide and equipment for $125 for 3 hours—but you don't go very far out. Super *pangas,* which have a shade cover and comfortable seats, start at around $180 for two people. Larger cruisers with bathrooms start at $240.

You can arrange sportfishing trips locally through hotels and tour agencies. David Jones of **The Fishermen's Fleet** (© **612/122-1313;** fax 612/125-7334; www.fishermensfleet.com) uses the locally popular *panga*-style fishing boat. He is superprofessional, speaks English, and truly understands area fishing. The average price is $225 for the boat, but double-check what the price includes—you may need to bring your own food and drinks.

WHALE-WATCHING Between January and March (and sometimes as early as Dec), 3,000 to 5,000 gray whales migrate from the Bering Strait to the Pacific coast of Baja. The main whale-watching spots are **Laguna San Ignacio** (on the Pacific, near San Ignacio), **Bahía Magdalena** (on the Pacific, near Puerto López Mateos—about a 2-hr. drive from La Paz), and **Scammon's Lagoon** (near Guerrero Negro).

Although it is across the peninsula on the Sea of Cortez, La Paz has the only major international airport in the area and thus has become a center of Baja's whale-watching excursions. Most tours originating in La Paz go to Bahía Magdalena, where the whales give birth in calm waters. Several companies arrange whale-watching tours originating in La Paz or other Baja towns or in the United States; 12-hour tours from La Paz start at around $106 per person, including breakfast, lunch, transportation, and an English-speaking guide. Make reservations at **Viajes Lybs,** 16 de Septiembre 408, between Revolución and Serdán (© **612/122-4680;** fax 612/125-9600).

Most tours from the United States offer birding, sea kayaking, and other close-to-nature experiences during the same trip. See "The Active Traveler," in chapter 2, for details.

You can go whale-watching without joining a tour by taking a bus from La Paz to Puerto López Mateos or Puerto San Carlos at Magdalena Bay (a 3-hr. ride) and hiring a boat there. It's a long trip to do in a day, but there are a few modest hotels in San Carlos. Check at the La Paz tourist office for information.

For a more in-depth discussion, see "Whale-Watching in Baja: A Primer" on p. 136.

ECOTOURS

A wide selection of ecotours and adventure activities are available through **Grupo Fun Baja,** Reforma 395, on the corner of Guillermo Prieto (© **612/121-5884** or 612/125-2366; www.funbaja.com; daily 8am–8pm). In addition to diving excursions (the company's specialty) they also offer ATV tours and kite surfing. **DeSea Adventures,** Marina Palmira L3, Carretera a Pichilingue Km 2.5 (© **612/121-5100;** www.desea baja.com), has a fleet of vehicles available and equipped for off-road adventures and also offers specialized Adventures Packages of preset itineraries for exploring the area that are either guided or self-driven. Their popular guided 1-day La Paz excursion

---

Snorkeling with Baja's Sea Lions

Among the many treasures of Baja Mexico, prime among them are the colonies of sea lions that live in the Sea of Cortez. These playful, curious sea creatures prove a powerful lure for many travelers to this area. One of the largest colonies is found at Los Islotes, a cluster of tiny red-rock islands north of La Paz, the desert capital of Baja, Mexico. The islands' claim to fame is that they're the year-round home to a colony or "rookery" of some 250 California brown sea lions.

Many tour operators in La Paz offer trips to Los Islotes, generally in *pangas*—the trip, by boat, takes about 2½ hours from La Paz. Here, the sea lions lay in the sun along the jagged rock shelves, bark out greetings to visitors, and occasionally belly-flop into the water.

Trip participants don wet suits and snorkels to join the sea lions, which will occasionally nip at your flippers or nuzzle you. They also seem to enjoy showing off their underwater antics and acrobatic skills.

California sea lions are considered to be the smartest of the pinnipeds, the class of mammals with flippers. The chocolate-brown "bulls" can weigh up to 1,000 pounds, and can occasionally become aggressive. These bulls seldom join the snorkelers; it is generally the moms or young pups that frolic in the waters with humans.

Among the operators offering sea-lion snorkeling trips is **Cortez Club,** at the La Concha Beach Resort (© **612/121-6120;** www.cortezclub.com). The full-day excursion departs at 8:30am and costs $70 per person, which includes wet suit, snorkel gear, and a box lunch, which you'll eat on the beach at Isla Partida. Dive trips are also available, with depths at Los Islotes averaging 7½ to 15m (25–49 ft.).

takes you to a local pottery workshop then on to the old mining town of El Triunfo to hike up to the mines and other historical points of interest. On the way home, there's a stop for lunch and a brief visit to a traditional weaver's shop. The tour costs $120, and includes guide, transportation, and lunch.

3 A Break from the Beaches: Exploring La Paz

Most tour agencies offer city tours of all of La Paz's major sights. Tours last 2 to 3 hours, include time for shopping, and cost around $15 per person.

HISTORIC LA PAZ

When Cortez landed here on May 3, 1535, he named it Bahía Santa Cruz. The name didn't stick. In April 1683, Eusebio Kino, a Spanish Jesuit priest, arrived and dubbed the place Nuestra Señora de la Paz (Our Lady of Peace). It wasn't until November 1, 1720, however, that Jaime Bravo, another Jesuit priest, set up a permanent mission. He used the same name as his immediate predecessor, calling it the Misión de Nuestra Señora de la Paz. The mission church stands on La Paz's main square on Revolución between Cinco de Mayo and Independencia, and today the city is called simply La Paz.

Museo de Antropología (Anthropology Museum) ⓡ   This museum features large, though faded, color photos of Baja's prehistoric cave paintings. There are also exhibits on various topics, including the geological history of the peninsula, fossils, missions, colonial history, and daily life. All information is in Spanish.

Corner of Altamirano and Cinco de Mayo. ⓒ **612/122-0162** or 612/125-6424. Free admission (donations encouraged). Daily 9am–6pm.

Biblioteca de las Californias   The small collection of historical documents and books at the Library of the Californias is the most comprehensive in Baja. The library sometimes shows free international films in the evening.

In the Casa de Gobierno, across the plaza from the mission church on Madero, between Cinco de Mayo and Independencia. For information, call the tourism office at ⓒ **612/122-2640.** Free admission. Mon–Fri 8am–3pm.

El Teatro de la Ciudad   The city theater is La Paz's cultural center, with performances by visiting and local artists. There's no extended calendar available, but bookings include small ballet companies, experimental and popular theater, popular music, and an occasional classical concert or symphony. Contact the box office for details and ticket prices.

Av. Navarro 700, corner of Independencia. ⓒ **612/125-0486.**

NATURE MUSEUMS OF LA PAZ

Increasingly, La Paz is drawing a number of travelers enchanted with the beauty of the area's diverse natural environment. Several new centers have emerged, combining entertainment with environmental education, which I've listed below. You may see information about an open-water **Dolphinarium** in La Paz, but it was closed after hurricanes damaged the facilities in 2003 and put the dolphins at risk (they were transferred to Dolphin Adventures in Puerto Vallarta, where they are now thriving). However, there is talk of repairing and reopening the facility at some point.

Aquarium ⓡ   The newest of La Paz's natural museums opened in late 2003 and offers opportunities to view the abundance of sea life found offshore. Among the Sea of Cortez species on display here are the Cortez angel and seahorses.

Pichilingue Km 5.5, next to the Hotel Concha. ⓒ **612/121-5872.** Admission $5 adults, $2 children. Daily 10am–2pm.

Downtown La Paz

To Airport

Bahia de La Paz

1 2 3
4 5

Alvaro Obregón

6

9
8 **10** **ⓘ**

To Ferry Terminal →

13

Manuel Pineda

Francisco Madero

7

11

Revolución de 1910

14

16 de Septiembre

12

Independencia

✝ **Cathedral**

Ignacio Allende

Aquiles Serdán

15

Antonio Rosales

16

5 de Mayo

19

20 →

Church ✝
Information ⓘ
Post Office ✉

Ignacio Altamirano

17
Degollado

Valentín Gómez Farías

18

Miguel Hidalgo y Costilla

ACCOMMODATIONS ■
Crowne Plaza **3**
Hacienda del Cortez **2**
Hotel Los Arcos **6**
Hotel Mediterrane **15**
La Concha Beach Resort **1**
Posada de las Flores **13**

Josefa Ortíz de Domínguez

Lic. Primo Verdad

Constitución

Marcelo Rubio R.

ATTRACTIONS ●
Antigua California **10**
Artesanías Cuauhtémoc
  (The Weaver) **5**
Biblioteca de las Californias **12**
Chinatown **9**

Dorian's **7**
El Teatro de la Ciudad **20**
Ibarra's Pottery **19**
Municipal Market **16**
Serpentarium **4**
The Anthropology Museum **18**

DINING ◆
Bismark II **17**
Caffe Expresso **8**
El Quinto Sol **11**
Trattoria La Pazta **14**

Cactus Sanctuary 𝄞   This 50-hectare (124-acre) natural reserve features 1,000m (over a half-mile) of marked pathways and self-guided tours with information about the plants and animals of La Paz's desert region. Fifty unique areas have been identified, which you can explore in consecutive order or any progression of your choosing. Route maps and guided tours are available as are descriptive signs for many of the plants. There's a surprising amount of wildlife to see here, from the many types of cacti to the numerous plants and animals that support this unique ecosystem. The sanctuary is in the Ejido El Rosario (an *ejido* is a village that is a community-owned piece of land). Go to the *ejido*'s *delegación* (main office), and they will provide you with a key to enter the reserve. Although the sanctuary itself has no phone or posted hours, you can contact its director, Dr. Héctor Nolasco, for information (ⓒ **612/124-0245;** hnolasco@cibnor.mx).

Ejido El Rosario. Free admission (donations encouraged). 45 min. south along Carretera Transpeninsular toward the town of El Triunfo, then 10 min. inland along a dirt road.

Serpentarium 𝄞   This mostly open-air natural museum offers plenty of opportunities to observe various species of reptiles that inhabit the region's ecosystem, including snakes, turtles, iguanas, lizards, and crocodiles.

Calles Brecha California and La Posada. ⓒ **612/123-5731.** Admission $3 adults, $1 children. Daily 10am–4pm. Go to the southernmost point of the *malecón* at Calle Abasola, where the last streetlights are. Just before the beach you'll see an unpaved street, which is Brecha California.

4 Shopping

La Paz has little in the way of folk art or other treasures from mainland Mexico. But the dense cluster of streets behind the **Hotel Perla,** between 16 de Septiembre and Degollado, abounds with small shops, some tacky, others quite upscale. This area also holds a very small but authentic **Chinatown** dating to the time when Chinese laborers were brought to settle in Baja. Serdán street, from Degollado south, offers dozens of sellers of dried spices, piñatas, and candy. Stores selling crafts, folk art, clothing, and handmade furniture and accessories lie mostly along the *malecón* (Alvaro Obregón) or a block or two in. The **municipal market,** at Revolución and Degollado, has little of interest to visitors. Something you're sure to notice if you explore around the central plaza is the abundance of stores selling electronic equipment, including stereos, cameras, and televisions. This is because La Paz is a principal port for electronic imports to Mexico from the Far East, and therefore offers some of the best prices in Baja and mainland Mexico.

Antigua California   This shop manages to stay in business as others come and go. It carries a good selection of folk art from throughout Mexico. It's open Monday to Saturday from 9:30am to 8:30pm, Sunday from 10am to 3pm. Paseo Alvaro Obregón 220, at Arreola. ⓒ **612/125-5230.**

Artesanías Cuauhtémoc (The Weaver)   If you like beautiful hand-woven tablecloths, place mats, rugs, and other textiles, it's worth the long walk or taxi ride to this unique shop where Fortunato Silva, an elderly gentleman, weaves wonderfully textured cotton textiles from yarn he spins and dyes himself. He charges far less than what you'd pay for equivalent artistry in the United States. Open Monday through Saturday from 10am to 3pm and 5 to 8pm, and Sunday from 10am to 1pm. Abasolo 3315, between Jalisco and Nayarit. ⓒ **612/122-4575.**

Dorian's   If you've forgotten essentials or want to stock up on duty-free perfumes or cosmetics, head for Dorian's, La Paz's major department store. La Paz is a duty-free port city, so prices are excellent. Dorian's carries a wide selection of stylish clothing, shoes, lingerie, jewelry, and accessories. Open daily from 10am to 9pm. 16 de Septiembre, between Esquerro and 21 de Agosto. ⓒ **612/122-8014.**

Ibarra's Pottery   Here, you not only shop for tableware, hand-painted tiles, and decorative pottery, you can watch it being made. Each piece is individually hand-painted or glazed, then fired. Open Monday to Friday from 9am to 3pm, and occasionally on Saturdays if they have a scheduled tour coming through—you can call to see if they're open on a particular Saturday. Guillermo Prieto 625, between Torre Iglesias and República. ⓒ **612/122-0404.**

5 Where to Stay

EXPENSIVE

Crowne Plaza ⓐ   Among La Paz's newest options in places to stay, this hotel offers travelers a comfortable sense of U.S. standards and modern conveniences. It's considered the best option for business travelers to the area, one of the few places in town with a full business center, Internet access, secretarial assistance, and meeting space. Vacationers will also enjoy the hotel's location on the marina as well as its range of helpful tour services and pleasant pool area. The clean, modern, and well-equipped rooms on three floors offer either views to the bay or overlooking the courtyard pool. Suites have a private balcony, and all have ocean views. The hotel is at the northern end of town, 3½ miles from downtown, at the Marina Fidepaz.

Lote A, Marina Fidepaz, P.O. Box 482, 23090 La Paz, B.C.S. ℂ 800/227-6963, 612/124-0830, or 612/124-0833. Fax 612/124-0837. www.crowneplaza.com. 108 units. High season $128–$135 double, $243 suite; low season $108–$120 double, $195 suite. AE, DC, MC, V. Free guarded parking. **Amenities:** Restaurant; 2 bars; pool; sauna; whirlpool; fitness center; full business center; concierge; tour desk; gift shop; room service; babysitting service; laundry service. *In room:* A/C, TV, coffeemaker, hair dryer, iron.

Posada de las Flores ⟨⟨ *Finds*   New owner Giuseppe Marceletti has continued the tradition of hospitality in this elegant B&B (formerly known as Posada Santa Fe), the best bet for travelers looking for a more refined place to stay in La Paz (at the northern end of the *malecón*). Each room is individually decorated with high-quality Mexican furniture and antiques, hand-loomed fabrics, and exquisite artisan details. Bathrooms are especially welcoming, with marble tubs and thick towels. Breakfast is served from 8 to 11am daily, and rates include wake-up service with in-room coffee.

Alvaro Obregón 440, 23000 La Paz, B.C.S. ℂ 612/125-5871. www.posadadelasflores.com. 8 units. $140 double; $199 suite; $450 master suite. Rates include American breakfast. MC, V. No children allowed. **Amenities:** Small pool; Internet service available through the office. *In room:* A/C, TV, minibar.

MODERATE

Hacienda del Cortez ⟨⟨   This unique beachfront boutique hotel offers guests highly personalized service in a comfortable, casual setting. The colonial-style hacienda is surrounded by tall palm trees and has a large beachfront swimming pool and *palapa* bar. Rooms are cozy, with colonial-style decor and antique details that make it feel less like a hotel and more like a guesthouse. The casita ("little house," or cottage) option is much larger, with a separate living room area. Guests congregate at the waterfront *palapa* bar, and the hotel's restaurant, featuring Mexican fare, is especially popular.

Nueva Reforma y Playa Sur, 23000 La Paz, B.C.S. ℂ 612/122-9999 or 612/122-9996. Fax 612/122-9997. www. haciendadelcortez.net. 25 units. High season $75–$115 double, $150 casita; low season $65–$95, double, $125 casita. MC, V. Free parking. **Amenities:** Restaurant; indoor/outdoor bar; pool; tour desk; Internet facility; room service; laundry service. *In room:* A/C, TV, coffeemaker.

Hotel Los Arcos ⟨⟨ *Value*   This three-story neocolonial-style hotel at the west end of the *malecón* is the best place for downtown accommodations with a touch of tranquillity. Los Arcos is functional in its furnishings and amenities, and the hotel's rambling nooks and crannies are filled with fountains, plants, and even rocking chairs that lend lots of old-fashioned charm. Most of the rooms and suites come with two double beds and a balcony overlooking the pool in the inner courtyard or the waterfront, plus coffeemaker and Jacuzzi tub. I prefer the South Pacific–style bungalows with thatched roofs and fireplaces in the back part of the property—in an appealing jungle garden shaded by large trees.

Alvaro Obregón 498, between Rosales and Allende (Apdo. Postal 112), 23000 La Paz, B.C.S. ℂ 800/347-2252 or 714/450-9000 in the U.S., or 612/122-2744. Fax 612/125-4313. www.losarcos.com. 130 units. $95 double; $105 suite; $75–$95 bungalow. AE, MC, V. Free guarded parking. **Amenities:** Restaurant; cafeteria; bar w/live music; 2 pools (1 heated); sauna; travel agency; desk for fishing information; room service; laundry; Ping-Pong tables. *In room:* A/C, TV, minibar.

La Concha Beach Resort 🏨🏨 This resort's setting, 10km (6¼ miles) north of downtown La Paz, on a curved beach ideal for swimming and watersports, is perfect. All rooms face the water and have double beds, balconies or patios, and small tables and chairs. Studio and three-bedroom condos with full kitchens are available on a nightly basis in the high-rise complex next door, and are worth the extra price for a family vacation. The hotel offers scuba, fishing, whale-watching, and a variety of other specialty packages.

Carretera a Pichilingue Km 5, 23000 La Paz, B.C.S. © **800/999-2252**, 612/121-6161, or 612/121-6344. Fax 612/122-8644. www.laconcha.com. 113 units. $95 double; $125 junior suite; $137–$259 condo. Weekly rates are available for condo rentals. AE, DC, MC, V. Free guarded parking. **Amenities:** Restaurant (w/theme nights); 2 bars; beachside pool; complete watersports center w/WaveRunners, kayaks, and paddleboats; beach club w/scuba program available; tour desk; free twice-daily shuttle to town; room service; laundry service. *In room:* A/C, TV.

INEXPENSIVE
Hotel Mediterrane 🏨🏨 Simple yet stylish, this unique inn mixes Mediterranean with Mexican, making a cozy place for couples or friends to share. All rooms face an interior courtyard and have white-tile floors and *equipal* furniture (a common type of Mexican furniture made from tanned leather and woven branches, rustic in style, and though inexpensive, durable and attractive), with colorful Mexican serapes draped over the beds. The location is great—just a block from the *malecón*. The adjacent Trattoria La Pazta restaurant (see "Where to Dine," below) is one of La Paz's best. Rates include the use of kayaks and bicycles for exploring the town and wireless Internet access. Those not traveling with their laptop can use the computer center, included with the rates. This is a gay-friendly hotel.

Allende 36, 23000 La Paz, B.C.S. ©/fax **612/125-1195**. www.hotelmed.com. 8 units. Low season $55–$60 double; high season $60–$75 double; year-round $80 suite. Weekly discounts available. AE, MC, V. **Amenities:** Sports equipment; wireless Internet access; computer center. *In room:* A/C, TV/VCR, minifridge (in some).

6 Where to Dine

Although La Paz is not known for culinary achievements, it has a growing assortment of small, pleasant restaurants that are good and reasonably priced. In addition to the usual seafood and Mexican dishes, you can find Italian, French, Spanish, Chinese, and even vegetarian offerings in town. Restaurants along the seaside *malecón* tend to be more expensive than those a few blocks inland. Generally, restaurant reservations are unnecessary, except perhaps during Easter and Christmas weeks.

MODERATE
Bismark II 🏨 SEAFOOD/MEXICAN Bismark excels at seafood; you can order fish tacos, chiles rellenos stuffed with lobster salad, marlin "meatballs" and paella, breaded oysters, or a sundae glass filled with ceviche or shrimp. The kitchen prepares extremely fresh dorado, halibut, snapper, or whatever else is in season in a number of ways. Chips and creamy dip are served while you wait. It's a good place to linger over a late lunch. The decor of pine walls and dark wood chairs is reminiscent of a country cafe.

Degollado and Altamirano. © **612/122-4854**. Breakfast $2–$5; main courses $4–$17. Daily 10am–10pm. Walk 7 blocks inland on Degollado to Altamirano.

Trattoria La Pazta 🏨🏨 ITALIAN/SWISS The trendiest restaurant in town, La Pazta gleams with black lacquered tables and white tile as the aromas of garlic and espresso float in the air. The menu features local fresh seafood such as pasta with squid in wine-and-cream sauce and crispy fried calamari. The lasagna is homemade, baked in a wood-fired oven. An extensive wine list complements the menu. La Pazta is also appealing for breakfast, or you can simply opt for an espresso and croissant. The restaurant is in front of the Hotel Mediterrane.

Allende 36, 1 block inland from the *malecón*. © 612/125-1195. Main courses $8–$11; breakfast $2–$4. AE, MC, V. Wed–Mon 7am–11pm.

INEXPENSIVE

Caffé Expresso FRENCH/CAFE   You'll feel you've suddenly been transported across the Atlantic and onto the Continent in this incongruous but welcome addition to La Paz. Indulge in any number of espresso coffee drinks, plus French and Austrian pastries, while sitting at marble-topped bistro tables listening to the jazz music playing in the background.

Av. Obregón and 16 de Septiembre. © 612/123-4373. Coffees and pastries $1–$3. No credit cards. Mon–Sat 7am–8pm; Sun 9am–3pm.

El Quinto Sol *(Finds* VEGETARIAN   Not only is this La Paz's principle health food market, it's a cheerful, excellent cafe for fresh-fruit *licuados* (shakes), tortas, and vegetarian dishes. Tables sit beside oversize wood-framed windows, with flowering planters in the sills. Sandwiches are served on whole-grain bread—also available for sale—and the potato tacos are an excellent way for vegetarians to indulge in a Mexican staple.

Av. Independencia and B. Domínguez. © 612/122-1692. Main courses $1.50–$6.50. No credit cards. Mon–Sat 7:30am–10pm; Sun 10am–4pm.

7 La Paz After Dark

A night in La Paz logically begins in a cafe along the *malecón* as the sun sinks into the sea—have your camera ready.

A favorite ringside seat at dusk is a table at **La Terraza,** next to the Hotel Perla (© 612/122-0777). La Terraza makes good, schooner-size margaritas. **Pelícanos Bar,** on the second story of the Hotel Los Arcos (© 612/122-2744), has a good view of the waterfront and a clubby, cozy feel. **Carlos 'n' Charlie's La Paz-Lapa** (© 612/122-9290) has live music on the weekends. **La Cabaña** (© 612/122-0777) nightclub in the Hotel Perla features Latin rhythms. It opens at 9:30pm daily, and there's a $5 minimum.

For dancing, a few of the hottest clubs are: **Video Disco Okey Lasser Club** (© 612/122-3133), Alvaro Obregón and Degollado, which plays dance music from the '70s to '90s. **Las Varitas** (© 612/125-2025), Independencia and Dominguez, plays Latin rock, ranchero, and salsa. Both are open from 9pm to 3 or 4am Thursday through Saturday (occasionally open earlier in the week as well), with cover charges around $3 (the charge may be waived or increased, depending on the crowd).

The poolside bar overlooking the beach at **La Concha Beach Resort** (© 612/121-6161 or 612/121-6344), Carretera a Pichilingue Km 5.5, is the setting for the ubiquitous Mexican fiesta Friday at 7pm. The price is $18, including tax and tips, for which you'll get a buffet dinner, drinks, and a show. It's a touristy event that's nevertheless very popular.

Mid-Baja: Loreto, Mulegé & Santa Rosalía

Halfway between the resort sophistication of Los Cabos (see chapter 4) and the frontier exuberance of Tijuana (see chapter 7) lies Baja's midsection, an area rich in history and culture. UNESCO has named the area's indigenous cave paintings a World Heritage Site, and the area was home to numerous Jesuit missions in the 1700s. These days, travelers come to experience the quiet side of Baja and its remote, wild natural beauty. The area is also known for its excellent sea kayaking, sportfishing, and hiking.

Overlooked by many travelers—except avid, informed sportfishers—**Loreto** is a rare gem that sparkles under the desert sky. Here, the purple hues of the Sierra de la Giganta mountains meet the indigo waters of the Sea of Cortez, providing a spectacular backdrop of natural contrasts for the town's historical past. **Mulegé** is, quite literally, an oasis in the Baja desert. The only freshwater river (Río Mulegé) in the peninsula flows through town; it's a lush, green place, with towering date palms, olive groves, citrus trees, and flowering gardens. And the port town of **Santa Rosalía,** while slightly past its prime, makes a worthy detour, with its pastel clapboard houses and unusual steel-and-stained-glass church designed by Gustave Eiffel (of Eiffel Tower fame).

The region is also a popular jumping-off point for many whale-watching tours; to find out when, where, and how to view these gentle giants, consult "Whale-Watching in Baja: A Primer," at the end of this chapter.

1 Loreto & the Offshore Islands ★★

389km (241 miles) NW of La Paz; 533km (330 miles) N of Cabo San Lucas; 1,125km (698 miles) SE of Tijuana

The unpretentious feel of the town of Loreto belies its historical importance. Loreto was the center of the Spanish mission effort during colonial times, the first capital of the Californias, and the first European settlement in the peninsula. Founded on October 25, 1697, it was Father Juan María Salvatierra's choice as the site of the first mission in the Californias. (California, at the time, extended from Cabo San Lucas in the south to the Oregon border in the north.) He held Mass beneath a figure of the Virgin of Loreto, brought from a town in Italy bearing the same name. For 132 years Loreto served as the state capital, until an 1829 hurricane destroyed most of the town. The state capital moved to La Paz (see chapter 5) the following year.

During the late 1970s and early '80s, the Mexican government saw in Loreto the possibility for another megadevelopment along the lines of Cancún, Ixtapa, or Huatulco. It invested in a golf course and championship tennis facility, modernized the town's infrastructure, and built an international airport and full marina facilities at

Puerto Loreto, 26km (16 miles) south of town. The economics, however, didn't make sense at the time, and few hotel investors and even fewer tourists came. In the past 2 years, however, this effort has been revitalized, and the area is seeing a welcome influx of flights, as well as the addition of its first new hotel in years, a stunning new Camino Real (p. 119). The Loreto Bay development company, which is building a real estate community south of Loreto, has been a major part of the renewed interest in the area, and will bring homes, condos, and other facilities to the region, with a rental program in place for vacation stays (© 877/TO-LORETO toll-free from the U.S. for rental information). It's still in its embryonic stage, but has contributed to making Loreto a place to keep your eye on; expect a growing awareness of the area and popularity among travelers looking for the next "new" place to go.

But for now, Loreto remains the wonderfully funky fishing village and well-kept secret it's been for decades. The celebration of the town's 300th anniversary in 1997 had the added benefit of updating the streets, plaza, and mission: Old Town Loreto is now a quaint showplace.

The main reasons to come to Loreto center on the Sea of Cortez and the five islands just offshore with their exceptional kayaking, sailing, diving, and fishing. Isla del Carmen and Isla Danzante are wonderful overnight sailing destinations, and kayakers launch here for trips to the offshore islands or down the remote coast of the Sierra de la Giganta to La Paz. An abandoned salt-mining town lies on the northwestern tip of Isla del Carmen, and rumors peg it as the site of a new hotel, complete with a landing strip. For the present, though, simply enjoy the island as it is—a remote sanctuary for desert wildlife.

ESSENTIALS
GETTING THERE & DEPARTING
BY PLANE   The **Loreto International Airport** (airport code: LTO; © 613/135-0499) is 6km (3¾ miles) southwest of Loreto. It is serviced by **AeroCalifornia** (© 800/237-6225 in the U.S., 613/135-0500, or 613/135-0555; fax 613/135-0566), which has direct flights from Los Angeles; **Aeromexico** (© 800/237-6639 in the U.S., or 613/135-1837; fax 613/135-1838), which has direct flights from Los Angeles, Ontario, San Diego, Phoenix, and Las Vegas; and **Alaska Airlines** (© 800/252-7522; www.alaskaair.com), which has flights from Los Angeles, San Francisco, and Spokane, Washington.

BY CAR   From La Paz (a 4½–5 hr. drive), take Carretera Transpeninsular northwest to Ciudad Constitución; from there, continue northeast on Carretera Transpeninsular to Loreto. This route takes you twice over the mountain range that stretches down the Baja peninsula, through mountain and desert landscapes, and into the heart of the old mission country. From Tijuana, travel south on Carretera Transpeninsular. The drive takes 17 to 20 hours straight into Loreto.

BY BUS   The bus station, or Terminal de Autobuses (© 613/135-0767), is on Salvatierra and Paseo Tamaral, a 10-minute walk from downtown. It's open 24 hours. Buses stop in Loreto en route to Santa Rosalía, Tijuana, Mexicali, Guerrero Negro, and La Paz. The trip to La Paz takes 5 hours. You can usually get a ticket for any bus, except during Easter, summer, and Christmas holidays, when buses tend to be more crowded. The bus terminal is a simple building and the staff there is very friendly and helpful.

The Lower Baja Peninsula

0   50 mi
0   50 km

Airport ✈
Beach ↗

Bahía de Sebastián Vizcaíno

Playa San Rafael

B. San Rafael

Bahía Tortugas

Guerrero Negro

Pto. Nuevo

Scammon's Lagoon

18

B. San Carlos

La Trinidad

Bahía Asunción
B. La Asunción

Guadalupe

B. Santa Ana

Gulf of California

DESIERTO DE

San Ignacio

Bahía San Hipólito

VIZCAINO

1

Santa Rosalía

Punta Chivato

Laguna de San Ignacio

Mulegé

SE. COYOTE

Bahía Concepción

PACIFIC OCEAN

La Purísima

San Isidro

B. San Basílio

Loreto

Isla Del Carmen

Boca La Soledad

Va. Ignacio Zaragoza

Ensenada Blanca Bay (Dazante Adventure Resort)

Pto. Adolfo Lopez Mateos

Ciudad Insurgentes

Sea of Cortez

Puerto San Carlos

B. Santa María

Ciudad Constitución

El Ciruelo

Isla San José

Bahía Magdalena

1

San Ignacio

B. Coyote

Isla La Partida

Isla Espíritu Santo

Isla Cerralvo

Pichilingue

Las Crúces

La Paz

San Pedro

La Ventana

B. de los Muertos

Buena Vista

19

Los Barriles

B. de Palmas

Todos Santos

SIERRA DE LA LAGUNA

La Rivera

1

Santiago

Miraflores

Cabo Pulmo

Cabo San Lucas

San José del Cabo

UNITED STATES

MEXICO

Gulf of Mexico

Mexico City ★

Area of Detail

0   500 mi
0   500 km

PACIFIC OCEAN

ORIENTATION

ARRIVING   At the airport, taxis (© **613/135-1255**) line up on the street to receive incoming passengers. They charge about $16 to Loreto, and the ride takes approximately 10 minutes.

If you plan to rent a car, Budget has a counter at the airport that's open during flight arrivals and a branch office in town. The branch is on Hidalgo between Pípila and López Mateos (© **613/135-1090;** daily 8am–1pm and 3–6pm). Advance reservations are not always necessary.

If you arrive at the bus station, it's about a 10-minute walk to the downtown area and a little farther to the hotels by the water. A taxi from the bus station to the hotels costs $2 to $5.

VISITOR INFORMATION   The city tourist-information office (© **613/135-0411**) is in the southeast corner of the Palacio de Gobierno building, across from the town square. It's open Monday through Friday from 9am to 3pm, and offers maps, local free publications, and other basic information about the area. Information is also available at www.gotoloreto.com, www.loreto.com, and www.loreto.com.mx.

CITY LAYOUT   Salvatierra is the main street that runs northeast, merging into Avenida Hidalgo toward the beach. Calle Playa (also referred to as Bulevar López Mateos or the *malecón*/boardwalk) runs parallel to the water, and it is along this road where you'll find many of the hotels, seafood restaurants, fishing charters, and the marina. Most of the town's social life revolves around the central square and the old mission, just off the central plaza. There's an old section of town along Salvatierra, between Madera and Playa, with mahogany and teak homes that date back to the 1800s.

GETTING AROUND   Most addresses in Loreto don't have a street number; the references are usually the perpendicular streets or the main square and the mission. There is no local bus service around town. Taxis or walking are your only options. The town is quite small and manageable for walking. Taxis are inexpensive, with average fares in town ranging from $1.50 to $2.50. The main taxi stand is on Salvatierra, in front of the El Pescador supermarket.

FAST FACTS: Loreto

Area Code The telephone area code is **613**.

Banks There is only one bank in Loreto. Come here to exchange currency. **Bancomer** (© **613/135-0315** or 613/135-0014) is on Francisco I. Madero, across the street from the Palacio Municipal (City Hall). Bank hours are Monday through Friday from 8:30am to 4pm. This is also the location of the only ATM in town. There is a *casa de cambio* (money-exchange house) on Salvatierra, near the main square.

Beach Safety The beaches are generally safe for swimming, with the main beach along the *malecón* (sea wall).

Emergencies Dial 060 for emergency assistance; **city police** can be reached at © **613/135-0035** (Paseo Tamaral, next to University of La Paz, Loreto Campus); and the **Red Cross** at © **613/135-1111**.

General Store **Super El Pescador,** on Salvatierra and Independencia (✆ 613/135-0060), is the best place to get toiletries, film, bottled water, and other basic staples as well as newspapers and telephone calling cards.

Internet Access **.Com Internet Cafe,** Francisco I. Madero next to Café Olé restaurant (✆ 613/135-1847), offers Internet access Monday through Saturday from 9am to 10pm. The cost is $2 for 30 minutes. **Caseta Soledad Internet Café,** Salvatierra s/n, in front of the bakery (✆ 613/135-0239), has Internet access at $3 per hour, plus long distance and fax services. It's open Monday to Saturday from 8am to 1pm and 4 to 7pm.

Marinas Loreto's marina for *pangas* (small fishing boats) is along the *malecón.* Cruise ships and other large boats anchor at Puerto Loreto, also known as Puerto Escondido, 26km (16 miles) south of Loreto. For details about the marina and docking fees, contact the Capitanía de Puerto in Loreto (✆ 613/135-0656 or 613/135-0465).

Medical Care Medical services are offered at the **Centro de Salud** hospital (✆ 613/135-0039), Salvatierra 68, near the corner with Allende. Open 24 hours, the cost per visit is $50, payable in cash only.

Parking Street parking is generally easy to find in the downtown area.

Pharmacy The **Farmacia del Rosario** (✆ 613/135-0670) is at Plaza Salvatierra, in front of supermarket El Pescador, and is open daily from 8am to 10pm. The **Farmacia de las Américas** (✆ 613/135-0670) is on the west corner of Independencia and Juárez, open 8am to 10pm daily.

Post Office The *correo* (✆ 613/135-0647) is at Deportiva between Salvatierra and Benito Juárez, and is open Monday through Friday from 8am to 3pm.

Taxis Taxis can generally be found parked on the north side of Loreto's main street, just east of the El Pescador market, and near large hotels. There are two taxi companies in Loreto, **Sitio Loreto** (✆ 613/135-0424) and **Sitio Juarez** (✆ 613/135-0915).

BEACHES & CRUISES

BEACHES   Beautiful beaches front Loreto and the hotels that surround it. The beaches are safe for swimming, with the main beach along the *malecón,* near El Chile Willie restaurant. It's a popular place for locals, especially on Sundays. Most visitors go to Loreto for the excellent sportfishing and other outdoor activities, so relaxing at the beach is one of the optional pleasures offered by this naturalist's paradise. For those seeking more pristine, secluded beaches, the options are unlimited in the several islands offshore. **Isla del Carmen** offers several particularly attractive beaches, with the best anchorage on the western shores of the island. You can either take one of the cruises mentioned below or hire a *lancha* (small wooden fishing boats available along the *malecón*) to take you there; the price depends on what you want and how sharp your bargaining skills are (the *lancheros,* or captains, take cash only).

CRUISES   More than cruises, Loreto offers island exploration tours that take in one, or a combination, of the five islands located just offshore. They usually offer the opportunity to visit sea lion colonies and do some snorkeling and beachcombing for

---

(Moments Festivals in Loreto

The feast of the patron saint of Loreto is celebrated September 5 to September 8, with a fair, music, dancing, and other cultural events, closing with the procession of the miraculous figure of the Virgin of Loreto. During the month of October, Loreto celebrates the anniversary of its founding with a series of cultural events that include music and dance. There is also a reenactment of the landing of the Spanish missionaries that is part of a popular festival held from October 19 to October 25.

---

around $40. Arrange cruises through a travel agency, your hotel, or call **Las Parras Tours** (© 613/135-1010; www.lasparrastours.com). Las Parras offers the widest selection of outdoor activities and tours. Among their cruise options are a 4-hour sailing day trip and a 2-hour sunset sailing trip. Prices are $39 and $15 respectively. It also offers an Island Skiff Trip, which takes you to Isla Coronado for snorkeling, relaxing on the white-sand beaches, and a visit to a sea lion colony. That tour costs $45, lasts 5 hours, and includes snacks and lunch. Each island is unique and offers a spectrum of activities such as sea kayaking, snorkeling, diving, hiking, or simply exploring the local desert flora and fauna (see "A Visit to Isla del Carmen," below).

LAND SPORTS

GOLF The 18-hole **Campo de Golf Loreto,** Bulevar Misión San Ignacio, Fraccionamiento Nopoló (© 613/133-0554 or 613/133-0788), is quite spectacular, and is probably the least crowded coastal golf course in the area. The back 9 holes are more challenging than the front 9, and the 14th hole is reputed to be particularly tough. Reservations are recommended. Prices are $51 for 18 holes and $39 for 9 holes, with an additional $36 for cart, $30 for caddy, and $22 for gear. The course is in the process of being redesigned by David Duval, so you can expect higher greens fees in the future—along with improved play.

HIKING There are virtually no formal trails in the Sierra de la Giganta, but the locals know the way to many magical spots in these towering mountains. Ask at **Deportes Blazer,** Hidalgo 18 (© 613/135-0911), or call **Las Parras Tours** (© 613/135-1010; www.lasparrastours.com) for help finding a guide or for current trail information.

HORSEBACK RIDING More practical for this terrain are the mule-riding excursions that visit the San Javier mission. These can be arranged through **Las Parras Tours** (© 613/135-1010; www.lasparrastours.com). It offers mule-trail tours during which you camp and sleep in different ranches in the surrounding area. These tours last 3 to 5 nights, with prices varying according to length, location, and amenities. Horseback riding tours are also available through this company, which offers the most options and the friendliest service.

SPORTING TOURS Trekking, hiking, mountain biking, and mule- and horseback riding tours are available through **Las Parras Tours** (© 613/135-1010; www.lasparrastours.com), where José Salas will be happy to explain the many options in detail. Mountain bikes can be booked for $5 per hour, or $25 for a full day. Local travel agencies also offer tours, but most likely will hire their guides from Las Parras Tours, the best-organized tour operator in Loreto.

The Loreto Area

To Mulege

Isla Coronado

Puerto de la Lancha

Loreto

Puerto Balandra

Salt Pond

Nopolo

Camino Real

Bahía Salinas

Isla del Carmen

Sea of Cortez

Bahía Marquer

Playa Juncalito

Punta Coyote

Punta Baja

Loreto Bay

Isla Danzante

Los Candeleros

Punta Candeleros

Dazante Adventure Resort

Isla Monserrate

Isla Santa Catalina

Transpeninsular Highway

To Ciudad Constitucion

Isla San Cosme

Punta San Cosme

Punta San Pasquel

Bahía Agua Verde

Punta San Marcial

UNITED STATES

THE BAJA PENINSULA

Area of Detail

MEXICO

Mexico City

0   500 mi
0   500 km

0   1/2 mi
0   1 km

TENNIS You can play tennis at the Nopolo Sports Center's **Centro Tenístico Loreto** (℗ 613/133-0129), also known as the John McEnroe Tennis Center, after its designer. There are eight courts, a pool, sun deck, stadium, racquetball court, and pro shop. Court fees are $9 per hour. The fee also gives you access to the pool. If you want to use the pool only, the access fee is $3 for the day. The center is open daily from 7am to 6pm.

WATERSPORTS & ACTIVITIES

SEA KAYAKING Kayaking season is October through April. **Las Parras Tours** (℗ 613/135-1010; www.lasparrastours.com) offers sit-on-top kayak tours for beginners ($45–$100). The more expensive tour visits three islands; the guide does all the hard work while you learn how to paddle close to shore and get to enjoy all the sights. The company also offers kayaking expeditions of 6 to 8 days, with camping on small islands and kayaking between them. They are fully guided with all gear provided, but you should take your own sleeping bag. The kayaking expeditions are approximately $100 per day per person. Puerto Loreto (also known as Puerto Escondido) is also an ideal starting point for experienced kayakers who want to reach Isla Monserrate; call Las Parras Tours for details. The company also offers kayak rentals that you can book by the hour ($5 single, or $7.50 double kayaks), half-day ($15 and $20), or full day ($25 and $30).

SNORKELING/DIVING   Several companies offer snorkeling; most island exploration trips include snorkeling, and trips to Isla del Carmen, Islas Coronados, Isla Monserrate, and Isla Catalina all include snorkeling opportunities. Some fishing trips carry snorkeling gear on board to give anglers a chance to check out the underwater world. For scuba diving, contact **Las Parras Tours** (© 613/135-1010; www.las parrastours.com); it offers several diving sites where you can admire the underwater bounty of the Sea of Cortez. The half-day trips cost $80 to $90 per diver, and an SSI-certified dive instructor guides all tours. Snacks are included, but any equipment needed, including tanks, is an extra charge (tanks/air cost $8, wet suit $10, BC (buoyancy compensator) $10, regulator $10, mask/fins $5, or a full equipment package when you book your dive tour is $20). The tour company recommends wearing a wet suit from November to May and a skin for the rest of the year. Las Parras also offers a 4-day resort course in diving ($300).

Finds A Visit to Isla del Carmen

Isla del Carmen is the largest of Loreto's offshore islands. It is mostly inaccessible and privately owned, so you'll need permission to go ashore. Access to Isla del Carmen is available through one of a number of tour companies in Loreto. Chose your company based on your preferred activity and mode of exploration (usually kayaking, sometimes hiking).

The island was once the site of an impressive salt-mining operation, but increased competition—not to mention the opportunity to earn a dollar from granting landing permissions to tourism purveyors—encouraged the company to shut down and refocus its economic endeavors. You can see the remains of the salt-mining town, completely abandoned in 1983, at the northeastern tip of the island.

Volcanic in origin, Isla del Carmen also has deposits of *coquina,* a limestonelike rock of cemented shell material that was quarried by the Jesuit missionaries for use in constructing the church and other buildings in Loreto. One favorite cove on Isla del Carmen is Puerto Balandra, where bold rock formations rising up like humpback whales frame crystal-blue water and ivory sand.

The craggy desert terrain offers a cornucopia of plant life, including elephant trees with their fragrant leaves and berries, desert asparagus (pickleweed), mesquite trees, jojoba, agave, cardón cacti, and passion flower vines. Be careful of the choya cacti, whose spines enter your skin in a crisscross pattern. To remove them, cut the spines from the plant, then pull them out one at a time.

The topography on the island alternates between salt-crusted ground, spongy surfaces—a sure sign that snakes, iguanas, and burrowing animals are nearby—and the rocky remains of former riverbeds. There is a variety of fauna as well, including a population of goats that were introduced to the island to provide a meat supply for its inhabitants. Feral cats, blacktailed hares, and birds that include osprey and heila woodpeckers are among the wildlife you'll regularly spot here.

Downtown Loreto

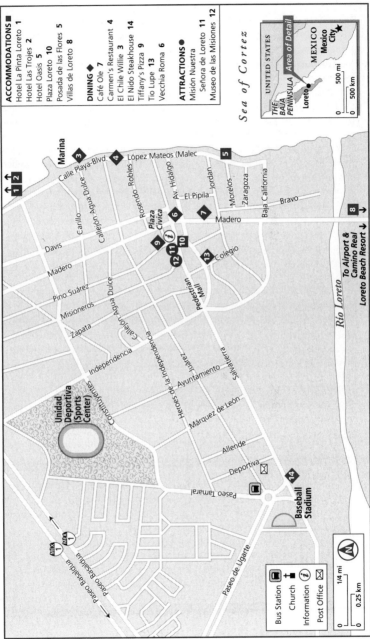

ACCOMMODATIONS ■
Hotel La Pinta Loreto **1**
Hotel Las Trojes **2**
Hotel Oasis **5**
Plaza Loreto **10**
Posada de las Flores **5**
Villas de Loreto **8**

DINING ◆
Café Ole **7**
Carmen's Restaurant **4**
El Chile Willie **3**
El Nido Steakhouse **14**
Tiffany's Pizza **9**
Tio Lupe **13**
Vecchia Roma **6**

ATTRACTIONS ●
Misión Nuestra
Señora de Loreto **11**
Museo de las Misiones **12**

Sea of Cortez

UNITED STATES

THE BAJA PENINSULA

Loreto

MEXICO

Mexico City

Area of Detail

0   500 mi
0   500 km

Marina

Calle Playa-Blvd.

López Mateos (Malec

Calle Playa Dulce

Callejón-Agua Dulce

Carrillo

Rosendo- Robles

Av. Hidalgo

El Pipila

Jordan

Morelos

Zaragoza

Baja California

Bravo

Davis

Plaza Cívica

Madero

Madero

Pino Suárez

Misioneros

Zapata

Independencia

Calle Agua Dulce

Callejón-Agua Dulce

Pedestrian Mall

Colegio

Heros de la Independencia

Juárez

Ayuntamiento

Salvatierra

Constituentes

Unidad Deportiva (Sports Center)

Márquez de León

Allende

Deportiva

Paseo Tamaral

Paseo de Ugarte

paseo Basdelua

paseo Basdelua

Baseball Stadium

To Airport & Camino Real Loreto Beach Resort →

Río Loreto

Bus Station
Church
Information
Post Office

0   1/4 mi
0   0.25 km

N

Finds Baja's Cave Paintings: An Exploration of the Mysterious

One fascinating excursion that demands good physical condition is a visit to the **aboriginal cave paintings of Baja.** The origin of these cave paintings is still unknown, with some researchers placing them as far back as 10,000 years old (during the Prehistoric Age), with a general consensus that they are at least 1,500 years old. They are so impressive that UNESCO has designated them a part of the historical patrimony of mankind.

The cave paintings are concentrated in the San Francisco de la Sierra and Santa Martha mountain ranges. It is believed that thousands of years ago, the shallow pools and oases that existed in this region allowed groups of people to survive here. The primitive rock paintings they left behind are the only examples of this kind of art on the North American continent. The cave paintings are spectacular murals done on rocks, with representations of larger-than-life humanlike and animal forms, in scenes that could be ritual ceremonies, pilgrimages, hunting, or in battle. The colors used are ochre, red, white, yellow, and black, with the faceless humanlike figures painted in red and black, standing with their arms extended and often depicted with unusual headpieces above their heads, possibly a symbol of an experience of a hallucinatory state. There is a strong magical-spiritual content to the paintings. Other figures appear to be jaguars, reptiles, deer-headed snakes, and human hands. Often the figures appear overlain on one another, meaning they were likely painted by various artists at different periods of time.

The first mention of the paintings was by the Jesuit missionary Francisco Javier Clavijero in 1789. Since then, scholars around the world have attempted to date and interpret these mystical scenes. Mexico's National

SPORTFISHING   The fishing near Loreto is exceptional, with a different sportfish for every season. Winter months are great for yellowtail, and spring is the time for roosterfish. During the summer, tie into big marlin, sailfish, tuna, dorado, and grouper. For something unusual, take advantage of the run of large Humboldt squid that pass inshore to spawn between Isla del Carmen and Isla Danzante during the fall. These 10-pound, ink-squirting creatures are hard fighting but good eating. The best fishing is said to be in the waters east of Isla del Carmen.

There are several different sportfishing operations in town. The least expensive way to enjoy deep-sea fishing is to pair up with another angler and charter a *panga* from the **Loreto Sportfishing Cooperative** at the main pier in Loreto, known as Barcena del Malecón (no phone). Prices range from $125 to $250 per boat, depending on the size and availability of shade. You can also arrange your trip in advance through most tour operators or contact the fleets directly. At **Arturo's Fleet,** Calle Juárez (*©* **613/ 135-0766**), trips cost $170 to $340, with rod rentals $10 each, and an extra charge for bait, drinks, and snacks. MasterCard and Visa are accepted, with a 5% surcharge. People with their own boats can launch at the ramp just north of the *malecón* in town or at Puerto Loreto, 26km (16 miles) south of town. If you plan on running out to

Institute of Anthropology (INAH) oversees these sites now and makes only selected sites open for public viewing, and even then, entry is only allowed with authorized guides.

Due to the summer rains and heat, it is recommended to visit between October and May. Guides can be found in the town of San Ignacio to take you to the cave known as La Pintada, known for the diversity and size of its paintings. However, La Pintada is a long and difficult trek. A more accessible option in the San Francisco de la Sierra is the cave known as El Raton, about 23 miles away on the Carretera Transpeninsular. From this cave, it's a short distance to another location, Las Flechas. Near Mulegé, your visit could include La Trinidad (an above-ground site), Piedras Pintas (a group of rocks with petroglyphs), and San Borjita cave.

The entire region where these paintings are located covers almost 7,500 square miles in the central part of the Baja peninsula. In the San Francisco de la Sierra, a grouping of over 300 sites is known as the Great Wall; it is the largest and most mysterious concentration of ancient rock paintings in the world.

Las Parras Tours (© 613/135-1010; www.lasparrastours.com) offers guided tours to these caves. Their tour lasts approximately 12 hours and takes you to the foothills of the Guadalupe mountains, between Loreto and Bahía de los Angeles, where you hike through the desert then swim in a couple of canyons before you reach the site. There is also an INAH museum in the area, which has displays and additional information about the cave paintings and the research which has been done on them.

Isla del Carmen, it's better to launch from Puerto Loreto, which cuts 10km (6 miles) off the crossing. For tackle, head to Deportes Blazer, Hidalgo 18, the catchall sporting-goods store in town.

WHALE-WATCHING ★★★   Loreto is the nearest major airport and city to Bahía Magdalena (Magdalena Bay), the southernmost of the major gray-whale-calving lagoons on the Pacific coast of Baja. For more information on popular whale-watching spots and tour operators, see "Whale-Watching in Baja: A Primer," later in this chapter. **Las Parras Tours** (© 613/135-1010; www.lasparrastours.com) conducts whale-watching trips to Magdalena Bay on the Pacific Coast to see gray whales ($120 for the 8-hr. trip) This trip includes an average of 2 hours in a skiff watching the whales; additional time in the skiff can be arranged by adding $60 per hour, divided by the number of people in your group. What makes this trip so special is the wealth of knowledge of the Las Parras guides about the natural history and culture of the area.

HISTORICAL LORETO & OTHER INTERESTING SITES

For cultural explorations in the area other than those listed below, contact **C&C Tours** (© 613/133-0151). Among the guided excursions this quality company offers are the Historic Loreto City Tour (morning and evening options available), Tabor

Canyon, Mulegé (see below for more on these areas), Primer Agua, and Wine & Cheese Party tours.

MISION NUESTRA SEÑORA DE LORETO   The first mission in the Californias was started in 1699. The catechization of California by Jesuit missionaries was based from this mission, and lasted through the 18th century. The inscription above the entrance reads CABEZA Y MADRE DE LAS MISIONES DE BAJA Y ALTA CALIFORNIA (Head and Mother of the Missions of Lower and Upper California). The current church, a simple building in the shape of a Greek cross, was finished in 1752 and restored in 1976. The original Virgen de Loreto, brought to shore by Padre Kino in 1667, is on display in the church's 18th-century gilded altar. The mission is on Salvatierra, across from the central square.

MUSEO DE LAS MISIONES   This museum is adjacent to the Misión Nuestra Señora de Loreto church (above) and is of equal or even greater interest. It has a small but complete collection of historical and anthropological exhibits. On display are interesting facts about the indigenous Guaycura, Pericúe, and Cochimí populations, along with accomplishments of the Jesuit missionaries—including their zoological studies, scientific writings, architectural sketches, and details of the role they played in the demise of indigenous cultures. Also on display are several religious paintings and sculptures dating to the 18th century. The museum, located at Salvatierra 16 (© **613/ 135-0441**), has a small shop where the INAH (Instituto Nacional de Antropología e Historia) sells books about the history of Mexico and Baja California. The museum is open Tuesday through Sunday from 9am to 1pm and 1:45 to 6pm. Admission is $3.

MISION SAN FRANCISCO JAVIER ⚓   About 2 hours from Loreto and in a section of the old Camino Real used by Spanish missionaries and explorers, this mission is one of the best-preserved, most spectacularly set missions in Baja—high in a mountain valley beneath volcanic walls. Founded in 1699 by the Jesuit priest Francisco María Píccolo, it was completed in 1758 and was the second mission established in California. The church was built with blocks of volcanic stone from the Sierra de la Giganta mountains. It is very well preserved, with its original walls, floors, gilded altar, and religious artifacts. Day tours from Loreto, organized by several local tour operators, visit the mission, with stops to view aboriginal cave paintings and an oasis settlement with a small chapel. The trips cost $40 to $65, and some offer mule riding and hiking options. If you are driving a high-clearance four-wheel-drive vehicle and are an experienced off-road driver, you can get there yourself by traveling south on Carretera Transpeninsular and taking the detour on Km 118. The 40km (25-mile) drive takes about 2 hours on a rocky, graded road.

PRIMER AGUA   A palm oasis in a fenced-off section of the Arroyo de San Javier, this serves as a prime picnic spot, complete with natural spring and swimming pool. You'll have to stop by the Nopoló FONATUR offices, Carretera Transpeninsular Km 111 (© **613/133-0245** or 613/133-0301), 2 days prior to your visit to make sure the oasis will be open to visitors on the day you plan your visit and to pay the entrance fee. Access is $10 per person, and it's open Thursday to Tuesday from 9am until 6pm. The oasis is closed on Wednesdays for pool cleaning. The road to Primer Agua is unpaved and graded, affording fairly easy access during the dry season. The entrance is 6km (3¾ miles) off Carretera Transpeninsular on the Km 114 detour.

SHOPPING

Quite frankly, you won't be coming to Loreto to shop, and if you do, you're going to be disappointed. Loreto has little in the way of shopping, either for basics or for folk art and other collectibles from mainland Mexico. There are a handful of the requisite shops selling souvenirs and some *artesanía*, all within a block of the mission. Some, such as the following, are better than others.

Conchita's Curios   This shop carries a fine selection of arts and crafts from throughout Mexico. Open daily from 9am to 8pm. The corner of Misioneros and Fernando Jordan. ℃ 613/135-1054.

El Alacrán   This shop also has a quality selection of arts and crafts, as well as inter-esting books about Baja, fine silver jewelry, and handmade and cotton clothing. Open Monday through Saturday from 9:30am to 1pm and 3 to 7pm. Salvatierra and Misioneros. ℃ 613/135-0029.

La Casa de la Abuela   "Grandma's House" offers better-than-average knickknacks with an emphasis on indigenous crafts. In the oldest house in Loreto, it also serves cof-fee, pastries, and light meals. Open Wednesday through Monday from 9am to 10pm. No credit cards. Salvatierra and Misioneros, across from the Mission. No phone.

La Iguana   Although Loreto doesn't have much of a gallery scene, this shop offers the best selection of finer art and art objects. Open daily from 9am to 8pm. Paseo Hidalgo s/n, at the corner of Fracc. Madero. ℃ 613/135-1355.

Lunenoma   This shop specializes in shells and mineral rocks, including necklaces made from the same. It's open daily from 1 to 8pm. In the cobblestone area of Salvatierra, behind the gazebo in Plaza Juarez. No phone.

Vesubio   Rustic Mexican furniture, as well as Mexican art and decorative items for the home, are featured at Vesubio. It's open Monday through Saturday from 9:30am to 1pm, and 4 to 8pm. Paseo Madero 56, at the corner of Paseo Baja California. ℃ 613/135-1132.

WHERE TO STAY

In general, accommodations in Loreto are the kind travelers to Mexico used to find regularly: inexpensive and unique, with genuinely friendly owner-operators. You'll be able to choose between a secluded resort, more casual beachfront inns, and even greater values in town.

EXPENSIVE

Camino Real Loreto Baja Beach & Golf Resort ★★★ *Kids*   Loreto's newest and most deluxe place to stay, the Camino Real is on its own private cove, on a lovely beach, with calm waters perfect for swimming. The hotel boasts the chain's stunning signature architecture, with bold colors and modern angles. The sleek guest rooms have stone floors and bright color accents. Master suites and presidential suites have large terraces and private Jacuzzis. The special services and recreational programs make this a great choice for families. Adjacent to Loreto's golf course, it's also ideal for any-one with a passion for the links. Five on-site dining choices plus 24-hour room serv-ice mean you never need to leave the premises, but the tour service, which specializes in area ecotours, will no doubt tempt you to do so. The upper-level Lobby Bar is a spectacular spot for a sunset cocktail.

Paseo de la Misión s/n, Nopolo 23880, Loreto, B.C.S. ℃ 800/873-7484 in the U.S., or 613/133-0010. www.camino real.com. 156 units. $140 standard double; $170 junior suite; $200 master suite. Meal plans available. AE, MC, V.

Amenities: 5 restaurants; 3 bars; swimming pool; golf course; fitness center; concierge desk w/nature tours; car-rental desk; tobacco shop; 24-hr. room service; child care; laundry service; Internet access. *In room:* A/C, satellite TV, minibar, hair dryer, safe.

Danzante Adventure Resort ★★★ *Finds*   This all-inclusive ecoresort offers guests everything that's wonderful about this area—sandy beaches, tranquillity, easy access to eco- and adventure activities—all in a lovely place to stay. It's 40km (25 miles) south of Loreto on serene Ensenada Blanca bay, also home to a tiny fishing village. The resort itself covers 10 acres and is comprised of nine hilltop suites perched in a rocky hill facing the sea. Each king or queen room has a large Mexican-tiled bath, beamed ceilings, handmade furnishings, large windows, and French doors that open onto a private thatched palm-covered terrace with hammocks. Laying in these hammocks, soaking in the view, seems to be the favored activity of guests, yet there's much more you can do here—most activities are included in the room rate, such as hiking, kayaking, snorkeling, and swimming at their secluded beach. Horseback riding is also available in the surrounding canyons, and diving, fishing, massage services, and excursions can be arranged for an additional charge. For meals, included in the room rate, they serve a delicious selection of seafood, local fruits and vegetables, and organic produce from the on-site garden. The resort is 100% solar powered, and is owned by a couple who counts among their many accomplishments published books on Mexico travel and diving, underwater documentaries, explorations for sunken treasure, and guiding adventure tours worldwide. This may be their best achievement yet.

Carretera Transpeninsular, at Ligui. Mailing address: P.O. Box 1166, Los Gatos, CA 95031. ✆ **408/354-0042** in the U.S. www.danzante.com. 9 units. $290 junior suite; all meals and activities included. MC, V. **Amenities:** Restaurant/bar; happy hour; hilltop freshwater swimming pool; tour services; lending library; telescope for stargazing; cell-phone at front desk. *In room:* Fan, hammock.

Posada de las Flores ★★★ *Finds*   The most exclusive hotel in Loreto conveniently sits adjacent to the main square, in the heart of historic Loreto. Every room is beautifully decorated with fine Mexican arts and crafts, including heavy wood doors, Talavera pottery, painted tiles, candles, and scenic paintings. The colors and decor are nouveau colonial, with rustic wood and tin accents. Large bathrooms have thick white towels and bamboo doors. Every detail has been carefully selected, including the numerous antiques tucked into corners. The Italian-owned and -operated hotel exudes class and refinement, from the general ambience to the wake-up service of coffee and pastries. The sophisticated service has a European style.

Salvatierra and Francisco I. Madero, Centro, 23880, Loreto, B.C.S. ✆ **877/245-2860** in the U.S., or 613/135-1162. www.posadadelasflores.com. 15 units. $140 standard; $200 junior suite. Rates include continental breakfast. 15% service charge in lieu of tips is added to your room, board, and bar bill. MC, V. Children under 16 not accepted. **Amenities:** 2 restaurants; bar; rooftop pool w/glass bottom; exclusive tours for guests. *In room:* A/C, TV, minibar, coffee maker, hair dryer, safe.

MODERATE

Hotel La Pinta Loreto ★★   On the beach and close to downtown, La Pinta offers spacious rooms with stone accents, heavy wood furnishings, and views of the offshore islands from individual terraces and private balconies. Accommodations are in two-story buildings that border a central pool and grassy courtyard. Twenty units have fireplaces. Pets are welcome.

Francisco I. Madero s/n, Playas de Loreto, 23880, Loreto, B.C.S. ✆ **800/800-9632** in the U.S., or 613/135-0025 or 612/135-0690. 48 units. $112 double w/fireplace; $89 hacienda-style double; $99 villa w/fireplace. Extra person $15. AE, MC, V. **Amenities:** Restaurant; 2 bars; swimming pool; tour desk; private fishing fleet. *In room:* A/C, TV.

My, what an inefficient way to fish.

Ring toss, good. Horseshoes, bad.

Faster! Faster! Faster!

We take care of the fiddly bits, from providing over 43,000 customer reviews of hotels, to helping you find our best fares, to giving you 24/7 customer service. So you can focus on the only thing that matters. Goofing off.

travelocity
You'll never roam alone.™

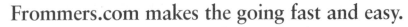

Frommers.com

So many places, so little time?

TOKYO 7766 miles
LONDON 3818 miles
4682 miles
TORONTO
5087 miles
SYDNEY 4947 miles
NEW YORK
LOS ANGELES 2556 miles
HONG KONG
5638 miles

Frommers.com makes the going fast and easy.

Find a destination. ✓ Buy a guidebook. ✓ Book a trip. ✓ Get hot travel deals.
Enter to win vacations. ✓ Check out the latest travel news.
Share trip photos and memories. ✓ And much more.

Frommers.com

Rated #1 Travel Web Site by *PC Magazine*®

Villas de Loreto 🐟   One of the best aspects of this comfortable hotel is the friendly staff that makes you feel right at home. The basic rooms have refrigerators and old-style Baja charm, with stone walls and rustic accents. The swimming pool has views of the five offshore islands. While the hotel welcomes families, it is more of a quiet getaway for nature lovers. It's on the beach, past the *arroyo* (small riverbed). Villas de Loreto is a smoke-free resort.

Antonio Mijares and Playa. Col. Zaragoza, 23880, Loreto, B.C.S. ⓒ **613/135-0586.** www.villasdeloreto.com. 13 units. $85–$96 double; $168 beach cabana double; $288 beach house double. Rates include continental breakfast. MC, V. **Amenities:** Restaurant/bar; swimming pool; bicycles; tour desk. *In room:* A/C, minifridge, coffeemaker.

INEXPENSIVE

Hotel Las Trojes 🐟   This unusual bed-and-breakfast is built from authentic wooden granaries *(trojes)* from the Tarascan Indians, brought over from the state of Michoacán. The rooms have wood interiors, wood floors, and ocean views. Each has a full bath. A path leads through a yard to the hotel's small, pebbly beach and beach bar, La Negrita. It's rustic and a little run-down, but the service is friendly and the experience quite nice for the price.

Calle Davis Norte s/n, 23880, Loreto, B.C.S. ⓒ **613/135-0277.** www.loreto.com/costa2.htm. 8 units. Dec–Mar $66 double; April–Nov $55 double. Rates include continental breakfast. No credit cards. **Amenities:** Bar; use of bicycles; tour services. *In room:* A/C, TV.

Hotel Oasis 🐟🐟   Fishermen who regularly visit this area seem to prefer this beachfront hotel, which caters to their needs with specialized services, excursions, and its own fleet of boats and equipment. In operation since 1960, Hotel Oasis has a friendly and knowledgeable staff. The simple but spacious rooms have two double beds and a private balcony or terrace, with either pool or ocean views. Summer rates with mandatory meal service are more expensive. It's on the beach at the south end of the *malecón*, close to restaurants, shops, and historic downtown. Their restaurant gets high marks from guests, and it even serves a 5am fisherman's breakfast.

Apdo. Postal 17. 23880, Loreto, B.C.S. ⓒ **800/497-3923** from the U.S., or 613/135-0211. Fax 613/135-0795. www.hoteloasis.com. 40 units. $79–$89 double; $114 suite. Bed and breakfast, as well as full meal plans available. Summer rates (including all meals) $149–$159 double; $234 suite. MC, V. Private parking. **Amenities:** Restaurant/bar; heated outdoor pool; travel desk; fishing services including boat and gear rentals. *In room:* A/C, coffee maker; TVs and phones on request.

Plaza Loreto   The location, just 1 block from the mission church, makes the Plaza Loreto easy to find and a perennial favorite. Well maintained and recently remodeled, the two-story motel frames a courtyard with shady seating areas. Each of the basic, clean rooms has one or two double beds, a table and two chairs, and a bathroom with shower. Here, you're a short walk from the mission, the museum, several good restaurants, and all the town's notable nightlife.

Paseo Hidalgo 2. Centro. 23880, Loreto, B.C.S. ⓒ **613/135-0280.** Fax 613/135-0855. www.loreto.com/hotelplaza. 24 units. $62 double; $73 triple. MC, V. **Amenities:** Travel agent, Internet access, tour desk, happy hour. *In room:* A/C, TV.

WHERE TO DINE

Loreto has a surprising variety of dining options given the town's small size and simple nature. Most menus feature some combination of seafood and Mexican cuisine, with ambience and price being the key variables. Among the exceptions is the beautiful **Vecchia Roma** (ⓒ **613/135-1162**), in the Posada de las Flores hotel, which serves authentic southern Italian cuisine prepared by chef Alessandro Bargelletti. It's open Monday through Saturday from 6 to 9pm, and reservations are required.

MODERATE

Carmen's Restaurant HAMBURGERS/SEAFOOD/MEXICAN This is a popular meeting place for the gringo community, with sports on the TV, barbecue options, ocean views, and a friendly proprietor. Along with Carmen's Snorkelburger, other popular choices are paella and barbecued tri-tips. Breakfast is served American style, and in ample portions. There's usually blues or jazz playing to accompany your meal.

Bulevar Costero López Mateos s/n (across from the *malecón*). ℭ 613/135-0577. Main courses $2.50–$8. No credit cards. Daily 7am–11pm.

El Chile Willie SEAFOOD/MEXICAN El Chile Willie serves an eclectic menu that emphasizes seafood in an appropriate setting—right at the water's edge. The extensive menu features choco clams (a local type of clam, not as bizarre as it sounds), clams Rockefeller, lobster served many different ways, and succulent fish filet baked in foil with tamarind herb sauce. Also available are chicken breast stuffed with *nopal* cactus, beef burger in barbecue sauce, and (the menu claims) the world's largest Mexican combo for two. During winter months, a semicircular oceanfront window keeps the cool air out while retaining the view; it opens when the weather warms. The place is lively, and its location on the main beach in town makes it great for people-watching, especially during weekend breakfast or lunch. From 4 to 6pm, El Chile Willie features a two-for-one happy hour with free appetizers.

Bulevar Costero López Mateos s/n. ℭ 613/135-0677. Main courses $3–$10. MC, V. Daily 10am–11pm.

El Nido Steakhouse STEAK/SEAFOOD The main link in a Baja chain of steak restaurants, El Nido satisfies hearty appetites. Its specialty is a thick cut of prime, tender beef served with the obligatory salad and baked potato. Seafood options are also available. It's on the main boulevard as you enter Loreto from Carretera Transpeninsular.

Salvatierra 154. ℭ 613/135-0027 or 613/135-0284. Main courses $6–$20. No credit cards. Daily 2–10:30pm.

Tio Lupe MEXICAN/SEAFOOD Elegant yet casual, this adobe-walled, thatched-roof restaurant offers great food in a comfortable atmosphere, surrounded by the works of modern Mexican artists. Although the construction is modern, the restaurant was built using traditional methods and local natural materials. Even the tables are made from cardón cacti. The menu features fairly standard Mexican dishes and seafood, but the *camarones casa de adobe,* a plate of grilled shrimp stuffed with cheese and wrapped in bacon, is delicious.

Paseo Hidalgo, between Independencia and Madero. ℭ 613/135-1882. Main courses $3–$14. No credit cards. Daily 11am–9:30pm.

INEXPENSIVE

Café Ole LIGHT FARE Along with specialty coffees, this breezy cafe is a good option for breakfast; try eggs with *nopal* cactus or hotcakes. A not-so-light lunch of a burger and fries, tacos, and some Mexican standards are also on the menu, as are *licuados* (fresh-fruit shakes).

Francisco I. Madero 14. ℭ 613/135-0496. Breakfast $2–$5. Sandwiches $2–$3.50. No credit cards. Mon–Sat 7am–10pm; Sun 7am–2pm.

Tiffany's Pizza PIZZA Tiffany's has created quite a following among locals and visitors alike with its thin-crust pizzas made with a variety of toppings, including homemade sausage and freshly made sauces. It's also popular for breakfast, with the fresh cinnamon buns the star attraction. It also serves espresso drinks, beer, and margaritas, and offers hotel delivery for pizza and buns (for buns, order the night before).

Paseo Hidalgo and Pino Suárez. (*C*) **613/135-0004.** Breakfast $2–$5. Pizzas $4–$10. No credit cards. Mon, Wed, Fri 11:30am–9:30pm; Tues, Thurs, Sat 11:30am–3pm; Sun 12:30–10pm.

LORETO AFTER DARK

Although the selection is limited, Loreto seems to offer a place for almost every nightlife preference—from rowdy beach pubs to an elegant billiard bar. Generally, though, closing time is around midnight.

The most elegant finish to an evening is at **Jarros y Tarros,** on Salvatierra, next to Deportes Blazer (just before crossing Francisco I. Madero; no phone). It has a few elegant pool tables as well as high round tables where you can sit and sip one of the many fine tequilas. Beers run about $2, mixed drinks $3. Open daily from 6pm to 2am, Jarros y Tarros plays exceptional contemporary Latin music and Mexican rock.

Mike's Bar, 2 blocks from the beach on Paseo Hidalgo (*C* **613/135-1126**), is an intimate, friendly place with "gringo bar" written all over it—it's very popular with North American visitors. It's great for sports and people-watching, and has live music most nights from 11:30 until closing. (It's open daily 11am–3am.) TV sports and beers are also a regular specialty at **Carmen's,** on the *malecón* (see "Where to Dine," above). The recently opened **California Bar,** on the cobblestone portion of Paseo Salvatierra, is a sports bar that dubs itself "Baja's Newest Old Bar." It features televised sports in a casual atmosphere.

And, as is the tradition in Mexico, Loreto's central plaza offers a free concert in the bandstand every Sunday evening.

2 Mulegé: Oasis in the Desert ★ ★

998km (619 miles) SE of Tijuana; 137km (85 miles) N of Loreto; 496km (308 miles) NW of La Paz; 710km (440 miles) NW of Cabo San Lucas

Verdant Mulegé offers shady cool in an otherwise scorching part of the world. Founded in 1705, it is home to one of the best-preserved and beautifully situated Jesuit missions in Baja. A visit is a worthwhile side trip, if only to take in the view. Mulegé is situated between two hills, in a valley where a creek runs down to the ocean. The landscape consists of immense palms, orchards, and tangles of bougainvillea.

Besides the respite of the landscape, Mulegé (pronounced "moo-leh-*hay*"), at the mouth of beautiful Bahía Concepción, has great diving, kayaking, and fishing. The origin of the name comes from the Cochimíes (indigenous inhabitants of the area), and means "big ravine of the white mouth." There are also several well-preserved Indian caves with stunning paintings, which can be reached by guided hikes into the mountains. Accommodations are limited and basic, and trailer parks are nearby. Good beach camping is also available just south of town along the Bahía Concepción, as is a landing strip for small planes.

ESSENTIALS

GETTING THERE & DEPARTING

BY PLANE   The closest international airport is in Loreto, 137km (85 miles) south. From Loreto, you'll need to rent a car or hire a taxi for the 1½-hour trip; taxis average $75 each way. Three airlines fly into Loreto: **AeroCalifornia** (*C* **800/237-6225** in the U.S., or 613/135-0500 or 613/135-0555; fax 613/135-0566) has direct flights from Los Angeles; **Aeromexico** (*C* **800/237-6639** in the U.S., or 613/135-1837; fax

613/135-1838; www.aeromexico.com) operates direct from Los Angeles, Ontario, San Diego, Phoenix, and Las Vegas; and **Alaska Airlines** (© **800/252-7522;** www.alaska air.com), which has flights from Los Angeles, San Francisco, and Spokane, Washington.

Small regional or private charter planes can get you all the way to town: **El Gallito,** a well-maintained, graded, 1,200m (4,000-ft.) airstrip, adjoins the Hotel Serenidad, Carretera Transpeninsular Km 30 (no phone, use radio frequency UNICOM 122.8). For additional information, contact the Comandancia del Aeropuerto in Loreto (© **613/135-0565**), from 7am to 7pm daily.

BY CAR   From Tijuana, take Carretera Transpeninsular direct to the Mulegé turnoff, 998km (619 miles) south (approximately 16 hr.). From La Paz, take Carretera Transpeninsular north, a scenic route that winds through foothills and then skirts the eastern coastline. The trip takes about 6 hours; it's roughly 496km (308 miles).

BY BUS   There is no bus station in Mulegé, but buses will pick up and drop off passengers on the main highway at the La Cabaña restaurant, at the "Y" entrance to town. Buses running south to Bahía Concepción, Loreto, and La Paz generally pass by about three times a day; buses traveling north to Santa Rosalía, Ensenada, and Tijuana have twice-daily service. Schedules are highly variable, but buses stay for about 20 minutes while dropping off and picking up passengers. Tickets to Tijuana average $30; the one-way fare to La Paz is about $12.

ORIENTATION

ARRIVING   If you arrive by bus, you will be dropped off at the restaurant at the entrance to town. From there, you can walk the few blocks downhill and east into town, or take a taxi. Taxis also line up around the plaza, and usually charge around $2 to $4 for a trip anywhere in town.

VISITOR INFORMATION   There is no official office, but tourist information is available at the office of the centrally located **Hotel Las Casitas,** Calle Francisco Madero 50 (© **615/153-0019**). The local laundry, **Efficient Lavamática Claudia,** at the corner of Zaragoza and Moctezuma (© **615/153-0057;** Mon–Sat 8am–6pm), is another prime source for local information, with a well-used community bulletin board. Use the bulletin board for gathering info rather than calling the laundry's phone number, because the staff can't answer questions—the board is a community service. Several maps that list key attractions, as well as a local biweekly English-language newspaper, the *Mulegé Post,* are available throughout town. Also of interest to serious travelers to Mulegé is Kerry Otterstrom's self-published book *Mulegé: The Complete Tourism, Souvenir, and Historical Guide,* available at shops and hotels in town.

The **State Tourism Office of Baja California Sur** can be reached by calling © **612/124-0199,** or you may contact the City of Mulegé (© **615/152-0148**).

CITY LAYOUT   Mulegé has an essentially east-west orientation, running from the Carretera Transpeninsular in the west to the Sea of Cortez. The Mulegé River (also known as Río Santa Rosalía) borders the town to the south, with a few hotels and RV parks along its southern shore. It's easy to find the principal sights downtown, where two main streets will take you either east or west; both border the town's central plaza. The main church is several blocks east of the plaza, breaking with the traditional layout of most Mexican towns. The Bahía Concepción is 11km (6¾ miles) south of town.

GETTING AROUND   There is no local bus service in town or to the beach, but you can easily walk or take a taxi. Taxis line up around the central plaza, or you can call the taxi dispatch at © **615/153-0420.**

Mulegé & Santa Rosalía Areas

Bicycles are available for rent from **Cortez Explorers,** Moctezuma 75-A (© **615/ 153-0500**). Prices start at $15 for the first day then drop to $10 per day for the first week, and $8 per day after that. It also has full dive- and snorkel-equipment rentals. It's open Monday through Saturday from 10am to 1pm and 4 to 7pm.

Mulegé is so small that it's easy to find anything you're looking for, even though most buildings don't have numbered addresses.

FAST FACTS: Mulegé

Area Code The telephone area code is **615**.

Banks Important note: There are no banks in Mulegé. Plan ahead or you'll need to drive to the bank in Loreto, about 1½ hours away.

Beach Safety Beaches in the area are generally tranquil and safe for swimming. The more protected waters of Bahía Concepción are especially calm. Avoid swimming at the mouth of the Mulegé River, which is said to be polluted.

Internet Access The Hotel Hacienda (p. 132) has a small Internet cafe; access is $3 per hour. **Cuesta Internet** cafe (Fracc. I. Madero s/n; © **615/153-0530**) offers service for $2 per hour, and is open Monday through Saturday from 9am to 10pm.

Medical Care Emergency medical services are offered by the **Mexican Red Cross** (© **615/153-0110**) and the Health Center ISSSTE (© **615/153-0298**).

Parking Street parking is generally easy to find in the downtown area. Note, however, that Mulegé's streets are very narrow and difficult for RVs and other large vehicles to navigate.

Pharmacy **Farmacia Ruben,** Calle Francisco Madero s/n, at the northwest corner of the central plaza (no phone), is a small drugstore with a sampling of basic necessities and medicines. The owner speaks some English. Across the plaza, **Supermercado Alba** (no phone) has a somewhat wider selection of other goods and toiletries. Both are open Monday through Saturday from 9am to 7pm.

Post Office The *correo* is at the intersection of calles Francisco Madero and General Martínez, on the north side of the street, opposite the downtown Pemex station (© **615/153-0205**). It is open Monday through Friday from 8am to 3pm, and Saturday from 8 to 11am.

BEACHES & OUTDOOR ACTIVITIES

Mulegé has long been a favorite destination for adventurous travelers looking for a place to relax and enjoy the diversity of nature. Divers, sportfishermen, kayakers, history buffs, and admirers of beautiful beaches all find reasons to stay in this oasis just a little longer.

BEACHES   To the north and east of Mulegé lies the Sea of Cortez, known for its abundance and variety of species of fish, marine birds, and sea mammals. To the north are the mostly secluded beaches of **Bahía Santa Inez** and **Punta Chivato,** both known for their beauty and tranquillity. Santa Inez is reachable by way of a long dirt road that turns off from Carretera Transpeninsular at Km 151. Twenty-five kilometers (16 miles) south is the majestic **Bahía Concepción,** a 48km-long (30-mile) body of water protected on three sides by more than 80km (50 miles) of beaches, and dotted with islands. The mountainous peninsula borders its crystal-clear turquoise waters to the east. Along with fantastic landscapes, the bay has numerous soft, white-sand beaches such as **Santispác, Concepción, Los Cocos, El Burro, El Coyote, Buenaventura, El Requesón,** and **Armenta.** Swimming, diving, windsurfing, kayaking, and other watersports are easily enjoyed, with equipment rentals locally available. Here's a rundown on some of the area beaches with restaurant service:

Punta Arena is accessible off Carretera Transpeninsular, at Km 119. A very good *palapa* restaurant is there, along with camping facilities and primitive beach *palapas.*

Playa Santispác, at Km 114, has a nice beachfront, lots of RVs in the winter, and two good restaurants (Ana's is the more popular).

Playa El Coyote is the most popular and crowded of the Bahía Concepción beaches. The restaurant El Coyote is on the west side of Carretera Transpeninsular at the entrance to this beach, .8km (½ mile) from the water; Restaurant Bertha's serves simple meals on the beachfront.

Playa Buenaventura, at Km 94, is the most developed of the beaches, with a large RV park, motel, convenience store, boat ramp, and public restrooms, along with George's Olé restaurant and bar.

Downtown Mulegé

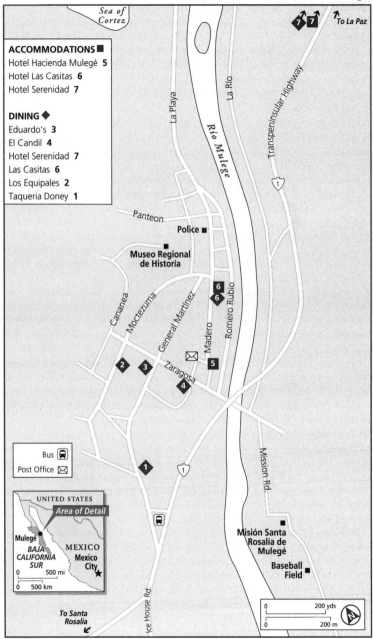

ACCOMMODATIONS ■
Hotel Hacienda Mulegé **5**
Hotel Las Casitas **6**
Hotel Serenidad **7**

DINING ◆
Eduardo's **3**
El Candil **4**
Hotel Serenidad **7**
Las Casitas **6**
Los Equipales **2**
Taqueria Doney **1**

Sea of Cortez

To La Paz

La Playa

La Río

Río Mulegé

Transpeninsular Highway

Panteon

Police ■

Museo Regional de Historía ■

Cananea

Moctezuma

General Martínez

Madero

Romero Rubio

Zaragosa

Bus 🚌
Post Office ✉

UNITED STATES
Area of Detail
Mulegé
BAJA CALIFORNIA SUR
MEXICO
Mexico City ★
0   500 mi
0   500 km

Misión Santa Rosalía de Mulegé ■

Baseball Field ■

Mission Rd.

Ice House Rd.

To Santa Rosalía

0   200 yds
0   200 m

FISHING   All of the hotels in town can arrange guided fishing trips to Punta Chivato, Isla San Marcos, or Punta de Concepción, the outermost tip of Bahía Concepción.

The best fishing in the area is for yellowtail, which run in the winter, and summer catches of dorado, tuna, and billfish like marlin and sailfish. Prices run $120 per day for up to three people in a *panga,* $180 for four in a small cruiser, or $200 and up for larger boats. **Mulegé Sportfishing** (© **615/153-0244** or 615/153-0482) organizes fishing trips in the area.

HIKING & PAINTED CAVE EXPLORATIONS ☆☆☆   One of the big attractions of this region are the large cave paintings in the Sierra de Guadalupe. UNESCO declared the cave paintings a World Heritage Site, and the locals take great pride in protecting them. Unlike many cave paintings, these are huge, complex murals. You are legally allowed to visit the caves only with a licensed guide.

The most popular series of caves is in **La Trinidad,** a remote rancho 29km (18 miles) west of Mulegé. After your guide drives you there, the hiking begins (count on hiking about 6km/3¾ miles) and getting wet. To reach the caves, several river crossings are necessary in spots deep enough to swim. Indeed, at one point, rock walls fringe a tight canyon, and there is no way through except by swimming. This river in Cañón La Trinidad allegedly is the source of the river that flows through Mulegé, although it disappears underground for many miles in between.

Among the representations of the cave murals are large deer silhouettes, and a human figure called the "cardón man" because of his resemblance to a cardón cactus.

Another favorite cave-art site is **San Borjitas.** To get there, you travel down a bad four-wheel-drive road to Rancho Las Tinajas, where your guide will take you on foot or by mule to the caves.

For about $35 per person (6 hr., minimum five people, lunch included), you can arrange for a guide in Mulegé to take you to La Trinidad; San Borjitas will cost around $50 per person (7 hr., two meals included). Check at Hotel Las Casitas or on the board of the local laundry for guide recommendations. One recommended guide is **Salvador Castro** (© **615/153-0232**).

SCUBA DIVING & SNORKELING   Although diving in the area is very popular, be aware that visibility right in Mulegé is marred by the fresh and not-so-fresh water that seems to flow into the sea from the numerous septic tanks in this area (do not swim or snorkel close to town). But as you head south into Bahía Concepción, there is excellent snorkeling at the numerous shallow coves and tiny offshore islands. Work the middle of the sandy coves looking for oysters and scallops. For bigger fish and colorful sea life, you'll have to swim out to deeper waters along the edges of each cove.

Boat diving around Mulegé tends to be around Punta de Concepción or north of town at Punta Chivato and the small offshore islands of Santa Inez and San Marcos. Numerous sites are perfect for both snorkeling and scuba. The marine life here is colorful—you're likely to see green moray eels, angelfish, parrotfish, and a variety of lobster. In addition, dolphins and other sea mammals are common sights. The best diving is between August and November, when the visibility averages 30m (98 ft.) and water temperatures are warmer (mid-80s/high 20s Celsius).

Bea and Andy Sidler's **Cortez Explorers,** Moctezuma 75-A (©/fax **615/153-0500;** www.cortez-explorer.com), bought out and took over the operations of the well-known Mulegé Divers, and maintains its reputation as one of the best-run dive operations in the state. If Mulegé has become known as a prime dive site in Baja, credit goes to this shop for its excellent prices and exceptional services. It has a great environmental consciousness, too. Cortez Explorers runs trips from a large, custom dive boat, and uses only well-maintained, current equipment.

Two-tank dive trips generally involve a 45-minute boat ride offshore and cost $60 to $80 per person, depending on the equipment needed. Snorkeling trips go for $30 to $35 (again, based on the need to rent equipment). Wet suits, jackets, and farmer johns are available, and they're necessary during winter months. Resort courses are also available, at a cost of $90.

SEA KAYAKING   Kayaks are the most popular and practical way to explore the pristine coves that dot this shoreline, and Bahía Concepción is a kayaker's dream—clear, calm water, fascinating shorelines, and lots of tempting coves to pull into, with white-sandy beaches.

Baja Tropicales, at Km 111 (Playa Escondido turnoff; 23km/14 miles south of the town of Mulegé; (℃) **615/153-0409** or 615/153-0320; ecomundo@aol.com), is Mulegé's undisputed kayak expert. It also rents kayaks to experienced paddlers for $20 to $45 per day, depending on the type of kayak—open top, sea kayaks, single, or tandem. Longer-term rentals are also available, as is full gear, including car racks and VHF radios. In addition, the company offers fully guided, ecologically oriented kayak tours in Bahía Concepción, and full-day Paddle, Snorkel, Dive & Dine excursions that combine a day of sporting fun with a seafood fiesta at the firm's *palapa* restaurant (the Kayak Kafe) on the beach. The trip, meal, and beverages cost $39, with a four-person minimum. The trip departs from the EcoMundo kayaking and natural history center, an extension of Baja Tropicales at Km 111, just south of Playa Santispác. No previous experience is necessary; complete instruction is given at the start of the tour. Baja Tropicales also offers 4- and 5-day trips around Bahía Concepción, down the coast, and even over in Scammon's Lagoon on Baja's west coast. They also offer campsites, and camping in their own tropical igloo *palapas* and cabañas, starting at $12 per night. Fresh water showers are available for $1.

WINDSURFING   Bahía Concepción, south of Mulegé, gets quite windy in the afternoon and has numerous coves for beginners to practice in. It has never developed the cachet with the hard-core sailboarding crowd that places like Buenavista and La Ventana have, but it's a worthy place to stop and rig up nevertheless.

EXPLORING MULEGE

MISION SANTA ROSALIA DE MULEGE   Founded in 1706 by Father Juan de Ugarte and Juan María Basaldúa, this site is just upstream from the bridge where the Carretera Transpeninsular crosses the Mulegé River. The original mission building was completed in 1766 to serve a local Indian population of about 2,000. In 1770, a flood destroyed nearly all the common buildings, and the mission was rebuilt on the site it occupies today, on a bluff overlooking the river. Built of stone, it is notable for its "L" formation. Its tower is several meters behind the main building. Although not the most architecturally interesting of Baja's missions, it remains in excellent condition and still functions as a Catholic church, although mission operations halted in 1828. Inside, there is a perfectly preserved statue of Santa Rosalía and a bell, both from the 18th century.

The mission is also a popular tour site. A lookout point 30m (98 ft.) behind the mission provides a spectacular vantage point for taking in the view of a grove of palm trees backed by the Sea of Cortez.

To reach the mission from town, take Calle Zaragoza (the longest north-south street in Mulegé) south, then cross the river using the small footbridge beneath the elevated highway bridge. Turn back sharply to the right and follow the dirt road through palm groves and up a graded path to the mission. The towers of the church will be visible.

MUSEO REGIONAL DE HISTORIA (REGIONAL MUSEUM OF HISTORY)
In 1907, a state penitentiary was built on a hill overlooking the town of Mulegé. About 20 years ago, a local historian and citizen's group established this small museum inside. The institution was known as the "prison without doors" because it operated on an honor system—inmates were allowed to leave every morning to work in town, on the condition that they return when the afternoon horn sounded. Escape attempts were rare, and when they occurred, the other prisoners pursued the escapees to bring them back. It functioned that way until the mid-1970s.

The museum (no phone) details the prison's operations and houses an eclectic collection of local historical artifacts. Admission is by donation, and hours are supposed to be Monday through Friday from 9am to 1pm, but have been known to vary. The museum is at the end of Calle Cananea.

SHOPPING
The town has a limited selection of shops, unless you're looking for basic groceries or auto parts. There are two exceptions:

Artesanías Cochimí   This shop sells the highest-quality selection of Mexican arts and decorative items in town, including pottery, silver jewelry, and handcrafted iron furniture. Shipping is available. Hours are Monday through Saturday from 9am to 6pm and Sunday from 10am to 2pm. If you call in advance, the owner will open at special hours. No credit cards. Calle Zaragoza and Moctezuma. (℃ **615/153-0378** or 615/153-0450.

Plantas Medicinales Sarah   If you're curious about or committed to natural health, this small but complete shop offers mineral salts, teas, powders, spirit waters, and herbs to care for your every ailment. Open Monday through Saturday from 9am to 1pm. No credit cards. Francisco Madero, across from the church. No phone.

WHERE TO STAY
Accommodations in Mulegé are basic but generally clean and comfortable. The biggest hotel in town, the Hotel Serenidad, has a recent history of closings due to ownership disputes with the local *ejido* (indigenous) community. It is open now, and claims to have resolved all questions of proprietorship.

EXPENSIVE
Punta Chivato ✶✶✶ *(Finds*   Not exactly in Mulegé, but near enough, is the elegant and tranquil Punta Chivato. Owned by the Posada de las Flores group, it's one of their three boutique hotels in Baja. Punta Chivato is 42km (26 miles) north of Mulegé, on Santa Ines bay. The hotel is on 3 hectares (7½ acres) fronting the Sea of Cortez, in one of the most beautiful settings you can imagine, a combination of desert landscape and aquamarine waters. The large and beautifully decorated guest rooms blend Mexican and colonial tastes. The eight standard rooms have garden views and a terrace with swing chairs. Junior suites are situated on the beach, with ocean views and porches with sun beds. Meals are included—there really are no other options nearby—and are served at scheduled times in the either the Hacienda Chivato air-conditioned restaurant, or at the outside *palapa* dining area. Resort activities include tennis, mountain biking, kayaking, snorkeling, and hiking, and fishing or boat rentals as well as excursions

Tips **Camping Bahía Concepción**

For many people who travel down Baja in RVs, Mulegé is the chosen destination, along with Bahía Concepción. Powdery white beaches, perfectly clear water, and plunging cliffs frame the big bay south of town, creating a coastline you might invent in a dream. It is still possible to just pull out onto some of the many beaches and camp, but an increasing number have been developed into more formal camping arrangements, and several have even turned into motor home colonies. Regardless, it's a stunning place, and camping in Mexico is much less structured than it is in the U.S., Canada, or the U.K.; you can't reserve in advance—sites are available on a first-come, first-served basis.

Driving south from Mulegé, the first beach camping you'll find is at **Playa Punta Arena,** 16km (10 miles) south of town. The beach isn't visible from the road, but like all the beaches here, it is nice. Though it's an RV spot, the rough dirt road keeps it from being overrun. You can rent a *palapa* right on the sand for around $5 per night. Camping is $3 per night.

A few more miles into the bay will bring you to **Playa Santispác.** It has a restaurant/bar, and many snowbirds pull their trailers onto the beach in the fall and stay through spring. Much better for tent campers is **Playa Los Cocos (Palm Beach),** 24km (15 miles) south of Mulegé. Although it's motor home–accessible, it's also very good for tents. Camping is $4 per night, and there are pit toilets and garbage receptacles. **Playa El Coyote,** 27km (17 miles) south of Mulegé, is also nice for tent camping. Sites are $4 per night.

arranged by the tour desk. The hotel has its own private airstrip (frequency 122.80), and offers fuel service. If you're coming from Loreto, the trip will take about 2½ hours and cost about $200 by taxi. *Note:* Children under 12 are not allowed here, and all rooms are nonsmoking.

Domocilio conocido, Punta Chivato, B.C.S. ℂ **615/153-0188.** Fax 615/155-5600. www.posadadelasflores.com. 18 units. $240–$270 double; $320–$350 junior suite. Rates include all meals. MC, V. Free parking; private airstrip available. **Amenities:** 2 restaurants; bar; swimming pool; tennis court; tour desk; video library; Internet satellite desk, satellite TV in public areas. *In room:* A/C, TV/VCR; minibar.

MODERATE

Hotel Serenidad 𝒜𝒜   Serenity, seclusion, and casual comfort are the hallmarks of the Serenidad, just south of town between the airstrip and a long stretch of beach. Low-rise, Mediterranean-style buildings border either Mulegé's largest pool (with *palapa* bar) or a courtyard. Most rooms have working fireplaces, and all have ceiling fans plus a large bathroom with a skylight. Decor is stylish for the area, and all rooms have a king-size bed, tile floors, and a small seating area with a glass-topped table and chairs. The larger casitas (bungalows) have two bedrooms and two baths, a small living area, and a terrace, making them ideal for families or friends traveling together.

The locally popular restaurant/bar has satellite TV, and on Saturdays the place fills up for the weekly pig roast and fiesta with mariachis, a regional specialty. The Serenidad has an adjacent RV park with 10 available spaces. It's on the south side of the mouth of the river, 4km (2½ miles) south of the town center, off the Carretera Transpeninsular. The hotel stays open year-round, but the restaurant closes for the month of September.

Carretera Transpeninsular Sur Km 30., P.O. Box 9, CP 23900 Mulegé, B.C.S. ② **615/153-0540.** Fax 615/153-0311. www.serenidad.com. 48 units. $72 double; $89 1-bedroom suite; $128 2-bedroom casitas. MC, V. Free parking; private airstrip available. **Amenities:** Restaurant/bar; swimming pool w/bar; telephone and fax service available through the front desk. *In room:* A/C.

INEXPENSIVE
Hotel Hacienda Mulegé 🍴 *Value*   A former 18th-century hacienda with double courtyards and a small, shaded swimming pool makes for a comfortable and value-priced place to stay. You couldn't be more centrally located in Mulegé, and the Hacienda is known for its popular bar, which also has satellite TV featuring sporting events. The bar closes for the night between 10 and 11pm, so it shouldn't keep you awake. The cozy restaurant with stone walls and a fireplace also has a pleasant patio. Rooms surround the courtyard and have beds with foam mattresses and brightly colored Mexican accents. Bathrooms are simple but large, with showers.

Calle Francisco Madero 3, Mulegé, B.C.S., ½ block east of the central plaza. ② **615/153-0021.** Fax 615/153-0046. 24 units. $35 per room. No credit cards. Free parking. **Amenities:** Restaurant/bar; small swimming pool; room service; laundry service; tourist guide services; currency exchange; fax available at front desk. *In room:* A/C, TV.

Hotel Las Casitas 🍴 *Value*   This long-standing favorite welcomes many repeat visitors, along with the local literati—it is the birthplace of Mexican poet Alan Gorosave. Rooms are in a courtyard just behind (and adjacent to) the Las Casitas restaurant, one of Mulegé's most popular. The basic accommodations have high ceilings, tile bathrooms, and rustic decor. Plants fill a small central patio for guests' use, but the more socially inclined gravitate to the restaurant and bar, which is open daily from 7am to 10pm. The place is especially lively on weekends—on Friday evenings there's a Mexican fiesta. The inn and restaurant are on the main east-west street in Mulegé, 1 block from the central plaza.

Calle Francisco Madero 50, Col. Centro 23900 Mulegé, B.C.S. ② **615/153-0019.** Fax 615/153-0190. **Amenities:** Restaurant/bar; tour desk. *In room:* A/C.

WHERE TO DINE
The must-have meal in Mulegé is the traditional pig roast. It's an event, with the pig roasted Polynesian-style in a palm-lined open pit for hours, generally while guests enjoy a few beers or other beverages. Homemade tortillas, salsas, an assortment of toppings, and the ubiquitous rice and beans accompany the succulent cooked pork. Remember—it's more than a pig, it's a party. The perennially popular pig roasts happen each Saturday night at both the **Las Casitas** restaurant (see below) and the **Hotel Serenidad** (see "Where to Stay," above). The meal costs about $10.

Another Mulegé—and Mexican—dining staple is the taco. The best are reportedly found at the taco stand adjoining Las Casitas or at the popular **Taquería Doney,** at Madero and Romero Rubio, just as you enter town, past the *depósito* (warehouse) on the right.

MODERATE
Las Casitas 🍴🍴 SEAFOOD/MEXICAN   Las Casitas remains a popular mainstay with both locals and visitors to Mulegé. The bar has a steady clientele day and night and often features special sporting events on satellite TV. Dine either in the interior stone-walled dining area or on its adjoining, plant-filled patio. Live music sometimes

plays from 6pm on, and Fridays feature a Mexican fiesta and buffet. If you're just dining off the menu, don't resist the fresh lobster for $10. The menu offerings are standard fare with an emphasis on fresh seafood, but the quality is good, and you can see the extra-clean exhibition kitchen as you enter.

Calle Francisco Madero 50. ✆ 615/153-0019. Breakfast $1.50–$4; main courses $3–$11. MC, V. Daily 7am–10pm.

Los Equipales 🦀 MEXICAN/SEAFOOD   First off, you won't find any *equipales* (rustic palm-and-leather bucket chairs) here. In their place, the restaurant has white faux-wicker chairs that are comfy but hardly authentic. This is one of Mulegé's ever-popular hangouts, with homestyle cooking matched by family-friendly service. Its second-story location offers diners the only lofty view in town, and this is the only place in Mulegé that serves complimentary chips and salsa with the meal. The specialties are traditional Mexican fare and Sonoran beef, especially barbecued ribs. Tropical drinks, like mango margaritas, are also popular.

Calle Moctezuma, 2nd floor. ✆ 615/153-0330. Main courses $3–$10. MC, V. Daily 8am–10pm.

INEXPENSIVE

Eduardo's MEAT/CHINESE   Eduardo's is known for its grilled meats—tender ribs, traditional *carne asada* (grilled marinated beef), and thick steaks, but it also serves an extensive buffet of Chinese food. White plastic chairs somewhat diminish the attractiveness of the stone-walled dining area, but the graciously friendly service compensates. Full bar service is also available. Across the street from the downtown Pemex station, the restaurant is currently only open on Sundays, but may expand its days of service, so check to see what the current schedule is.

General Martínez. ✆ 615/153-0258. Main courses $3–$10. No credit cards. Sun 2–9pm.

El Candil MEXICAN   Filling platters of traditional Mexican fare at reasonable prices are the specialty of this casual restaurant, which has been run by the same family for more than 3 decades. Tacos are always popular, but the best of the house is the heaping Mexican combination plate.

Zaragoza 8, near the central plaza. No phone. Main courses $2–$8. No credit cards. Mon–Sat 11am–11pm; Sun 1–8pm.

MULEGE AFTER DARK

Mulegé's nightlife pretty much centers on the bars of the Hacienda Hotel and Las Casitas, in town. In addition, **La Jungla Bambú,** at the corner of General Martínez and Zaragoza (no phone) is an American-style sports bar gone tropical. For dancing, **Plaza José San Antonio** (directly behind Las Casitas) serves up a fresh selection of disco several nights a week in their garden-setting *palapa.* Also, The **Pick Up Bar,** on the corner by the town square, seems to attract a lively group of English-speaking revelers, and the staff is generally helpful and fun. Also of note is the bar at the **Hotel Serenidad.**

3 A Side Trip from Mulegé: Santa Rosalía

61km (38 miles) N of Mulegé

In an arroyo north of Mulegé you'll find Santa Rosalía, a unique mining town dating to 1855. Founded by the French, the town has a decidedly European architectural ambience, though a distinctly Mexican culture inhabits it. Pastel clapboard houses surrounded by picket fences line the streets, giving the town its nickname, *ciudad de madera* (city of wood). Its large harbor and the rusted ghost of its copper-smelting facility dominate the central part of town bordering the waterfront.

The town served as the center for copper mining in Mexico for years; a French company, Compañía de Boleo (part of the Rothschild family holdings), obtained a 99-year lease in the 1800s. Mexican President Porfirio Díaz originally granted the lease to the German shipping company Casa Moeller, which sold the mining operation rights to the Rothschild family but retained exclusive rights to transport ore from the mine. The agreement was that in exchange for access to the rich deposits of copper the company would build a town, the harbor, and public buildings, and establish a maritime route between Santa Rosalia and Guaymas, creating employment for Mexican workers. Operations began in 1885 and continued until 1954, when the Mexicans regained the use of the land through legislation. During the French operation, more than 644km (399 miles) of tunnels were built underground and in the surrounding hills, primarily by Indian and Chinese laborers. Following the reversion of the mining operations to the Mexican government, the facility was plagued with problems, including the alleged leakage of arsenic into the local water supply, so the plant was permanently closed in 1985.

The French influence is apparent everywhere in Santa Rosalía—especially in the colonial-style wooden houses. The French also brought over thousands of Asian workers who have since integrated into the local population (Chinese cuisine is still particularly popular here) along with the German and French residents. The French administrators built their homes on the northern Mesa Francia, the part of town where you'll find the museum and historic buildings, while the Mexican residents settled on the southern Mesa Mexico. The town still has a noticeably segregated feel.

Today, Santa Rosalía, with a population of 14,000, is notable for its man-made harbor—the recently constructed Marina Santa Rosalía, complete with concrete piers, floating docks, and full docking accommodations for a dozen ocean cruisers. Santa Rosalía is the main seaport of northern Baja, directly across from Guaymas. A ferry link established during the mining days still operates between the two ports. Because this is the prime entry point of manufactured goods into Baja, the town abounds with autoparts and electronic appliance stores, along with shops selling Nikes and sunglasses.

The town has no real beach to speak of, and fewer recreational attractions. The rusted, dilapidated smelting foundry, railroad, and pier all border the docks and give the town an abandoned, neglected atmosphere.

EXPLORING SANTA ROSALIA

The principal attraction in Santa Rosalía is the **Iglesia de Santa Barbara,** a structure of galvanized steel designed by Gustave Eiffel (of Eiffel Tower fame) in 1884. It was originally created for the 1889 Paris World Expo, where it was displayed as a prototype for what Eiffel envisioned as a sort of prefab mission. The concept never took off, and the structure was left in a warehouse in Brussels, where it was later discovered and sent to Baja by officials of the mining company. Section by section the church was transported then reassembled in Santa Rosalía in 1897. The somber gray exterior belies the beauty of the intricate stained-glass windows viewed from inside.

Along with the church, the other obligatory site to see is the **Ex-Fundación del Pacífico,** or **Museo Histórico Minero de Santa Rosalía.** In a landmark wooden building, it houses a permanent display of artifacts from the days of Santa Rosalía's mining operations. There are miniature models of the town and its buildings, old accounting ledgers and office equipment, and samples of the minerals extracted from

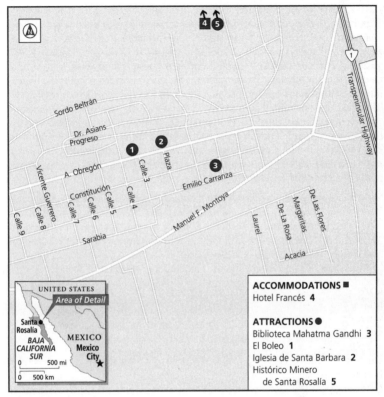

ACCOMMODATIONS ■
Hotel Francés **4**

ATTRACTIONS ●
Biblioteca Mahatma Gandhi **3**
El Boleo **1**
Iglesia de Santa Barbara **2**
Histórico Minero
  de Santa Rosalía **5**

local mines. It's open Monday through Saturday from 8:30am to 2pm and 5 to 7pm. Admission is $1.50.

Bordering the museum are the most attractive of the clapboard houses, painted in a rainbow of delicious colors—mango, lemon, blueberry, and cherry. The wood used to construct these houses was the return cargo on ships that transported copper to refineries in Oregon and British Columbia during the 1800s.

Other sites of note are the Plaza Benito Juárez, or central *zócalo* (square) that fronts the Palacio Municipal, or City Hall, an intriguing structure of French colonial design. The streets of Constitución, Carranza, Plaza, and Altamirano border the square. Just down Constitución is the **Biblioteca Mahatma Gandhi,** more notable for the uniqueness of its name in Mexico than for the library itself, which is the only one in operation between Ensenada and La Paz. The library has a permanent exhibition of historic photos on display.

WHERE TO STAY & DINE

Santa Rosalía has one of the best bakeries in all of Baja—**El Boleo** (✆ **615/152-0310**)—which has been baking tasty and crusty mini French baguettes (it's likely the term "boleo," signifying this popular Mexican bread, was coined here) since the late 1800s. It's on Avenida Obregón at Calle 3, 3 blocks west of the church, and is open daily from 8am to 9pm.

Hotel Francés ⭐⭐   Founded in 1886, the Hotel Francés once set the standard of hospitality in Baja Sur, welcoming European dignitaries and hosting the French administrators and businessmen of the mining operations. Today, it has a worn air of elegance but retains its position as the most welcoming accommodation in Santa Rosalía. The lobby, restaurant/bar, and colonial-style wraparound veranda make up the front part of the building. Rooms are in the back, with wooden porches and balconies that overlook a small courtyard pool. Each room has individually controlled air-conditioning plus windows that open for ventilation. Floors are wood-planked, and the bathrooms are beautifully tiled, although small. Security boxes and telephone service are available in the lobby. The restaurant is open daily, but currently only for breakfast from 7am to noon; check to see whether it has added other meals.

Calle Jean Michel Cousteau s/n, Santa Rosalía B.C.S. ⓒ/fax **615/152-2052**. 17 units. $54 single or double. No credit cards. Free parking. **Amenities:** Restaurant/bar; small pool. *In room:* A/C, TV, no phone.

4 Whale-Watching in Baja: A Primer

Few sights inspire as much reverence as close contact with a whale in its natural habitat. The thrill of seeing one of these giant inhabitants of the sea up close is a life-changing event for many people, and few places in the world can offer as complete an experience as Mexico's Baja peninsula. The various protected bays and lagoons on the Pacific coast are the preferred winter waters for migrating gray whales as they journey south to mate and give birth to their calves.

While the entire Pacific coast of the Baja peninsula offers opportunities for whale sightings, the experience is particularly rewarding in the protected areas of the El Vizcaíno Biosphere Reserve, where a large number of whales can be seen easily. This area encompasses the famous Laguna Ojo de Liebre—also known as Scammon's Lagoon—close to Guerrero Negro, Laguna San Ignacio, and Bahía Magdalena.

Because these protected waters offer ideal conditions for gray whales during the winter, the neighboring towns have developed the necessary infrastructure and services to accommodate whale-watchers. Avid eco- and adventure-lovers seem to follow their own migratory patterns and arrive at these shores between January and March to gaze in awe at the gentle cetaceans.

WHAT YOU'LL SEE

Gray whales are the favorite species for whale-watchers because they tend to swim and feed mostly in coastal shallows, occasionally resting with their abdomens on the bottom, while their close relatives prefer to frequent the deeper realms of the ocean. Whale-watching in one of Baja's lagoons can be truly exciting—at times, gray whales appear to be on all sides, displaying the full spectrum of typical whale behavior.

Watchers might be showered with a cloud of water from a whale spouting (clearing its blowhole) or might witness an enormous male spyhopping—lifting its head vertically out of the water, just above eye level, to pivot around before slipping back into the water. Perhaps the most breathtaking spectacle of all is a breach, when a whale propels itself out of the water and arches through the air to land on its back with a splash. These gray whales are known to be so friendly and curious that they frequently come up to the whale-watching boats and stay close by, sometimes allowing people to pet them.

To be close to these magnificent creatures is a privilege. Above all, respect their environment and their integrity as inhabitants of the marine world.

⌒Tips Should I Take a Tour or Hire a Boat?

You'll often get a better deal if you hire a local *panga* operator; head down to the local pier to price it. Expect to pay anywhere from $30 to $45 per person for a day trip with a local guide (plus a tip for good service); an organized tour can run almost double that price. It's always a good idea to check for licensed, experienced operators (they must have photo-ID credentials showing they are licensed tour guides) who know how to approach the whales with calm, caution, and respect for the environment. The most important thing about whale-watching is to enjoy it while practicing guidelines that ensure both your safety and the safety of the whales. (We've recommended several tour operators and organizations below.)

WHICH TOWN? WHICH TOUR?

Regardless of where you decide to stay in Baja, you most likely will easily find tours to the whale-watching areas of Bahía Magdalena and the lagoons of Ojo de Liebre and San Ignacio. (For whale-watching tours that depart from La Paz, see chapter 5.) If you want to center your visit on whale-watching, the best places to visit are Guerrero Negro, San Ignacio, Ciudad Constitución, Puerto San Carlos, and Puerto López Mateos.

While the above-mentioned towns have basic facilities, Loreto may actually be the wisest base to choose; it has a well-developed tourist infrastructure and a number of lovely resort hotels. From here, whale-watching cruises along the Pacific coast are easily accessible. The trips take you by road to Bahía Magdalena, where you board a skiff to get up close to the gentle giants. En route you get a chance to view the spectacular desert landscape; guides offer a wealth of natural and historical information. Locally based **Las Parras Tours** (© 613/135-1010; www.lasparrastours.com) offers excellent excursions. Another is the U.S.-based **Baja Expeditions,** 2625 Garnet Av., San Diego, CA 92109 (© 800/843-6967, or 612/125-3828 in La Paz). Prices for package trips from Loreto run $95 to $125 per person for a daylong trip.

Guerrero Negro sits on the dividing line between southern and northern Baja. It has a modest but well-developed tourism infrastructure in an otherwise industrial town (it's the site of the world's largest evaporative saltworks). Despite the industrial nature of the town, the lagoon where gray whales calve and spend the winter has remained safe and has witnessed a remarkable comeback of this almost-extinct species. This is partly because the salt produced in Guerrero Negro is shipped from an offshore artificial island, built away from the whale area, and also because of the designation of the area as part of the El Vizcaíno Biosphere Reserve in 1988.

San Ignacio is a small town built by the Spaniards in the middle of a palm oasis and is full of Jesuit history. It is the ideal point of departure for **Laguna San Ignacio** ✶✶, 74km (46 miles) southwest of the town. The San Ignacio lagoon is an excellent spot for whale-watching because it is common for whales in this area to approach the small whale-watching boats, occasionally coming close enough to allow you to touch them.

Bahía Magdalena is another spot preferred by wintering gray whales. Two towns on the bay's shore offer whale-watching tours. **Puerto López Mateos,** on the northern shore, is the closest town to the whales' calving areas. Accommodations are limited to a few modest hotels and restaurants, but several boat operators offer tours. For

The Bloody History of a Whale-Watching Haven

Forty kilometers (25 miles) southwest of Guerrero Negro is **Laguna Ojo de Liebre,** also known as Scammon's Lagoon. It takes its name from an infamous whaler, Charles Melville Scammon, who followed a pod of gray whales into Laguna Ojo de Liebre. Taking advantage of geography—the lagoon has a very narrow mouth—he managed to slaughter the entire lot by using explosive harpoons. Before Scammon's "accomplishment," gray whales had remained safe from whalers because of their aggressive nature when under attack. But after Scammon's massacre, scores of whalers hopped on the bloody bandwagon, killing an estimated 10,000 gray whales in less than 20 years, bringing the population close to extinction. (In an ironic turn of events, Scammon became a naturalist of some note later in life and wrote an important book about whales and the whaling industry.) The gray whales have made a remarkable comeback in the last 20 years, however—so much so that they are now off the endangered-species list.

recommendations, contact the **Unión de Lancheros y Servicios Turísticos del Puerto** (© 613/131-5114), an association of fishing-boat operators on Adolfo López Mateos, or the **Sociedad Cooperativa de Servicios Turísticos** (© **613/131-5112,** 613/131-5198, or 613/131-5066; ask for Señor Francisco).

Puerto San Carlos offers a more developed tourism infrastructure, with well-appointed hotels and restaurants, trailer parks, travel agencies, a bus station, and other services. To arrange a tour, try **Viajes Mar y Arena,** Puerto La Paz s/n (© **613/136-0076,** 613/136-0599, 613/136-0676, or 613/137-8093).

Ciudad Constitución, the largest of the three towns, is 61km (38 miles) inland. It has a well-developed tourism infrastructure, with tour organizers that offer daily whale-watching tours during the season.

GETTING THERE   To get to Puerto López Mateos, take the only road going west from Loreto for about 121km (75 miles). When you arrive in the town of Insurgentes, turn right and continue 2.4km (1½ miles) to the Puerto López Mateos exit. Turn left and continue 34km (21 miles) to Puerto López Mateos. To get to Puerto San Carlos, take the same road west to Insurgentes, then drive south about 24km (15 miles) until you reach Ciudad Constitución. From Ciudad Constitución, take the exit marked PUERTO SAN CARLOS, and continue the remaining 63km (39 miles) to town. Both routes are well paved and maintained.

7

Northern Baja: Tijuana, Rosarito Beach & Ensenada

The region that holds Mexico's most infamous border crossing also claims to be the birthplace of the original Caesar salad and the margarita. Who could resist that? This trip into northern Baja California combines the boisterous (Tijuana), the beachy (Rosarito Beach), and the beautiful (Ensenada), three towns that comprise some of the most important introductions to Mexico.

Long notorious as a party-hard border town, 10-block Tijuana has cleaned up its act a bit on its way to becoming a full-scale city with explosive population growth. The town's traditional lures—the legendary nightlife and hardcore souvenir shopping—are now augmented by a

number of family-friendly sports and cultural attractions.

For a more tranquil experience, the resort town of Rosarito Beach remains a laidback beach destination despite spending time in Hollywood's spotlight as the location where much of the movie *Titanic* was filmed (see "En Route from Rosarito to Ensenada," later in this chapter).

Continue south past stellar surf breaks, golf courses, and fish-taco stands, and the lovely town of Ensenada emerges, a favored port of call with plenty of appeal for active travelers. Take time to travel inland from Ensenada to explore Mexico's emerging wine country.

EXPLORING NORTHERN BAJA

If you have a car, it's easy to venture into Baja Norte from Southern California for a few days' getaway. Since 1991, American car-rental companies have allowed customers to drive their cars into Baja. Whether you drive your own car or a rented one, you'll need Mexican auto insurance in addition to your own; it's available at the border in San Ysidro or through the car-rental companies (see "Getting Around" in chapter 2).

It takes relatively little time to cross the international border in Tijuana, but be prepared for a delay of an hour or more on your return to the United States through San Diego—with increased security measures for entering the U.S., this is an especially diligent point of entry. If you take local buses down the Baja coast (which is possible), the delays come en route rather than at the border.

1 Tijuana: Bawdy Border Town

26km (16 miles) S of San Diego

Don't expect to find the Mexico of your fantasies—charming, sun-dappled town squares and churches blanketed in bougainvillea; women in colorful embroidered skirts and blouses—in infamous Tijuana, Mexico's first point of entry from the West Coast of the U.S. You're more likely to encounter a dynamic city with a decidedly urban culture, a profusion of U.S.–inspired goods and services, and relentless hawkers playing to the thousands of tourists who come for a taste of old Mexico.

Like many burgeoning cities in developing nations, Tijuana is a mixture of new and old, rich and poor, modern and traditional. But Tijuana is increasingly an important city in Mexico; the population has swelled to nearly two million, making it the second-largest city on the Pacific coast of North America (after Los Angeles). Despite obvious signs of widespread poverty, the town claims one of the lowest unemployment rates in the country, thanks to the rise in *maquiladoras,* the foreign-owned manufacturing operations that continue to proliferate under NAFTA (North American Free Trade Agreement). High-rise office buildings testify to increased prosperity, as does the emergence of a white-collar middle class that shops at modern shopping centers away from the tourist zone. And the availability of imported goods and the lure of a big-city experience draw visitors.

Tijuana has long been renowned for its hustling, carnival-like atmosphere and easily accessible decadence, a reputation stemming from its early notoriety as a playground of illicit pleasures during the U.S. Prohibition, when scores of visitors flocked here to the site of the world's largest saloon bar, The Whale. Not long after, the $10-million Hotel Casino de Agua Caliente—the first "megaresort" in Mexico—attracted Hollywood stars and other celebrities with its casino, greyhound racing, and hot-springs spa.

But Tijuana's "sin city" image is gradually morphing as the city develops into a more culturally diverse destination. Vineyards associated with the growing wine industry are nearby, and an increasing number of museums and other cultural offerings are joining the traditional sporting attractions of greyhound racing and bullfights.

GETTING THERE & DEPARTING

A visit to Tijuana requires little in the way of formalities—no passport or tourist card is currently required of people who stay less than 72 hours in this border zone. However, this policy is currently under review and may change by December 2006, requiring passports of anyone entering the U.S. from the border. If you plan to stay longer than 72 hours, you must have a tourist card, available free of charge from the border crossing station or from any immigration office.

BY PLANE **AeroCalifornia** (© **800/237-6225** in the U.S., or 664/684-2100) has nonstop or direct flights from Los Angeles; **Aeromexico** (© **800/237-6639** in the U.S., 664/683-2700, or 664/638-8444; www.aeromexico.com) has connecting flights from Houston, New York, Culiacán, Hermosillo, Guadalajara, La Paz, and Mexico City. **Mexicana** (© **800/531-7921** in the U.S., or 664/634-6566; www.mexicana. com) has direct or connecting flights from Guadalajara, Los Angeles, Mexico City, and Cancún.

BY CAR If you plan to visit only Tijuana and are arriving from Southern California, you should consider leaving your car behind, since traffic can be challenging. One alternative is to walk across the border; you can either park your car in one of the safe, long-term parking lots on the San Diego side for about $12 a day, or take the San Diego Trolley (see below for more information) to the border. Once you're in Tijuana, it's easier to get around by taxi than to take on the local drivers. Cab fares from the border to downtown Tijuana run about $5. You can also charter a taxi to Rosarito for about $20 (one-way) or to Ensenada for $100 (one-way).

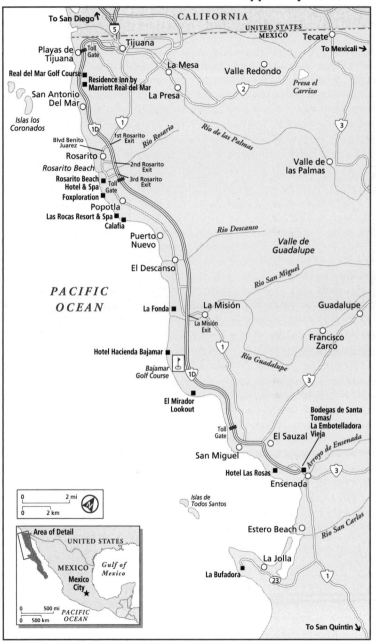

The Upper Baja Peninsula

CALIFORNIA

To San Diego↑

UNITED STATES
MEXICO

Tecate

To Mexicali →

Playas de Tijuana

Toll Gate

Tijuana

La Mesa

Valle Redondo

Presa el Carrizo

Real del Mar Golf Course

Residence Inn by Marriott Real del Mar

San Antonio Del Mar

La Presa

Islas los Coronados

1D

Blvd Benito Juarez

1st Rosarito Exit

Rio Rosario

Rio de las Palmas

Valle de las Palmas

Rosarito

Rosarito Beach

2nd Rosarito Exit

Rosarito Beach Hotel & Spa

Toll Gate

3rd Rosarito Exit

Foxploration

Popotla

Rio Descanso

Valle de Guadalupe

Las Rocas Resort & Spa

Calafia

Puerto Nuevo

El Descanso

Rio San Miguel

PACIFIC OCEAN

La Fonda

La Misión

Guadalupe

La Misión Exit

Francisco Zarco

Hotel Hacienda Bajamar

Bajamar Golf Course

1D

Rio Guadalupe

El Mirador Lookout

Bodegas de Santa Tomas/ La Embotelladora Vieja

Toll Gate

El Sauzal

Arroyo de Ensenada

San Miguel

Hotel Las Rosas

Ensenada

0   2 mi
0   2 km

Islas de Todos Santos

Estero Beach

Rio San Carlos

Area of Detail

UNITED STATES

La Jolla

MEXICO

Gulf of Mexico

La Bufadora

Mexico City ★

23

0   500 mi

0   500 km

PACIFIC OCEAN

To San Quintin ↘

To reach Tijuana from the U.S., take I-5 south to the Mexican border at San Ysidro. The 18-mile (29km) drive from downtown San Diego takes about half an hour.

Many car-rental companies in San Diego allow customers to drive their cars into Baja California, at least as far as Ensenada. Cars from **Avis** (✆ **800/331-1212** or 619/688-5000; www.avis.com) may be driven as far as the 28th parallel and Guerrero Negro, the dividing line that separates Baja into two states, North and South. **Cabaja Auto Rentals** (✆ **888/470-7368** or 619/470-7368; www.cabaja.com), with locations in San Diego and Alpine, has perhaps the best rates and vehicles to take into Baja, and it allows its cars to be driven the entire 1,610km (1,000-mile) stretch of the Baja peninsula. You can even book a one-way rental to Los Cabos. Daily rates for economy cars are $55; convertibles are $100; 4×4 SUV daily rates range from $130 to $160. All rates include Mexican insurance and 100 miles per day. San Diego's **Bob Baker Ford** (✆ **619/297-5001,** ext. 9; http://ford.bobbaker.com and click on "Rental Cars") also allows its cars to be driven anywhere in Baja.

Keep in mind that if you drive in, you'll need Mexican auto insurance in addition to your own. You can get it in San Ysidro, just north of the border at the San Ysidro exit; from your car-rental agency in San Diego; or from a AAA office if you're a member.

From the south, take the Carretera Transpeninsular north to Tijuana. It's a long and sometimes difficult drive.

BY TROLLEY   From the San Diego border, you also have the option of taking the bright-red trolley in San Ysidro at the Plaza Las Americas and getting off in Tijuana at Revolución and Calle 2 (it's nicknamed the Tijuana Trolley for good reason). It's simple, quick, and inexpensive; the one-way trolley fare is $2. The last trolley leaving for San Ysidro departs downtown around midnight; the last returning trolley from San Ysidro is at 1am. On Saturday, the trolley runs 24 hours. Departures leave about every 30 minutes.

BY BUS   **Five Star Tours,** in San Diego at the intersection of Broadway and Kettner (✆ **619/232-5049;** fax 619/575-3075; www.fivestartours.com), offers specialized trips across the border. For $50 for the first person and $5 per extra person, the company will take you across the border, recommend shops and restaurants, or take you to the Cultural Center, then pick you up to return to San Diego at a pre-established time. You must make reservations 24 hours in advance, and as trips are catered to individual desires, arrangements and pick-up locations are confirmed when you book your trip.

Also from San Diego, **Contact Tours** (✆ **619/477-8687**) offers a tour to Tijuana for $29, including stops at the must-see tourist sights, including Avenida Revolución, and stops for shopping and lunch. It's not a regularly scheduled tour, so call ahead to check departure dates and times.

Mexicoach (✆ **664/685-1440;** www.gototijuana.com) specializes in cross-border transportation at a cost of just $2.50 each way. It's open daily from 5:30am to 9pm, with departures every 15 to 20 minutes from 8am to 9pm, 365 days per year. Board the bus at the Border Station Parking (next to the San Diego Factory Outlet Center, a huge outlet mall right near the border crossing—you can't miss it) or from the trolley's (see above) last stop at the border, and it will take you to the Tijuana Tourist Terminal (✆ **664/685-1470**) on Avenida Revolución, between calles 6 and 7. Returns to the border leave from the same terminal. These buses also travel to Rosarito Beach ($6 each way) and the Tijuana Bullring-by-the-Sea ($4 each way). Note that the special bus lanes through the border are also, on average, much faster than the car lanes.

Tijuana

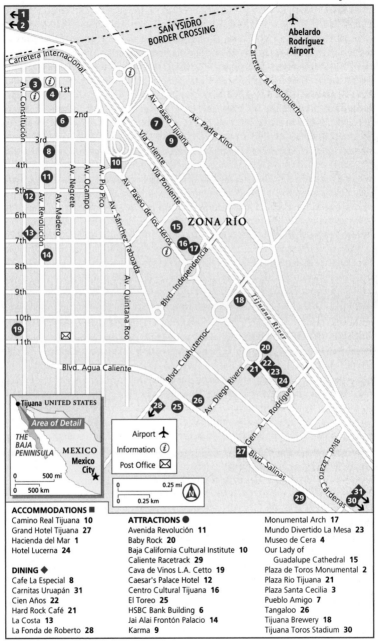

ACCOMMODATIONS ■
Camino Real Tijuana **10**
Grand Hotel Tijuana **27**
Hacienda del Mar **1**
Hotel Lucerna **24**

DINING ◆
Cafe La Especial **8**
Carnitas Uruapán **31**
Cien Años **22**
Hard Rock Café **21**
La Costa **13**
La Fonda de Roberto **28**

ATTRACTIONS ●
Avenida Revolución **11**
Baby Rock **20**
Baja California Cultural Institute **10**
Caliente Racetrack **29**
Cava de Vinos L.A. Cetto **19**
Caesar's Palace Hotel **12**
Centro Cultural Tijuana **16**
El Toreo **25**
HSBC Bank Building **6**
Jai Alai Frontón Palacio **14**
Karma **9**

Monumental Arch **17**
Mundo Divertido La Mesa **23**
Museo de Cera **4**
Our Lady of
  Guadalupe Cathedral **15**
Plaza de Toros Monumental **2**
Plaza Rio Tijuana **21**
Plaza Santa Cecilia **3**
Pueblo Amigo **7**
Tangaloo **26**
Tijuana Brewery **18**
Tijuana Toros Stadium **30**

ORIENTATION

ARRIVING   Upon arrival at the airport, buy a ticket inside the building for a taxi, which can be shared by up to five passengers. It costs about $9 to and from anywhere in the city. Public buses to downtown Tijuana, marked CENTRO, are also available and cost 45 ¢ per passenger. The airport is about 8km (5 miles) east of the city.

The major car-rental agencies all have counters at the airport, open during flight arrivals: **Avis** (℗ **800/331-1212** from the U.S., or 664/683-2310; www.avis.com); **Budget** (℗ **800/527-0700** from the U.S., or 664/683-2905; www.budget.com); **Hertz** (℗ **800/654-3131** from the U.S., or 664/683-2080; www.hertz.com); and **National** (℗ **800/328-4567** from the U.S., or 664/683-8115; www.nationalcar.com). Advance reservations are not always necessary, but they are recommended, especially since you can usually get a better rate if you make your reservation in the U.S.

If you've come to Tijuana via the San Diego Trolley or if you leave a car on the U.S. side of the border, you will walk through the border crossing. The first structure you'll see on your left is a Visitor Information Center, open daily from 9am to 7pm; ask for a copy of the *Baja Visitor* magazine and the *Baja Times.* From here, you can easily walk into the center of town or take a taxi.

Taxicabs in Tijuana are easy to find and are available at most of the visitor hot spots. It's customary to agree upon the rate before stepping into the cab, whether you're going just a few blocks or hiring a cab for the afternoon. One-way rides within the city cost between $4 and $10, and tipping is optional. Some cabs are "local" taxis, frequently stopping to take on or let off other passengers during your ride; they are less expensive than private cabs and are more likely to be minivans that seat multiple passengers.

VISITOR INFORMATION   Prior to your visit, you can write for information, brochures, and maps from the **Tijuana Convention & Visitors Bureau,** P.O. Box 434523, San Diego, CA 92143-4523. You can also get a preview of events, restaurants, and more online at **www.seetijuana.com**. Once in Tijuana, pick up visitor information at the **Tijuana Tourism Board,** Paseo de los Héroes 9365, Zona Río (℗ **888/775-2417** toll-free in the U.S., or 664/686-1345; www.seetijuana.com). You can also try the **National Chamber of Commerce** (℗ **664/685-8472;** Mon–Fri 9am–2pm and 4–7pm). Its offices are at the corner of Avenida Revolución and Calle 1, and its staff is extremely helpful with maps and orientation, local events of interest, and accommodations; in addition, the Tijuana Tourism Board provides legal assistance for visitors who encounter problems while in Tijuana.

Tijuana has several **Visitor Information Centers.** The facility at the San Ysidro border (℗ **664/683-1405**) is open Monday through Saturday 8am to 5pm and Sunday 8am to 3pm. An office at the Mexico entrance across the pedestrian crossing bridge (℗ **664/683-4987**) is open Monday through Saturday 9am to 5pm and Sunday from 8am to 3pm. On Avenida Revolución, between calles 3 and 4 (℗ **664/685-2210**), is another office, open Monday through Thursday 10am to 4pm, and Friday through Sunday 10am to 7pm. The office at Via de la Juventud 8800, office 23–25, in the Centro Commercial Viva Tijuana (℗ **664/973-0430**), is open Monday through Friday 8am to 8pm and Saturday and Sunday 9am to 6pm. A visitor information module at the Tijuana Airport (℗ **664/683-8244**) is open daily 8am to 3pm.

For additional information online, visit www.tijuanaonline.org and www.baja.gob.mx.

Tijuana has a special **tourist assist number** (℗ **078;** this is a free call) to help visitors with special needs. The following countries have **consulate offices** in Tijuana:

the **United States** (℡ **664/622-7400**), **Canada** (℡ **664/684-0461**), and the **United Kingdom** (℡ **664/681-7323** or 664/686-5320).

FAST FACTS: Tijuana

Area Code The local telephone area code is **664**.

Banks Banks exchange currency during business hours, generally Monday through Friday from 8:30am to 6pm and Saturday from 9am to 2pm. Major banks with ATMs and *casas de cambio* (money-exchange houses) are easy to find in all the heavily trafficked areas discussed in this book. The currency of Mexico is the peso, but you can easily visit Tijuana (or Rosarito and Ensenada for that matter) without changing money since dollars are accepted virtually everywhere.

Climate & Weather Tijuana's climate is similar to Southern California's: Don't expect sweltering heat just because you're south of the border, and remember that the Pacific waters won't be much warmer than off San Diego. The first beaches you'll find are about 24km (15 miles) south of Tijuana.

Emergencies Dial ℡ **078** to reach **Tourist Assist**; ℡ **066** to reach the **Police** or **Red Cross**. Both are free calls. To reach the Green Angels (a government service that travels the roadways of Mexico looking for cars with problems, equipped to make minor repairs and only charging for parts used or gas consumed) servicing the Tijuana area, call ℡ **664/624-3479**.

Internet **CyberNet**, Av. Las Palmas 4713-4 (℡ **664/608-4075**; www.cybernet cafe.8k.com), has Internet access, computer rentals, scanners, and printers available in its cafe. Online access is $2.50 per hour, and it's open Monday through Friday 8am to 10pm, Saturdays from 10am to 6pm. Another option is **El Portal Café Internet**, Bulevar Díaz Ordaz 12649, Local 6, 2nd floor (℡ **664/ 681-2735**), which charges $3 per hour. It's open Monday through Saturday 8am to 10pm, Sundays 10am to 6pm.

Pharmacy **Sanborn's** (℡ **664/688-1462**) is a 24-hour megastore with a 24-hour pharmacy. It has several locations in Tijuana; one is at the corner of Avenida Revolución and Calle 8. Numerous discount pharmacies are also found along avenidas Constitución and Revolución.

Taxes & Tipping A value-added tax of 10%, called **IVA** *(Impuesto al Valor Agregado),* is added to most bills, including those in restaurants. This does not represent the tip; the bill will read "IVA incluído," but you should add about 15% for the tip if the service warrants.

Taxis To call a **Radio Taxi**, call ℡ **664/600-4900**; **Yellow Cabs (Taxis Amarillos)** can be reached by calling ℡ **664/682-4617**. You might also want to try catching a "local" combi taxi (VW vans that drive along a particular route; similar to a bus but traveling on more routes and transporting multiple passengers).

EXPLORING TIJUANA

One of the first major tourist attractions below the border is also one of the strangest—the **Museo de Cera (Wax Museum),** Calle 1 no. 8281 (downtown), at the corner of Madero (℡ **664/688-2478**). Featured statues include the eclectic mix of

Whoopi Goldberg, Frida Kahlo, Laurel and Hardy, and Bill Clinton arranged in an exhibit otherwise dominated by figures from Mexican history. If you aren't spooked by the not-so-lifelike figures of Aztec warriors, brown-robed friars, Spanish princes, and 20th-century military leaders (all posed in period dioramas), step into the Chamber of Horrors, where wax werewolves and sinister sadists lurk in the shadows. When the museum is mostly empty, which is most of the time, the dramatically lit Chamber of Horrors can be a little creepy. This side-street freak show is open daily from 10am to 6pm, and admission is $1.50.

For many visitors, Tijuana's "main event" is the bustling **Avenida Revolución,** the street whose reputation precedes it. Since its construction in 1889, Avenida Revolución has been a mecca for tourists visiting Tijuana. In the 1920s, American college students, servicemen, and hedonistic tourists discovered "La Revo" as a bawdy center for illicit fun. Since then, however, some of the original attractions have fallen by the wayside: Gambling was outlawed in the 1930s, back-alley cockfights are also illegal, and the same civic improvements that gave Revolución trees, benches, and wider sidewalks also vanquished the girlie shows whose barkers once accosted passersby. Don't expect staid and sedentary, however: Drinking and shopping are the main order of business these days; while revelers from across the border knock back tequila shooters and dangle precariously from the upstairs railings of glaring bars, bargain hunters peruse the never-ending array of goods (and not-so-goods) for sale. You'll find the action between calles 1 and 9; the information centers (mentioned earlier) are at the north end, and the landmark jai alai palace anchors the southern portion. To help make sense of all the tchotchkes sold here, see "Shopping," below.

Although the lightning-paced indoor ballgame jai alai (pronounced "*high* ah-*lye*") is no longer played here, it's still worth a visit to the **Jai Alai Frontón Palacio,** Avenida Revolución at Calle 8 (© **664/685-3687,** 664/688-0125, or 619/231-1910 in San Diego), for its exquisite neoclassical architecture. Built in 1925, the building for years was the site of jai alai matches, an ancient Basque tradition incorporating elements of tennis, hockey, and basketball. Now the arena is used just for cultural events or occasional boxing matches.

Another building of architectural interest on Avenida Revolución (at Calle 2) is the **HSBC Bank Building**. One of Tijuana's oldest private buildings, the structure was built in 1929 to resemble the French Nouveau style popular in the early 1900s.

Visitors can be easily seduced—then quickly repulsed—by tourist-trap areas like Avenida Revolución, but it's important to remember that there's more to Tijuana than American tourism. If you're looking to see a different side of Tijuana, the best place to start is the **Centro Cultural Tijuana (Tijuana Cultural Center),** Paseo de los Héroes at Mina (© **664/687-9600;** www.cecut.gob.mx). You can easily spot the ultramodern complex, designed by irrepressible modern architect Pedro Ramírez Vásquez, by its centerpiece gigantic sand-colored dome housing an OMNIMAX theater, which screens various 45-minute films (subjects range from science to space travel). The center also houses the **Museo de las Identidades Mexicanas (Museum of Mexican Identities)** permanent collection of artifacts from pre-Hispanic times through the modern political era, plus a gallery for visiting exhibits that has included everything from the works of artist Diego Rivera to a well-curated yet disturbing exhibit chronicling torture and human-rights violations through the ages. Music, theater, and dance performances take place in the center's concert hall and courtyard, and there's also a cafe and an excellent museum bookshop. Call to check the concert schedule during your visit. The center also holds the new **Museo de las Californias (Museum of the Californias),** with exhibits that trace the history of the Californias, dating back to prehistoric times. The center is open daily from 10am to 7pm. Admission to the museum's permanent exhibits is free; there's a $2 charge for the special-event gallery, and tickets for OMNIMAX films are $4 for adults and $2.50 for children. The OMNIMAX theater is open Monday through Friday 1 to 9pm, and Saturdays and Sundays 10am to 9pm.

The Cultural Center may sound like a field trip for schoolchildren, but it's a must-see, if only to drag you away from tourist kitsch and into the more sophisticated **Zona Río (river area)** of Tijuana. While there, stop to admire the wide, European-style **Paseo de los Héroes.** The boulevard's intersections are gigantic *glorietas* (traffic circles), at the center of which stand statuesque monuments to leaders ranging from Aztec Emperor Cuauhtémoc to Abraham Lincoln. Navigating the congested *glorietas* will require your undivided attention, however, so it's best to pull over to admire the monuments. The Zona Río also has some classier shopping options, a colorful local marketplace, and the **Baja California Cultural Institute,** which has exhibits showcasing the culture of the region. It's at 10151 Centenario Av. (© **664/683-5922**).

The ultimate kid destination in Tijuana is **Mundo Divertido La Mesa,** 15035 Vía Rápida Poniente, Fracc. San José (© **664/701-7133** and -7134). Literally translated, it means "fun world," and one parent described it as the Mexican equivalent of "a Chuck E. Cheese's restaurant built inside a Malibu Grand Prix." You get the idea—noisy and frenetic, it's the kind of place kids dream about. Let them choose from miniature golf, batting cages, a roller coaster, a kid-size train, a video game parlor, a bowling alley, movie theaters, and go-carts. There's a food court with tacos and hamburgers; if you're in luck, the picnic area will be festooned with streamers and piñatas for some fortunate child's birthday party. The park is open weekdays noon to 9pm, Saturday and Sunday 11am until 10pm. Admission is free, and several booths inside sell tickets for the various rides.

The fertile valleys of northern Baja produce most of Mexico's finest wines; many high-quality vintages are exported to Europe but most are not available in the U.S. For an introduction to Mexican wines, stop into **Cava de Vinos L.A. Cetto (L.A. Cetto Winery),** Av. Cañón Johnson 2108, at Avenida Constitución Sur (© **664/685-3031** or 664/685-1644; www.lacetto.com). Shaped like a wine barrel, this building's striking

---

Moments **First Crush: The Annual Harvest Festival**

If you enjoyed a visit to L.A. Cetto, Tijuana's winery (see above) or Ensenada's Bodegas de Santo Tomás (p. 166), then you might want to return during the **Fiesta de la Vendimia (Harvest Festival),** held each year in late August or early September. Set among the endless vineyards of the fertile Valle de Guadalupe, the day's events include the traditional blessing of the grapes, wine tastings, live music and dancing, riding exhibitions, and a country-style Mexican meal. L.A. Cetto offers a group excursion from Tijuana (about an hour's drive); San Diego's Baja California Tours (© **800/336-5454** or 858/454-7166) also organizes a daylong trip from San Diego.

facade was fashioned from old oak aging barrels in an inspired bit of recycling. The entrance has a couple of wine presses (ca. 1928) that Don Angel Cetto used back in the early days of production. His family still runs the winery, which opened the impressive visitor center in 1993. L.A. Cetto bottles both red and white wines, some of them award winners, including petite sirah, Nebbiolo, and cabernet sauvignon. Most bottles cost about $5; the special reserves are a little more than $10. The company also produces tequila, brandy, and olive oil, all for sale here. Admission is $2.50 for a tour and generous tasting (for those 18 and older only; those under 18 are admitted free with an adult but cannot taste the wines), $3 with souvenir wine glass. L.A. Cetto is open Monday through Friday 9:30am to 6:30pm, and Saturday 9:30am to 5:30pm. Tours run Monday through Friday 10am to 1:30pm and 4 to 6pm, and Saturday 10am to 4pm as necessity dictates.

If your tastes run more toward *cerveza* than wine, plan to visit the **Cerveza Tijuana brewery**, Fundadores 2951, Col. Juarez (© **664/684-2406** or 664/638-8662; www.tjbeer.com). Here, guided tours (by prior appointment) demonstrate the beer-making process at the brewery, where all beers are made from a select group of hops and malt. The family who owns the company has a long tradition of master brewers who worked in breweries in the Czech Republic and brought their knowledge back home to Tijuana. Cerveza Tijuana was founded in January 2000, and now has select distribution in the U.S. Its lager, dark, and light beers are all available to sample in the adjoining European-style pub, which features karaoke on Monday and Tuesday nights and live music Wednesday through Saturday. A menu of appetizers and entrees is also available. It's open Monday to Saturday 10am to 2am.

SIGHTS OF INTEREST   Tijuana's long and varied history has given rise to a number of intriguing sites of interest. Here are a few of my favorites:

Although the original **Caesar's Palace Hotel,** Av. Revolución 1059, at Calle 5 (© **664/685-1666**), is one of Tijuana's oldest hotels, its real claim to fame is as the birthplace of the Caesar salad (see "Tossed in Tijuana?" below).

The oldest church in Tijuana is the **Catedral de Nuestra Senora de Guadalupe (Our Lady of Guadalupe Cathedral),** in front of City Hall, at Paseo Centenario 10150 and Josefa Ortiz de Domínguez, in Zona Río (© **664/682-4577;** www.nuevacatedraldetijuana.org). First inaugurated in 1902 as a parish church, it was appointed cathedral status in 1964, at which time an expanded construction began, which was completed in the mid-1970s. A more recent expansion began in 2001 and is still underway. When finished, the renovated cathedral will seat 3,000, with standing room for 14,000. Its hallmark will be a brilliant white obelisk bell tower 25 stories high in front of a large statue of the Virgin of Guadalupe, Mexico's patron saint. Mass is celebrated Monday through Friday at 8am and 7pm, Saturdays at 7pm, and Sundays at 9am, noon, and 6pm.

A modern symbol of Tijuana, the **Monumental Arch** (also referred to as the Tijuana or Millennium Arch, or Monumental Clock) was constructed to celebrate the millennium, and has become a source of local debate as to whether it's loved or hated (its modern architecture leaves some with a bad taste in their mouth, as it sits in a historical district). It's at the mouth of Plaza Santa Cecilia, where Calle 1 meets Avenida Revolución.

Plaza Santa Cecilia, also known as Arguello Square, is Tijuana's oldest plaza; at Calle 1 and Avenida Revolución, near the Tourist Assistance kiosk, it is the only plaza in the city that is on a transverse street from the original city-planning grid. Today it's

Tossed in Tijuana?

Local legend has it that local restaurateur Caesar Cardini tossed the first Caesar salad here on July 24, 1924. Julia Child herself saw him whip up a tableside version as a young child. The only problem is that Giacomo Junia, a chef in Chicago, is said to have created a similar dish, named it in honor of the great Roman emperor, in 1903. So which is the original? It's a toss-up—both legends live on.

home to a variety of colorfully painted restaurants and shops, and you'll almost always find a mariachi band playing for tips. At the center of the plaza is a monument to Santa Cecilia, the patron saint of musicians.

SPECTATOR SPORTS

BASEBALL Enjoy the all-American pastime Mexico-style, at the grand new stadium for the **Tijuana Toros,** Río Eufrates s/n, in the Col. Capistrano neighborhood. For a schedule visit www.torostijuana.com. Tickets range in price from $1.50 to $13 and are available for purchase at the stadium.

BULLFIGHTING While some insist this spectacle promotes a cruel disregard for animal rights, others esteem it as a richly symbolic drama involving the courage Ernest Hemingway called "grace under pressure." Whatever your opinion, bullfighting has a prominent place in Mexican heritage and is even considered an essential element of the culture. The skill and bravery of matadors is closely linked with cultural ideals regarding machismo, and some of the world's best perform at Tijuana's two stadiums. The season runs from May through September, with events held Sundays at 4:30pm and at other scheduled times. Ticket prices range from $17 to $40 (the premium seats are on the shaded side of the arena) and can be purchased at the bullring or in advance from San Diego's **Five Star Tours** (© 619/232-5049). **El Toreo** stadium (© 664/686-1510; www.bullfights.org; open only during performances) is 3.2km (2 miles) east of downtown on Bulevar Agua Caliente at Avenida Diego Rivera. **Plaza de Toros Monumental,** or Bullring-by-the-Sea (© 664/680-1808; www.plazamonumental. com), is 10km (6 miles) west of downtown on Highway 1-D (before the first toll station); it perches at the edge of both the ocean and the California border. You can take a taxi easily to El Toreo—fares are negotiable, and around $10 one-way from downtown should be fair. You can also negotiate a fare to Bullring-by-the-Sea, which will range anywhere from $12 to $25, depending on the bargaining mood of the taxi driver.

DOG RACING There's satellite wagering on U.S. horse races at the majestic **Caliente Racetrack,** Bulevar Agua Caliente 12027, 4.8km (3 miles) east of downtown, but these days only greyhounds actually kick up dust at the track. Races are held daily at 7:45pm, with Saturday and Sunday matinees at 2pm. General admission is free, but bettors in the know congregate in the comfortable Turf Club; admission there is $10, refundable with a wagering voucher. For more information, call © 664/633-7300, 664/685-7833, or 619/231-1910 in San Diego. For other racing information, call © 800/PICK-BAJA.

GOLF Once favored by golfing celebrities and socialites (and a very young Arnold Palmer) who stayed at the now-defunct Agua Caliente Resort, the **Tijuana Country Club,** Bulevar Agua Caliente at Avenida Gustavo Salinas (© 664/681-7855), is near the Caliente Racetrack and behind the Grand Hotel Tijuana; it's about a 10-minute drive from downtown. The course is well maintained and frequented mostly by business travelers staying at nearby hotels, many of which offer golf packages (see Grand Hotel Tijuana in "Where to Stay," below). Weekend greens fees are $40 per person, and optional cart rental is $20 per cart; club rental is $20, with caddies an additional $20 plus tip. Ask for seasonal specials. Stop by the pro shop for balls, tees, and a limited number of other accessories; the clubhouse also has two restaurants (complete with cocktail lounges). The **Real del Mar Golf Resort & Country Club** is in the resort development of the same name, on the Pacific coast just 20 minutes from downtown Tijuana, Carretera Escénica Tijuana-Ensenada Km 19.5 (© **664/631-3670;** www.realdelmar.com.mx). The golf course features a challenging 6,400 yards of play interspersed with five lakes and three canyons, challenging players of all levels. Rates for play are: Monday through Thursday $39 for 9 holes, $59 for 18 holes, and $35 for 18 holes at twilight; Fridays and Saturdays $49 for 9 holes, $69 for 18 holes, and $40 for 18 holes at twilight. Discounts are available for seniors. Real del Mar has a hacienda-style clubhouse, with a pro shop and snack bar. Also on-site are a full spa, equestrian center, shopping, and a restaurant.

SHOPPING

Tijuana's biggest attraction is shopping—ask any of the 44 million people who cross the border each year to do it. They come to take advantage of reasonable prices on a variety of merchandise: terra cotta and colorfully glazed pottery, woven blankets and serapes, embroidered dresses and sequined sombreros, onyx chess sets, beaded necklaces and bracelets, silver jewelry, leather bags and huarache sandals, rain sticks (bamboo branches filled with pebbles that simulate the patter of raindrops), hammered-tin picture frames, thick drinking glasses, novelty swizzle sticks, Cuban cigars, and Mexican liquors like Kahlúa and tequila. You're permitted to bring $400 worth of purchases back across the border (sorry, no Cuban cigars allowed), including 1 liter of alcohol or three bottles of wine per person.

When most people think of Tijuana, they picture **Avenida Revolución,** which appears to exist solely for the extraction of dollars from American visitors. Dedicated shoppers quickly discover that most of the curios spilling out onto the sidewalk look alike, despite the determined seller's assurances that their wares are the best in town. Browse for comparison's sake, but for the best souvenir shopping, duck into one of the many *pasajes,* or passageway arcades, where you'll find items of a slightly better quality and merchants willing to bargain. Some of the most enjoyable *pasajes* are on the east side of the street between calles 2 and 5; they also provide a pleasant respite from the quickly irritating tumult of Avenida Revolución.

An alternative is to visit **Sanborn's,** on Avenida Revolución between calles 8 and 9 (© **664/688-1462**), a branch of the Mexico City department store long favored by American travelers. It sells an array of regional folk art and souvenirs, books about Mexico in both Spanish and English, and candies and fresh sweet treats from the bakery—and you can have breakfast in the sunny cafe. It's open Monday through Saturday from 7am to 1am, and Sundays from 7am to 11pm.

One of the few places in Tijuana to find better-quality crafts from a variety of Mexican states is **Tolán,** Avenida Revolución between calles 7 and 8 (© **664/688-3637**). In addition to the obligatory selection of standard Avenida Revolución souvenirs, you'll find blue glassware from Guadalajara, glazed pottery from Tlaquepaque, crafts from the Oaxaca countryside, and distinctive tilework from Puebla. Prices at Tolán are fixed, so you shouldn't try to bargain the way you can in some of the smaller shops and informal stands.

If a marketplace atmosphere and spirited bargaining are what you're looking for, head instead to **Mercado de Artesanías** (crafts market), Calle 2 and Avenida Negrete, where over 200 stalls of vendors selling pottery, clayware, clothing, and other crafts from throughout Mexico fill an entire city block.

A more sophisticated selection of Mexican handicrafts is found in the three stores featuring **Mexico Mexico Mexico** products. One of the largest distributors of goods crafted by artisans across Mexico, you'll find a broad selection of quality wares including Talavera ceramics from Puebla, Oaxacan black clay pottery, Huichol bead art, hand-blown glassware from Tonala, Day of the Dead curios, *alebrijos* (fantasy animal figurines), and works of art made from *milagros,* small silver religious offerings. Shop locations in Tijuana include **El Campanario,** Av. Revolución 952 (no phone), **El Girasol,** Av. Revolución 964 (no phone), and **H. Arnold,** Av. Revolución 1067 (© **664/685-2338**); or you can also purchase online, through the above listed website.

Shopping malls are as common in Tijuana as in any big American city; you shouldn't expect to find typical souvenirs there, but shopping alongside residents and other intrepid visitors is often more fun than feeling like a sitting-duck tourist. One of the biggest, and most convenient, is **Plaza Río Tijuana,** Paseo de los Héroes 96 at Avenida Independencia, Zona Río (© **664/684-0402**), an outdoor plaza anchored by several department stores and featuring dozens of specialty shops and casual restaurants. **Plaza Agua Caliente,** Bulevar Agua Caliente 4558, Col. Aviación (© **664/681-7777**) is a more upscale shopping center, and in addition to fine shops and restaurants, it is known for its emphasis on health and beauty, with day spas, gyms, and doctors offices in abundance here.

Other shopping malls are listed at www.seetijuana.com/tijuanasite/shopping_centers.htm.

On the other side of Paseo de los Héroes from Plaza Río Tijuana is **Plaza del Zapato,** a two-story indoor mall filled with only *zapato* (shoe) stores. Though most are made with quality leather rather than synthetics, inferior workmanship ensures they'll likely last only a season or two. But with prices as low as $30, why not indulge?

For a taste of everyday Mexico, visit **Mercado Hidalgo,** 1 block west of Plaza del Zapato at avenidas Sánchez Taboada and Independencia, a busy indoor-outdoor marketplace where vendors display fresh flowers and produce, sacks of dried beans and chiles by the kilo, and a few souvenir crafts (including some excellent piñatas). Morning is the best time to visit the market, and you'll be more comfortable paying with pesos, since most sellers are accustomed to a local crowd.

WHERE TO STAY

When calculating room rates, always remember that hotel rates in Tijuana are subject to a 12% tax.

Tips Where to Park in Tijuana

Plaza Río Tijuana has ample free parking and is just across the street from the Cultural Center, where private lots charge $5 to $8 to park.

EXPENSIVE

Camino Real Tijuana ⭐⭐⭐ The Camino Real is Tijuana's newest hotel, with the hallmark architectural style and use of bold colors that define this luxury Mexican hotel chain. It's popular especially with business travelers, and its location in the Zona Río makes it ideal for shopping or cultural excursions to the city. It's also close to the most sophisticated dining and nightlife in Tijuana. Rooms are both elegant and spacious. The sixth floor is dedicated to Camino Real Club Level rooms, which have a private reception, upgraded rooms and a selection of amenities including complementary continental breakfast buffets and afternoon cocktails and appetizers. The contemporary lobby showcases renowned Mexican artists, and two restaurants offer both a casual and an upscale dining option. There are a variety of packages available, including weekend escape, seasonal bullfight, and honeymoon packages.

Paseo de los Héroes 10305, Zona Río, 22320 Tijuana, B.C. ℰ **877/215-3051** in the U.S., or 664/633-4000 in Tijuana. Fax 664/633-4001. www.caminoreal.com/tijuana. 263 units. $175 double; $215 Grand Club rooms, $230–$450 suites. AE, MC, V. Free parking. **Amenities:** 2 restaurants; lobby bar; fitness room; concierge; travel agency; business center; 24-hr. room service; laundry and dry cleaning. *In room:* A/C, TV, dataport, minibar, hair dryer, iron, safe.

Grand Hotel Tijuana ⭐ Popular with business travelers, visiting celebrities, and for society events, this hotel has some of the best-maintained public and guest rooms in Tijuana, which helps make up for what it lacks in regional warmth. You can see the hotel's 32-story mirrored twin towers from all of the surrounding city. Modern and sleek in design, it opened in 1982—at the height of Tijuana's prosperity—under the name Fiesta Americana, a name locals (and many cab drivers) still use. Rooms have spectacular views of the city from the higher floors. The top three floors have been converted into the Grand Club Level, with VIP access, private reception, upgraded rooms, and a selection of amenities including DSL Internet access, fax machines in the room, and complementary continental breakfast buffets and afternoon appetizers and wine. A new Vegas-like lobby gives way to several ballrooms and an airy atrium that serves elegant international cuisine at dinner and weekend brunch. Next to the atrium is a casual Mexican restaurant, beyond which the Vegas resemblance resumes with an indoor shopping arcade. The hotel offers a golf package for $82 per person—it includes one night's lodging with a welcome cocktail and a round of 18 holes (including cart) at the adjacent Tijuana Country Club.

Agua Caliente 4500, Tijuana (P.O. Box BC, Chula Vista, CA 92012). ℰ **866/472-6385** in the U.S., or 664/681-7000 in Tijuana. Fax 664/681-7016. www.grandhoteltij.com.mx. 422 units. $135 double; $195 Grand Club room; $230–$750 suite. AE, MC, V. Free underground parking. **Amenities:** 2 restaurants; lobby bar; heated pool; tennis courts; fitness center; sauna; concierge; tour desk; business center; shopping arcade; 24-hr. room service; laundry and dry cleaning; sports and race book (off-track betting). *In room:* A/C, TV, dataport, minibar, iron, safe.

MODERATE

Hacienda del Mar ⭐ If you prefer to keep a little distance between you and the hustle and bustle of downtown Tijuana, this clean, comfortable hotel in Tijuana's beach zone is an excellent value. It's just 20 minutes from the action in downtown TJ and is almost adjacent to the seaside bullring. Rooms, with carpeting, are clean and comfortable. Two suites have private Jacuzzis. The staff at this privately owned hotel is bilingual and very helpful. Special weekly rates are offered.

Paseo Playas 116, 22320 Playas de Tijuana, B.C. ℰ **888/675-2927** in the U.S., or 664/630-8603 in Tijuana. Fax 664/630-8603. www.ventanarosahotels.com. 60 units. $45–$55 double; $75–$85 junior suite. MC, V. Free secured parking. **Amenities:** Restaurant; bar; heated pool; concierge; laundry and dry cleaning. *In room:* A/C, TV, safe.

Hotel Lucerna ⟨★⟩   Once the most chic hotel in Tijuana, Lucerna now feels slightly worn, but the place still has personality. The flavor here is Mexican colonial—wrought-iron railings and chandeliers, rough-hewn heavy wood furniture, brocade wallpaper, and traditional tiles. The hotel is in the Zona Río, away from the noise and congestion of downtown, so a quiet night's sleep is easily attainable, and it's just two blocks from the Plaza Río Tijuana shopping center (see above). All the rooms in this five-story hotel have balconies or patios but are otherwise unremarkable. Sunday brunch is served outdoors by the swimming pool; there's also a coffee shop that provides room service. The staff is friendly and attentive.

Av. Paseo de los Héroes 10902, Zona Río, Tijuana. ℂ 800/582-3762 in the U.S., or 664/634-2000. www.hotel-lucerna.com.mx. 167 units. $85 double; $90 suite. AE, DC, MC, V. **Amenities:** 2 restaurants; 2 bars; swimming pool; fitness center; tour desk; business center; room service; laundry service. *In room:* A/C, TV, coffeemaker, hair dryer, iron.

Residence Inn by Marriott Real del Mar ⟨★★⟩   If being in the center of downtown is a bit too much Tijuana for you, this hotel offers a location that is near enough to the city's action while also being in its own tranquil setting, complete with golf course. Real del Mar is a resort and residential development about 10 miles south of Tijuana, across the highway from the ocean. In addition to golf, it has an equestrian center, spa, and shopping. The Marriott brand is, of course, familiar to American travelers, and you can expect the same standards of quality and comforts in this one, though it's more upscale than most Residence Inns, and you have your choice of two room categories (studios or suites). All suites offer ocean views, fireplaces, and small but complete kitchens—more closely resembling small apartments than hotel rooms. These units are ideal for families or extended stays in the area and are worth the splurge. Two restaurants are available for dining; the Patio Brasserie overlooks the golf course and is open for breakfast and lunch, while Rincon de San Roman, under the direction of a Paris-educated chef, serves Continental cuisine for lunch and dinner.

Carretera Escénica Tijuana-Ensenada Km. 19.5, 22605 Tijuana. ℂ 800/803-6038 in the U.S., or 664/631-3670. Fax 664/631-3677. www.realdelmar.com.mx. 75 units. $119–$129 double or studio; $149–$159 suite. Golf and spa packages available. Complimentary on-site parking. AE, MC, V. **Amenities:** 2 restaurants, swimming pool; tennis court; exercise room; tour desk; room service; daycare; laundry service; grocery shopping service. *In room:* A/C, TV, Internet access, kitchen, coffeemaker, hair dryer, iron.

WHERE TO DINE
EXPENSIVE

Cien Años ⟨★★★⟩ MEXICAN   This is an elegant and gracious Zona Río restaurant offering artfully blended Mexican flavors (tamarind, poblano chile, mango) in stylish presentations. Try chile rellenos stuffed with shrimp in lobster sauce, delicate *calabaza* (squash-blossom) soup, or *huitlacoche* (corn mushroom) tamales. The most adventurous diners can sample garlicky ant eggs or buttery *guisanos* (cactus worms). If you're interested in true haute cuisine, the buzz around Tijuana is all about this place.

Calle José María Velasco 1407. ℂ **664/633-3900** or 664/634-7262. Main courses $12–$30. AE, MC, V. Daily 8am–11pm.

La Costa ⟨★⟩ MEXICAN-STYLE SEAFOOD   Fish gets top billing here, starting with hearty seafood soup. There are combination platters of half a grilled lobster, stuffed shrimp, and baked shrimp; fish filet stuffed with seafood and cheese; and several abalone dishes. Its reputation as one of the best seafood restaurants in Tijuana has won it a strong local following.

Calle 7 no. 8131 (just off Av. Revolución), Zona Centro. ℂ **664/685-8494.** Main courses $8–$20. AE, MC, V. Daily 10am–11pm.

MODERATE

Hard Rock Cafe AMERICAN/MEXICAN   Had an overload of Mexican culture? Looking for a place with all the familiar comforts of home? Then head for the Tijuana branch of this ubiquitous watering hole, which promises nothing exotic; it serves the standard Hard Rock chain menu, which admittedly features an outstanding hamburger, in the regulation Hard Rock setting (dark, clubby, walls filled with rock-'n'-roll memorabilia). While the restaurant's street presence is more subdued than most Hard Rock locations, you'll still spot the trademark Caddie emerging from above the door. Prices are in line with what you'd see in the U.S.—and therefore no bargain in competitive Tijuana.

Av. Revolución 520 (near Calle 1), Zona Centro. ⓒ 664/685-0206. Menu items $5–$10. AE, MC, V. Daily 11am–2am.

INEXPENSIVE

Cafe La Especial MEXICAN   Tucked away in a shopping *pasaje* at the bottom of some stairs (turn in at the taco stand of the same name), this restaurant is a well-known shopper's refuge and purveyor of home-style Mexican cooking at reasonable (though not dirt-cheap) prices. The gruff, efficient waitstaff carry out platter after platter of *carne asada* served with fresh tortillas, beans, and rice—it's La Especial's most popular item. Traditional dishes like tacos, enchiladas, and burritos round out the menu, augmented by frosty cold Mexican beers.

Av. Revolución 718 (between calles 3 and 4), Zona Centro. ⓒ 664/685-6654. Menu items $4–$12. MC, V. Daily 9am–10pm.

Carnitas Uruapán 🐷🐷 MEXICAN   *Carnitas*—marinated pork roasted on a spit till falling-apart tender, then served in chunks with tortillas, salsa, cilantro, guacamole, and onions—is a beloved dish in Mexico and the main attraction at Carnitas Uruapán. It serves the meat by the kilo (or portion thereof) at long, communal wooden tables to a crowd of mostly locals. A half-kilo of carnitas is plenty for two people and costs around $12, including beans and that impressive array of condiments. It's a casual feast without compare, but vegetarians need not apply. This branch is in the fashionable Zona Río. Another location, which specializes in seafood as well, is on Paseo de los Héroes at Avenida Rodríguez (no phone).

Bulevar Díaz Ordaz 12650 (across from Plaza Patria), La Mesa. ⓒ 664/681-6181. Menu items $2.50–$8. No credit cards. Daily 8am–5am.

La Fonda de Roberto 🐷🐷 MEXICAN   Although its location may seem out of the way on the map, this modest restaurant's regular appearances on San Diego "Best Of" lists attest to its continued appeal. A short drive (or taxi ride) from downtown Tijuana, La Fonda's colorful dining room opens onto the courtyard of a kitschy 1960s motel, complete with retro kidney-shaped swimming pool. The festive atmosphere is perfect for enjoying a variety of regional Mexican dishes, including decent chicken mole and generous portions of *milanesa* (beef, chicken, or pork pounded paper thin, then breaded and fried). A house specialty is *queso fundido,* deep-fried cheese with chiles and mushrooms, served with a basket of freshly made corn tortillas.

In the La Sierra Motel, 2800 Cuauhtémoc Sur Oeste (Av. 16 de Septiembre, on the old road to Ensenada). ⓒ 664/686-4687. Most dishes $5–$11. MC, V. Tues–Sat 10am–10pm.

TIJUANA AFTER DARK

Avenida Revolución is the center of the city's nightlife; many compare it with Bourbon Street in New Orleans during Mardi Gras—except here it's a regular occurrence,

Finds **A Northern Baja Spa Sanctuary**

One of Mexico's best-known spas is in northern Baja, just 58km (36 miles) south of San Diego. Its location chosen for the area's perfect climate, **Rancho La Puerta** 𝒜𝒜 opened in 1940 as a "health camp," among the pioneers of the modern spa and fitness movement. (The rates at the time were $18 a week—but you had to bring your own tent!)

Much has changed since then. Today the ranch occupies 3,000 acres of lush oasis surrounded by pristine countryside, which includes a 2.4-hectare (6-acre) organic garden. Cottages can accommodate up to 150 guests per week, and the ranch has a staff of almost 400. Each cottage has its own patio garden and is decorated with Mexican folk art. Inside the rooms are spacious living room–size seating areas, desks, CD players, hair dryers, robes, and safes, and most rooms have fireplaces.

Three swimming pools, four tennis courts, five hot tubs, saunas, steam rooms, and 11 gyms for aerobic and restorative classes are only a part of the common facilities. Separate men's and women's health centers offer the full range of spa services. Hiking trails surround the resort, and there's even a full-size replica of the ancient labyrinth found in Chartres Cathedral, for moving meditation. There are also several lounges and shared spaces, including the library, with thousands of books to browse; an evening movie lounge; a recreation room; and for those who can't conceive of totally disconnecting, the E-center, with 24-hour access to the Internet.

Rancho La Puerta runs weeklong programs—Saturday through Saturday—emphasizing a mind/body/spirit philosophy. Prices begin at $2,080 for the week during the summer, and at $2,460 for the week from mid-September to June. Included in the rates are all classes, meals, evening programs, and use of facilities. You can book shorter stays (3 nights or more) if within 2 weeks of your visit; rates will be prorated on a nightly basis.

For reservations contact Rancho La Puerta, Carretera a Tijuana Km 5 "A," 21440, Tecate, B.C.N., or P.O. Box 69, Tecate, CA 91980 (© **800/443-7565** in the U.S., or 665/654-1155 at the ranch; fax 665/654-1108; www.rancholapuerta.com). MasterCard and Visa are accepted.

not a once-a-year blowout. Tijuana has several lively discos; perhaps the most popular is **Baby Rock,** 1482 Diego Rivera, Zona Río (© **664/634-2404;** www.babyrocktj.com), a cousin to Acapulco's lively Baby O, which features everything from Latin rock to rap. It's open 9pm to 3am daily, with a cover charge of $12 on Saturdays.

Also popular in Tijuana are sports bars, featuring wagering on events from all over the United States as well as races from Tijuana's Caliente track. The most popular of these bars cluster in the **Pueblo Amigo** and **Vía Oriente** areas and around **Plaza Río Tijuana** in the Zona Río, a new center designed to resemble a colonial Mexican village. Also in Zona Río is the chic club **Karma,** Paseo de los Héroes 954713 (© **664/900-6063;** Thurs–Sat 9pm–3am). Just beyond Zona Río you'll find **Tangaloo,** Av. Monterrey 3215 (© **664/681-8091;** www.tangaloo.com; Thurs–Sun 9pm–4am), a hip club featuring DJs spinning electronic dance music with a changing theme each Saturday night. Three of the town's hottest clubs, **Rodeo de Media Noche** (⟨℃ 664/ 682-4967; Thurs–Sun 9pm–4am), **Balak** (⟨℃ 664/682-9222 or 664/607-3566; Thurs–Sat 9pm–4am), and **Señor Frogs** (⟨℃ 664/682-4962; www.senorfrogs.com; daily noon–4am; no cover), are in the Pueblo Amigo shopping mall, which is less than 3.2km (2 miles) from the border in the Zona Río district, a short taxi ride or—during daylight hours—a pleasant walk.

2 Rosarito Beach & Beyond: Baja's First Beach Resorts

55km (34 miles) S of San Diego; 29km (18 miles) S of Tijuana

Just a 20-minute drive south of Tijuana and a complete departure in ambience, Rosarito Beach is a tranquil, friendly beach town. It also gained early renown during the U.S. Prohibition, when the elegant Rosarito Beach Hotel catered to Hollywood stars. This classic structure still welcomes numerous guests, despite the fact that its opulence has lost some luster. Hollywood has likewise played a major part in Rosarito's recent renaissance—it was the location for the soundstage and filming of the Academy Award–winning *Titanic.* The Titanic Expo museum at **Foxploration!** here continues to draw fans of the film (see "En Route from Rosarito to Ensenada," below).

Two roads run between Tijuana and Ensenada (the largest and third-largest cities in Baja)—the scenic, coast-hugging toll road (marked CUOTA, or 1-D) and the free but slower-going public road (marked LIBRE, or 1). We strongly recommend starting out on the toll road (pay at each *caseta,* or toll booth; pesos are more common but dollars are accepted), but use the free road along Rosarito Beach if you'd like to easily pull on and off the road to shop or look at the view. The beaches between Tijuana and Rosarito are also known for excellent surf breaks.

You can also take **Mexicoach** (⟨℃ 664/685-1440; www.gototijuana.com) to Rosarito, leaving your car on the U.S. side of the border. Board the bus shuttle service at the Border Station Parking (next to the San Diego Factory Outlet Center) or from the Trolley's last stop at the border (see "Getting There & Departing" on p. 140), and it will take you to the Tijuana Tourist Terminal, Av. Revolución, between calles 6 and 7 (⟨℃ 664/685-1470; www.rosaritobeachexpress.com), where you can continue on to Rosarito. The cost from San Ysidro direct to Rosarito is $12 each way; from the Tijuana Tourist Terminal to Rosarito is $6 each way. It's open daily from 5:30am to 9pm, with departures every 15 to 20 minutes from 8am to 9pm, 365 days per year. Returns to the border leave from the same terminal. Another option is to travel direct from San Diego to Rosarito on **Baja Express** (⟨℃ 619/232-5040, or 619/230-5049). Pickups can be arranged with 1-day advance scheduling from downtown San Diego, Mission Valley, Coronado, or Chula Vista. Round trips start at $25.

VISITOR INFORMATION   Try **Baja California Tourism Information** (⟨℃ 800/ 522-1516 in California, Arizona, or Nevada; 800/225-2786 in the rest of the U.S. and Canada; or **619/298-4105** in San Diego; www.baja.gob.mx). This office provides advice and makes hotel reservations throughout Baja California. You can also contact the local **Secretaria de Turísmo,** Carretera Libre Tijuana-Ensenada Km 28 (⟨℃ 800/ 962-2252 in the U.S., 01-800/025-6288 toll-free in Mexico; www.rosarito.org). The office is open Monday through Friday from 8am to 8pm, and Saturday and Sunday from 9am to 1pm. Special **tourist aid** service is available by calling **664/612-0200.**

Rosarito Beach

PACIFIC OCEAN

To Tijuana

Ensenada Al Mar

Primero de Mayo

12 de Mayo

San Francisco

Manuel Avila Camacho

Mision San Gabriel

Vicente Guerrero

Tecate

Tijuana

20 de Noviembre

toll road

Laurel

Sauce

Ebano

Cedro

Abeto

Alamo

Cipres

Olivo

Rousseau

Mar Mediterraneo

Mar del Norte

Benito Juárez

Acacias

Roble

Encino

Eucalipto

Palma

Magnolia

Nogal

Cleofas Ruiz

Alfredo Bontil

Alta Tension

To Foxploration

Rosarito Beach

UNITED STATES

Area of Detail

THE BAJA PENINISULA

MEXICO

Mexico City

0   500 mi

0   500 km

ACCOMMODATIONS ■
Hotel Brisas del Mar **1**
Rosarito Beach Hotel & Spa **4**

DINING ◆
El Nido **3**
Papas & Beer **2**

0   0.25 mi

0   0.25 km

EXPLORING ROSARITO BEACH

Once a tiny resort town that remained a secret despite its proximity to Tijuana, Rosarito Beach saw an explosion of development in the prosperous '80s and has now settled down into its own spirited personality. One reason its popularity persists is because of its location—it's the first beach resort town south of the border, and party-minded tourists aren't always too discriminating. (This should give you an idea of the crowd to expect on holiday weekends and during school breaks.)

Reputation is another draw: For years the **Rosarito Beach Hotel & Spa** (see "Where to Stay," below), built around 1927, was the preferred hideaway of celebrities and other fashionable Angelenos. Movie star Rita Hayworth and her husband Prince Aly Khan vacationed here, and Paulette Goddard and Burgess Meredith were married at the resort. Although the hotel's entry still features the gallant inscription POR ESTA

PUERTA PASAN LAS MUJERES MAS HERMOSAS DEL MUNDO ("Through this doorway pass the most beautiful women in the world"), today's vacationing starlets are more often found at resorts on Baja's southern tip. While the glimmer (as well as the glamour) has worn off, the Rosarito Beach Hotel is still the most interesting place in town, and nostalgia buffs will want to stop in for a look at some expert tile- and woodwork as well as the panoramic murals throughout the lobby. Check out the colorful Aztec images in the main dining room, the magnificently tiled restrooms, and the glassed-in bar overlooking the sparkling pool and beach, or peek into the original owner's mansion on the property (now home to a spa and gourmet restaurant).

Rosarito Beach has caught the attention of Hollywood for years; most recently, the megahit *Titanic* was filmed here in a state-of-the-art production facility. *Titanic*'s allure is fading fast, however, and the former set was remodeled into an interactive museum with broader appeal (see "En Route from Rosarito to Ensenada," below).

If it's not too crowded, Rosarito is a good place to while away a few hours. You can swim or horseback ride at the beach; have a drink at the local branch of Ensenada's enormously popular Papas & Beer (see "Rosarito Beach After Dark," below); shop for souvenirs along the Old Ensenada Highway just south of town; or dine on fish tacos or tamales from any one of a number of family-run stands along Bulevar Benito Juárez, the town's main (and only) drag.

SHOPPING

The dozen or so blocks north of the Rosarito Beach Hotel abound with the stores typical in Mexican border towns; curio shops, cigar and *licores* (liquor) stores, and *farmacias* (where drugs like Viagra, Retin-A, Prozac, and many more are available at low cost and without a prescription). Rosarito has also become a center for carved furnishings—plentiful downtown along Bulevar Benito Juárez—and pottery, best purchased at stands along the old highway, south of town. A reliable but more expensive furniture shop is **Casa la Carreta,** Km 29.5, on the old road south of Rosarito (ⓒ **661/612-0502;** www.casalacarreta.net), where you can see plentiful examples of the best workmanship—chests, tables, chairs, headboards, cabinets, and cradles.

The **Casa Torres Museum Store** (at the Rosarito Beach Hotel shopping center; ⓒ **661/612-1008**) has been around since 1969 selling museum-quality handicrafts from throughout Mexico. Find carved wooden masks, beaded Huichol art, Day of the Dead curios, and more. An adjoining duty-free store sells perfumes, liquors, and cosmetics.

WHERE TO STAY

Hotel Brisas del Mar 🦋 *Value* This clean, friendly hotel is close to everything in Rosarito and just a 3-minute walk to the beach. It's also a good value. The rooms in this two-story hotel are basic, but highlights of the hotel are its semi-chic lounge-style bar and the friendly, attentive staff. If you don't have to be on the beach, this is the best bet in town.

Bulevar Benito Juárez 22, 22710 Playas de Rosarito, B.C. Mexico. ⓒ **888/871-3605** in the U.S., or 661/612-2546. www.ventanarosahotels.com. 71 units. $75–$115 double. MC, V. Secured free parking. **Amenities:** Restaurant; bar; heated Jacuzzi and pool, plus a separate kids' pool; laundry service. *In room:* A/C, TV, safe.

Rosarito Beach Hotel & Spa 🦋🦋 *Value* Although this once-glamorous resort has been holding steady since its heyday, the vestiges of vacationing movie stars, a casino, and 1920s elegance have been all but eclipsed by the glaring nighttime neon and partymania that currently define the former retreat. Despite the resort's changed personality, unique features of artistic construction and lavish decoration remain, setting it apart from the rest along a wide stretch of a family-friendly beach. The hotel draws a mixed crowd. The stately on-site home of the original owners has been transformed into the full-service Casa Playa Spa, where massages and other treatments are only slightly less costly than in the U.S.

You'll pay more for an ocean view, and more for the newer, air-conditioned rooms in the tower; the older rooms in the poolside building may only have ceiling fans, but they prevail in the character department, with hand-painted trim and original tile. Although the rooms are slightly worn, they are large and comfortable.

Bulevar Benito Juárez, Zona Centro, 22710 Rosarito, B.C. Mexico (P.O. Box 430145, San Diego, CA 92143). © 800/ 343-8582 or 1-866/ROSARITO in the U.S., or 661/612-0144. Fax 661/612-1125. www.rosaritohotel.com. 280 units. $69–$129 double Sept–June; $89–$139 double July–Aug and U.S. holidays. 2 children under 12 stay free in parent's room. Packages available. MC, V. Free parking. **Amenities:** 2 restaurants; bar; 2 swimming pools; racquetball and tennis courts; playground; room service. *In room:* TV.

WHERE TO DINE

While in Rosarito, you may want to try **Chabert's** (Continental) or the more casual **Azteca Restaurant** (Mexican), both in the Rosarito Beach Hotel. Early risers out for a stroll can enjoy fresh, steaming-hot tamales (with a variety of stuffings), a traditional Mexican breakfast treat sold from sidewalk carts for around 50¢ each.

El Nido ⟨☆☆⟩ MEXICAN/STEAKS   One of the first eateries in Rosarito, El Nido remains popular with visitors unimpressed by the flashier, neon-lit joints that pop up to please the college-age set. The setting here is Western frontier, complete with rustic candles and rusting wagon wheels; sit outside in the enclosed patio or opt for the dark, cozy interior warmed by a large fireplace and open grill. The mesquite fire is constantly stoked to prepare the grilled steaks and seafood that are El Nido's specialty; the menu also includes free-range (and superfresh) quail and venison from the owner's ranch in the nearby wine country. Meals are reasonably priced and generous, including hearty bean soup, American-style green salad, baked potatoes, and all the fresh tortillas and zesty salsa you can eat.

Bulevar Benito Juárez 67. © 661/612-1430. Main courses $5.50–$20. No credit cards. Daily 8am–11pm.

ROSARITO BEACH AFTER DARK

Because the legal drinking age in Baja is 18, the under-21 crowd from Southern California tends to flock across the border on Friday and Saturday nights. The most popular spot in town is **Papas & Beer** (© 661/612-0444; www.papasandbeer.com) on Rosarito Beach. It's a relaxed, come-as-you-are type club on the beach, just a block north of the Rosarito Beach Hotel. Even for those young in spirit only, it's great fun, with open-air tables and a bar surrounding a sand volleyball court. It's open daily all year long from 11am to 3am. Or choose from several other adjacent clubs, each offering booming music, spirited dancing, and all-night-long energy. Cover charges vary depending on the season, the crowd, and the mood of the staff. The **Salon Méxican** (© 661/612-0144), in the Rosarito Beach Hotel, attracts a slightly more mature crowd, with live music on Friday, Saturday, and Sunday nights. It also serves a buffet-style dinner.

3 En Route from Rosarito to Ensenada

A few miles south of Rosarito proper lies the seaside production site of the 1997 megablockbuster *Titanic*. A 240m-long (787-ft.) *Titanic* replica was constructed for filming, and many local citizens served as extras in the movie. Although the gargantuan ship was sunk and destroyed during filming, soundstages still contain partial sets (like a first-class hallway) and numerous props, including lifeboats, furnishings, and crates from dockside scenes. Fox Studio's **Foxploration!,** Carretera Libre Tijuana-Ensenada Km. 32.5 (© **866/369-2252** from the U.S., or 661/614-0110 or -9418; www.foxploration. com), is an interactive museum which covers several acres and can hold up to 3,000 visitors, with exhibits in the Cinemagico section that showcase the art of making movies. Hands-on exhibits demonstrate everything from optical illusions to computer generation of special effects. Props and scenery from various Fox Studio movie sets are on view throughout, but the star attraction is the Titanic Expo, with a wealth of memorabilia and props from the movie. The steady flow of curious visitors prompted the opening of Foxploration! It's open Wednesday to Sunday from 9am to 5:30pm (daily around holidays and during busy seasons). Admission is $12 for adults, $9 for children 3 to 11. There's a food court with Dominos, Subway, and Starbucks on premises.

Leaving Rosarito, drive south on the toll highway or the local-access old road that parallels it. In addition to the curious juxtaposition of ramshackle villages and luxurious vacation homes, you'll pass a variety of restaurants and resorts—this stretch of coastline has now surpassed Rosarito in drawing the discriminating visitor. Many places are so Americanized, however, that you'll feel as though you never left home, so my favorites are the funkier, more colorfully Mexican places, like Calafia restaurant, Puerto Nuevo lobster village, and La Fonda resort (see "Where to Stay" and "Where to Dine," below). After La Fonda, be sure to get back on the toll road, because the old road veers inland and you don't want to miss what's coming next.

Development falls off somewhat for the next 24km (15 miles), but the coastline's natural beauty picks up. You'll see green meadows running down to meet white-sand beaches and wild sand dunes as you skirt rocky cliffs reminiscent of the coast at Big Sur. The ideal place to take it all in is **El Mirador lookout,** about 18km (11 miles) south of La Fonda. Feel the drama build as you climb up the stairs and gasp at the breathtaking view, which sweeps from the deep-blue open sea past steep cliffs and down the curved coastline to Salsipuedes Point, around which Ensenada lies. If vertigo doesn't trouble you, look straight down from El Mirador's railing, and you'll see piles of automobiles lying where they fell before the El Mirador lookout was built. Whether the promontory was a popular suicide spot or merely a junkyard with an enticing twist is best left to urban legend-makers; it nevertheless reinforces your sense of a different culture—nowhere in image-conscious California would that twisted pile of metal be left on the rocks.

After a few miles farther south on the toll road, you'll come to a sign for SAL-SIPUEDES BAY (the name means "leave if you can"). The dramatic scenery along the drive ends here, so you can take the exit if you want to turn around and head north again. If you plan to do some camping, head down the near-mile-long, rutted road to

---

Biking the Northern Baja Coast

The stretch of coast between Rosarito and Ensenada is so lovely that many bicyclists are tempted to ride along the smooth, paved highways. Twice a year you can do so in company. The two towns host a biannual event each spring and fall, the Rosarito Ensenada Bike Ride, one of the largest and longest running cycling events in the world. The 50-mile course offers breathtaking views of the Pacific coastline. For schedules and more information, visit www.rosaritoensenada.com.

Fun Fact **The Bartender Who Launched a Thousand Hangovers**

The Rancho La Gloria hotel and restaurant claims to be the birthplace of the margarita. Here's the deal: Carlos "Danny" Herrera says he invented the drink in 1948 for movie starlet Marjorie King, who allegedly fared badly if she drank any type of alcohol other than tequila. But she didn't want to appear unladylike by downing straight tequila—so Danny added fresh lime juice and Cointreau to soften the taste for Margarita, as she was known south of the border. The libation quickly gained popularity with fellow hotel guests and Hollywood friends Phil Harris and Alice Faye. Soon the concoction was being mixed up at La Plaza, a hotel in La Jolla, California, before making its way to Los Angeles and eventual beverage superstardom.

Salsipuedes Campground set under olive trees on a cliff. Each campsite has a fire ring and costs $5 a day (day use is also $5). There's a natural rock tub with hot-spring water at the campground and some basic cottages that rent for $30 a day. There is no easy access to the beach, known for its good surfing, from the campground.

Ensenada, with its shops, restaurants, and winery, is another 24km (15 miles) away.

NEARBY GOLF

Bajamar (© **800/311-6067** in the U.S., or 646/155-0152), 32km (20 miles) north of Ensenada, is a self-contained resort with 27 truly spectacular holes of golf. It's the place to go if you want to feel just like you're in the United States. Conceived as a planned community with vacation homes and a country club, Bajamar suffered when the bottom dropped out of '80s speculation, leaving a lot of unbuilt house pads on cul-de-sacs behind the grandiose guardhouse. The main attraction is now the golf club and sister hotel, which play host to high-level retreats, conventions, and Asian tourists attracted by great golf deals. Featuring oceanfront Scottish-style links reminiscent of the courses on the Monterey Peninsula, Bajamar lets you combine any two of its three 9-hole courses. Public greens fees for 18 holes (including mandatory cart) are $75 Sunday through Thursday, and $89 Friday or Saturday. Hotel guests pay $5 less, but the **Hotel Hacienda Bajamar** (see "Where to Stay," below) offers a bevy of golf packages. Services include a pro shop, putting and chipping greens, a driving range, and an elegant bar and restaurant.

WHERE TO STAY

Hotel Hacienda Bajamar ★★   Situated 32km (20 miles) north of Ensenada, Hacienda Bajamar is tucked away in the Bajamar golf resort and community. Popular with business conventions and family gatherings, Bajamar is as Americanized as it gets, and so is its hotel, near the clubhouse. The hotel is built like an early Spanish mission, with an interior outdoor plaza and garden surrounded by long arcades shading guest-room doorways. The 27 holes of golf are the main draw. The long road from the highway is lined with signs for phases of the surrounding vacation-home development that never really got off the ground. Rooms and suites are very spacious and comfortable, with vaguely colonial furnishings and luxurious bathrooms. A variety of golf packages are available, including pricing for couples with only one golfer. For greens fees, see "Nearby Golf," above.

Tips Surfing, Northern Baja Style

From California and beyond, surfers come to the northern Baja coastline for perpetual right-breaking waves, cheap digs and eats, and *Endless Summer*–type camaraderie.

Undoubtedly, the most famous surf spot in all of Mexico is Killers, at Todos Santos Island. This was the location of the winning wave in the 1997–98 K2 Challenge (a worldwide contest to ride the largest wave each winter—and be photographed doing it). Killers is a very makeable wave for confident, competent surfers. To get there you'll need a boat. You can get a lift from the local *panga* (skiff) fleet, for about $100 for the day. That's pretty much the going rate, and the tightly knit Ensenada *pangueros* aren't eager to undercut each other. It's about 16km (10 miles) out to the island; there you'll anchor and paddle into the lineup. You must bring everything you'll need—food, drink, sunscreen, and so on.

Other less radical and easier-to-reach spots include Popotla, just south of Rosarito, where you'll walk to the beach through the Popotla trailer park. Calafia, also just a mile or two south of Rosarito, has a reeling right point that can get extremely heavy. San Miguel is the point break just south of the final tollbooth on the highway into Ensenada. It's an excellent wave but generally crowded.

If you're a surfer looking to get your bearings or a spectator wanting to get your feet wet, stop by Inner Reef (Km 34½; no phone). Opened in 1998 by a friendly Southern California expat named Roger, this tiny shack offers all the essentials: wax, leashes, patch kits, surfboard sales and rentals, even expert repairs at bargain prices. Roger is there from noon until sunset every day in summer, and from Wednesday to Sunday in winter.

Hwy. 1-D, Km 77.5 (mailing address: 416 W. San Ysidro Bulevar, Suite L-732, San Ysidro, CA 92173). © **800/311-6067** U.S., or 646/155-0151. www.golfbajamar.com. 80 units. $84–$112 double; $184–$208 suite. Children under 12 stay free in parent's room. Golf packages available. AE, MC, V. Complimentary parking. **Amenities:** Restaurant; heated swimming pool; tennis courts; spa; concierge; tour desk; business center; room service; laundry and dry cleaning. *In room:* A/C, TV, dataport, minibar, hair dryer, iron.

La Fonda ✦ *(Value* Just as American-style Las Rocas has its staunch devotees, plenty of folks are loyal to La Fonda's rustic rooms, which don't have minibars, state-of-the-art TVs, or phones. What they do have is an adventuresome appeal unlike any other northern Baja coast resort, a place for people who truly want to get away from it all. Relaxation and romance are the key words at this small hotel and restaurant, which opened in the '50s and hasn't changed a whole lot since. Perched cliffside above a wide, sandy beach, all of La Fonda's rooms have wide-open views of the breaking surf below. Although there are some newer motel-style rooms, the older apartments with fireplaces (some with kitchenettes) have more charm. To reach them, guests use narrow winding staircases, much like the pathway down to the sand. The best rooms are numbers 18 to 22, closest to the sand and isolated from the main building; ask for one of these when you reserve. During particularly cold months, unheated La Fonda can get chilly—an important consideration. At the very least, be sure you're in a room with a fireplace.

Ensenada is a scenic 45-minute drive south and Puerto Nuevo a mere 13km (8 miles) up the road—if you decide you need to leave this hideaway at all.

Hwy. 1-D, Km 59, La Misión exit. (Mailing address: P.O. Box 430268, San Ysidro, CA 92143.) No phone. 26 units. $55 standard; $75 deluxe (w/fireplace and/or full kitchen). No credit cards. Write for reservations; allow 2 weeks for response. **Amenities:** Restaurant/bar (see "Where to Dine," below). *In room:* TV.

Las Rocas Resort & Spa ☆☆   This polished hotel is run by an American, for Americans, and it shows. English is spoken fluently everywhere, and there are only as many signs in Spanish as you'd expect to see in Los Angeles. Built in Mediterranean style, with gleaming white stucco, cobalt-blue accents, and brightly painted tiles everywhere, Las Rocas has a lovely setting perched above the sea. There's no beach below the rocky edge, but the hotel's two oceanfront infinity-edge swimming pools and three secluded whirlpool lagoons more than make up for it. The thatched-roof *palapa* in the poolside garden serves tropical drinks and snacks, and swaying palms rustle throughout the property. Like most Baja resorts, Las Rocas is oriented toward the sea, so all rooms have an oceanfront private terrace. The rooms and suites are very nicely furnished in Mexican colonial style, and bathrooms are well equipped and beautifully tiled. There's quite a selection of rooms types to select from: Junior suites come with a king bed, fireplace, kitchenette (with refrigerator, microwave, coffeemaker, and sink) as well as a living room area. Penthouse rooms have a private Jacuzzi-for two on the balconies, in addition to the amenities of the junior suite. Regular rooms are basic but clean, and the oceanview balcony is a plus. The restaurant makes outstanding guacamole, which you can order by the bowl for chip-dipping at the indoor or poolside bar. The restaurant offers spa-cuisine options and a popular Sunday brunch served from 7:30am to 3pm. The spa is a highlight, with daily yoga classes and a full menu of massages, facials, and body treatments to select from. To get here, take the second Rosarito exit off the toll road, then drive 10km (6 miles) south, or follow the free road south from Rosarito; Las Rocas will be on the right.

Carretera Libre Tijuana-Ensenada Km 38.5, Playas de Rosarito, B.C. 22710. ℂ **888/527-7622** in the U.S., or 661/614-0357. www.lasrocas.com. 74 units. Low season $74 double, $114 junior suite; $149 penthouse suite; high season $89 double, $134 junior suite, $219 penthouse suite. *Note:* High season rates include all weekends. Senior discounts, as well as spa and yoga packages, available. MC, V. Secured free parking. **Amenities:** Restaurant; bar; heated Jacuzzi and pool; separate kids' pool; laundry service. *In room:* A/C, TV, safe; suites also have kitchenette and coffeemaker.

WHERE TO DINE

A bit less than 5km (3 miles) south of Rosarito Beach, elaborate stucco portals beckon drivers to **Calafia** (ℂ **661/612-1581**), a restaurant and trailer park that isn't visible from the highway. We don't recommend the dismal accommodations, but Calafia's restaurant (daily 8am–11pm; MasterCard and Visa are accepted) is worth a stop, if only to admire the impressive setting above the crashing surf. Your meal is served at tables on terraces, balconies, and ledges wedged into the rocks all the way down to the bottom, where an outdoor dance floor and wrecked Spanish galleon sit on the beach. At night, when the outdoor landings are softly lit and the mariachis' gentle strumming complements the sound of crashing waves, romance is definitely in the air. The menu is standard Mexican fare with the addition of some Americanized dishes like fajitas, but it's all prepared well and served with fresh, warm tortillas and good, strong margaritas. Calafia serves breakfast, lunch, and dinner daily.

A trip down the coast just wouldn't be complete without stopping at **Puerto Nuevo,** a tiny fishing town with nearly 30 restaurants—all serving exactly the same thing. Some 40 years ago the fishermen's wives here started serving local lobsters from the kitchens of their simple shacks; many eventually added small dining rooms to their homes or built proper restaurants. The result is a lobster lover's paradise, where a feast of lobster, beans, rice, salsa, limes, and fresh tortillas costs around $10. Puerto Nuevo is 19km (12 miles) south of Rosarito on the Old Ensenada Highway (parallel to the toll Carretera Transpeninsular)—just drive through the arched entryway, park, and stroll the town's three or four blocks for a restaurant that suits your fancy. Some have names, and some don't; **Ortega's** is one of the originals, and has expanded to five locations within the village. There's also **La Casa de la Langosta (House of Lobster),** which even opened a branch in Rosarito Beach. But regulars prefer the smaller, family-run spots, where mismatched dinette sets and chipped plates underscore the earnest service and personally prepared dinners.

About 16km (10 miles) farther south of Puerto Nuevo, roughly halfway between Rosarito and Ensenada, is the **La Fonda** hotel and restaurant (no phone; see "Where to Stay," above). Plenty of San Diegans make the drive Sunday mornings for La Fonda's outstanding buffet brunch, an orgy of meats, traditional Mexican stews, *chilaquiles* (a saucy egg-and-tortilla scramble), fresh fruits, and pastries. Breakfast, lunch, and dinner are always accompanied by a basket of Baja's best flour tortillas (try rolling them with some butter and jam at breakfast). The best seating is under thatched umbrellas on La Fonda's tiled terrace overlooking the breaking surf; live music keeps the adjacent bar jumping on Friday and Saturday nights (strolling mariachis entertain the rest of the time). House specialties include banana pancakes, pork chops with salsa verde, succulent glazed ribs, and a variety of seafood; plan to walk off your heavy meal along the sandy beach below, accessible by a stone stairway. Relaxing ambience coupled with exceptionally good food and service make La Fonda a must-stop along the coast. Sunday brunch is around $12 a person; main courses are otherwise $4 to $15. Open daily from around 9am to 10pm; Sunday's buffet brunch is from 10am to 3:30pm.

4 Ensenada: Port of Call 🖈

135km (84 miles) S of San Diego; 110km (68 miles) S of Tijuana

Ensenada is an attractive, classic town on a lovely bay surrounded by sheltering mountains. About 40 minutes from Rosarito, it's the kind of place that loves a celebration. Almost any time you choose to visit, the city is festive—be it for a bicycle race or a seafood festival.

One of Mexico's principal ports of call, Ensenada welcomes half a million visitors a year who are attracted to its beaches, excellent sportfishing, nearby wineries, and surrounding natural attractions.

GETTING THERE   After passing through the final tollbooth, Highway 1-D curves sharply toward downtown Ensenada. Watch out for brutal metal speed bumps slowing traffic into town—they're far less forgiving on the average chassis than those in the U.S.!

VISITOR INFORMATION   The **Tourist and Convention Bureau booth** (© **646/178-2411**) is at the western entrance to town, where the waterfront-hugging Bulevar Lázaro Cárdenas—also known as Bulevar Costero—curves away to the right. The booth is open daily from 9am till dusk and can provide a downtown map, directions to major nearby sites, and information on special events throughout the city. As

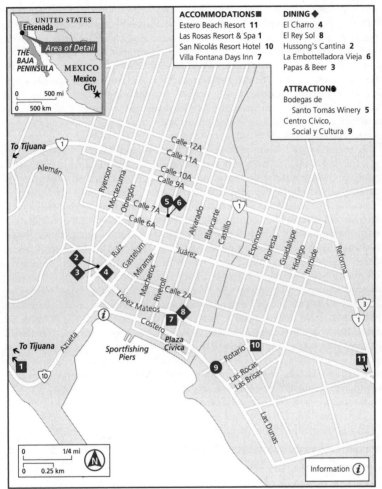

ACCOMMODATIONS■
Estero Beach Resort **11**
Las Rosas Resort & Spa **1**
San Nicolás Resort Hotel **10**
Villa Fontana Days Inn **7**

DINING ◆
El Charro **4**
El Rey Sol **8**
Hussong's Cantina **2**
La Embottelladora Vieja **6**
Papas & Beer **3**

ATTRACTION●
Bodegas de
  Santo Tomás Winery **5**
Centro Cívico,
  Social y Cultura **9**

in most of the commonly visited areas of Baja, one or more employees speak English fluently. Eight blocks south you'll find the **State Secretary of Tourism,** Bulevar Lázaro Cárdenas 1477, Government Building (© **646/172-3022;** fax 646/172-3081), which is open Monday through Friday from 9am to 7pm, Saturday from 10am to 3pm, and Sunday from 10am to 2pm. Both offices have extended hours on U.S. holidays. Taxis park along López Mateos.

EXPLORING ENSENADA

Ensenada is technically a "border town," but part of its appeal is its multilayered vitality born out of being concerned with much more than tourism. The bustling port consumes the entire waterfront—beach access is north or south of town—and the Pacific fishing trade and agriculture in the fertile valleys surrounding the city dominate the economy. Try not to leave Ensenada without getting a taste of its true personality; for example, stop by the indoor-outdoor fish market at the northernmost corner of the harbor where each day, from early morning to midday, merchants and housewives gather to assess the day's catch—tuna, marlin, snapper, plus many other varieties of fish and piles of shrimp from the morning's haul.

Outside the market is the perfect place to sample the culinary craze of Baja California, the Baja fish taco. Several stands prepare this local treat; strips of freshly caught fish are battered and deep fried, then wrapped in corn tortillas and topped with shredded cabbage, cilantro, salsa, and various other condiments. They're delicious, cheap, and filling, and it's easy to see why surf bums and collegiate vacationers consider them a Baja staple.

Elsewhere in town, visit the **Bodegas de Santo Tomás Winery,** Av. Miramar 666 at Calle 7 (© **646/178-2509;** www.santo-tomas.com). While most visitors to Mexico are quite content quaffing endless quantities of cheap *cerveza* (beer), even part-time oenophiles should pay a visit to this historic winery—the oldest in Mexico and the largest in all of Baja. It uses old-fashioned methods of processing grapes grown in the lush Santo Tomás Valley, first cultivated by Dominican monks in 1791. A 45-minute tour introduces you to low-tech processing machinery, hand-hammered wood casks, and cool, damp stone aging rooms; it culminates in an invitation to sample several Santo Tomás vintages, including an international-medal-winning cabernet and delightfully crisp sparkling blanc de blanc. The wood-paneled, churchlike tasting room is adorned with paintings of mischievous altar boys being scolded by stern friars for pilfering wine or ruining precious grapes. Anyone used to the pretentious, assembly-line ambience of trendier wine regions will relish the friendly welcome and informative tour presented here. Tours in English start Monday through Saturday at 10am, 11am, noon, 1pm, and 3pm. Admission is $6, including a tasting of three low-priced wines; $10 more gets you a souvenir wineglass and a tasting of 12 high-priced wines. Wines for sale cost $6.50 to $26 a bottle. *Note:* Most of the winery's product is exported for the European market.

Be sure to poke around Santo Tomás a bit after your tour concludes. The little modern machinery installed here freed up a cavernous space now used for monthly jazz concerts, and a former aging room has been transformed into La Embotelladora Vieja (The Old Aging Room) restaurant (see "Where to Dine," below). Across the street stands La Esquina de Bodegas (The Corner Wine Cellar), former aging rooms for Santo Tomás: The industrial-style building now functions as a gallery showcasing local art, with a skylit bookstore on the second level and a small cafe (punctuated by giant copper distillation vats) in the rear.

Ensenada's primary cultural center is the **Centro Cívico, Social y Cultura,** Bulevar Lázaro Cárdenas at Avenida Club Rotario. The impressive Mediterranean building was formerly Riviera del Pacífico, a glamorous 1930s bayfront casino and resort frequented by Hollywood's elite. Tiles in the lobby commemorate "Visitantes Distinguidos 1930–1940," including Marion Davies, William Randolph Hearst, Lana Turner, Myrna Loy, and Jack Dempsey. Now used by the Rotary Club as offices and for cultural and social events, the main building is open to the public. Elegant hallways and ballrooms evoke bygone elegance, and every wall and alcove glows with original murals depicting Mexico's colorful history. Lush formal gardens span the front of the building, and there's a small art gallery on one side. Through the lobby, facing an inner courtyard, is Bar Andaluz, which is open to the public sporadically. It's an intimate, dark-wood place where you can just imagine someone like Papa Hemingway holding cocktail-hour court beneath that colorful toreador mural.

A NEARBY ATTRACTION

South of the city, a 45-minute drive along the rural Punta Banda peninsula, is one of Ensenada's major attractions: **La Bufadora**, a natural sea spout in the rocks. With each incoming wave, water is forced upward through the rock, creating a geyser whose loud grunt gave the phenomenon its name (*la bufadora* means "buffalo snort"). Local fishermen who ply these waters have a much more lyrical explanation for this roaring blowhole. According to local legend, a mother gray whale and her calf were just beginning their migration from the safety of Baja's San Ignacio lagoon to Alaska. As they rounded Punta Banda, the curious calf squeezed into a sea cave, only to be trapped. The groan that this 21m-high (70-ft.) blowhole makes every time it erupts is the sound of the stranded calf still crying for his mother, and the tremendous spray is his spout.

From downtown Ensenada, take Avenida Reforma south (Carretera Transpeninsular) to Highway 23 west. It's a long, meandering drive through a semi-swamplike area untouched by development; look for grazing animals, bait shops, and fishermen's shacks along the way. La Bufadora is at the end of the road, and once parked ($1 per car in crude dirt lots), you must walk downhill to the viewing platform, at the end of a 540m (1,771-ft.) pathway lined with souvenir stands. In addition to running a gauntlet of determined vendors featuring the usual wares, visitors can avail themselves of inexpensive snacks at the sole restaurant there, including tasty fish tacos. Visitation is enormous, but long-standing plans to pave the dirt parking lots and build permanent restaurants and shops have yet to become a reality.

For a guided walking tour of downtown Ensenada, shopping tours, or tours to the wine country, you can also contact **Jatay Tours** (© **646/172-2246** or 646/107-4373).

SPORTS & OUTDOOR ACTIVITIES

FISHING   Ensenada, which bills itself as "the yellowtail capital of the world," draws sportfishermen eager to venture out from the beautiful Bahía de Todos Santos (Bay of All Saints) in search of the Pacific's albacore, halibut, marlin, rockfish, and sea bass. A wooden boardwalk parallel to Bulevar Lázaro Cárdenas (Costero) near the northern entrance to town provides access to the sportfishing piers and their many charter-boat operators. Open-party boats leave early, often by 7am, and charge around $35 per person, plus an additional fee (around $5) for the mandatory fishing license. Nonfishing passengers must, by law, also be licensed. Those disinclined to comparison shop the boats can make advance arrangements with San Diego–based **Baja California Tours** (© **619/454-7166**). In addition to daily fishing excursions, it offers 1- to 3-night packages including hotel, fishing, some meals, and transportation from San Diego.

HIKING   Ensenada is the gateway city to the **Parque Nacional Constitución de 1857.** On the spine of the Sierra de Juárez, the park was once a heavily used mining area, but most of the mines are now defunct. In contrast to the dry and sometimes desolate surroundings of much of the northern peninsula, the 5,000-hectare (12,350-acre) preserve averages about 1,200m (3,936 ft.) in altitude and is covered in places with pine forests. The most idiosyncratic thing, however, is the sight of a good-size lake in an alpine setting. The park has no developed trails other than a 10km (6.2-mile) one that circumnavigates the lake, Laguna Hanson, but there are endless opportunities for blazing your own. To get to the park, take Highway 3 south from Ensenada and exit at the graded dirt access road at Km 55. The park entrance road (35km/22 miles to the park entrance) is gravel and generally well maintained but can be really rough after a rainy year. If the entrance is staffed, you'll be asked for a modest entrance fee.

The **Parque Nacional Sierra San Pedro Mártir** is to Baja California what Yosemite is to Alta California. Almost 72,000 hectares (177,840 acres) of the highest mountains on the peninsula have been preserved here. The highest, Picacho del Diablo (Devil's Peak), rises to 3,095m (10,152 ft.). Views from the summit encompass both oceans and an immense stretch of land. Best of all, it's virtually unvisited, something that sets it apart from the normal national park experience in Los Estados Unidos.

Farther south on Carretera Transpeninsular from Ensenada, you'll come to a signed turnoff for the park at Km 140, soon after you pass the little town of Colonet. The sign also says OBSERVATORIO. Fill up with gas in Colonet—there is no more until you exit this way again—and reset your trip odometer at the turnoff. In between, it's entirely possible to put on a gas-guzzling 242km (150 miles) of rugged driving. It's 76km (47 miles) to the park entrance.

You'll find a high alpine realm of flower-speckled meadows, soaring granite peaks, and year-round creeks. Official trails are few and far between, so wander at your own risk, but anyone who's good with a map and compass can have a great time hiking. Cow trails (yes, cows in a national park) are numerous. Four year-round creeks drain the park and make great destinations. Picacho del Diablo is a difficult but rewarding overnight hike and long scramble. Always remember that you're in one of the most rugged and remote places in all of Baja, and with the lack of marked trails, it's quite likely that if you get lost or hurt, nobody will come looking for you.

For other adventure tours in the region, contact **Expediciones de Turismo Ecológico y de Aventura,** Bulevar Costero 1094–14, Centro (© **646/178-3704;** www.mexonline.com/ecotur.htm), which runs hiking, mountain bike, ATV, and other adventure tours in the region.

SEA KAYAKING   The rocky coastline of Punta la Banda is a favorite first trip for beginning ocean kayakers due to its several secluded beaches, sea caves, and terrific scenery. Many kayakers use La Bufadora as a launching point to head out to the Todos Santos Islands. It's about 11km (7 miles) from La Bufadora to the southern and larger of the two islands. The first 4.8km (3 miles) follow a rocky coast to the tip of Punta la Banda. From here you'll need to size up the wind, the waves, and the fog. If the coast is clear, take a compass and begin the 6km (4-mile) open-water crossing. Bring water and camping gear to spend a night on the pristine island. **Dale's La Bufadora Dive Shop** (© **646/154-2092**) has kayak rentals and is open weekends or by prior reservation. **Expediciones de Turismo Ecológico y de Aventura,** Bulevar Costero 1094–14, Centro (© **646/178-3704;** www.mexonline.com/ecotur.htm) offers guided kayak trips, including a full kayak expedition through the Bay of Los Angeles.

SCUBA DIVING & SNORKELING   La Bufadora is a great dive spot with thick kelp and wonderful sea life. Get underwater and zoom through lovely kelp beds and rugged rock formations covered in strawberry anemones and gypsy shawl nudibranchs. You may also spot spiny lobsters and numerous large fish. It's possible to swim right over to the blowhole (see "A Nearby Attraction," above), but use extreme caution in this area—you don't want to end up like that mythical whale calf. **Dale's La Bufadora Dive Shop** (© **646/154-2092**) is on shore at the best entry point. The staff will set you up with fills (for air tanks) and advice.

Several dive shops in Ensenada, including **Almar,** Av. Macheros 149 (© **646/178-3013**), will arrange boat dives to the Todos Santos islands, which sit at the outer edge of Todos Santos Bay. The diving here is similar to the diving at Catalina or the other

California Channel Islands—lots of fish, big kelp, urchins, and jagged underwater rock formations. The visibility varies widely depending on the swell.

SURFING   Only the best and boldest surfers challenge the waves off Islas de Todos Santos, two islands about 19 km (12 mi) west of Ensenada, considered to be some of the best surf on the coast. Waves can reach 9m (30 ft.) in winter, and surfers must hire a *panga* to take them to the waves. You'll find gentler but still challenging waves at San Miguel and Salsipuedes. For local surf reports and gear rental, visit the **San Miguel Surf Shop,** Avenida López Mateos at Calle Ruiz, Centro (© 646/178-1007), the most popular local surf shop

SHOPPING

Ensenada's equivalent of Tijuana's Avenida Revolución is crowded Avenida López Mateos, which runs roughly parallel to Bulevar Lázaro Cárdenas (Costero); the highest concentration of shops and restaurants is between avenidas Ruiz and Castillo. Beggars fill this street, and sellers are less likely to bargain here than in Tijuana—they're used to gullible cruise-ship buyers in Ensenada. However, compared to Tijuana, there is more authentic Mexican art- and craftwork in Ensenada, pieces imported from rural states and villages where different skills are traditionally practiced. Though from the outside it looks dusty and unlit, **Pacific Jewelry,** Av. López Mateos 725 (© 646/178-3191), is a treasure trove of fine jewelry, with quality gemstones and creative designs.

You'll see colorfully painted glazed pottery wherever you go in northern Baja. It ranges in quality, from sloppy pieces quickly painted with a limited palette to intricately designed, painstakingly painted works evocative of Tuscan urns and pitchers. The best prices are at the abundant roadside stands lining the old road south of Rosarito.

WHERE TO STAY

Estero Beach Resort ⭐ (Kids)   About 10km (6¼ miles) south of downtown Ensenada, this sprawling complex of rooms, cottages, and mobile-home hookups is popular with families and active vacationers. The bay and protected lagoon at the edge of the lushly planted property are perfect for swimming and launching sailboards; there's also tennis, horseback riding, volleyball, and a game room with Ping-Pong and billiards. The guest rooms are a little worn, but no one expects fancy here. The beachfront restaurant serves a casual mix of seafood, Mexican fare, hamburgers, fried chicken, and omelets. Some suites and 5 of the 15 cottages have kitchenettes, and some can easily accommodate a whole family.

Estero Beach. (Mailing address: Apdo. Postal 86, Ensenada, B.C., Mexico.) © 646/176-6225. www.hotelestero beach.com. 94 units. $95–$156 double; $75–$120 cottage sleeping 2; $448 presidential suite. From Ensenada, take Carretera Transpeninsular south; turn right at ESTERO BEACH sign. MC, V. **Amenities:** Restaurant; pool w/2 Jacuzzis; tennis court; game room; Mexican art museum and shop. *In room:* TV.

Las Rosas Hotel & Spa ⭐⭐   One of the most modern hotels in the area, Hotel Las Rosas still falls short of most definitions of luxurious, yet the pink oceanfront hotel 3.2km (2 miles) north of Ensenada is the favorite of many Baja aficionados. It offers most of the comforts of an upscale American hotel—which doesn't leave room for much Mexican personality. The atrium lobby is awash in pale pink and sea-foam green, a color scheme that pervades throughout—including the guest rooms, sparsely furnished with quasitropical furniture. Some rooms have fireplaces and/or in-room whirlpools, and all have balconies overlooking the pool and ocean. One of the resort's main photo ops is the infinity swimming pool that overlooks and appears to merge with the Pacific Ocean beyond. If you're looking to maintain the highest comfort level possible, this should be your hotel choice.

Carretera Transpeninsular, 3.2km (2 miles) north of Ensenada. (Mailing address: Apdo. Postal 316, Ensenada, B.C., Mexico.) 𝒞 646/174-4310. 47 units. $126–$190 double. Children under 12 $16; extra adult $22. MC, V. Amenities: Restaurant; cocktail lounge; swimming pool; tennis and racquetball courts; basic workout room; cliff-top hot tub; business center w/Internet; tour desk; room service; massage; laundry service. In room: A/C, TV.

San Nicolás Resort Hotel   Most rooms at this modern motor inn face the courtyard or have balconies overlooking the swimming pool—and the place is surprisingly quiet for being right on the main drag. The hotel also has a disco and a branch of Caliente Sports Book, where you can gamble on games and races throughout the U.S.

Av. López Mateos and Guadalupe, Ensenada. (Mailing address: P.O. Box 437060, San Ysidro, CA 92073-7060.) 𝒞 646/176-1901. Fax 646/176-4930. www.sannicolas.com.mx. 147 units. $99–$134 double; $146–$291 suite. Extra person $10. AE, MC, V. Amenities: Restaurant; cocktail lounge; swimming pool. In room: A/C, TV.

Villa Fontana Days Inn   This motel is notable for its out-of-place architecture—who'd expect a peak-roofed, gabled, New England–style structure in a land dominated by red-tiled roofs? Otherwise this bargain-priced motel is unremarkable though it is well and cleanly run by the Days Inn chain. It has a small pool and enclosed parking. Most of the 65 rooms have showers, rather than tubs, in the bathrooms. Ask for a room at the back, away from street noise.

Av. López Mateos 1050, Ensenada. 𝒞 800/4-BAJA-04 in the U.S., or 646/178-3434. www.villafontana.com.mx. 65 units. Summer $60 double; $115 suite. Rates are higher on holidays, lower Tues–Thurs, and in winter. Rates include continental breakfast. Internet discounts available. AE, MC, V. Amenities: Pool. In room: A/C, TV.

WHERE TO DINE

El Charro _Kids_ MEXICAN   You'll recognize El Charro by its front windows: Whole chickens rotate slowly on the rotisserie in one while a woman makes tortillas in the other. This little place has been here since 1956 and looks it, with charred walls, a ceiling made of split logs, and giant piñatas hanging from the walls above the concrete floor. The simple fare consists of such dishes as half a roasted chicken with fries and tortillas, or _carne asada_ (grilled marinated beef) with soup, guacamole, and tortillas. Kids are welcome; they'll think they're on a picnic. Wine and beer are served, and beer is cheaper than soda.

Av. López Mateos 475 (between Ruiz and Gastellum). 𝒞 646/178-2114. Menu items $5–$12; lobster $20. No credit cards. Daily 11am–2am.

El Rey Sol _Kids_ FRENCH/MEXICAN   Opened by French expatriates in 1947, the family-run El Rey Sol has long been considered Ensenada's finest eatery. Decked out like the French flag, this red, white, and blue building is a beacon on busy López Mateos. Wrought-iron chandeliers and heavy oak farm tables add to the country-French ambience, but the menu's prices and sophistication belie the casual decor. House specialties include seafood puff pastry; baby clams steamed in butter, white wine, and cilantro; chicken in brandy and chipotle-chile cream sauce; tender grilled steaks; and homemade French desserts. Portions are generous, however, and always feature fresh vegetables from the nearby family farm. Every table receives a complimentary platter of appetizers at dinnertime; lunch is a hearty three-course meal.

Av. López Mateos 1000 (at Blancarte). 𝒞 646/178-1733. Reservations recommended for weekends. Main courses $9–$19. AE, MC, V. Daily 8:30am–10:30pm.

Diving with Great White Sharks in Baja

For anyone who still draws a pause when they hear the theme from Jaws, read no further: This is no adventure for the faint of heart. Off the coast of Baja, one can go cage diving with great white sharks at Isla Guadalupe. More than an extreme sport, this activity actually supports shark science. **Absolute Adventures–Shark Diver** (© **888/405-3268**, 415/404-6144, or 415/235-9410 in the U.S.; www.sharkdiver.com) is led by Patrick Douglas, an adventure guide who has teamed up with scientists in Baja Mexico and Southern California to fuse ecotourism with research. Dives take place at Isla Guadalupe, a 158-sq.-km (109-sq.-mile) island 242km (150 miles) off-shore of the Pacific coast of Mexico, roughly south of San Diego and west/northwest of Punta Eugenia on the Baja California peninsula. Sur-rounded by deep water, as much as 3,600m (11,808 ft.) between the island and the mainland, the island is home to a stunning array of wildlife, includ-ing one of the world's most accessible populations of great white sharks.

The great white shark (Carcharodon carcharias) occurs naturally in all temperate marine waters, and is usually between 3 and 4m (10 and 13 ft.) long, although it can grow to 6.5m (21 ft.) and weigh over 1,800kg (2 tons). They are among the most feared predators in the world, known for their fearsome sudden attacks. Great whites typically surprise their prey by rush-ing from below and grasping the victim with a powerful, large bite. If the bite is not fatal, the prey is usually left to weaken or die through blood loss, at which time the white shark returns and consumes its prey. Shark diving allows shark enthusiasts to observe the world of great whites, as well as the array of other marine life in the area, in their natural environment. Absolute Adventures claims to use the largest shark cages in existence—4.5 to 9.3 sq. m (50 to 100 sq. ft) in size—which are used to create a discernable barrier that the sharks quickly recognize so divers may safely view and pho-tograph the sharks. The four-man shark cages are constructed using high-grade materials and a state-of-the-art fabrication processes. The 5-day live aboard-cage diving expeditions take place on one of their two full-time shark diving vessels, and range in price from $2,350 to $2,550 per person, depending on which vessel you choose: the "laid-back" or "upscale" adven-ture (one offers sleeping bunks, the other air-conditioned staterooms). The program supports large-scale research programs involving researchers from Mexico (Centro Interdisciplinario de Ciencias del Mar) and University of Cal-ifornia–Davis, in Northern California.

La Embotelladora Vieja ★★★ (Finds) FRENCH/MEXICAN   If you're planning to splurge on one fine meal in Ensenada (or all of northern Baja for that matter), this should be the place to do it. Hidden on an industrial side street and attached to the Bodegas de Santo Tomás winery, it looks more like a chapel than the elegant restau-rant it is. Sophisticated diners will feel right at home in the stylish setting, a former winery aging room now resplendent with red oak furniture (constructed from old wine casks), high brick walls, and crystal goblets and candlesticks on linen tablecloths.

The wine list is exemplary, featuring bottles from Santo Tomás and other Baja vintners, and the "Baja French" menu features dishes carefully crafted to include or complement wine. Look for appetizers like abalone ceviche or cream of garlic soup followed by grilled swordfish in cilantro sauce, filet mignon in port wine–Gorgonzola sauce, or quail with tart sauvignon blanc sauce.

Av. Miramar 666 (at Calle 7). (©) 646/174-0807. Reservations recommended for weekends. Main courses $8–$20. AE, MC, V. Mon–Sat noon–10pm.

ENSENADA AFTER DARK

No discussion of Ensenada would be complete without mentioning **Hussong's Cantina,** Av. Ruiz 113, near Avenida López Mateos (©) **646/178-3210**); just like the line from *Casablanca,* "everyone goes to Rick's," everyone's been going to Hussong's since the bar opened in 1892. Nothing much has changed in the last century plus—the place still sports Wild West–style swinging saloon doors, a long bar to slide beers along, and strolling mariachis bellowing to rise above the din of revelers. There's definitely a minimalist appeal to Hussong's, which looks as if it sprang from a south-of-the-border episode of *Gunsmoke.* Beer and tequilas at astonishingly low prices are the main order of business. Be aware that hygiene and privacy are a low priority in the restrooms.

While the crowd (a pleasant mix of tourists and locals) at Hussong's can really whoop it up, they're amateurs compared to those who frequent **Papas & Beer,** Avenida Ruiz near Avenida López Mateos (©) **646/178-4231**), across the street. A tiny entrance leads to the upstairs bar and disco, where the music is loud and the hip young crowd is definitely here to party. Happy patrons hang out of the second-story windows calling out to their friends and stop occasionally to eat *papas* (french fries) accompanied by local beers. Papas & Beer has quite a reputation with the Southern California college crowd and has opened a branch in Rosarito Beach (see "Rosarito Beach After Dark" on p. 159). You've probably noticed bumper stickers for these two quintessentially Baja watering holes, but they don't just give them away. In fact, each bar has several souvenir shops along Avenida Ruiz.

EXPLORING THE VALLE DE GUADALUPE— MEXICO'S WINE COUNTRY

Beyond the lure of Tijuana and tequila, an exploration of Mexico's wine country, in the northern Baja peninsula, makes for an offbeat and intriguing side trip to the area. A 29km (18-mile) drive northeast of Ensenada along Highway 3 will bring you to the Valle de Guadalupe (Guadalupe Valley), the heart of Mexico's small but blossoming wine industry. Although most connoisseurs tend to be dismissive of Mexico's wine efforts, in recent years the production and quality have made quantum leaps, and several Mexican vintages have earned international acclaim.

Spanish missionaries first introduced wine to Baja California in 1701, when a Jesuit priest, Father Juan de Ugarte, planted the peninsula's first grape vines. In 1791, the first vineyards were established in these fertile valleys at Misión Santo Thomas. In 1888, the Santa Tomás winery was established, giving birth to Mexico's wine country.

It wasn't until the 1970s that commercial wineries entered the area, with the establishment of the Domecq and L.A. Cetto operations—two of Mexico's largest wine producers, which until recently specialized in inexpensive, mass-produced wines. It was the opening of the boutique winery **Monte Xanic** in the late 1980s that brought the culture of fine wines to the area, and to Mexico.

Wine Country

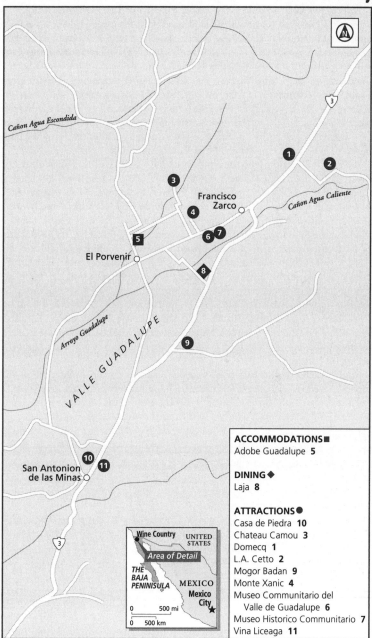

ACCOMMODATIONS ■
Adobe Guadalupe **5**

DINING ◆
Laja **8**

ATTRACTIONS ●
Casa de Piedra **10**
Chateau Camou **3**
Domecq **1**
L.A. Cetto **2**
Mogor Badan **9**
Monte Xanic **4**
Museo Communitario del
    Valle de Guadalupe **6**
Museo Historico Communitario **7**
Vina Liceaga **11**

Cañon Agua Escondida

Francisco
Zarco

Cañon Agua Caliente

El Porvenir

Arroyo Guadalupe

VALLE GUADALUPE

San Antonion
de las Minas

Wine Country
UNITED
STATES
Area of Detail
THE
BAJA
PENINISULA
MEXICO
Mexico
City

0   500 mi
0   500 km

The Valle de Guadalupe is in the "world wine strip," a zone of lands with the climate and porous soil that result in ideal conditions for grape growing—similar to those found in Northern California, France, Spain, and Italy. Northern Baja's dry, hot summers and cool, humid winters added to a stream of cool breezes make the conditions in Guadalupe Valley especially conducive for vineyards, similar to what you would find in the Mediterranean. The most common wines found here include chenin blanc, colombard, sauvignon blanc, and chardonnay among the whites, and cabernet sauvignon, merlot, Barbera, Nebbiolo, and zinfandel among the reds. However, the region's limited rainfall and water supply will likely limit its growth, meaning it is likely to remain the picturesque place it is today rather than growing into a tourist-oriented culture in the way Napa Valley has evolved.

In 1905, the Mexican government granted political asylum to 100 families from Russia, who arrived in Guadalupe Valley to cultivate grapes. These were the pioneers of grape cultivation in the area, and many of the present-day residents are descendents of those Russian families. The **Museo Comunitario del Valle de Guadalupe,** on Francisco Zarco (**©** **646/155-2030**), has displays and artifacts from this curious time of cultural conversion. It even has a small adjoining restaurant that serves traditional Russian food. Just across the street is the **Museo Histórico Comunitario,** affiliated with Mexico's INAH (National Institute of Anthropology and History). Although small in scale, it has informative displays of the indigenous Kumiai culture of the region, and more about the influence of the Russian immigrants in the Valley of Guadalupe. The museum is open Tuesday through Sunday from 10am to 5pm (**©** **646/178-2531**).

The best time to visit the Valle de Guadalupe is in late August, during Las Fiestas de la Vendimia (Harvest Festivals). Various vineyards schedule a multitude of activities during the festivals, including tastings, classical music concerts, and Masses celebrating the harvest.

Note that most of the roads in the Valle de Guadalupe are dirt-surfaced, so an SUV is the preferred vehicle to explore the area in. The area's only fully paved road is Highway 3 (to Tecate), which cuts through the valley. Most of the wineries and attractions are just off this scenic road, which is lined with vineyards and olive orchards.

WINERY TOURS

Winery tours are available at most of the region's wineries, with some having more structure than others. Especially if you visit the smaller wineries, you'll find you may be the only visitor, meaning you'll enjoy personal attention. But before you snap up cases of the vintages you taste, keep in mind that customs limit you to taking only three bottles back across the U.S. border.

Scheduled winery tours are offered by **Baja California Tours** (**©** **800/336-5454** or 858/454-7166 in the U.S.; www.bajaspecials.com). Tours include visits to several wineries, a historical overview of the valley, transportation from the border, and lunch. They also have overnight tours, including during the annual Harvest Festival.

I've listed below a few of the more popular wineries you may want to visit on your own.

Bodegas de Santo Tomás is Baja's oldest winery. They offer daily tours and wine tastings at 11am, 1, and 3pm for $2. They are in Ensenada, at Av. Miramar 666 (**©** **646/178-2509,** 646/174-0836, or -0829; www.santo-tomas.com).

Casa de Piedra offers free tours and wine tastings through its small but celebrated vineyard Monday through Friday 10am to 2pm and Saturdays from 10am to noon.

Large groups may be accommodated by appointment. It's in Valle de Guadalupe, at Km. 86.5, Highway 3 to Tecate (© **646/155-3097;** www.vinoscasadepiedra.com).

Chateau Camou has free tours and wine tastings Monday through Friday from 10am to 2pm and Saturdays from 10am to noon. Large groups may be accommodated by appointment. This winery has beautiful gardens and panoramic views of the valley. It's in Francisco Zarco, Valle de Guadalupe, just off Highway 3 to Tecate (© **646/177-2221;** www.chateau-camou.com.mx).

Domecq hosts free wine tastings and tours Monday through Friday 10am to 4pm and Saturdays from 10am to 1:30pm. They have a gift shop and picnic areas on premises. Domecq is in Valle de Guadalupe at Km. 73, on Highway 3 to Tecate (© **646/ 155-2249;** www.vinos-domecq.com.mx).

L.A. Cetto, one of the largest and most commercial wineries in the region, offers free wine tastings and tours daily from 10am to 4pm. There's also a gift shop and picnic areas on site in Valle de Guadalupe at Km. 73.5 on Highway 3 to Tecate (© **646/ 155-2264;** www.lacetto.com).

Mogor Badan, a boutique winery, offers tours and wine tastings by appointment only. They're in Valle de Guadalupe, Rancho El Mogor, Km. 86.5 on Highway 3 to Tecate (©/fax **646/177-1484**).

Monte Xanic is a true jewel of a winery to visit, with wine tastings and tours (costing $2) available by appointment Monday through Friday from 10am to 4pm and Saturdays from 9am to 12:30pm. These are considered by many to be Mexico's finest wines in Francisco Zarco, Valle de Guadalupe, just off Highway 3 to Tecate (© **646/ 174-6769** or 646/174-6155; www.montexanic.com).

Vina Liceaga has by-appointment wine tastings and tours available on Saturdays at 1pm. Don't miss their award-winning merlot. Still in Valle de Guadalupe, at Km 93 on Highway 3 to Tecate (© **646/184-0126** or 646/184-1184; www.vinosliceaga.com).

WHERE TO STAY

Adobe Guadalupe ★★★ *Finds*   One of the few places to stay in Guadalupe Valley, Adobe Guadalupe is both an intimate inn and a boutique winery. Six private bedrooms and a stunning interior courtyard comprise this lovely mission style structure situated on 26 hectares (65 acres) of vineyard, which grows cabernet sauvignon, merlot, Nebbiolo, cabernet Franc, Tempranillo, shiraz, and a bit of Viognier grapes. The vineyards were started in 1998, and their first harvest was in 2000. Rooms are cozy and comfortable, with rough-hewn Mexican furnishings and antiques. Rates include breakfast, which is served in the kitchen from 8 to 10am daily. You may also reserve dinner, at a cost of $50 per person, which includes a four-course meal accompanied by their own wines ($35 without wine). After you've had your fill of traipsing through vineyards or sampling wines, you can relax by the pool or read a book by the courtyard fountain.

Hwy. 1-D, Km 77.5. (Mailing address: 416 W. San Ysidro Bulevar, Suite #L-732, San Ysidro, CA 92173.) © **649/ 631-3098** in the U.S., or 646/155-2094. www.adobeguadalupe.com. 6 units. $150 double, includes breakfast. AE, MC, V. To find Adobe Guadalupe, once you've arrived in the town of Guadalupe along Highway 3, turn left just past the river (Francisco Zarco). The pavement will soon end, but continue for about 5.6km (3½ miles), past the Monte Xanic and Chateau Camou wineries. At the stop sign (adjacent to the Unidad Médica Familiar building), turn right and continue .8km (½ mile) more. Adobe Guadalupe will be on your right. **Amenities:** Dining room; heated swimming pool and Jacuzzi; concierge; picnic area. *In room:* A/C, TV.

WHERE TO DINE

Laja ★★★ *Finds* GOURMET MEXICAN   Under the direction of former Four Seasons chef Jair Tellez, this extraordinary gem of a gourmet restaurant (which has won accolades from the major Southern California publications) is reason enough to visit the valley. Set in a lovely adobe and stone building with picture windows overlooking the valley, Laja, with its own herb garden and small vineyard, serves a daily fixed menu of four to eight courses featuring local fresh produce and wines.

On Hwy. 3 Km. 83, Francisco Zarco, Valle de Guadalupe. ℂ **646/155-2556.** Reservations required. Main courses $25–$40. No credit cards. Thurs–Fri and Sun 1:30–6pm; Sat 1:30–8:30pm.

Appendix A:
Baja in Depth

The entire country of Mexico stretches nearly 3,220km (1,996 miles) from east to west and more than 1,600km (992 miles) north to south. Only one-fifth the size of the United States, its territory includes trackless deserts in the north, dense jungles in the south, thousands of miles of lush seacoast and beaches along the Pacific and Caribbean, and the central highlands, crisscrossed by mountain ranges.

The Baja peninsula was once a part of mainland Mexico, and perhaps its physical separation has helped contribute to the sense of cultural separation from the rest of its homeland. Although no matter where you go in Mexico the sense of national pride runs deep, in Baja there is also a close sense of kinship with its neighbor to the north—the U.S. state of California, which, of course, was once part of Mexico itself.

Today, many travelers to Baja claim this region feels more like an extension of Southern California than it does Mexico. This is especially true in the Los Cabos area, at the very tip of Baja, where a large and growing expat community of Americans has taken up residence. There, English is as common as Spanish, and dollars are the preferred form of currency. This isn't as prevalent in the mid- and northern parts of Baja, especially in the central rural areas.

Still, Baja has a cultural identity unique to itself. It has always been a rugged and often inhospitable land, and has been, through the years, as much a home to pirates, outlaws, and adventurers as to anyone. The ability to survive here has given rise to a sturdy soul in the inhabitants of this region, something that continues to be a sense of pride.

No one knows much about the ancient inhabitants of the Baja peninsula other than that they left a remarkable collection of dramatic paintings on the walls of caves in central Baja's mountainous region. These mystical paintings of faceless human and animal forms, despite all that we now know, seem to defy interpretation. Although the date of these paintings, as well as their meaning, remains unclear, the art they left behind is a stunning expression of a rich and complex cosmological view.

There is also limited knowledge of the indigenous tribes who lived here at the time of the arrival of the Spanish explorers, but what is clear is that they were less than welcoming. The first known European ship to arrive to these shores was the *Concepción* in 1534, under sail by a group of mutineers who landed in La Paz. Natives killed the majority, and the few survivors brought back tales of caches of black pearls found on a rugged island. Hernán Cortez, who was leading the Spanish Crown's conquest of Mexico, organized further explorations, which ultimately ended in a similar fate. He finally succeeded in financing an expedition led by Captain Francisco de Ulloa that charted what is now known as the Sea of Cortez, establishing the fact that this was not an island but a peninsula.

For these reasons and more, the Baja is an intriguing place. Most travelers to the area will be drawn to its cobalt-blue waters and desert landscapes, but for more adventurous souls, what will ultimately hold your attention is the vast and mysterious interior section of the peninsula, and the strength of character it requires to survive and thrive there. This may no longer be the "no man's land" which once characterized it, yet Baja remains a rugged region (outside the resort areas), one that invites you to challenge yourself to test your personal limits.

1 The Land & Its People

SOCIAL MORES   American and English travelers have often observed that Mexicans have a different conception of time—that life in Mexico obeys slower rhythms. This is true, and yet few observers go on to explain what the consequences of this are for the visitor to Mexico. This is a shame, because an imperfect appreciation of the difference causes a good deal of misunderstanding between tourists and locals.

On several occasions, Mexican acquaintances have asked me why Americans grin all the time. At first I wasn't sure what to make of the question and only gradually came to appreciate what was at issue. As the pace of life for Americans, Canadians, and others has quickened, they have come to skip some of the niceties of social interaction. When walking into a store, many Americans simply smile at a clerk and launch right into a question or request. The smile, in effect, replaces the greeting. In Mexico, it doesn't work that way. Mexicans misinterpret this American manner of greeting. After all, a smile when there is no context can be ambiguous; it can convey amusement, smugness, or superiority.

One of the most important pieces of advice I can offer travelers is this: Always give a proper greeting when addressing Mexicans. Don't try to abbreviate social intercourse. Mexican culture places a higher value on proper social form than on saving time. A Mexican must at least say *"¡Buenos días!"* or a quick *"¿Qué pasó?"* (or its equivalent) to show proper respect. When an individual meets up with a group, he will greet each person separately, which can take quite a while. For us, the polite thing would be to keep our interruption to a minimum and give a general greeting to all.

Mexicans, like most people, will consciously or subconsciously make quick judgments about individuals they meet. Most divide the world into the *bien educado* (well raised and cultured), and the *mal educado* (poorly raised). Unfortunately, many visitors are reluctant to try out their Spanish, preferring to keep exchanges to a minimum. Don't do this. To be categorized as a foreigner isn't a big deal. What's important in Mexico is to be categorized as one of the cultured foreigners and not one of the barbarians. This makes it easier to get the attention of waiters, hotel desk clerks, and people on the street.

TODAY'S BAJA CULTURE & PEOPLE   The Baja peninsula was for years one of Mexico's least populated regions. With the exception of the stretch of coast between Tijuana and Ensenada, which began attracting spirited travelers from the U.S. during Prohibition with its more lenient liquor laws, only a small number of hardy souls resided in the central and southern parts of the peninsula working as ranchers or fishermen. Even La Paz, the capital of Baja, was considered a minor shell of a port, with a limited citizenry.

It wasn't until the Carretera Transpeninsular (Hwy. 1) was completed in 1973, connecting Tijuana with Cabo San Lucas, that opportunities for growth opened up. Prior to that, it took 10 days to travel the rugged dirt roads between Tijuana and La Paz (today—at a speed of 80kmph/50 mph, which is not always possible, and with limited rest stops—it would take 23 hr.). The population in the southern region exploded following this event, and the area has flourished ever since. This has been aided in large part by Fonatur's (Mexico's tourism infrastructure secretariat) focus on investing in the Los Cabos area to create another center of tourism for Mexico. The area south of Loreto, also known as Puerto Escondido, has also been a focus of Fonatur investment efforts, recently revitalized with the Loreto Bay real estate project.

Because Baja's geography created a natural barrier to growth for so many years, you'll find that many of Baja's inhabitants are transplants from the north or from other parts of Mexico, most a mix of foreign and indigenous ancestry. In addition to the European settlers, who included sea-weary sailors who jumped ship, the early pioneers of Baja included Chinese immigrants brought here to work, a colony of Russian refugees granted political asylum who came to the Valle de Guadalupe, and French miners who settled in Santa Rosalía. Their descendents have greatly contributed to the multicultural spirit of Baja.

However, there remains a sense of separatism to this culture, and as such, you may not find the locals as naturally warm and welcoming to visitors as you'll find in other parts of Mexico. What you will often encounter, though, is an eagerness by locals to share their knowledge of the natural treasures of Baja—whether it be the unique desert flora, the rich underwater life, or survival skills in this challenging terrain. Most of Baja's long-term residents appear to be inherently respectful of the surrounding nature.

BAJA'S GEOGRAPHY The Baja peninsula is long, narrow piece of land dominated by mountain ranges and desert terrain. The length of the peninsula extends 1,300km (806 miles) from the U.S.-Mexico border to its southernmost tip. Its widest point across land is at the border itself, which measures 193km (120 miles), while the narrowest part,

near the southern tip, extends just 45km (28 miles) from the Bay of La Paz in the east to the Pacific Ocean in the west. Its total coastal area, including the Pacific Ocean, Sea of Cortez, and many coves and inlets, measures about 4,800km (2,976 miles) of shoreline. Throughout Baja, mountains rise up in a succession of ranges, with a total of 23 named ranges. The four primary ranges are: the **Sierra de San Pedro Mártir, Sierra de Juárez, Sierra de la Giganta,** and the **Sierra de la Laguna.** The highest peak in Baja is the **Picacho del Diablo (Devil's Peak),** which reaches an elevation of 3,095m (10,152 ft.). More than 65% of Baja's total land area is classified as desert, although—truly a land of contrasts—it also boasts pine (conifer) forests in its northern mountainous regions.

NATURAL LIFE & PROTECTED AREAS There are two national parks in Baja, which are considered some of the most beautiful sites within the state. The **Parque Nacional Constitución de 1857** is within the Sierra de Juárez mountain range, in the extreme north of the peninsula, at an average altitude of 1,650m (5,412 ft.), with a surface area of 5,000 hectares (12,372 acres). In it, you'll find diverse pine forests with some trees growing to heights of over 30m (98 ft.), as well as Laguna Hanson, also known as Laguna de Juárez, a lake in the park's interior (note that due to diminished rainfall in recent years, the lake is currently dry). The area was declared a national park in 1962, and in 1983 it became a part of the country's protected natural areas. Within the park, you can enjoy hiking, mountain climbing, biking, bird-watching, stargazing, and other activities. Two Pro-Natura-designed roads allow you to admire the beauty of the park from elevated vantage points. Camping is available here, and there are a few rustic cabins for rent throughout the park system. Two ecotourism ranches, Rodeo del Rey and Los

Bandidos, are also within the park, offering rustic rooms as well as campsites and related services. An information booth with maps is just past the entry point; a per-vehicle entry charge applies.

The **Parque Nacional Sierra San Pedro Mártir,** 210km (130 miles) southeast of Ensenada, has elevations that range from 1,000 to over 3,048m (3,280–9,997 ft.). Its surface area covers 72,000 hectares (177,840 acres) of pine forests. The park is managed by the Baja California State Government and it is home to Mexico's National Astronomical Observatory, UNAM. Among the highlights of a visit here include a 2km (1.2-mile) hike up to the El Altar viewpoint, at a 2,888m (9,473 ft.) elevation, where both the Pacific Ocean and Sea of Cortez can be seen. In the southeast portion of the park is the highest peak in Baja, Picacho del Diablo (Devil's Peak), at an elevation of 3,095m (10,152 ft). It's a popular place for mountain climbing and rappelling. Snow is common here in the winter, and no services are available once you're inside the park, so its essential to bring your own supplies. Camping areas, restrooms, and forest ranger services are available.

Within these parks, you'll see pine, fir, cypress, and poplar forests. Wild fauna found here may include ram, cougar, blacktailed deer, bobcats, royal eagles, owls, and the California condor.

2 A Look at Mexico's Past

PRE-HISPANIC CIVILIZATIONS

The earliest Mexicans were Stone Age hunter-gatherers from the north, descendants of a race that had probably crossed the Bering Strait and reached North America around 12,000 B.C. They arrived in what is now Mexico by 10,000 B.C. It is likely that Baja was inhabited by human populations well before mainland Mexico, as Baja was the logical termination point for the coastal migration route followed by Asian groups crossing the Bering Strait. The San Dieguito culture migrated south into Baja somewhere between 7000 and 5000 B.C. Sometime between 5200 and 1500 B.C., in what is known as the **Archaic period,** they began practicing agriculture and domesticating animals.

THE PRE-CLASSIC PERIOD (1500 B.C.–A.D. 300) Eventually, agriculture improved to the point that it could support large communities and free some of the population from agricultural work. A

Dateline

- 10,000–1500 B.C. Archaic period: hunting and gathering; later, the dawn of agriculture: domestication of chiles, corn, beans, avocado, amaranth, and pumpkin. Mortars and pestles in use. Stone bowls and jars, obsidian knives, and open-weave basketry developed. Possible dating of the cave paintings of central Baja, believed to have been created by nomadic indigenous tribes.

- 1500 B.C.–A.D. 300 Pre-Classic period: Olmec culture develops large-scale settlements and irrigation methods. Cities spring up. Olmec influence spreads over other cultures in the Gulf Coast, central and southern Mexico, Central America, the lower Mexican Pacific Coast, and the Yucatán. Several cities in central and southern Mexico begin the construction of large ceremonial centers and pyramids. The Maya develop several city-states in Chiapas and Central America.

- A.D. 300–900 Classic period: Broad influence of Teotihuacán culture and the establishment there of a truly cosmopolitan urbanism. Satellite settlements spring up across central Mexico and as far away as Guatemala. Trade and cultural interchange with civilization emerged that we call the **Olmec**—an enigmatic people who settled the lower Gulf Coast in what is now Tabasco and Veracruz. Anthropologists regard them as the mother culture of Mesoamerica because they established a pattern for later civilizations in a wide area stretching from northern Mexico into Central America. The Olmec developed the basic calendar used throughout the region, established a 52-year cycle (which they used to schedule the construction of pyramids), established principles of urban layout and architecture, and originated the cult of the jaguar and the sanctity of jade. They may also have bequeathed the sacred ritual of "the ball game"—a universal element of Mesoamerican culture.

One intriguing feature of the Olmec was the carving of colossal stone heads. We still don't know what purposes these heads served, but they were immense projects; the basalt from which they were sculpted was mined miles inland and transported to the coast, probably by river rafts. The heads share a rounded, baby-faced look, marked by a peculiar, high-arched lip—a "jaguar mouth"—that is an identifying mark of Olmec sculpture.

The Maya civilization began developing in the Yucatán during the late pre-Classic period, around 500 B.C. Our understanding of this period is sketchy, but Olmec influences are apparent everywhere. The Maya perfected the Olmec calendar and, somewhere along the way, developed an ornate system of hieroglyphic writing and early architectural concepts. Two other civilizations began the rise to prominence around this time: the people of Teotihuacán, just north of present-day Mexico City, and the Zapotec of Monte Albán in the valley of Oaxaca.

In Baja, the San Dieguito culture either developed into, or was superceded by, the Yumano culture, believed to be the creators of the rock paintings and petroglyphs found on the central interior of the peninsula. The Yumanos made use of more sophisticated hunting equipment as well as fishing nets, and also created ceramics. Paintings also indicate a fundamental knowledge of astronomy and depict solstice celebrations. Descendants of this culture were the Indians found living here by the Spanish in the 16th century.

THE CLASSIC PERIOD (A.D. 300–900) The flourishing of these three civilizations marks the boundaries of this period—the heyday of pre-Columbian Mesoamerican artistic and cultural achievements. These include the pyramids and palaces in Teotihuacán; the ceremonial center of Monte Albán; and

the Maya and the Zapotec flourish. The Maya perfect the calendar and improve astronomical calculations. They build grandiose cities at Palenque, Calakmul, and Cobá, and in Central America.

■ **900** Post-Classic period begins: More emphasis is placed on warfare in central Mexico. The Toltec culture emerges at Tula and replaces Teotihuacán as the dominant city of central Mexico. Toltec

influence spreads to the Yucatán, forming the culture of the Itzaés, who become the rulers of Chichén Itzá.

■ **909** This is the date on a small monument at Toniná (near San Cristóbal de las Casas), the latest date yet discovered, symbolizing the end of the Classic Maya era.

■ **1325–1470** Aztec capital Tenochtitlán is founded; Aztecs begin military campaigns in the Valley of

Mexico and then thrust farther out, subjugating the civilizations of the Gulf Coast and southern Mexico.

■ **1516** Gold found on Cozumel during aborted Spanish expedition of Yucatán Peninsula arouses interest of Spanish governor in Cuba, who sends Juan de Grijalva on an expedition, followed by another led by Hernán Cortez.

continues

the stelae and temples of Palenque, Bonampak, and the Tikal site in Guatemala. Beyond their achievements in art and architecture, the Maya made significant discoveries in science, including the use of the zero in mathematics and a complex calendar with which the priests could predict eclipses and the movements of the stars for centuries to come.

The inhabitants of **Teotihuacán** (100 B.C.–A.D. 700), near present-day Mexico City, built a city that, at its zenith, is thought to have had 100,000 or more inhabitants. It was a well-organized city, covering 23 sq. km (9 sq. miles), built on a grid with streams channeled to follow the city's plan.

Farther south, the **Zapotec,** influenced by the Olmec, raised an impressive civilization in the region of Oaxaca. Their two principal cities were **Monte Albán,** inhabited by an elite of merchants and artisans, and **Mitla,** reserved for the high priests.

THE POST-CLASSIC PERIOD (A.D. 900–1521)

Warfare was the most conspicuous activity of the civilizations that flourished in this period. Social development was impressive but not as cosmopolitan as the Maya, Teotihuacán, and Zapotec societies. In central Mexico, a people known as the **Toltec** established their capital at Tula in the 10th century.

They revered a god known as **Tezcatlipoca,** or "smoking mirror," who later became an Aztec god. The Toltec maintained a large military class divided into orders symbolized by animals. At its height, Tula may have had 40,000 people, and its influence spread across Mesoamerica. By the 13th century, however, the Toltec had exhausted themselves, probably in civil wars and in battles with the invaders from the north.

THE CONQUEST

In 1517, the first Spaniards arrived in what is today known as Mexico and skirmished with Maya Indians off the coast of the Yucatán Peninsula. One of the fledgling expeditions ended in shipwreck, leaving several Spaniards stranded as prisoners of the Maya. The Spanish sent out another expedition, under the command of **Hernán Cortez,** which landed on Cozumel in February 1519. Cortez inquired about the gold and riches of the interior, and the coastal Maya were happy to describe the wealth and splendor of the Aztec empire in central Mexico. Cortez promptly disobeyed all orders of his superior, the governor of Cuba, and sailed to the mainland.

Cortez arrived when the Aztec empire was at the height of its wealth and power. **Moctezuma II** ruled over the central and southern highlands and extracted tribute

- **1519** Conquest of Mexico begins: Hernán Cortez and troops make their way along Mexican coast to present-day Veracruz.
- **1521** Conquest is complete after Aztec defeat at Tlatelolco.
- **1521–24** Cortez organizes Spanish empire in Mexico and begins building Mexico City on the ruins of Tenochtitlán.

- **1532** Cortez launches the first exploration to Baja, then believed to be an island. The expedition is unsuccessful, with ships intercepted by pirates.
- **1534** The *Concepción* makes landfall near present-day La Paz, under charge of a group of mutineers; most are killed by the indigenous inhabitants of the area.
- **1539** Capt. Ulloa explores the entire perimeter of the

Sea of Cortez, establishing that Baja is not an island, as believed, but a peninsula.
- **1541** Cortez is recalled to Spain, never to return to Mexico.
- **1565** Trade routes between Acapulco and Manila are established, with Baja becoming an important stopping point along this route, which lasted for over 250 years. It was also the site of ongoing pirating, which

from lowland peoples. His greatest temples were literally plated with gold and encrusted with the blood of sacrificial captives. Moctezuma was a fool, a mystic, and something of a coward. Despite his wealth and military power, he dithered in his capital at Tenochtitlán, sending messengers with gifts and suggestions that Cortez leave. Meanwhile, Cortez blustered and negotiated his way into the highlands, always cloaking his real intentions. Moctezuma, terrified by the military tactics and technology of the Spaniard, convinced himself that Cortez was in fact the god Quetzalcoatl making his long-awaited return. By the time the Spaniards arrived in the Aztec capital, Cortez had gained some ascendancy over the lesser Indian states that were resentful tributaries to the Aztec. In November 1519, Cortez confronted Moctezuma and took him hostage in an effort to leverage control of the empire.

In the middle of Cortez's dangerous game of manipulation, another Spanish expedition arrived with orders to end Cortez's authority over the mission. Cortez hastened to meet the rival's force and persuade them to join his own. In the meantime, the Aztec chased the garrison out of Tenochtitlán, and either they or the Spaniards killed Moctezuma. For the next year and a half, Cortez laid siege to Tenochtitlán, with the help of rival Indians and a decimating epidemic of smallpox, to which the Indians had no resistance. In the end, the Aztec capital fell, and when it did, all of central Mexico lay at the feet of the conquistadors.

Cortez began his explorations of Baja California in 1532. Looking across from western Mexico, they believed Baja to be an island, and so declared the sea the Mar de Cortez (Sea of Cortez). The first explorations failed, succumbing to pirates. The first Spanish ship recorded to have reached Baja was in 1534 when the *Concepción,* under the leadership of a mutinous crew, landed at present-day La Paz, only to be attacked by indigenous inhabitants while refilling their water stocks. A few members of the crew returned to the ship and sailed back to the mainland, where they told Cortez of an island rich with black pearls, fueling his desires for further explorations. In 1539, one expedition, under the direction of Capt. Francisco de Ulloa, explored the entire perimeter of the Sea of Cortez, establishing the fact that Baja was not an island, but was a peninsula.

The Spanish Conquest started as a pirate expedition by Cortez and his men, unauthorized by the Spanish crown or its governor in Cuba. The Spanish king legitimized Cortez following his victory

becomes an embarrassment to the Spanish crown.

- **1535–1821** Viceregal period: 61 viceroys appointed by King of Spain govern Mexico. Control of much of the land ends up in the hands of the Catholic Church and the politically powerful.
- **1697–1767** Jesuit Mission period of Baja, during which 20 missions were established for the purpose of converting the indigenous populations to Christianity.
- **1810–21** War of Independence: Miguel Hidalgo starts movement for Mexico's independence from Spain but is executed within a year; leadership and goals change during the war years, but Agustín de Iturbide outlines a compromise between monarchy and republic.
- **1822** First Empire: Iturbide ascends throne as Emperor of Mexico, loses power after a year, and loses life in an attempt to reclaim throne.
- **1824–64** Early Republic period, characterized by almost perpetual civil war between federalists and centralists, conservatives and liberals, culminating in the victory of the liberals under Juárez.
- **1833–47** Mexican-American War results in the loss of

continues

over the Aztec and ordered the forced conversion to Christianity of this new colony, to be called **New Spain.** Guatemala and Honduras were explored and conquered, and by 1540, the territory of New Spain included possessions from Vancouver to Panama. In the 2 centuries that followed, Franciscan and Augustinian friars converted millions of Indians to Christianity, and the Spanish lords built huge feudal estates on which the Indian farmers were little more than serfs. The silver and gold that Cortez looted made Spain the richest country in Europe.

THE MISSION PERIOD

Among the subsequent expeditions sent by the Spanish crown, many included Catholic priests seeking to establish missions for converting the native cultures to Christianity. Padre Juan Maria Salvatierra was the first to succeed in establishing a permanent settlement on the Baja peninsula, when he founded the mission Nuestra Senora de Loreto in 1697, at the site of present-day Loreto. This began the Jesuit Mission period in Baja, which lasted until 1767, during which 20 missions were established, stretching from the southern tip of Baja into central Baja near present-day Cataviña. The mission system worked by offering protection to

the natives by the Church and the Spanish crown, in exchange for submitting to religious instruction. If they were not in agreement, they were generally punished or massacred. Those who did agree assisted in the building of the mission, which became a place of refuge. In addition to religious instruction, natives also learned European farming techniques and other trades. Unlike their counterparts on the mainland, none of the Jesuit priests operating in Baja ever produced a text recording the indigenous languages. During the mission years, repeated epidemics of smallpox, syphilis, and measles, combined with those who lost their lives in rebellions, decimated the local populations, leaving Baja primarily to the new European settlers. The Jesuit missions were followed by missions established by the Franciscans and Dominicans, leading to a more diverse population of European cultures. By the end of the 18th century, it was estimated that the native population in Baja numbered fewer than 5,000.

THE COLONIAL PERIOD

Back on the mainland, Hernán Cortez set about building a new city upon the ruins of the old Aztec capital. To do this he collected from the Indians the tributes once paid to the Aztec emperor, many of these rendered in labor. This arrangement, in

huge amounts of territory to the U.S. by Mexico. In 1847 Mexico City falls to U.S. troops. The Treaty of Guadalupe Hidalgo was signed in 1848, in which Mexico conceded not only the Río Grande area of Texas but part of New Mexico and all of California for a payment of U.S. $25 million and the cancellation of all Mexican debt.

- **1849** The California Gold Rush lures many Mexicans and Indians from the Baja peninsula to seek their fortunes in California, reducing Baja's already scarce population, and transforming it into a haven for outlaws, pirates, and renegades.
- **1864–67** Second Empire: The French invade Mexico in the name of Maximilian of Austria, who is appointed Emperor of Mexico. Juárez

and the liberal government retreat to the north and wage war with the French forces. The French finally abandon Mexico and leave Maximilian to be defeated and executed.
- **1872–76** Juárez dies, and political struggles ensue for the presidency.
- **1877–1911** Porfiriato: Porfirio Díaz, president/dictator of Mexico for 33 years, leads country to modernization by encouraging foreign

one form or another, became the basis for the construction of the new colony. But diseases brought by the Spaniards decimated the native population over the next century and drastically reduced the pool of labor.

Cortez soon returned to Spain and was replaced by a governing council, and, later, the office of viceroy. Over the 3 centuries of the colonial period, 61 viceroys governed Mexico while Spain became rich from New World gold and silver—chiseled out by Indian labor. The colonial elite built lavish homes in Mexico City and in the countryside. They filled their homes with ornate furniture, had many servants, and adorned themselves in imported velvets, satins, and jewels.

A new class system developed. Those born in Spain considered themselves superior to the *criollos* (Spaniards born in Mexico). Those of other races and the *castas* (mixtures of Spanish and Indian, Spanish and African, or Indian and African) occupied the bottom rungs of society. It took great cunning to stay a step ahead of the avaricious Crown, which demanded increasing taxes and contributions from its fabled foreign conquests. Still, wealthy colonists prospered enough to develop an extravagant society.

However, discontent with the mother country simmered for years over social and political issues: taxes, royal monopolies, the bureaucracy, Spanish-born citizens' advantages over Mexican-born subjects, and restrictions on commerce with Spain and other countries. In 1808, Napoleon invaded Spain and crowned his brother Joseph king in place of Charles IV. To many in Mexico, allegiance to France was out of the question; discontent reached the level of revolt.

INDEPENDENCE

The rebellion began in 1810, when **Father Miguel Hidalgo** gave the *grito,* a cry for independence, from his church in the town of Dolores, Guanajuato. The uprising soon became a full-fledged revolution, as Hidalgo and Ignacio Allende gathered an "army" of citizens and threatened Mexico City. Although Hidalgo ultimately failed and was executed, he is honored as the Father of Mexican Independence. Another priest, José María Morelos, kept the revolt alive with several successful campaigns through 1815, when he, too, was captured and executed.

After the death of Morelos, prospects for independence were rather dim until the Spanish king who replaced Joseph Bonaparte decided to make social reforms in the colonies. This convinced the conservative powers in Mexico that they didn't need Spain after all. With their tacit

investment in mines, oil, and railroads. Mexico witnesses the development of a modern economy and a growing disparity between rich and poor. Social conditions, especially in rural areas, become desperate.
- **1911–17** Mexican Revolution: Francisco Madero drafts revolutionary plan. Díaz resigns. Leaders jockey for power during period of great violence, national upheaval, and tremendous loss of life.
- **1920** U.S. Prohibition, in which the manufacture, sale, and consumption of alcoholic beverages is made a federal offense, is a boon to Baja, with Americans rushing across the border into Tijuana and northern Baja to buy liquor and drink in cantinas. It also initiates an era of organized crime and sees the establishment of casinos and brothels.
- **1917–40** Reconstruction: Present constitution of Mexico is signed; land and education reforms are initiated and labor unions strengthened; Mexico expropriates oil companies and railroads. Pancho Villa, Zapata, and presidents Obregón and Carranza are assassinated.

continues

approval, Agustín de Iturbide, then commander of royalist forces, changed sides and declared Mexico independent and himself emperor. (Spain, already losing its imperial power due to conflicts in Europe, could no longer hang on to Mexico, nor could the new king afford to wage war.) Before long, however, internal dissension brought about the fall of the new emperor, and Mexico was proclaimed a republic.

Political instability engulfed the young republic and Mexico waged a disastrous war with the United States and lost half its territory. A central figure was **Antonio López de Santa Anna,** who assumed the leadership of his country no fewer than 11 times and was flexible enough in those volatile days to portray himself variously as a liberal, a conservative, a federalist, and a centralist. He probably holds the record for frequency of exile; by 1855 he was finally left without a political comeback and ended his days in Venezuela.

Political instability persisted, and the conservative forces, with some encouragement from Napoleon III, hit upon the idea of inviting in a Habsburg to regain control (as if that strategy had ever worked for Spain). They found a willing volunteer in Archduke Maximilian of Austria, who accepted the position of Mexican emperor with the support of French troops. The ragtag Mexican forces defeated the French force—a modern, well-equipped army—in a battle near Puebla (now celebrated annually as **Cinco de Mayo**). A second attempt was more successful, and Ferdinand Maximilian Joseph of Habsburg became emperor. After 3 years of civil war, the French were finally induced to abandon the emperor's cause; Maximilian was captured and executed by a firing squad near Querétaro in 1867. His adversary and successor (as president of Mexico) was **Benito Juárez,** a Zapotec Indian lawyer and one of the great heroes of Mexican history. Juárez did his best to unify and strengthen his country before dying of a heart attack in 1872; his impact on Mexico's future was profound, and his plans and visions bore fruit for decades.

THE PORFIRIATO & THE REVOLUTION

A few years after Juárez's death, one of his generals, **Porfirio Díaz,** assumed power in a coup. He ruled Mexico from 1877 to 1911, a period now called the Porfiriato. He stayed in power by imposing repressive measures and courting the favor of powerful nations. Generous in his dealings with foreign investors, Díaz became, in the eyes of most Mexicans, the archetypal *entreguista* (one who sells out his country for private gain). With foreign

- **1940** Mexico enters contemporary period of political stability and makes steady economic progress. Quality of life improves, although problems of corruption, inflation, national health, and unresolved land and agricultural issues continue.
- **1952** The Territory of Northern Baja California becomes Mexico's 29th state.
- **1973** Carretera Transpeninsular (Hwy. 1) opens, connecting Tijuana to Cabo San Lucas. This leads to serious growth in Baja, and the following year, Baja California Sur becomes Mexico's 30th state.
- **1994–97** Mexico, Canada, and the United States sign the North American Free Trade Agreement (NAFTA). An Indian uprising in Chiapas sparks countrywide protests over government policies concerning land distribution, bank loans, health, education, and voting and human rights.
- **2000** Mexico elects Vicente Fox, of the PAN party, president.

investment came the concentration of great wealth in few hands, and social conditions worsened.

In 1910, Francisco Madero called for an armed rebellion that became the **Mexican revolution** (*La Revolución* in Mexico; the revolution against Spain is the *Guerra de Independencia*). Díaz was sent into exile; while in London, he became a celebrity at the age of 81, when he jumped into the Thames to save a drowning boy. He is buried in Paris. Madero became president but was promptly betrayed and executed by **Victoriano Huerta.** Those who had answered Madero's call responded again—to the great peasant hero **Emiliano Zapata** in the south, and to the seemingly invincible **Pancho Villa** in the central north, flanked by Alvaro Obregón and Venustiano Carranza. They eventually put Huerta to flight and began hashing out a new constitution.

For the next few years, the revolutionaries Carranza, Obregón, and Villa fought among themselves; Zapata did not seek national power, though he fought tenaciously for land for the peasants. Carranza, who was president at the time, betrayed and assassinated Zapata. Obregón finally consolidated power and probably had Carranza assassinated. He, in turn, was assassinated when he tried to break one of the tenets of the Revolution—no reelection. His successor, Plutarco Elias Calles, learned this lesson well, installing one puppet president after another, until **Lázaro Cárdenas** severed the puppeteer's strings and banished him to exile.

Until Cárdenas's election in 1934, the outcome of the revolution remained in doubt. There had been some land redistribution, but other measures took a back seat to political expediency. Cárdenas changed all that. He implemented massive redistribution of land and nationalized the oil industry. He instituted many reforms

and gave shape to the ruling political party (now the **Partido Revolucionario Institucional,** or PRI) by bringing a broad representation of Mexican society under its banner and establishing mechanisms for consensus building. Most Mexicans practically canonize Cárdenas.

MODERN MEXICO

The presidents who followed were noted more for graft than for leadership. The party's base narrowed as many of the reform-minded elements were marginalized. Economic progress, a lot of it in the form of large development projects, became the PRI's main basis for legitimacy. In 1968, the government violently repressed a democratic student movement. Police forces shot and killed an unknown number of civilians in the Tlatelolco section of Mexico City. Though the PRI maintained its grip on power, it lost all semblance of being a progressive party. In 1985, a devastating **earthquake in Mexico City** brought down many of the government's new, supposedly earthquake-proof buildings, exposing shoddy construction and the widespread government corruption that fostered it. The government's handling of the relief efforts also drew heavy criticism. In 1994, a political and military **uprising in Chiapas** focused world attention on Mexico's great social problems. A new political force, the Ejército Zapatista de Liberación Nacional or EZLN (Zapatista National Liberation Army), has skillfully publicized the plight of the peasant. Adding to the troubles of that year, Luis Donaldo Colosio, the PRI's popular presidential candidate, was shot to death while campaigning in Tijuana in March of 1994. In the ensuing investigation, top-ranking party officials, including standing president Carlos Salinas' own brother, Raúl, were implicated, bringing to light the extent of interparty power struggles within the PRI.

In the years that followed, opposition political parties grew in power and legitimacy. Facing pressure and scrutiny from national and international organizations, and widespread public discontent, the PRI had to concede defeat in state and congressional elections throughout the '90s. The party began choosing its candidates through primaries instead of through appointment. But in the presidential elections of 2000, Vicente Fox, candidate for the opposition party PAN, won by a landslide. In hindsight, there was no way that the PRI could have won in a fair election. For most Mexicans, a government under the PRI was all that they had ever known.

Since then, Mexico has been sailing into the uncharted waters of coalition politics. The three main parties, PRI, PAN, and PRD, have grown into their new roles within a more open, more transparent political system. To their credit, the sailing has been much smoother than many observers predicted. But the real test will be weathering the economic slowdown that accompanied the downturn in the U.S. economy, and in carrying out the next presidential elections, in 2006.

3 Art & Architecture 101

Mexico's artistic and architectural legacy reaches back more than 3,000 years. Until the conquest of Mexico in A.D. 1521, art, architecture, politics, and religion were intertwined. Although the European conquest influenced the style and subject of Mexican art, this continuity remained throughout the colonial period.

PRE-HISPANIC FORMS

Mexico's **pyramids** were truncated platforms crowned with a temple. Many sites have circular buildings, such as El Caracol at Chichén Itzá, usually called the observatory and dedicated to the god of the wind. El Castillo at Chichén Itzá has 365 steps—one for every day of the year. The Temple of the Magicians at Uxmal has beautifully rounded and sloping sides. Evidence of building one pyramidal structure on top of another, a widely accepted practice, has been found throughout Mesoamerica.

Throughout Mexico, carved stone and mural art on pyramids served a religious and historic function rather than an ornamental one. **Hieroglyphs,** picture symbols etched on stone or painted on walls or pottery, functioned as the written language of the ancient peoples, particularly the Maya. By deciphering the glyphs, scholars allow the ancients to speak again, providing us with specific names to attach to rulers and their families, and demystifying the great dynastic histories of the Maya. For more on this, read *A Forest of Kings* (Morrow, 1990), by Linda Schele and David Freidel, and *Blood of Kings* (George Braziller, 1986), by Linda Schele and Mary Ellen Miller. Good hieroglyphic examples appear in the site museum at Palenque.

Pre-Hispanic cultures left a wealth of fantastic painted **murals and cave paintings,** most of which are remarkably preserved, in the central mountain region concentrated in the San Francisco de la Sierra and Santa Martha mountains. Most depict a combination of faceless human forms and animal forms, in apparent depictions of ritualistic ceremonies. Their origin remains a mystery. Over 300 cave paintings are concentrated in an area known as the Great Wall, in the San Francisco de la Sierra—it's the largest concentration of ancient rock paintings in the world.

SPANISH INFLUENCE

With the arrival of the Spaniards, new forms of architecture came to Mexico.

Many sites that were occupied by indigenous groups at the time of the conquest were razed and in their place appeared Catholic churches, public buildings, and palaces for conquerors and the king's bureaucrats. In the Yucatán, churches at Izamal, Tecoh, Santa Elena, and Muná rest atop former pyramidal structures. Indian artisans, who formerly worked on pyramidal structures, were recruited to build the new buildings, often guided by drawings of European buildings. Frequently left on their own, the indigenous artisans implanted traditional symbolism in the new buildings: a plaster angel swaddled in feathers, reminiscent of the god Quetzalcoatl, and the face of an ancient god surrounded by corn leaves. They used pre-Hispanic calendar counts—the 13 steps to heaven or the nine levels of the underworld—to determine how many florets to carve around church doorways.

To convert the native populations, New World Spanish priests and architects altered their normal ways of teaching and building. Often before a church was built, an open-air atrium was constructed to accommodate large numbers of parishioners for services. *Posas* (shelters) at the four corners of churchyards were another architectural technique unique to Mexico, again to accommodate crowds. Because of the language barrier between the Spanish and the natives, church adornment became more explicit. Biblical tales came to life in frescoes splashed across church walls. Christian symbolism in stone supplanted that of pre-Hispanic ideas as the natives tried to make sense of it all. Baroque became even more baroque in Mexico and was dubbed **churrigueresque** or **ultrabaroque.** Exuberant and complicated, it combines Gothic, baroque, and plateresque elements.

Almost every major town in the Baja peninsula has the remains of a **mission** nearby. Many were built in the 17th century following the early arrival of Jesuit friars. Prime examples include the **Misión Nuestra Señora de Loreto,** the first mission in the Californias, started in 1699. The catechization of California by Jesuit missionaries was based from this mission, and lasted through the 18th century. About 2 hours from Loreto, in a section of the old Camino Real used by Spanish missionaries and explorers, is **Misión San Francisco Javier,** one of the best-preserved, most spectacularly set missions in Baja—high in a mountain valley beneath volcanic walls. Founded in 1699 by the Jesuit priest Francisco María Píccolo, it was the second mission established in California, completed in 1758. The original building of the **Misión Santa Rosalía de Mulegé,** founded in 1706 by Father Juan de Ugarte and Juan María Basaldúa, was completed in 1766, but in 1770, a flood destroyed nearly all the common buildings, and the mission was rebuilt on the site it occupies today, on a bluff overlooking the river. Although not the most architecturally interesting of Baja's missions, it remains in excellent condition and still functions as a Catholic church, although mission operations halted in 1828. Inside, there is a perfectly preserved statue of Santa Rosalía and a bell, both from the 18th century.

When Porfirio Díaz became president in the late 19th century, the nation's art and architecture experienced another infusion of European sensibility. Díaz idolized Europe, and he commissioned a number of striking European-style public buildings, including many opera houses. He provided European scholarships to promising young artists who later returned to Mexico to produce Mexican-subject paintings using techniques learned abroad.

In Baja, Díaz granted the Compañía de Boleo (part of the Rothschild family holdings) a 99-year lease to the rich deposits of copper in the area surrounding Santa Rosalía in exchange for the company building a town, the harbor, public buildings, and establishing a maritime route between the port and Guaymas, meant to create employment for Mexican workers. The architectural influence of Santa Rosalía is decidedly European, and no more so than in its church, the **Iglesia de Santa Barbara,** a structure of galvanized steel designed by Gustave Eiffel (of Eiffel Tower fame) in 1884. It was originally created for the 1889 Paris World Expo, where it was displayed as a prototype for what Eiffel envisioned as a sort of prefab mission. The structure eventually made its way to Santa Rosalía in 1897, where its somber gray exterior belies the beauty of the intricate stained-glass windows viewed from inside.

THE ADVENT OF MEXICAN MURALISM

As the Mexican Revolution ripped the country apart between 1911 and 1917, a new social and cultural Mexico was born. In 1923, Minister of Education José Vasconcelos was charged with educating the illiterate masses. As one means of reaching people, he invited **Diego Rivera** and several other budding artists to paint Mexican history on the walls of the Ministry of Education building and the National Preparatory School in Mexico City. Thus began the tradition of painting murals in public buildings, which you will find in towns and cities throughout Mexico.

4 Religion, Myth & Folklore

Mexico is predominantly Roman Catholic, a religion introduced by the Spaniards during the conquest of Mexico. Despite its preponderance, the Catholic faith in many places in Mexico (Chiapas and Oaxaca, for example) has pre-Hispanic undercurrents. You need only visit the *curandero* section of a Mexican market (where you can purchase copal, an incense agreeable to the gods; rustic beeswax candles, a traditional offering; the native species of tobacco used to ward off evil; and so on) or attend a village festivity featuring pre-Hispanic dancers to understand that supernatural beliefs often run parallel with Christian ones in Mexico.

Mexico's complicated mythological heritage from pre-Hispanic religion is full of images derived from nature—the wind, jaguars, eagles, snakes, flowers, and more—all intertwined with elaborate mythological stories to explain the universe, climate, seasons, and geography. Most groups believed in an underworld (not a hell), usually containing 9 levels, and a heaven of 13 levels—which is why the numbers 9 and 13 are so mythologically significant. The solar calendar count of 365 days and the ceremonial calendar of 260 days are significant as well. How one died determined one's resting place after death: in the underworld (*Xibalba* to the Maya), in heaven, or at one of the four cardinal points. For example, men who died in battle or women who died in childbirth went straight to the sun. Everyone else first had to make a journey through the underworld.

Appendix B:
Useful Terms & Phrases &
a Guide to Mexico's Food & Drink

1 Basic Vocabulary

Most Mexicans are very patient with foreigners who try to speak their language; it helps a lot to know a few basic phrases. I've included simple phrases for expressing basic needs, followed by some common menu items.

ENGLISH-SPANISH PHRASES
BASIC PHRASES

English	Spanish	Pronunciation
Good day	**Buen día**	bwehn *dee*-ah
Good morning	**Buenos días**	*bweh*-nohss *dee*-ahss
How are you?	**¿Cómo está?**	*koh*-moh ehss-*tah*?
Very well	**Muy bien**	mwee byehn
Thank you	**Gracias**	*grah*-syahss
You're welcome	**De nada**	deh *nah*-dah
Good-bye	**Adiós**	ah-*dyohss*
Please	**Por favor**	pohr fah-*vohr*
Yes	**Sí**	see
No	**No**	noh
Excuse me	**Perdóneme**	pehr-*doh*-neh-meh
Give me	**Déme**	*deh*-meh
Where is . . . ?	**¿Dónde está . . . ?**	*dohn*-deh ehss-*tah*?
the station	**la estación**	lah ehss-tah-*syohn*
a hotel	**un hotel**	oon oh-*tehl*
a gas station	**una gasolinera**	*oo*-nah gah-soh-lee-*neh*-rah
a restaurant	**un restaurante**	oon res-tow-*rahn*-teh
the toilet	**el baño**	el *bah*-nyoh
a good doctor	**un buen médico**	oon bwehn *meh*-dee-coh
the road to . . .	**el camino a/hacia . . .**	el cah-*mee*-noh ah/*ah*-syah
To the right	**A la derecha**	ah lah deh-*reh*-chah
To the left	**A la izquierda**	ah lah ees-*kyehr*-dah
Straight ahead	**Derecho**	deh-*reh*-choh
I would like	**Quisiera**	key-*syeh*-rah

English	Spanish	Pronunciation
I want	**Quiero**	*kyeh*-roh
to eat	**comer**	koh-*mehr*
a room	**una habitación**	*oo*-nah ah-bee-tah-*syohn*
Do you have . . . ?	**¿Tiene usted . . . ?**	tyeh-neh oo-*sted?*
a book	**un libro**	oon *lee*-broh
a dictionary	**un diccionario**	oon deek-syow-*nah*-ryo
How much is it?	**¿Cuánto cuesta?**	*kwahn*-toh *kwehss*-tah?
When?	**¿Cuándo?**	*kwahn*-doh?
What?	**¿Qué?**	keh?
There is	**(¿)Hay (. . . ?)**	eye?
(Is there . . . ?)		
What is there?	**¿Qué hay?**	keh eye?
Yesterday	**Ayer**	ah-*yer*
Today	**Hoy**	oy
Tomorrow	**Mañana**	mah-*nyah*-nah
Good	**Bueno**	*bweh*-noh
Bad	**Malo**	*mah*-loh
Better (best)	**(Lo) Mejor**	(loh) meh-*hohr*
More	**Más**	mahs
Less	**Menos**	*meh*-nohss
No smoking	**Se prohibe fumar**	seh proh-*ee*-beh foo-*mahr*
Postcard	**Tarjeta postal**	tar-*heh*-ta pohs-*tahl*
Insect repellent	**Repelente contra insectos**	reh-peh-*lehn*-te cohn-trah een-*sehk*-tos

MORE USEFUL PHRASES

English	Spanish	Pronunciation
Do you speak English?	**¿Habla usted inglés?**	*ah*-blah oo-*sted* een-*glehs?*
Is there anyone here who speaks English?	**¿Hay alguien aquí que hable inglés?**	eye *ahl*-gyehn ah-*kee* keh *ah*-bleh een-*glehs?*
I speak a little Spanish.	**Hablo un poco de español.**	*ah*-bloh oon *poh*-koh deh ehss-pah-*nyohl*
I don't understand Spanish very well.	**No (lo) entiendo muy bien el español.**	noh (loh) ehn-*tyehn*-doh mwee byehn el ehss-pah-*nyohl*
The meal is good.	**Me gusta la comida.**	meh *goo*-stah lah koh-*mee*-dah
What time is it?	**¿Qué hora es?**	keh *oh*-rah ehss?
May I see your menu?	**¿Puedo ver el menú (la carta)?**	*pueh*-do vehr el meh-*noo* (lah *car*-tah)?

English	Spanish	Pronunciation
The check, please.	**La cuenta, por favor.**	lah *quehn*-tah pohr fa-*vorh*
What do I owe you?	**¿Cuánto le debo?**	*kwahn*-toh leh *deh*-boh?
What did you say?	**¿Mande?** (formal)	*mahn*-deh?
	¿Cómo? (informal)	*koh*-moh?
I want (to see) . . .	**Quiero (ver) . . .**	*kyeh*-roh (vehr)
a room	**un cuarto** or **una habitación**	oon *kwar*-toh, *oo*-nah ah-bee-tah-*syohn*
for two persons	**para dos personas**	*pah*-rah dohss pehr-*soh*-nahs
with (without) bathroom	**con (sin) baño**	kohn (seen) *bah*-nyoh
We are staying here	**Nos quedamos aquí**	nohs keh-*dah*-mohss ah-*kee*
only . . .	**solamente . . .**	soh-lah-*mehn*-teh
one night.	**una noche.**	*oo*-nah *noh*-cheh
one week.	**una semana.**	*oo*-nah seh-*mah*-nah
We are leaving . . .	**Partimos (Salimos) . . .**	pahr-*tee*-mohss (sah-*lee*-mohss)
tomorrow.	**mañana.**	mah-*nya*-nah
Do you accept . . . ?	**¿Acepta usted . . . ?**	ah-*sehp*-tah oo-*sted*
traveler's checks?	**cheques de viajero?**	*cheh*-kehss deh byah-*heh*-roh?
Is there a	**¿Hay una**	eye *oo*-nah lah-*vahn*-deh-*ree*-ah
laundromat . . . ?	**lavandería . . . ?**	
near here?	**cerca de aquí?**	*sehr*-kah deh ah-*kee*
Please send these clothes to the laundry.	**Hágame el favor de mandar esta ropa a la lavandería.**	*ah*-gah-meh el fah-*vohr* deh mahn-*dahr* ehss-tah *roh*-pah a lah lah-*vahn*-deh-*ree*-ah

NUMBERS

1	**uno** (*ooh*-noh)		17	**diecisiete** (dyess-ee-*syeh*-teh)
2	**dos** (dohss)		18	**dieciocho** (dyess-ee-*oh*-choh)
3	**tres** (trehss)		19	**diecinueve** (dyess-ee-*nweh*-beh)
4	**cuatro** (*kwah*-troh)		20	**veinte** (*bayn*-teh)
5	**cinco** (*seen*-koh)		30	**treinta** (*trayn*-tah)
6	**seis** (sayss)		40	**cuarenta** (kwah-*ren*-tah)
7	**siete** (*syeh*-teh)		50	**cincuenta** (seen-*kwen*-tah)
8	**ocho** (*oh*-choh)		60	**sesenta** (seh-*sehn*-tah)
9	**nueve** (*nweh*-beh)		70	**setenta** (seh-*tehn*-tah)
10	**diez** (dyess)		80	**ochenta** (oh-*chehn*-tah)
11	**once** (*ohn*-seh)		90	**noventa** (noh-*behn*-tah)
12	**doce** (*doh*-seh)		100	**cien** (syehn)
13	**trece** (*treh*-seh)		200	**doscientos** (do-*syehn*-tohs)
14	**catorce** (kah-*tohr*-seh)		500	**quinientos** (kee-*nyehn*-tohs)
15	**quince** (*keen*-seh)		1,000	**mil** (meel)
16	**dieciseis** (dyess-ee-*sayss*)			

TRANSPORTATION TERMS

English	Spanish	Pronunciation
Airport	**Aeropuerto**	ah-eh-roh-*pwehr*-toh
Flight	**Vuelo**	*bweh*-loh
Rental car	**Arrendadora de autos**	ah-rehn-da-*doh*-rah deh *ow*-tohs
Bus	**Autobús**	ow-toh-*boos*
Bus or truck	**Camión**	ka-*myohn*
Lane	**Carril**	kah-*reel*
Nonstop	**Directo**	dee-*rehk*-toh
Baggage (claim area)	**Equipajes**	eh-kee-*pah*-hehss
Intercity	**Foraneo**	foh-rah-*neh*-oh
Luggage storage area	**Guarda equipaje**	*gwar*-dah eh-kee-*pah*-heh
Arrival gates	**Llegadas**	yeh-*gah*-dahss
Originates at this station	**Local**	loh-*kahl*
Originates elsewhere	**De paso**	deh *pah*-soh
Stops if seats available	**Para si hay lugares**	*pah*-rah see eye loo-*gah*-rehs
First class	**Primera**	pree-*meh*-rah
Second class	**Segunda**	seh-*goon*-dah
Nonstop	**Sin escala**	seen ess-*kah*-lah
Baggage claim area	**Recibo de equipajes**	reh-*see*-boh deh eh-kee-*pah*-hehss
Waiting room	**Sala de espera**	*sah*-lah deh ehss-*peh*-rah
Toilets	**Sanitarios**	sah-nee-*tah*-ryohss
Ticket window	**Taquilla**	tah-*kee*-yah

POSTAL GLOSSARY

Airmail   **Correo Aéreo**

Customs   **Aduana**

General delivery   **Lista de correos**

Insurance (insured mail)   **Seguro (correo asegurado)**

Mailbox   **Buzón**

Money order   **Giro postal**

Parcel   **Paquete**

Post office   **Oficina de correos**

Post office box (abbreviation)   **Apdo. Postal**

Postal service   **Correos**

Registered mail   **Registrado**

Rubber stamp   **Sello**

Special delivery, express   **Entrega inmediata**

Stamp   **Estampilla** or **timbre**

2 Menu Glossary

Achiote   Small red seed of the *annatto* tree.

Achiote preparado   A Yucatecan-prepared paste made of ground *achiote*, wheat and corn flour, cumin, cinnamon, salt, onion, garlic, and oregano.

Agua fresca   Fruit-flavored water, usually watermelon, cantaloupe, chia seed with lemon, hibiscus flour, rice, or ground melon-seed mixture.

Antojito   Typical Mexican supper foods, usually made with *masa* or tortillas and having a filling or topping such as sausage, cheese, beans, and onions; includes such things as tacos, tostadas, *sopes,* and *garnachas.*

Atole   A thick, lightly sweet, hot drink made with finely ground corn and usually flavored with vanilla, pecan, strawberry, pineapple, or chocolate.

Botana   An appetizer.

Buñuelos   Round, thin, deep-fried crispy fritters dipped in sugar.

Carnitas   Pork deep-cooked (not fried) in lard and then simmered and served with corn tortillas for tacos.

Ceviche   Fresh raw seafood marinated in fresh lime juice and garnished with chopped tomatoes, onions, chiles, and sometimes cilantro.

Chayote   A vegetable pear or mirliton, a type of spiny squash boiled and served as an accompaniment to meat dishes.

Chiles en nogada   Poblano peppers stuffed with a mixture of ground pork and beef, spices, fruits, raisins, and almonds. Can be served either warm—fried in a light batter—or cold, sans the batter. Either way it is then covered in walnut-and-cream sauce.

Chiles rellenos   Usually poblano peppers stuffed with cheese or spicy ground meat with raisins, rolled in a batter, and fried.

Churro   Tube-shaped, breadlike fritter, dipped in sugar and sometimes filled with *cajeta* (milk-based caramel) or chocolate.

Cochinita pibil   Pork wrapped in banana leaves, pit-baked in a *pibil* sauce of *achiote,* sour orange, and spices; most common in the Yucatán.

Enchilada   A tortilla dipped in sauce, usually filled with chicken or white cheese, and sometimes topped with *mole* (*enchiladas rojas* or *de mole*); tomato sauce and sour cream (*enchiladas suizas*—Swiss enchiladas); covered in a green sauce (*enchiladas verdes*); or topped with onions, sour cream, and guacamole (*enchiladas potosinas*).

Escabeche   A lightly pickled sauce used in Yucatecan chicken stew.

Frijoles refritos   Pinto beans mashed and cooked with lard.

Garnachas   A thickish small circle of fried *masa* with pinched sides, topped with pork or chicken, onions, and avocado, or sometimes chopped potatoes and tomatoes.

Gorditas   Thick, fried corn tortillas, slit and stuffed with choice of cheese, beans, beef, or chicken, with or without lettuce, tomato, and onion garnish.

Horchata   Refreshing lightly sweetened drink made of ground rice or melon seeds, ground almonds, and cinnamon.

Huevos mexicanos   Scrambled eggs with chopped onions, hot green peppers, and tomatoes.

Huitlacoche   Sometimes spelled "cuitlacoche." A mushroom-flavored black fungus that appears on corn in the rainy season; considered a delicacy.

Manchamantel   Translated, means "tablecloth stainer." It's a stew of chicken or pork with chiles, tomatoes, pineapple, bananas, and jicama.

Masa   Ground corn soaked in lime, it's the basis for tamales, corn tortillas, and soups.

Mixiote   Rabbit, lamb, or chicken cooked in a mild chile sauce (usually chile ancho or pasilla) and then wrapped like a tamal and steamed. It is generally served with tortillas for tacos, with traditional garnishes of pickled onions, hot sauce, chopped cilantro, and lime wedges.

Pan de muerto   Sweet bread made around the Days of the Dead (Nov 1–2) in the form of mummies or dolls, or round with bone designs.

Pan dulce   Lightly sweetened bread in many configurations, usually served at breakfast or bought in any bakery.

Papadzules   Tortillas stuffed with hard-boiled eggs and seeds (pumpkin or sunflower) in a tomato sauce.

Pibil   Pit-baked pork or chicken in a sauce of tomato, onion, mild red pepper, cilantro, and vinegar.

Pipián   A sauce made with ground pumpkin seeds, nuts, and mild peppers.

Poc chuc   Slices of pork with onion marinated in a tangy sour orange sauce and charcoal-broiled; a Yucatecan specialty.

Pulque   A drink made of fermented juice of the maguey plant; best in the state of Hidalgo and around Mexico City.

Quesadilla   Corn or flour tortillas stuffed with melted white cheese and lightly fried.

Queso relleno   Translated as "stuffed cheese," this dish consists of a mild yellow cheese stuffed with minced meat and spices; it's a Yucatecan specialty.

Rompope   Delicious Mexican eggnog, invented in Puebla, made with eggs, vanilla, sugar, and rum.

Salsa verde   An uncooked sauce using the green tomatillo puréed with spicy or mild hot peppers, onions, garlic, and cilantro.

Sopa de flor de calabaza   A soup made of chopped squash or pumpkin blossoms.

Sopa de lima   A tangy soup made with chicken broth and accented with fresh lime; popular in Yucatán.

Sopa de tortilla   A traditional chicken broth–based soup, seasoned with chiles, tomatoes, onion, and garlic, served with crispy fried strips of corn tortillas.

Sopa tlalpeña (or *caldo tlalpeño*)   A hearty soup made with chunks of chicken, chopped carrots, zucchini, corn, onions, garlic, and cilantro.

Sopa tlaxcalteca   A hearty tomato-based soup filled with cooked *nopal* cactus, cheese, cream, and avocado, with crispy tortilla strips floating on top.

Sope   Pronounced "*soh*-peh." An *antojito* similar to a *garnacha* except spread with refried beans and topped with crumbled cheese and onions.

Tacos al pastor   Thin slices of flavored pork roasted on a revolving cylinder dripping with onion slices and the juice of fresh pineapple slices. Served in small corn tortillas, it's topped with chopped onion and cilantro.

Tamal   Often incorrectly called a tamale (*tamal* is singular; *tamales* is plural), this dish consists of a meat or sweet filling rolled with fresh *masa* wrapped in a corn husk or banana leaf and steamed.

Tikin xic   Also seen on menus as "tik-n-xic" and "tikik chick," it is a charbroiled fish brushed with *achiote* sauce.

Torta   A sandwich, usually on *bolillo* bread, typically with sliced avocado, onions, tomatoes, and a choice of meat and often cheese.

Xtabentun   Pronounced "shtah-behn-*toon*," this is a Yucatecan liquor made of fermented honey flavored with anise. It comes *seco* (dry) or *crema* (sweet).

Zacahuil   Pork leg tamal, packed in thick *masa,* wrapped in banana leaves, and pit-baked, sometimes pot-made with tomato and *masa;* it's a specialty of mid- to upper Veracruz.

3 Food

Authentic Mexican food differs dramatically from what is frequently served in the United States under that name. For many travelers, Mexico will be new and exciting culinary territory. Even grizzled veterans will be pleasantly surprised by the wide variation in specialties and traditions offered from region to region.

Despite regional differences, some generalizations can be made. Mexican food usually isn't pepper-hot when it arrives at the table (though many dishes have a certain amount of piquancy, and some home cooking can be very spicy, depending on a family's or chef's tastes). Chiles and sauces add piquant flavor after the food is served; you'll never see a table in Mexico without one or both of these condiments. Mexicans don't drown their cooking in cheese and sour cream, a la Tex-Mex, and they use a great variety of ingredients. But the basis of Mexican food is simple—tortillas, beans, chiles, squash, and tomatoes—the same as it was centuries ago, before the Europeans arrived. Although geographically separated from the mainland, Baja's culinary customs mirror those of the mainland in this regard.

For information on food and drink safety, see "Treating & Avoiding Digestive Trouble" on p. 21.

THE BASICS

TORTILLAS   Traditional tortillas are made from corn that's boiled in water and lime and then ground into *masa* (a grainy dough), patted and pressed into thin cakes, and cooked on a hot griddle known as a *comal.* In many households, the tortilla takes the place of a fork and spoon; Mexicans merely tear them into wedge-shaped pieces, which they use to scoop up their food. Restaurants often serve bread rather than tortillas because it's easier, but you can always ask for tortillas. A more recent invention from northern Mexico is the flour tortilla, which is seen less frequently in the rest of Mexico.

ENCHILADAS   The tortilla is the basis of several Mexican dishes, but the most famous of these is the enchilada. The original name for this dish would have been *tortilla enchilada,* which simply means a tortilla dipped in a chile sauce. In like manner, there's the *entomatada* (tortilla dipped in a tomato sauce) and the *enfrijolada* (in a bean sauce). The enchilada began as a very simple dish: A tortilla is dipped in chile sauce (usually with ancho chile) and then into very hot oil, and then is quickly folded or rolled on a plate and sprinkled with chopped onions and a little *queso cotija* (crumbly white cheese) and served with a few fried potatoes and carrots. You can get this basic enchilada in food stands across the country. I love them, and if you come across them in your travels, give them a try. In restaurants you get the more elaborate enchilada, with different fillings of cheese, chicken, pork, or even seafood, and sometimes in a casserole.

TACOS   A taco is anything folded or rolled into a tortilla, and sometimes a double tortilla. The tortilla can be served either soft or fried. *Flautas* and quesadillas are species of tacos. For Mexicans, the taco is the quintessential fast food, and the taco stand *(taquería)*—an ubiquitous sight—is a great place to get a filling meal. See the section "Eating Out: Restaurants, *Taquerías* & Tipping," below, for information on taquerías.

What's Cooking in Baja

Although the culinary traditions of Baja California are not the most notable of Mexico, the region does bring to the table several notable specialties. The olives and olive oil produced in the Valle de Guadalupe are byproducts of the grape harvests of the region, and specially cured varieties are found in the area. Also found in this valley is traditional Russian cuisine, including dark bread and soft cheese. Near Ensenada, an abundance of seafood is harvested, including abalone, oysters, mussels, clams, shrimp, and lobster. Lobster, of course, is the featured item along the beach at Puerto Nuevo, where it is traditionally served grilled with tortillas, lime, and rice and beans. Tijuana—and specifically the Caesar's Palace Hotel—claims to be the birthplace of the Caesar salad. Fish tacos, found throughout Baja, are prepared deep-fried in a light batter and topped with a spicy mayonnaise-based salsa. And to top it all off, Tijuana is where the ubiquitous margarita first made its appearance, that tempting concoction of tequila, Cointreau, and lime served in a salt-rimmed glass.

FRIJOLES   An invisible "bean line" divides Mexico: It starts at the Gulf Coast in the southern part of the state of Tamaulipas and moves inland through the eastern quarter of San Luis Potosí and most of the state of Hidalgo, then goes straight through Mexico City and Morelos and into Guerrero, where it curves slightly westward to the Pacific. To the north and west of this line, the pink bean known as the *flor de mayo* is the staple food; to the south and east, including all of the Yucatán, the standard is the black bean.

In private households, beans are served at least once a day and, among the working class and peasantry, with every meal, if the family can afford it. Mexicans almost always prepare beans with a minimum of condiments—usually just a little onion and garlic and perhaps a pinch of herbs. Beans are meant to be a contrast to the heavily spiced dishes. Sometimes they are served at the end of a meal with a little Mexican-style sour cream (heavy whipping cream that sometimes tastes sweet).

Mexicans often fry leftover beans and serve them on the side as *frijoles refritos*. "Refritos" is usually translated as refried, but this is a misnomer—the beans are fried only once. The prefix "re" actually means "well" (as in thoroughly).

TAMALES   You make a tamal by mixing corn masa with a little lard, adding one of several fillings—meats flavored with chiles (or no filling at all)—then wrapping it in a corn husk or in the leaf of a banana or other plant, and finally steaming it. Every region in Mexico has its own traditional way of making tamales. In some places, a single tamal can be big enough to feed a family, while in others they are barely 3 inches long and an inch thick.

CHILES   Many kinds of chile peppers exist, and Mexicans call each of them by one name when they're fresh and another when they're dried. Some are blazing hot with only a mild flavor; some are mild but have a rich, complex flavor. They can be pickled, smoked, stuffed, stewed, chopped, and used in an endless variety of dishes.

MEALTIME

MORNING The morning meal, known as *el desayuno,* can be something light, such as coffee and sweet bread, or something more substantial: eggs, beans, tortillas, bread, fruit, and juice. It can be eaten early or late and is always a sure bet in Mexico. The variety and sweetness of the fruits on offer is remarkable, and you can't go wrong with Mexican egg dishes.

MIDAFTERNOON The main meal of the day, known as *la comida* (or *almuerzo*), is eaten between 2 and 4pm. Stores and businesses close for the meal, and most people go home to eat and perhaps take a short afternoon siesta before going about their business. The first course is the *sopa,* which can be either soup *(caldo)* or rice *(sopa de arroz)* or both; then comes the main course, which ideally is a meat or fish dish prepared in some kind of sauce and served with beans, followed by dessert.

EVENING Between 8 and 10pm, most Mexicans have a light meal called *la cena.* If eaten at home, it is something like a sandwich, bread and jam, or perhaps a couple of tacos made from some of the day's leftovers. At restaurants, the most common thing to eat is *antojitos* (literally, "little cravings"), a general label for light fare. *Antojitos* include tostadas, tamales, tacos, and simple enchiladas, and are big hits with travelers. Large restaurants offer complete meals as well. In Baja, popular *antojitos* include *menudo* (a thick soup of cow's feet and stomachs, seasoned with chiles, oregano, and chopped onion), *huaraches* (a flat , thick oval-shaped tortilla, topped with fried meat and chiles), and *chalupas* (a crisp whole tortilla, topped with beans, meat, and other toppings).

EATING OUT: RESTAURANTS, *TAQUERIAS* & TIPPING

First of all, I feel compelled to debunk the widespread myth that the cheapest place to eat in Mexico is in the market. Actually, this is almost never the case. You can usually find better food at a better price without going more than 2 blocks out of your way. Why? Food stalls in the marketplace pay high rents, they have a near-captive clientele of market vendors and truckers, and they get a lot of business from many Mexicans for whom eating in the market is a traditional way of confirming their culture.

On the other side of the spectrum, avoid eating at those inviting sidewalk restaurants that you see beneath the stone archways that border the main plazas. These places usually cater to tourists and don't need to count on getting any return business. But they are great for getting a coffee or beer.

Most nonresort towns have one or two restaurants (sometimes one is a coffee shop) that are social centers for a large group of established patrons. These establishments over time become virtual institutions and change comes very slowly. The food is usually good, standard fare cooked as it was 20 years ago, and the decor is simple. The patrons have known each other and the staff for years, and the *charla* (banter), gestures, and greetings are friendly, open, and unaffected. If you're curious about Mexican culture, eating and observing the goings-on in one of these places will be fun for you.

During your trip, you're sure to see many ***taquerías*** (**taco joints**), which function as Mexican fast food joints. These are generally small places with a counter or a few tables set around the cooking area; you get to see exactly how the cooks make their tacos before deciding whether to order. Most tacos come with a little chopped onion and cilantro but not tomato and lettuce. Find one that seems popular with the locals and where the cook performs with brio (a good sign of pride in the product). Sometimes there will be a woman making the tortillas right there (or working the *masa* into *gorditas, sopes,* or *panuchos* if these are also served). You will never see men doing this—this is perhaps the strictest gender division in Mexican society. Men may do all other cooking and kitchen tasks, and work with prepared tortillas, but they will never be found working *masa.*

For lunch, the main meal of the day, many restaurants offer a multicourse blue-plate special called **comida corrida** or **menú del día.** This is the least expensive way to get a full meal.

In Mexico, you need to ask for your check; it is generally considered inhospitable to present a check to someone who hasn't requested it. If you're in a hurry to get somewhere, ask for the check when your food arrives.

The **tipping** situation is about the same as in the United States, though you'll sometimes find a 15% **value-added tax** on restaurant meals, which shows up on the bill as "IVA." This is a boon to arithmetically challenged tippers, saving them from undue exertion.

To summon the waiter, wave or raise your hand, but don't motion with your index finger, which is a demeaning gesture that may even cause the waiter to ignore you. Or if it's the check you want, you can motion to the waiter from across the room using the universal pretend-you're-writing gesture.

Most restaurants do not have **nonsmoking sections;** when they do, we mention it in the reviews. But Mexico's wonderful climate allows for many open-air restaurants, usually set inside a courtyard of a colonial house, or in rooms with tall ceilings and plenty of open windows.

4 Drinks

All over Mexico you'll find shops selling *jugos* (juices) and *licuados* (smoothies) made from several kinds of tropical fruit. They're excellent and refreshing. You'll also come across *aguas frescas*—water flavored with hibiscus, melon, tamarind, or lime. Soft drinks come in more flavors in Mexico than in any other country I know, and the Pepsi and Coca-Cola taste the way they did in the United States years ago, before the makers started adding corn syrup. Mexican coffee is generally good, and **hot choco-late** is a traditional drink, as is *atole*—a hot, corn-based beverage that can be sweet or bitter.

Of course, Mexico has a proud and lucrative **beer**-brewing tradition, and you will find a few of its more notable breweries in Baja, including Tecate and the boutique Tijuana Brewery. A lesser-known brewed beverage is *pulque,* a pre-Hispanic drink made from the fermented juice of a few species of maguey or agave. Mostly you find it for sale in *pulquerías* (a type of liquor store specializing in the sale of fermented spir-its) in central Mexico. It is an acquired taste, and not every gringo acquires it. **Mezcal** and **tequila** also come from the agave. Tequila is a variety of mezcal produced from the *A. tequilana* species of agave in and around the area of Tequila, in the state of Jalisco. Mezcal comes from various parts of Mexico and from different varieties of agave. The distilling process is usually much less sophisticated than that of tequila, and, with its stronger smell and taste, mezcal is much more easily detected on the drinker's breath. In some places such as Oaxaca, it comes with a worm in the bottle; you are supposed to eat the worm after polishing off the mezcal. But for those teeto-talers out there who are interested in just the worm, I have good news—you can find these worms for sale in Mexican markets when in season. *¡Salud!*

Index

See also Accommodations and Restaurant indexes, below.

RESTAURANTS

Frommer's
Italy 2006

The only guide independent travelers need to make smart choices, avoid rip-offs, get the most for their money, and travel like a pro.

FROMMER'S® NATIONAL PARK GUIDES

Algonquin Provincial Park
Banff & Jasper
Family Vacations in the National
  Parks

Grand Canyon
National Parks of the American West
Rocky Mountain

Yellowstone & Grand Teton
Yosemite & Sequoia/Kings Canyon
Zion & Bryce Canyon

FROMMER'S® MEMORABLE WALKS

Chicago
London

New York
Paris

San Francisco

FROMMER'S® WITH KIDS GUIDES

Chicago
Hawaii
Las Vegas
New York City

Ottawa
San Francisco
Toronto

Vancouver
Walt Disney World® & Orlando
Washington, D.C.

SUZY GERSHMAN'S BORN TO SHOP GUIDES

Born to Shop: France
Born to Shop: Hong Kong, Shanghai
  & Beijing

Born to Shop: Italy
Born to Shop: London

Born to Shop: New York
Born to Shop: Paris

FROMMER'S® IRREVERENT GUIDES

Amsterdam
Boston
Chicago
Las Vegas
London

Los Angeles
Manhattan
New Orleans
Paris
Rome

San Francisco
Seattle & Portland
Vancouver
Walt Disney World®
Washington, D.C.

FROMMER'S® BEST-LOVED DRIVING TOURS

Austria
Britain
California
France

Germany
Ireland
Italy
New England

Northern Italy
Scotland
Spain
Tuscany & Umbria

THE UNOFFICIAL GUIDES®

Beyond Disney
California with Kids
Central Italy
Chicago
Cruises
Disneyland®
England
Florida
Florida with Kids
Inside Disney

Hawaii
Las Vegas
London
Maui
Mexico's Best Beach Resorts
Mini Las Vegas
Mini Mickey
New Orleans
New York City
Paris

San Francisco
Skiing & Snowboarding in the West
South Florida including Miami &
  the Keys
Walt Disney World®
Walt Disney World® for
  Grown-ups
Walt Disney World® with Kids
Washington, D.C.

SPECIAL-INTEREST TITLES

Athens Past & Present
Cities Ranked & Rated
Frommer's Best Day Trips from London
Frommer's Best RV & Tent Campgrounds
  in the U.S.A.
Frommer's Caribbean Hideaways
Frommer's China: The 50 Most Memorable Trips
Frommer's Exploring America by RV
Frommer's Gay & Lesbian Europe

Frommer's NYC Free & Dirt Cheap
Frommer's Road Atlas Europe
Frommer's Road Atlas France
Frommer's Road Atlas Ireland
Frommer's Wonderful Weekends from
  New York City
Retirement Places Rated
Rome Past & Present

THE NEW TRAVELOCITY GUARANTEE

EVERYTHING YOU BOOK WILL BE RIGHT, OR WE'LL WORK WITH OUR TRAVEL PARTNERS TO MAKE IT RIGHT, RIGHT AWAY.

*To drive home the point,
we're going to use the word "right" in every single sentence.*

Let's get right to it. Right to the meat! Only Travelocity guarantees everything about your booking will be right, or we'll work with our travel partners to make it right, right away. Right on!

Here's a picture taken smack dab right in the middle of Antigua, where the guarantee also covers you.

The guarantee covers all but one of the items pictured to the right.

For example, what if the ocean view you booked actually looks out at a downright ugly parking lot? You'd be right to call – we're there for you. And no one in their right mind would be pleased to learn the rental car place has closed and left them stranded. Call Travelocity and we'll help get you back on the right track.

Now, you may be thinking, "Yeah, right, I'm so sure." That's OK; you have the right to remain skeptical. That is until we mention help is always right around the corner. Call us right off the bat, knowing that our customer service reps are there for you 24/7. Righting wrongs. Left and right.

Now if you're guessing there are some things we can't control, like the weather, well you're right. But we can help you with most things – to get all the details in righting,* visit **travelocity.com/guarantee**.

*Sorry, spelling things right is one of the few things not covered under the guarantee.

I'd give my right arm for a guarantee like this, although I'm glad I don't have to.

travelocity
You'll never roam alone.

IF YOU BOOK IT, IT SHOULD BE THERE.

Only Travelocity guarantees it will be, or we'll work with our travel partners to make it right, right away. So if you're missing a balcony or anything else you booked, just call us 24/7. **1-888-TRAVELOCITY**

travelocity

You'll never roam alone